PHILIPPIKA

Marburger altertumskundliche Abhandlungen 55,1

Herausgegeben von
Joachim Hengstl, Torsten Mattern,
Robert Rollinger, Kai Ruffing
und Orell Witthuhn

2013

Harrassowitz Verlag · Wiesbaden

Legal Documents in Ancient Societies (LDAS) 1

The Letter

Law, State, Society and the Epistolary Format in the Ancient World

Proceedings of a Colloquium
held at the American Academy in Rome 28–30.9.2008

Edited by
Uri Yiftach-Firanko

2013
Harrassowitz Verlag · Wiesbaden

Gedruckt mit Unterstützung der Emil und Arthur Kießling Stiftung für Papyrusforschung.

Bibliografische Information der Deutschen Nationalbibliothek
Die Deutsche Nationalbibliothek verzeichnet diese Publikation in der Deutschen Nationalbibliografie; detaillierte bibliografische Daten sind im Internet über http://dnb.dnb.de abrufbar.

Bibliographic information published by the Deutsche Nationalbibliothek
The Deutsche Nationalbibliothek lists this publication in the Deutsche Nationalbibliografie; detailed bibliographic data are available in the internet at http://dnb.dnb.de.

For further information about our publishing program consult our website http://www.harrassowitz-verlag.de

Printed on permanent/durable paper.
Printing and binding: ⊕ Hubert & Co., Göttingen
Printed in Germany

ISSN 1613-5628
ISBN 978-3-447-06764-5

Table of Contents

List of Abbreviations

AbB	Altbabylonische Briefe in Umschrift und Übersetzung
AE	Archaiologike Ephemeris, ekdidomenē tēs Archaiologikēs Hetaireias
Aegyptus	Aegyptus. Rivista italiana di egittologia e di papirologia
AfO	Archiv für Orientforschung
AJA	American Journal of Archaeology
AJPh	American Journal of Philology
AMI	Archäologische Mitteilungen aus Iran. Ergänzungsband
AncW	The Ancient World
Ann. Camerino	Annali della Facoltà Giuridica dell'Università di Camerino
ASNP	Annali della Scuola Normale Superiore di Pisa
AOAT	Alter Orient und Altes Testament
APF	Archiv für Papyrusforschung und verwandte Gebiete
ArOr	Archiv Orientální
AS	Assyriological Studies
AUCT	Andrews University Cuneiform Texts
AUPA	Annali del Dipartimento di Storia del Diritto. Università degli Studi di Palermo
BaM	Baghdader Mitteilungen
BASP	The Bulletin of the American Society of Papyrologists
BATSH	Beiträge zu den Ausgrabungen von Tall Šeḫ Ḥamad
BCH	Bulletin de correspondance hellénique, École Française d'Athènes
BICS	Bulletin of the Institute of Classical Studies of the University of London
BiOr	Bibliotheca Orientalis
BN	Beiträge zur Namenforschung
BZAW	Beihefte zur Zeitschrift für die alttestamentliche Wissenschaft
CCG	Cahiers du Centre Gustave-Glotz
CÉ	Chronique d'Égypte
Chiron	Chiron. Mitteilungen der Kommission für alte Geschichte und Epigraphik des Deutschen Archäologischen Instituts

ClAnt	Classical Antiquity
CM	Cuneiform Monographs
CNI	Carsten Niebuhr Institute of Ancient Near Eastern Studies
CQ	Classical Quarterly
CW	The Classical World
DHA	Dialogues d'histoire ancienne
Dike	Dike. Rivista di storia del diritto greco ed ellenistico
DMOA	Documenta et Monumenta Orientis Antiqui
FAOS	Freiburger altorientalische Studien
FIRA	Fontes iuris Romani antejustiniani
FM	Florilegium Marianum
FoSub	Fontes et subsidia ad Bibliam pertinentes
G&R	Greece and Rome
HAW	Handbuch der Altertumswissenschaft
HdO	Handbuch der Orientalistik
Hermes	Hermes. Zeitschrift für klassische Philologie
Hesperia	Hesperia. The Journal of the American School of Classical Studies at Athens
HSPh	Harvard Studies in Classical Philology
Index	Index. Quaderni camerti di studi romanistici
IVRA	Iura. Rivista internazionale di diritto romano e antico
JAOS	Journal of the American Oriental Society
JARCE	Journal of the American Research Center in Egypt
JBL	Journal of Biblical Literature
JCS	Journal of Cuneiform Studies
JEOL	Jaarbericht van het Vooraziatisch-Egyptisch Genootschap Ex Oriente Lux
JHS	Journal of Hellenic Studies
JJP	Journal of Juristic Papyrology
JNES	Journal of Near Eastern Studies
Labeo	Labeo. Rassegna di diritto romano
LAPO	Littératures Anciennes du Proche-Orient
MAIBL	Mémoires de l'Académie des Inscriptions et Belles-lettres
MARI	Mari. Annales de Recherches Interdisciplinaires
MBPR	Münchener Beiträge zur Papyrusforschung und antiken Rechtsgeschichte

MC	Mesopotamian Civilizations
MDAI	Mémoires de la Délégation Archéologique en Iran
MDOG	Mitteilungen der Deutschen Orient-Gesellschaft zu Berlin
Mesopotamia	Mesopotamia. Rivista di archeologia, epigrafia e storia orientale antica
MVN	Materiali per il vocabolario neosumerico
NABU	Nouvelles assyriologiques brèves et utilitaires
NAPR	Northern Akkad Project Reports
OAAS	Old Assyrian Archives, Studies
OBO	Orbis Biblicus et Orientalis
OIP	Oriental Institute Publications
OLA	Orientalia Lovaniensia Analecta
OMRO	Ouheidkundige mededelingen uit het Rijksmuseum van Oudheden te Leiden
PIHANS	Publications de l'Institut Historique et Archéologique Néerlandais de Stamboul
Phoenix	Phoenix. Bulletin uitgegeven door het Vooraziatisch-Egyptisch Genootschap Ex Oriente Lux
RA	Revue d'assyriologie et d'archéologie orientale
RAN	Revue archéologique de Narbonnaise
RBL	Review of Biblical Literature
RE	Paulys Realencyclopädie der classischen Altertumswissenschaft
REA	Revue des études anciennes
RHD	Revue historique de droit français et étranger
RIDA	Revue internationale des droits de l'antiquité
RIMA	The Royal Inscriptions of Mesopotamia. Assyrian periods
RIME	The Royal Inscriptions of Mesopotamia. Early periods
RlA	Reallexikon der Assyriologie
SAA	State Archives of Assyria
SAAB	State Archives of Assyria Bulletin
SAAS	State Archives of Assyria Studies
SAOC	Studies in Ancient Oriental Civilization
SBL MS	Society of Biblical Literature, Monograph Series
SBAW	Sitzungsberichte der Bayerischen Akademie der Wissenschaften. Philosophisch-philologische und historische Klasse

TAPhA	Transactions and Proceedings of the American Philological Association
TCS	Texts from Cuneiform Sources
TR	Tijdschrift voor Rechtsgeschiedenis = Revue d’histoire du droit
TUAT	Texte aus der Umwelt des Alten Testaments
WVDOG	Wissenschaftliche Veröffentlichungen der Deutschen Orient-Gesellschaft
WZKM	Wiener Zeitschrift für die Kunde des Morgenlandes
YOS	Yale Oriental Series, Babylonian Texts
ZA	Zeitschrift für Assyriologie und Vorderasiatische Archäologie
ZABR	Zeitschrift für altorientalische und biblische Rechtsgeschichte
ZPE	Zeitschrift für Papyrologie und Epigraphik
ZRG	Zeitschrift für Rechtsgeschichte
ZSSRA	Zeitschrift der Savigny-Stiftung für Rechtsgeschichte. Romanistische Abteilung

Foreword

The group *Legal Documents in Ancient Societies* was established in 2008 to enhance collaboration among students of everyday documentation in the Ancient Near East, Ancient Egypt, the Greek and Hellenistic world, and the Roman State down to late Antiquity. A key means of achieving this goal is a series of annual meetings, focusing each on a different topic. The first meeting, held at the *American Academy in Rome* on 28 – 30. 9. 2008, focused on the study of different documentary applications of the letter from the third millennium BCE to late Antiquity. The twelve papers delivered in the meeting illustrated how letters were applied for similar purposes in different civilizations, sometimes millennia apart. Dominique Charpin, Ingo Kottsieper and James Sickinger, for example, demonstrated how royal state-apparatus applied letters for administrative purposes in the old Babylonian period, the Persian empire, and the Greek and Hellenistic world. Eva Cancik and Ingo Kottsieper discussed the application of letters in the administration of Justice in 13th century BCE Assyria and the Persian period. Sophie Démare-Lafont, Edward Harris and Éva Jakab showed how the application of letters promoted complex economic activities extending over different states and continents. The reader of this volume can study these cross-cultural phenomena and will undoubtedly pinpoint others.

The papers delivered in Rome enabled the participants to pinpoint evolution in the position of the letter as a legal document in the Greek and Roman world. Letters began to be written in the Greek world in the archaic period, probably not long after the introduction of the Greek alphabet. But at first letters, and perhaps writing in general, were treated with suspect as a means to be employed by free states or their citizens for the documentation of their everyday activity. This fact was demonstrated by the papers of Paola Ceccarelli and James Sickinger. Besides, even if letters could be, and were certainly used on a regular basis for different purposes, early letters as discussed and cited by Edward Harris do not exhibit an established format that would indicate their independent use as a routine instrument for the documentation of everyday, particularly legal activities. Things changed in this respect in the Hellenistic period. Not only did letters become, as shown by James Sickinger, an established and acceptable means of issuing decrees by Hellenistic monarchs. The letter also became a routine type of legal document, recording legal acts whose performance was not attended by witnesses, and which gave rise to an obligation solely by virtue of the fact that the document was written by the prospective debtor in person. The result of this change, the *cheirographon*, was discussed in most papers focusing on the Hellenistic, Roman and Byzantine period.

Mark Depauw and Katelijn Vandorpe studied the evolution of the Demotic and Greek letter format as an established type of legal document in Persian and Ptolemaic Egypt. Sophie Kovarik studied the final triumph of the letter format, in the

Byzantine period, as *the* default means of documentation of legal activities. Andrea Jördens showed how the *cheirographon*—originally written by just one of the parties and therefore recording his obligations, but not those of the addressee of the document—was transformed, on occasions, into a "normal" legal document, recording obligations of both parties alike. Finally, Éva Jakab studied the reception of the *cheirographon* into Roman legal practice and theory. This last issue was also taken up by Johannes Platschek, whose paper focused on the procedural implications of contracts that were entered upon informally and were occasionally given evidence of in letters, as opposed to those entered upon by formal acts created within *ius civile.*

Sources quoted in this volume are abbreviated according to the conventions in each field of research. Ancient Near Eastern sources are abbreviated by S. Démare-Lafont and E. Cancik-Kirschbaum according to the conventions given in R. Borger, *Handbuch der Keilschriftliteratur, 3 vol.*, Berlin, 1967–1975, while D. Charpin's article follows those of the *Archives Babyloniennes, XXe–XVIIe Siècles av. J.-C.* (www.archibab.fr.). Classical literary sources, if abbreviated, are abbreviated according to routine conventions that can be found, for example, at http://iam.classics.unc.edu/main/help/P.html. Greek inscriptions are cited according to the conventions of the *Supplementum Epigraphicum Graecum* (SEG), and are also available at http://dge.cchs.csic.es/lst/2lst3.htm. Greek and Demotic papyri are cited according to the conventions of the *Checklist of Editions of Greek, Latin, Demotic and Coptic Papyri, Ostraca and Tablets* (http://scriptorium.lib.duke.edu/papyrus/texts/clist_papyri.html). Aramaic texts discussed by I. Kottspieper are cited according to the conventions established by Porten-Yardeni 1986–1999.

Thanks are due to people and institutes who made the meeting and the publication of this volume possible: The *Institute for the Study of the Ancient World at New York University*, which sponsored the meeting, the *American Academy in Rome* which hosted us in its course, the *Emil und Arthur Kießling Stiftung für Papyrusforschung*, which offered financial support for the publication of the present volume, Professor Hans-Albert Rupprecht, who made this financial support possible, Dr. Kai Ruffing, who accepted this book for publication in the distinguished series *Philippika. Marburger altertumskundliche Abhandlungen*. I would also like to thank the participants in the meeting for the oral and written versions of their papers as they are published in this volume and to the members of the steering committee of the group *Legal Documents of Ancient Societies,* Sophie Démare-Lafont, Mark Depauw, Michele Faraguna, Éva Jakab and Dennis P. Kehoe for their advice, as well as for their moral and practical support. Special thanks are due to Roger S. Bagnall, without whose support and guidance the idea of our group would have never been materialized.

Uri Yiftach-Firanko

Jerusalem, July 2012

Introduction

A: The Letter as a Genre in Mesopotamia (S. Démare-Lafont)

In the Ancient Near East, the earliest account of a letter dates to the end of the third millennium BCE. According to the Sumerian epic *Enmerkar and the Lord of Aratta*, dating to this period, Enmerkar, king of Uruk in archaic times, sent a series of messages, ultimatums, to his opponent, the king of Aratta (in Iran). The latter was to acknowledge Enmerkar's suzerainty. As the last message was too long to be memorized, Enmerkar decided to inscribe his words on a tablet which would be read by his emissary. Consequently, the text reports, "The Lord of Kullab (= Enmerkar) smoothed clay with the hand and set down the words on it in the manner of a tablet. While up to then there had been no one setting down words on clay, now, on that day, under that sun, thus it verily came to be ; the lord of Kullab set down words on clay, thus it verily came to be !"[1] The epistolary genre was born.

Letters were in use in any literate or semi-literate society. They were understood as a written conversation. In Mesopotamia, letters are composed for utilitarian causes. Whether issued by kings, diplomats, administrative officers, merchants or women, letters are not drafted for gossip; they are meant to convey important pieces of information. The style of the letter can be informal and direct or plumy and literary, depending on its period, environment and authors: pedants in need of recognition flaunt their culture; housewives issue repeated reproaches to their husbands; zealous administrators give the king account of their management; traders call for their unpaid debts and humans promise the gods to honor them if they put an end to their sufferings. Regardless, however, of this great variety of styles and contents, cuneiform letters do exhibit several common features: they are usually written on a single tablet, are covered with an envelope and contain no date nor place of drafting; letters start with an address stating the names of the addressee and of the writer, sometimes also their titles, and a greeting formula. The standard pattern is as follows:

> To PN (my Lord)
> say:
> thus (speaks) PN_2 (your servant).
> May you have a long-lasting life ! / May GN and GN_2 keep you alive / in good health for the sake of mine ![2]

In the past, scholars drew from the above formulae that letters were meant to be read aloud by the messenger to the addressee. This view has now been largely revisited:

1 See the edition by Kramer 1952: 36–9 ll. 504–6 and the translation by Jacobsen 1987: 312.

2 On the various forms of greetings in Mesopotamian letters, see Salonen 1971.

as a significant part of the population is now assumed to have been literate, we conclude that many senders probably wrote their correspondence in person, without resorting to the services of a scribe.[3] At the same time, the oral background always remains manifested and pivotal; the heading formula shows that the letter is conceptualized as the written form of silent words. The first letter in Mesopotamian history, sent by Enmerkar to the king of Aratta, contains a message described as a "spoken word" (inim-du$_{11}$-ga).[4]

Indeed, epistolary style replicates sometimes everyday expressions, dialogues, fits of passion or endless sentences full of personal names and confused facts, just like in a desultory conversation. Such is the case for instance in the correspondence of the Assyrian merchants,[5] at the beginning of the second millennium, or in the letters of the Syrian dignitaries from the kingdom of Mari,[6] while the contemporary exchanges between Hammurabi and his officers in Babylonia focus on administrative rather than narrative aspects and testify to a certain sobriety in style and vocabulary.[7] The spirit of the Mari letters reappears in the Middle-Assyrian administrative correspondence of the Great vizir Aššur-iddin, excavated at Dur-katlimmu.[8] Later, in the 14th century BC, the abundant correspondence of the Egyptian pharaoh with the Mesopotamian royal courts meets complex language conventions based on allusions and insinuations typical of diplomatic speech,[9] which can already be observed in the Mari documentation.[10] In the first millennium, the curtness of the reports sent by the governors and the scholars (doctors, astrologists, exorcists ...) to the Assyrian king[11] contrasts with the petitions for comeback written by deposed courtiers, real pieces of literary works combining scholarship and flattery.

Legal historical study is naturally commonly based on evidence provided by laws and legal documents. Still, laws and legal documents are highly standardized and formulized and leave for this reason a variety of spheres and modes of legal activity unattested. This is where the epistolary documentation sets in. Letters convey precious insight into concrete and vivid situations that are not dealt with in laws and contracts[12]; they fill gaps and give the sociological background that is lacking in the

3 See Charpin 2008: 52–60 and his article in this volume.

4 Kramer 1952: 40–1, ll. 540–1: en-aratta^{ki}-ke$_4$ im-ma igi i-ni-in-bar, inim-du$_{11}$-ga "The Lord of Aratta looked at the clay, the spoken word".

5 See lastly Veenhof 2008.

6 See Durand 1997–2000.

7 See for instance the correspondence of Šamaš-hazir, in charge with management of the fields belonging to the royal domain in Larsa under Hammurabi, partially studied by Pecha 1999; see also the letters of Sin-iddinam, former personal secretary of the king and governor of the province of Larsa, in particular the edition by van Soldt 1994: n° 5–48, 50, 52.

8 Cancik-Kirschbaum 1996.

9 Moran 1987.

10 See Lafont 1992 and Sasson 2001.

11 See for instance Hunger 1992 and Parpola 1997.

12 Kraus 1977.

legal texts. Thus for instance, thanks to the letters excavated in the Anatolian trading station of Kaniš[13] we can get a rather precise idea of the commercial law prevailing among the Assyrian merchants in the 19th century BC: the most frequent commercial contract, called *naruqqum*, is attested in two tablets only.[14] Yet its current use is attested in numerous letters sent from Aššur to Kaniš. The same body of texts also repeatedly alludes to a commercial legislation inscribed on a stele that remains to be found.[15]

The use of letters among the average, ordinary population is rather restricted. With the exception of merchants, who regularly send letters because of their commercial activities, commons do not write to exchange private news. They resort to this means of communication only to convey a precise piece of information, usually in connection with a trial, wherefore the use of epistolary documentation (especially Old Babylonian) is particularly fruitful for the study of judgments and rules of procedure.[16] But as a whole, letters concern the "public" area and deal with matters such as diplomatic, administration or political life.

The richness of this genre is made very clear in the articles of D. Charpin and E. Cancik-Kirschbaum here: both authors shed light on many technical aspects resorting to administrative or judicial practices. But beyond these data, which are essential to improve our understanding of law in practice, letters offer also a broader picture of the legal culture of a place or an area. For instance, the study of the metalanguages handled by the kings in the 14th century BC illuminates the political codes among the great powers in the middle of the second millennium (Egypt, Mitanni, Babylonia, Hatti and Assyria).[17] The three articles presented in this volume focus on the judicial (E. Cancik-Kirschbaum, D. Charpin) and the administrative (S. Démare-Lafont) aspects contained in the Mesopotamian letter, a major genre in the legal culture of the Ancient Near East.

Charpin's paper reviews the various forms of letters during the Old Babylonian Period (first half of the second millennium): along with letter-orders for everyday administration, petitions to the king, royal edicts and rescripts, the letter is also a means of proof, acting as a substitute for the person of the witness. Cancik-Kirschbaum deals with a small group of Middle-Assyrian legal summonses, involving the narrow circle of royal officers during the reign of Tukulti-Ninurta I, and exhibiting a high degree of orality in their style, consistent with the oral nature of the arbitration procedure. Démare-Lafont discusses three examples of administrative letters in order to illustrate the three administrative patterns documented throughout the Meso-

13 See the analysis of Veenhof 1999 and Démare-Lafont 2008.
14 One of these tablets is unpublished, the other one was republished by Hecker 1999.
15 See Veenhof 1995.
16 For a preliminary approach, see Démare-Lafont 2003.
17 About language and metalanguage in the El-Amarna letters, see Liverani 1999: 314–8 and Liverani 2000.

potamian history: the bureaucratic management in use during the Neo-Sumerian empire (end of the third millennium); the family approach of the Amorite kingdom of Mari (18th century BC); the imperial type represented by the Neo-Assyrian kingship (8th–7th centuries BC).

B: Classical Greece and Persia (Michele Faraguna)

As for the Greek world, Edward Harris, Paola Ceccarelli and James Sickinger have sketched a coherent picture of the role and the statute of the letter from the archaic period until Hellenism emphasizing a number of generally accepted fundamental aspects. For our purposes, four points can be singled out as follows:

1. Letter writing is relatively poorly attested in archaic and classical Greece down to the second half of the fifth century.
2. The letter is not codified as an autonomous genre until the beginning of the fourth century: no epistolary language, no standard introductory and closing formulae appear until then; letters as a literary genre are also entirely a product of the fourth century. The earlier "letters" we possess are mere oral messages conveyed in a written form. In this respect, a typical example is provided by the letter of Achillodoros from Berezan, discussed by Edward Harris, where the use of pronouns is at first sight confusing and can be justified only on the assumption that the letter is actually conceived as an oral message addressed to Protagoras (hence the vocative ὦ Πρωταγόρη) and is meant to be read aloud by the addressee. It moreover incorporates a second message to Anaxagoras, where the sender is consistently referred to in the third person. The verb identifying the document as a "letter" is in this case ἐπιστέλλω, whose meaning is ambiguous for it can signify both "to command" and "to send a letter". In Herodotus' *Histories* letters are similarly introduced by a vocative and by formulae such as ὁ δεῖνα τάδε λέγει which are the same as those employed to introduce oral messages.
3. There is no attestation of the publication of "official" letters on stone until the end of the fourth century, although a royal chancellery existed in Macedonia since at least 343 BC, when Eumenes was active as γραμματεύς (Nep. *Eum.* 1.5; cf. Plut. *Eum.* 1.4; Arr. 5.24.6; 7.4.6). Such Hellenistic documents, however, stemmed from kings and other dynasts. Leaving covering letters and a few other marginal cases aside, the use of the letter form to convey official decisions by Greek *poleis* can altogether be considered rather infrequent and does not at any rate start before the second half of the third century BC.
4. The situation outlined above is the product of the political and diplomatic style typical of Greek cities which enacted public decisions in the form of decrees voted by the *demos* and, if needed, had their contents disseminated by heralds and envoys, whereas letters as a type of document were perceived as having clear despotic associations and were typical of tyrants and autocrats.

Within this framework, some elements still remain open to debate and require further elaboration building on Paola Ceccarelli's fundamental point that "it is important to differentiate between public and private communication, between type of letters and occasions, while at the same time bearing in mind the generic and socio-political context within which a reference to a letter is made" (cf. p. 85)

To begin with the quantitative aspect, it is correct to stress that, as far as archaic and classical attestations of letters are concerned, they are limited in number but we should not be over-pessimistic. The *corpus* of letters on lead tablets and *ostraka* from the Greek world is steadily increasing, as excavators are nowadays more aware of them, and has more than doubled over the past twenty years. Twenty nine texts, spanning, chronologically, from the mid-sixth to the fourth century BC and, geographically, from the Black Sea Region to the Western Mediterranean, are presently known (for an updated list see Dana 2007: 68–69; Eidinow & Taylor 2010: 50–61). Some of these are badly fragmentary, others have only been reported and still await publication but seven documents can be dated to the second half of the sixth century and six to the fifth century. This is rather striking.

As for their contents, these early letters usually convey instructions either for the administration of the household or for business and trade purposes. Some texts from the Pontic area are interesting because, among other things, they provide the first attestation of chattel slavery in the region. A letter from Phanagoria, in particular, is about the sale of a παῖς. Graffiti on potsherds from Attica bear instructions such as "Thamneus, put the saw under the threshold of the garden gate", "Boy, bring other new couches for Phalantos", "Eumelis, come as quickly as you can". A fourth-century letter from Torone is about the shipment of a load of wood. They are generally short and do not seem to be the product of elite social groups.

Paradoxically, the first reference to writing in Greek literature, and the only reference to the use of writing in the Homeric poems, which, as is well known, portray the world of the heroes as a society where writing had no significance at all, is the famous Bellerophon episode (*Il.* 6.167–170). It revolves around a letter, written with σήματα (not γράμματα) λυγρά in a folded *pinax* bearing instructions for the death of the person who had to deliver it, a typically oriental theme. It can thus be suggested that when the Greeks learnt the use of the alphabetic script they did not simply learn to master a technique but also became familiar with the ways and the contexts in which it could be put to use and to which it belonged. *Deltos*, *byblos*, *arrhabon* and possibly *habax* are, in different degrees, all words of certain or probable Semitic origin. We also have some examples of Phoenician letters, for instance a letter on a papyrus from Saqqara dated to the sixth century (Donner & Röllig 2002: no. 50). Against this background, it also needs to be stressed that some of the earliest texts in our *corpus* of letters appear to be fairly sophisticated documents employing technical language and reflecting the complexity of trading operations in archaic Greece.

The best examples are the two texts examined by Edward Harris in his paper. His main argument that Greek law did not develop the concept of agency is largely built on the testimonies provided by some archaic letters on lead. To strengthen his important point that there was little "vertical specialization" in the Greek economy and that slaves and partners were sufficient to conduct overseas trade in an effective way a passage from Demosthenes' *Against Phormio* can be quoted to the effect that Chrysippos, having extended a maritime loan to Phormio, entrusted him a letter to deliver to his slave and to a partner (ἔχων ἐπιστολὰς παρ' ἐμοῦ, ἃς ἔδωκ' αὐτῷ ἀπενεγκεῖν τῷ παιδὶ τῷ ἐμῷ παραχειμάζοντι ἐκεῖ καὶ κοινωνῷ τινί) instructing them, as soon as the goods were unshipped, to inspect them and keep an eye on them (Dem. 34.8). Here, again, trade is carried out relying on a slave, permanently based in the Pontus, and a κοινωνός. There is no sign of an agent, for which there was no Greek word. The letter of Apatourios, in particular, referring to a legal case which could be solved by means of the consultation of διφθέρια seems to be the product of a surprisingly literate and to some extent document-minded society. Concerning its interpretation, it may well be that the role of Apatourios could simply be that of a ναύκληρος entrusted with the transport of a shipment of goods and that the part played by Meno in the affair has generally been overlooked, although the nature of the relationship between the three characters involved, Leanax, Apatourios and Meno, still remains obscure.

Another important testimony which deserves closer attention is a fragment of Euripides' *Palamedes*, one of the civilizing heroes, or πρῶτοι εὑρηταί, to whom Greek tradition assigned the "invention" of writing. In this fragment, probably in an ἀγών opposing him to Odysseus, Palamedes boasts about the benefits accruing from the use of alphabetic writing and singles out three functions and purposes for which his "invention" had proved useful, namely overseas correspondence, wills and the solving of legal disputes (Eur. fr. 578 Kannicht). In a recently published essay Paola Ceccarelli showed that the choice of the three functions performed by writing was functional to the plot of the tragedy – and that, according to the version of the myth accepted by Euripides, the reference to letter writing was somehow ironical since Palamedes' death was itself caused by the discovery of a forged letter (Ceccarelli 2002). Notwithstanding this, it is clear that in selecting such uses of writing Euripides could not refer to something which was not meaningful for his audience, as wills and legal disputes obviously were. Letter writing may not have been commonplace, as Christophe Pébarthe recently suggested ("banale") (2006: 81–88), but it must have been part of peoples' everyday experience.

It is not by chance that letters appear in the works of Herodotus and Thucydides and that, despite the rhetorical *topoi* emphasizing Spartan illiteracy, Spartan leaders are portrayed as communicating by means of *epistolai* and of the *skytale* starting from the early fifth century. For Athens, on the contrary, we apparently have to wait until the last quarter of the fifth century and we may assume that it was the Peloponnesian War and the continuously expanding geographical dimension of the war theatre that made written communication between *strategoi* and the assembly necessary.

The reason for the very limited use of private letters as a means of proof in the orators' speeches therefore probably lies in their ephemeral character and in their being easily prone to falsification or manipulation. To some extent, the same can be said about wills which have a rather ambiguous status in the Athenian courts as they were usually deposited with a third party and their authenticity could only be certified by witnesses so that forgeries were not infrequent. A letter is for instance mentioned in Antiphon's *On the murder of Herodes* where the argument aims at showing that the document was unlikely to be authentic on two accounts: first, that the bearer, unlike in the situation described, was not usually informed of the contents of the message and, second, that letters were usually necessary when the message was too long to be remembered. It is however interesting to note that the latter statement does not seem to correspond to the evidence of our epigraphic letters and that we are probably confronted with a rhetorical *topos* of judicial oratory.

In the light of this, the absence of "official" letters as an instrument of communication at a political and interstate level is even more striking. A typical example of the diplomatic practices of Greek *poleis*, even within an imperial context, is offered by the Athenian decree enforcing the use of Attic coins, weights and measures in the cities of the Delian League. Here, after the decree had been voted, heralds, κήρυκες, one for each of the administrative districts of the empire, were to be selected to disseminate τὰ ἐψηφισμένα, the provisions of the decree, among the allied communities. Every city, even against the will of the local *demos*, was then to set up a copy of the decree in its agora (*IG* I^3 1453 = ML 45).

Considering that the Persian Empire was the only available model for the Athenians when they created their own *arche* (Raaflaub 2009)—and no doubt Persian procedures did work as a model for the modalities of the assessment and collection of tribute—their different approach to diplomatic relations becomes rather evident. The only possible explanation for this phenomenon lies in an ideological construct, the Greeks' deeply rooted belief that, in spite of more and more widespread literacy and written communication, politics and decision-making in a city-state could only be conducted orally in the assembly—Aristotle in the *Politics*, for instance, rejects the possibility that a city with a huge population, an *ethnos* or a megalopolis such as Babylon, could form a *polis* for, he observes, who could be the herald of such a community? (1326b2–7)—and that democracy entailed equality and open access to information, ἐς μέσον καταθεῖναι τὰ πράγματα, βουλεύματα πάντα ἐς τὸ κοινὸν ἀναφέρειν in Herodotus' words (3.80.2 and 6).

On the contrary, as stressed by James Sickinger diplomacy conducted by means of letters, consistently with the etymology of the term *epistole*, was perceived as secretive and "private" and therefore had autocratic associations and overtones which made it unsuitable within a Greek context. There is thus a continuous thread connecting Herodotus' *Histories*, where letter writing belongs with autocratic rulers such as the Persian kings, the Egyptian pharaoh Amasis and Greek tyrants (Polykrates, Histiaios and Aristagoras) as well as ambiguous characters like Themistokles, down to Demosthenes, where Athenian freedom of speech, παρρησία, is contrasted with Philip's commands conveyed in the form of ἐπιστολαί, and to Hellenism, where letters were one of the most common means for rulers to convey instructions to their Greek subjects, to enforce constitutional changes, to arbitrate disputes, to grant privileges and, finally, to intervene in religious matters.

Ingo Kottsieper's contribution, analyzing the corpus of Aramaic letters under the name of the well-documented Persian satrap Arsames (late fifth century BC), provides a striking counterpoint to the Greek picture and illustrates the role of letters in the complex workings of the Achaemenid imperial administration. All documents are written on leather apart from one which is on papyrus. They can be divided on the basis of formal criteria into two groups. In the first group, the name of the sender and of the recipient are followed by a greetings formula, whereas in the second the latter is consistently missing and at the end of the document there is a note: "X knows this order, Y is the scribe". Notwithstanding such differences, the texts were in some cases written by the same hand and clearly were the product of the same chancellery.

By comparing the formal aspects and the contents of the two types of documents, the author shows that the differences reflected their different nature. The documents of the first group were letters addressed by Arsames to officials who were *not* under his authority and whose decisions the satrap was trying to influence. Thus, they were not legal documents nor were their contents legally binding. This was, however, the case for the letters of the second group, adjudicating legal disputes or authorizing expenditure or the supply of rations to officials in the satrap's administration. Unlike the others, these documents issued orders and the decisions they carried were legally binding. The person who "knew the order" and, presumably, had been responsible for issuing it and the "scribe" acted as witnesses and guarantors for the authenticity of the document. The formula at the end of the text also made it impossible to manipulate its contents, for example by introducing unauthorized additions after the seal had been broken.

As for the royal correspondence in the Hellenistic kingdoms, one of the questions posed by James Sickinger in his paper concerns the definition of the fundamental typological characters distinguishing a letter from other forms of royal commands such as the διαγράμματα. He is right in identifying Alexander's settlement concerning the territory of Philippi as a *diagramma*, a royal edict conveyed to the city either by Antipatros, Alexander's governor of Macedonia, or, perhaps, by Philippian envoys who had petitioned Alexander (hence, in this document, Alexander is always referred to in the third person) (*SEG* 34.664). In a similar way, Alexander's document concerning constitutional and military matters in Chios, which displays a remarkably authoritarian tone, and is defined as "strongly interventionist" by Rhodes and Osborne in their collection of *Greek Historical Inscriptions* (Oxford 2003, nr. 84), was again a *diagramma*, the prescript παρὰ βασιλέως 'Αλε[ξάνδρ]ου Χίω[ν τῶι] δήμωι having been added when the king's rulings were published on a stele in Chios.

The style and forms of royal *epistolai* thus developed at a slow pace in the last decades of the fourth century, although the difference between *epistolai* and *diagrammata* remained less clear-cut than we might expect. As a rule *diagrammata* were "general laws" promulgated by the king and covered different matters; they were formally divided into paragraphs (in our inscriptions, as a matter of fact, we never find the whole text of a *diagramma* but excerpts of the provisions relevant for the community which published them). Elias Bickerman aptly defined the *diagramma* as a *lex satura*. It had no prescript and no addressee and it was in force as soon as it had been promulgated. It was also a source of law in that all communities subject to the king had to conform to it and modify their civic laws accordingly. Commands were expressed with verbs in the infinitive. Royal letters, on the contrary, had a more limited scope and were usually addressed to a subject *polis* in response to a particular request and they were written in the first person in epistolary form with full use of the standard formulae.

That the contours of these different types of documents were sometimes blurred and that there was a sort of grey area of overlap is, however, shown for example by two Macedonian inscriptions dealing with religious matters. The first, quoted by James Sickinger, is a stele, dated to 248 BC, containing the texts of three letters from Demetrios II to Harpalos, the *epistates* of Beroia, ruling, among other things, that certain revenues of the sanctuary of Herakles which the city had misappropriated be returned to the sanctuary and granting the priest of the sanctuary *ateleia* (*EKM* I, 3, ll. 4–8 and 14–17). The second inscription, dated to 187 BC, is again a composite document preserving instructions concerning the property of Sarapis in Thessalonike. In the covering letter introducing the new provision the term *diagramma* is explicitly mentioned (Hatzopoulos 1996: no. 15). The two inscriptions are thus very similar in content but their typology is clearly different.

In spite of their more courteous, civilized tone, the provisions of an *epistole* were no less authoritative, nor authoritarian, than those of a *diagramma*. In a recently published letter of Eumenes II to the *katoikountes* of Tyriaion in Phrygia (post 188 BC) granting the community the status of a polis, king Eumenes openly underlines that the request of the petitioners is of no little consequence and that it is only in the power of his own word and decision νομίζεσθαι πολίτευμα, in other words to recognize their status as a *polis*, which, he points out, he has already done in another ἐπιστολή (*SEG* 47.1745). Along similar lines, in his second letter to the *tagoi* and the polis of Larissa Philip V made it clear that the enlargement of the citizen body had to be enforced κατὰ τὴν παρ' ἐμοῦ ἐπιστολήν and the ensuing decree that the Larisseans voted to comply stated that the *tagoi* were to have the names of the new citizens inscribed κατὰ τὰν ἐπιστολὰν τοῦ βασιλέως (*SIG*³ 543).

What is clear, however, is that a royal letter was generally part of an ongoing dialogue, and one should say, a subtle power game, between the king and a subject city. Greek cities voted honors (crowns, gilded statues, cults) for a king and sent envoys to announce the honors which they had decreed and, at the same time, to present some request in exchange. The king would reply in letter form accepting such honors and ruling over the matter of the petition. The publication of the king's letter by the city and the commemoration of the king's benefactions on stone would enhance his honor and dignity. It is important to stress, as noted by James Sickinger, that honors were always granted in the form of decrees and the contents were illustrated and glossed over orally to the recipient by ambassadors. In an article, first published in 1985, J.-M. Bertrand (1990) brilliantly showed the different ways Greek *poleis* managed to integrate royal commands, conveyed in letter form, into their political discourse behaving as if they still enjoyed absolute independence and were not part of a more complex political universe. In a kind of game of pretence, the Greeks thus clung to their traditional political style and to their ideological constructs throughout their history, even when they had lost their freedom and had to live as subjects under powerful monarchies.

C: Greco-Roman Egypt and the Roman World (Uri Yiftach-Firanko)

As the preceding pages have shown, letters were used for the documentation of everyday activity in every literate society. This was also the case, naturally, in the Greco-Roman world.[18] Now however we encounter a new phenomenon: in the Hellenistic period emerges in the Greek East a new type of legal document: *cheir,* or *cheirographon.* The lexical rendering of the adjective *cheirographos / cheirographon* is *written with the hand, holograph, manuscript.*[19] It is commonly used to denote any autograph acknowledgment by a contracting party. This acknowledgement does not necessarily take the form of a letter: in the Delphic manumission inscriptions as well as in Roman Puteoli it probably does not.[20] Yet in Ptolemaic and Roman Egypt *cheirographon* becomes the *terminus technicus* for a contract drafted in a letter format. Just like every letter, the *cheirographon* is opened with the address clause: "A (debtor) to B (creditor) greeting". But the *cheirographon* contains in its final form none of the routine courtesies to be found in regular letters. It focuses, rather, on documenting an account, by the debtor, of the act that brought about the contractual bond, and encompasses also other clauses typical in contracts, in particular the execution (*praxis*) and validity (*kyria*) clauses.[21] The *cheirographon* ends with the date clause. The greeting ἔρρωσο ("fare well"), which appears at the end of regular letters, is left out of the *cheirographon.*

The above scheme evolves in the course of the second century BCE (compare, e.g., P.Erasm. 12, 152 BCE—Kaine, Arsinoites), and reaches maturity in its last quarter, a period in which it is attested, in its mature form, throughout Egypt. P. Adler 4 (109 BCE—Ptolemais) exhibits its features:

> "Psemminis, son of [...]os, to [Horos, son of Nechoutes, gr]eeting. [I acknowledge that I received from you three (?) talents of copper coinage (?), free of interest (?)]. The[se are] what is still lowing to you according to the contract of Taïsis, your daughter, which I shall repay to you up to Pachon 30

18 Cf., e.g., P.Mich. VIII 512 (early III CE—Alexandria (?)); CPR XXV 9 (late V-early VI CE—Herakleopolites).

19 LSJ^9 s.v. p. 1985. Preisigke, WB II 733: *Handschriftlich.*

20 Cf., e.g., FD III 6.14 (20 – 46 CE); FIRA III no. 130 and Jakab, 221, n. 21.

21 Cf., e.g., P.Dion. 32.17–8 (*praxis*), 18–20 (*kyria*) (107 BCE—Hermopolites).

of the [year] 9 without trial and judgement. And if I do not return them by the fixed time, I shall give you the same twice over compulsorily. And you shall have the right of execution (*praxis*) both upon me and upon all my property as if in accordance with a legal decision. Dionysios, son of Archidemos, of the demos Berenike, wrote on behalf of Psemminis by his request as he is illiterate. Year 8 Tybi 24".[22]

The emergence of the *cheirographon* is of far reaching implications, as for the first time a legal act (i.e. the act recorded in the *cheirographon*) was made evident without its attendance by witnesses or performance before a public organ. The actionability of the act was entirely based on the fact that the document recording it was drafted in theory by the debtor in person, in his own hand. This change reflects an entirely new attitude towards the concept of writing. Its social, cultural and legal consequences go beyond those studied in this book.

In the five centuries following the creation of the *cheirographon*, it exhibits, in Egypt at least, remarkable uniformity and popularity, in particular in documents recording credit and sale-related transactions. Accordingly, among 464 loan contracts dating to the Roman period before Diocletian, nearly one third, 153 in all, are structured as *cheirographa*. In some regions, such as the Oxyrhynchite nome, the *cheirographon* stands out as the routine format for the documentation of loans (45 of 68 early-Roman Oxyrhynchite loan contracts are structured as *cheirographa*).

Most early Roman *cheirographa* exhibit several common features: besides the structure already reported above, most of them are also drafted not by a professional scribe but, in theory at least, by the declaring party (i.e. the prospective debtor) in person; they are drafted in a single copy, which is kept by the creditor in the course of the contract and returned to the debtor or obliterated after the settlement of the debt; *cheirographa* also do not record witnesses, or the registration or deposition of the document in an archive[23] and their format is narrow, their width measuring around 15 cm. with between 25 and 30 letters a line.[24] This description applies to most early Roman *cheirographa*, in particular to those stemming from the Arsinoite

22 [Ψεμμῖνις. . . . .]ο̣υ | [Ὥρωι Νεχούτου (?) χα]ίρει̣ν̣. | [ὁμολογῶ ἔχειν παρὰ σοῦ] | [χαλκοῦ νομίσματος τάλ (?)]|[αν]τ̣α̣ [τρία ἄ]τ̣[ο]κ̣α̣. (?) τ̣[αῦτα δέ] | ἐστιν ἃ̣ π̣ροσωφιλη̣τ̣ο̣ (read προσωφείλετό) | σοι πρὸς τὴν συνγραφὴν | [Τ]αι̣|[σ]ε̣[ως] (?) τῆς θυγατρ̣[ός] | [σο]υ, ἃ καὶ ἀποδ̣[ώ]σ̣[ω] σ̣ο̣ι̣ | ἕ̣ω̣ς Παχὼν λ τοῦ θ̣ [(ἔτους)] | [ἄν]ε̣υ̣ κ̣ρ̣ίσεως καὶ δίκης· | ἐ̣ὰν δὲ μὴ ἀπο̣δ̣ῶ{ι} σοι | ἕως τοῦ ἀφωρισμένου χρόνου̣ | [ἀ]ποτίσω σοι τὰ προγεγραμ|μ̣ένα διπλ̣ᾶ ἐ̣π̣ά̣ν̣‹αγ›κ̣ο̣ν̣ | [ε]ἶ̣ναι δέ σοι τὴν πρᾶξιν̣ [ἔ]κ τε ἐμοῦ καὶ ἐκ τῶν | ὑπαρχόντ̣ω̣ν μοι πάντω̣ν̣ | πράσ‹σ›οντι καθάπερ | ἐ̣γ δίκης. ἔγραψεν ὑπὲρ | τοῦ Ψεμμίνιος Διονύ̣σ̣ιος | [Ἀ]ρχεδήμου Βερενικεὺς | [ἀ]ξιωθεὶς ὑπ ᾽ αὐτοῦ διὰ τὸ | μ̣ὴ εἰδέναι γράμματα. | (ἔτους) η Τῦβι κδ. Translation according to P.*Adler* p. 17.

23 The only exception to that rule are the *cheirographa* of the archive of Dionysios son of Kephalas, of late second century Akoris. Cf., e.g., P.Dion. 32 (107 BCE—Hermopolites) and Vandorpe below, 178.

24 Cf., e.g., P.Tebt. II 387 (73 CE—Tebtynis).

nome, but they are not valid everywhere. In a recent article (Yiftach-Firanko, 2009) I argued that in the early Roman period the scheme of the *cheirographon* was employed by professional scribes located in private scribal offices near the *Sarapeion* in the city of Oxyrhynchos. The scribes may have registered the contents of the document in their files. In both these respects, the Oxyrhynchite *cheirographa* are precursors of the 'new *cheirographon*', a scheme of the *cheirographon* applied by professional scribes called *tabelliones* throughout Egypt, starting from the reign of Diocletian.

The present volume contains six articles focusing on the use of the letter format as a legal document in the Greco-Roman world. Four, by Depauw, Jördens, Kovarik and Vandorpe, focus on Egypt; another two, by Jakab and Platschek, on Rome and Roman law. Depauw's article focuses on the Demotic epistolary format. Depauw first aims at clearing some methodological ambiguities, especially the identification as a contract of epistolary style of every contract that can not be formally identified as stemming from a notary office. Depauw discerns three types of documents: notary contracts (*sẖ*), contracts of epistolary format (*š*ʿ*.t*), and a large group of hybrid contracts leaning in some respects upon the notary contracts. Depauw first offers a clear definition of the scheme of letters in the Persian period: (1) the location of the date formula at the end of the contract, (2) the absence of the designation of the ruling pharaoh but the designation of the day, (3) the opening formula *ḫrw A m-bꜣḥ B* 'the voice of A before B' or A *smꜣ*ʿ *r* B (*m-bꜣḥ* G) 'A greets B (before the god G)', (4) the frequent absence of witnesses. In three cases these letters are of legal contents, making just a tiny fraction of the extant corpus of legal documents of the Persian period.

Depauw then studies the evolution of the letter format in the early Ptolemaic period (most conspicuously the introduction of the formula A *pꜣ nty ḏd (n* B*)* 'A is the one who says to B', which also appears in this period in notary contracts). In this period too, contracts of epistolary format make just 1% of our finding. A relative popularity is only evident after 150 BCE, a period in which 14% of the contracts are written in the epistolary style. In this period, Depauw notes two significant developments, which coincide with similar changes in the Greek sphere: (1) the *š*ʿ*.t* is expected to be written by the debtor in person, (2) witnesses generally become dispensable.

K. Vandorpe places the *cheirographon* in the broader context of types of documentation, Greek and Demotic alike, that were used for recording loans in the Ptolemaic period. Vandorpe's synopsis shows how the contents of each type of document prevalent in the Ptolemaic *chora* was offered security: she discusses witnesses, the existence of a *scriptura interior*, the types of clauses present in each type of contract, the format of the document (broad or narrow) and, in particular perhaps, how different forms of registration of the contents of the documents in a state or temple archive secured the terms of the contract. Vandorpe analyses, from the above viewpoints, first the older, more formal and more public types of documents that already emerge in the third century BCE: the double document, the Greek agoranomic document, and the Demotic temple contract. Then she moves on to the direct predecessor of the *cheirographon*, the 'informal *cheirographon*' as she terms it, to Demotic non-notarial acknowledgements of debt of the third century BCE, and finally discusses the formal *cheirographon* and the Demotic autograph acknowledgment of the late Ptolemaic period.

Vandorpe shows how the registration of the contract as well as the types of clauses commonly incorporated in it affected the scopes of its application. The *cheirographon* was commonly registered in an archive (so Vandorpe, see however above 23), and absorbed all types of clauses originating from the more formal, older types of documents. Among these clauses it was especially the *praxis* clause that made the *cheirographon* valid, she argues, according to the Greek law of the *chora*, and encouraged contracting parties to use the *cheirographon* for the documentation of all types of transactions, cheap and expensive alike. Vandorpe compares this strong position of the *cheirographon* with that of the contemporary Demotic autograph contract: here the clause placing the debtor's property as security for the debt, that is the Demotic equivalent to the Greek *praxis* clause, was generally omitted, and the contract was therefore generally used for the documentation of less valuable transactions.

As indicated above, in the Roman period the *cheirographon* became one of the key types of legal documents in Egypt. Its key features, scopes of application, and treatment by the state have all been dealt with, in brief, by H.J. Wolff,[25] but a more comprehensive study is required. At this stage it is sufficient to note several phenomena that anticipate two features of the later Roman *cheirographon* discussed by Jördens and Kovarik. The early Roman *cheirographon* is generally drafted by the debtor in person. Yet this is not always the case. The *cheirographon* is also consistently applied by professional scribes. This is the case in second century Arabia, as well as in first and second century Oxyrhynchos, and may thus account for the introduction of the *cheirographon* as the default format in legal documents issued by the *tabelliones* from the late third century CE onwards, a phenomenon discussed by Sophie Kovarik. The *cheirographon* was also drafted in a single copy that was kept, in the duration of the contract, in the hands of the creditor. As such, the *cheirographon* was suitable for the documentation of obligations entered upon by the debtor, but not those of the creditor. This state of affairs changed in late antiquity: from the third century onwards *cheirographa* are occasionally drafted in two, three and even four copies, and are as such also capable of documenting the obligations of multiple contractual parties, a phenomenon studied by A. Jördens.

Kovarik's survey focuses on the evolution of the *cheirographon* from the fourth through the eighth century CE. In late antiquity, the format of the *cheirographon* became the routine scheme employed by professional scribes called *tabelliones*. However, the new *cheirographon* was differently structured from the early Roman one. The date clause, which formerly appeared at the end of the contract, was now placed at its beginning, and the contract also recorded the name of the *tabellio* in charge,

25 Wolff 1978: 106–14.

and eventually also recorded witnesses. The new format was eventually regulated by law, in four constitutions of the emperor Justinian in 528, 537 and 538 CE, but it was introduced much earlier, initially in the reign of the emperor Diocletian. Still, as Kovarik has shown, the formation of the sixth-century *cheirographon* was a long process, which took different pace in different regions, in the course of which it influenced, and was influenced by, other types of widespread schemes.

A. Jördens focuses on a unique phenomenon. The *cheirographon* is commonly formulated as a letter by the prospective debtor to the prospective creditor. As such it is especially suitable for the documentation of obligations of the former, rather than those of the latter. This unilaterality finds expression also in the formulation of the address clause: "A (debtor) to B (creditor) greeting". Yet in thirty-four or thirty-five *cheirographa* dating from the second century onwards we find a different formulation: "A and B to each other greeting". Jördens first discusses the regional and diachronic distribution of the mutual *cheirographon* alongside other types of legal documents expressing the parties' mutual obligations. Jördens argues that bilaterality was especially stressed where the parties were of equal social standing, and where the parties' family or community aspired at maintaining oversight of the transaction documented. With regard to the *cheirographon*, Jördens stresses the role the bilateral formulation played in contracts of association, barter agreements, and agreements relating to the delegation of liturgies.

Éva Jakab's contribution takes us into the field of Roman law and legal practice. The first section of Jakab's paper focuses on the application of the *cheirographon* in everyday practice, as documented in the writings of the jurisprudents and in the *tabulae* stored in the files of the bank of the Suplicii in Puteoli (TPSulp.). The Roman *cheirographon* records the creation of debt. Its scheme is different from that of its Egyptian counterpart. It has no epistolary background: it contains no address clause, and is introduced by the formula *scripsi me acepisse*, vel sim. Yet the Roman *cheirographon* does share three important features of its Egyptian counterpart: its formulation is subjective (written in the first person singular); if the debtor is literate it is supposed to be autograph; the act is not attended by witnesses. The *cheirographon* was of Greek origin, and was integrated into the Roman contractual system, its composition creating an *obligatio stricti iuris*. If the *cheirographon* recorded a loan, the creditor could alternatively sue on account of the *numeratio*. Very frequently the *cheirographon* also recorded the act of *stipulatio*, thus according the creditor a third procedural means of retrieving at least some elements of the debt.

Jakab's second section focuses on the *epistula*. Contrary to the *communis opinio*, which tends to view the *epistula* and the *cheirographon* as synonymous term, Jakab's analysis proves that the *epistula* was an actual letter with legal contents. Just as the letter, the *epistula* is written by the contracting party in person, and presumes common social background between the author and the addressee, the main difference being that the *epistula* documents legal acts or states of affairs (thus resembling the evidence discussed, e.g., by D. Charpin and E. Harris). The *epistula* does not focus on loans. In the cases discussed by Jakab stand out *depositum*, *mandatum* and *manumissio*, but the *epistula* can be used for the documentation of any transaction whatsoever. Some of the transactions recorded in *epistulae* are very complex, involving three and more different persons. Unlike the *cheirographon*, the composition of an *epistula* also does not create an obligation; it is drawn up for evidentiary purposes only.

The paper of J. Platschek focuses on an issue already discussed by Jakab, the existence of two different forms of giving evidence of a debt, and assuming the commitment to its return. These two acts could be performed through a formal act of *stipulatio*. In that case the action for recovering the debt was *ex stiuplatu* or a *condictio*, both remedies anchored in *ius civile*. Alternatively, if no *stipulatio* was undertaken but the debtor could give evidence of his commitment to return the debt differently, the creditor would not benefit from a civilian remedy, but the praetor would grant him an *actio de pecunia constituta*, which would allow him to be compensated for any damage he suffered due to the failed payment.

Certain liabilities involving debts could result both from the civilian and formal act of the *stipulatio* and informally, e.g., by means of a letter, yet the remedies of which the creditor could avail himself were rigidly set apart: a creditor who received *stipulatio* was not allowed to resort to the *actio de pecunia constituta*, say in the case that the *stipulatio* turned defective. This is a remarkable rule compared with the remedies placed at the debtor's disposal for defending himself against a claim of the debt after it has already been settled: if the debt was returned through an *accepilatio*—that is the formal act terminating a debt created through a *stipulatio*—and the *accepilatio* turned for some reasons defective, the debtor could still apply for his defense the remedies provided by the praetor in the case of informal defrayment.

La lettre comme instrument de l'administration royale en Mésopotamie

Sophie Démare-Lafont (Paris)

La correspondance administrative est, de tout temps, un genre *a priori* austère et rébarbatif. Le style souvent redondant et la terminologie technique indigeste des technocrates modernes peuvent en effet décourager le citoyen de bonne volonté. Pourtant, les codes linguistiques mis en œuvre dans ce type de lettre présentent une certaine uniformité selon l'administration concernée et sont autant de marqueurs sociaux qui en disent aussi long sur la personnalité des protagonistes que sur les méandres des institutions publiques.

La même conclusion vaut pour les lettres administratives mésopotamiennes, qui se révèlent très stimulantes par la description concrète et vivante qu'elles fournissent sur les agissements des fonctionnaires et leurs méthodes. La principale qualité de ces tablettes est de mettre en avant les hommes plutôt que les institutions, et à travers eux, les modèles politiques dans lesquels s'inscrivent leurs fonctions. En effet, les milliers de textes émanant directement de l'administration, qu'elle soit royale ou locale, sont soit des bordereaux d'enregistrement pour la réception ou la livraison de denrées, de matières premières ou d'objets, soit des tablettes comptables. Ces documents permettent de restituer les opérations effectuées, les bilans d'exploitation, les gestions de stock et les procédures de contrôle. Mais par nature, ils ne disent rien sur la formation des agents en poste, ni sur leurs compétences ou leurs mérites ; il est parfois difficile aussi d'y trouver des indications sur les effectifs d'un service, la longévité du personnel en place ou la marge de manœuvre dont il dispose. C'est au contraire dans les lettres que ces renseignements ont le plus de chances d'être trouvés, à travers des cas d'espèce dont on peut espérer qu'ils sont représentatifs de leur époque et de leur milieu. Par recoupement avec d'autres dossiers, les profils de certaines fonctions et les carrières de certains personnages peuvent être reconstitués.

D'une manière générale, les sources mésopotamiennes soulignent une association constante entre les gens de pouvoir – issus de la famille royale, des élites locales ou du monde du palais – et le milieu des scribes, ces spécialistes de la gestion écrite qui maîtrisent l'usage des normes quantifiées. La royauté essaye ainsi, dans la mesure du possible, de combiner fidélité politique et qualification professionnelle dans la composition de son administration.

À partir de ce cadre commun à toutes les périodes de l'histoire cunéiforme, trois approches différentes de l'administration peuvent être dégagées, correspondant à trois époques particulièrement prolifiques :

- l'approche bureaucratique, typique de l'empire néo-sumérien à la fin du troisième millénaire, documentée par des tablettes provenant du sud, dans la région d'Ur ;
- l'approche familiale, représentative de la royauté amorrite au XVIIIe s. av. J.-C. et illustrée par les textes du royaume de Mari en Syrie ;
- l'approche impériale, caractéristique des sources néo-assyriennes des VIIIe-VIIe s. av. J.-C. provenant de Ninive.

Ces trois modèles sont autonomes et ne doivent pas être analysés de manière évolutive. Ils sont le reflet de trois conceptions différentes de la gestion des affaires publiques : la troisième dynastie d'Ur a construit un régime où les mécanismes administratifs occupent un rôle essentiel alors que l'idéologie tient une place relativement secondaire ; les rois de Mari ont développé une forme de pouvoir inspirée des liens lignagers d'origine bédouine et des prérogatives du chef de famille sur ses dépendants ; l'empire néo-assyrien a donné à la monarchie une dimension absolutiste qui s'est répercutée sur le fonctionnement de l'administration centrale et de la cour royale.

À ces trois catégories correspondent trois genres de lettres : les mandements (ou *letter-orders*), les lettres proprement dites et les placets. Bien qu'ils soient tous les trois attestés à la plupart des époques[1], ils n'en reflètent pas moins la tendance dominante de chacun des trois modèles énumérés plus haut. Trois personnages ont été choisis pour incarner ces trois visages de l'administration et illustrer tout le profit qu'apporte la lecture de la correspondance pour la compréhension de la culture administrative mésopotamienne.

1. Babati à l'époque néo-sumérienne (XXIe s. av. J.-C.)

Le corpus des lettres administratives néo-sumériennes compte plus d'un demi-millier de textes édités, généralement très courts (5 à 8 lignes) et ordonnant au(x) destinataire(s) de livrer un objet, de libérer un individu ou d'exécuter un travail.

Il est très rare que ces textes donnent une information détaillée sur les protagonistes. Le plus souvent, ces documents laconiques sont rédigés sans formule de salutation ni de bénédiction. L'adresse ne comporte en général que le nom du destinataire, sur le modèle « Dis à NP », et il arrive même qu'aucun nom ne figure. Le ton du message est impersonnel et presque familier, et son contenu est rédigé à la 3e personne du singulier, quoique les utilisations des 2e et 1e personnes soient fréquentes. La principale caractéristique des lettres administratives d'Ur III réside dans leur formule d'exhortation finale. La plus répandue est une expression qu'on peut traduire par « Pas de discussion » (nam-mi-gur-re, litt. « Qu'il ne revienne pas

1 Voir ici-même la contribution de D. Charpin pour les mandements et les placets à l'époque paléo-babylonienne.

(sur cet ordre) »), mais on trouve aussi des variantes pittoresques comme « Urgent ! » (a-ma-ru-kam litt. « C'est le déluge ! ») ou « Je t'en prie » (a-ba šeš-gu_{10}-gin_7 litt. « Qui est comme mon frère ? »). La date est rarement mentionnée, en revanche le sceau de l'expéditeur est déroulé théoriquement sur toutes les lettres ou leurs enveloppes[2].

Une catégorie particulière de lettres est représentée par la correspondance royale des souverains avec leurs fonctionnaires en poste dans l'empire. Cet ensemble de vingt-quatre tablettes est constitué – et c'est un fait unique dans la documentation cunéiforme – de textes apocryphes, tous rédigés à l'époque paléo-babylonienne[3] et appartenant à une tradition scribale extérieure à Isin. Les nombreux anachronismes ont conduit certains spécialistes à douter globalement de l'historicité du contenu de ces lettres, dont certaines ont été réécrites voire composées à l'époque paléo- et même médio-babylonienne[4]. Toutefois, s'il faut en effet manier avec prudence les informations transmises par ces sources, on ne peut leur dénier pour autant toute valeur historique (voir infra pp. 33s.).

Les données fournies par les mandements administratifs et les lettres royales ne se recoupent pas habituellement. Il est donc remarquable de disposer d'un cas où ces deux catégories épistolaires se combinent pour illustrer la carrière et les fonctions d'un grand serviteur de l'Etat : Babati. Ce dignitaire, issu d'un puissant clan du Nord de la Mésopotamie, fut rattaché à la famille royale par le mariage de sa sœur, Abi-simti, à un roi de la dynastie – certainement Šulgi – à qui elle donna un héritier au trône, Šu-Sin[5]. C'est ce souverain qui offrit à Babati un sceau énumérant une liste impressionnante de titres : archiviste (šadubba)[6], chef de l'administration royale (šà-tam lugal), gouverneur militaire (šagina) de Maškan-šarrum (une ville située à l'Est du Tigre et au Nord d'Ešnunna), gouverneur civil (ensí) d'Awal, une localité voisine, inspecteur des canaux d'irrigation et responsable administratif de divers terroirs appartenant aux deux reines (Abi-simti la reine-mère et Kubatum l'épouse

2 Sur les lettres d'Ur III, voir Sollberger 1966, à compléter avec Lafont 1990, Michalowski 1993: 52–118 et Huber 2001 et désormais l'édition de référence Michalowski 2011.

3 D'après leur grammaire et leurs colophons, les textes sont datés entre le milieu du règne de Rim-Sin et la fin de celui de Samsu-iluna, soit une période comprise entre les années 1790 et 1712 av. J.-C., sauf un exemplaire tardif de Suse. Cf. Michalowski 2011: 46 fn. 20.

4 Pour un point bibliographique sur cette question, cf. Huber 2001: 170. Voir maintenant Michalowski 2011 pour une mise en contexte historique de ces lettres. Je remercie B. Lafont pour les utiles mises à jour qu'il m'a signalées et pour ses commentaires sur ce dossier.

5 Sur Abi-simti, voir Dahl 2007: 10, 17 et 21. L'inscription originale du sceau de Babati (Frayne 1997: 340–1 n° 32) établit clairement qu'Abi-simti est la mère de Šu-Sin, mais ne dit rien sur l'identité de son royal époux. Abi-simti porte le titre de reine durant la dernière année du règne d'Amar-Sin mais il pourrait s'agir d'une désignation honorifique, qu'elle conserve dans les textes datés de son successeur Šu-Sin.

6 La lecture et le sens de ce terme sont très discutés. Voir les mises au point de Michalowski 1976: 50 et Borger 2004: 346 et tout dernièrement la traduction « high commissioner » de Michalowski 2011: 345 et 386.

de Šu-Sin)[7]. Le personnage a connu une ascension remarquable puisque, sous le règne d'Amar-Sin, il n'était attesté que comme « scribe » (dubsar), terme qui ne correspond pas à une profession mais plutôt à une fonction administrative. On sait en effet qu'il fut chargé pendant six ans, au début du règne d'Amar-Sin, de réceptionner les offrandes régulières à Drehem pour le compte de divers temples de Nippur.

C'est sans doute vers cette époque qu'il faut situer deux billets administratifs qui, de manière très atypique, sont consécutifs. Ils sont rédigés avec la sobriété propre à ce genre épistolaire, ce qui rend leur interprétation factuelle difficile; mais il est clair qu'ils se rapportent aux mêmes protagonistes et à la même affaire.

> « Dis à Nani de prendre auprès d'Urmes la tablette de Babati concernant 216 000 litres de grain. J'ai interrogé Babati ; qu'il (Nani) le déduise des comptes et qu'il détruise la tablette (de la dette) d'Urmes. (Sous une érasure) Pas de discussion ! »[8].
>
> « Dis à Nani : concernant la tablette de Babati que Urmes devait apporter, il y a du nouveau. Lu-enna a (maintenant) la tablette d'Urmes. Qu'il règle (l'affaire) et qu'on n'en parle plus. Babati ne t'a rien dit ? »[9].

Nani est un archiviste (šadubba) de Girsu, contemporain de Babati puisqu'il exerça ses activités durant les règnes d'Amar-Sin et de Šu-Sin[10]. Urmes est en revanche impossible à identifier, ce nom étant très répandu dans l'onomastique d'Ur III.

L'énorme quantité de grain mentionnée dans le premier texte rappelle les volumes comparables qui circulent entre les diverses villes provinciales, notamment pour la gestion des offrandes aux temples supervisée par Babati. Les 2160 hectolitres de grain cités ici pourraient constituer un reliquat de ces denrées. Cette hypothèse est confortée par le fait que le reste de la documentation concernant Babati n'évoque plus jamais cette activité bureaucratique. On le voit au contraire impliqué dans d'autres tâches plus politiques, coïncidant avec l'occurrence de son titre d' « archiviste » (šadubba).

Il est ainsi évoqué dans une lettre adressée à Šulgi, second roi de la dynastie, par le marchand Ur-DUN[11], qui raconte comment, dévalisé par des brigands et confronté à l'indifférence des autorités locales, il s'est tourné vers deux dignitaires voyageant dans les régions frontalières de l'Est : Arad-mu le chancelier et Babati l'archiviste

7 Pour l'édition du sceau, voir Goetze 1963: 22–3 n° 43 et Buchanan & Hallo 1981: 250–1, 453 n° 654.

8 Sollberger 1966: n° 165, réédité par Michalowski 1993: n° 88.

9 Lafont 1990: 169 n° 2. La présente traduction suit la version de Michalowski 1993: n° 89.

10 Il est attesté avec cette fonction entre AS 5 et ŠS 9 (cf. Lafont 1990: 168) ; on sait par ailleurs que Babati gère les offrandes aux temples de Nippur durant les six premières années d'Amar-Sin (cf. Çiğ Kizilyay & Salonen 1954: n° 552 et Owen 1975: n° 234).

11 YBC 5011, édité par Michalowski 1976: 216–20 n° 14 et Michalowski 2011 n° 11. Commentaire par Neumann 1992: 88–9; voir aussi Neumann 2006: 17–8 n° 5.

(šadubba), dont la présence s'explique par la charge de gouverneur militaire qu'il exerçait à Maškan-šarrum, une ville située dans la même zone géographique.

Šulgi cite encore Babati dans une lettre à Išbi-Erra, roi d'Isin, dans laquelle il reprend son titre d'archiviste et vante ses qualités personnelles : « lui (Babati) qui m'est comme un grand-père, un ancien, un conseiller qui sait vraiment donner des conseils »[12].

Preuve de la confiance que lui accordait le régime, il fut également chargé de la construction du mur contre les Amorrites durant la troisième année du règne de Šu-Sin. Une lettre de ce souverain à Šarrum-bani[13], un officier militaire commandant la garnison de Muriq-Tidnim, expose les lourdes récriminations royales à son encontre. À peine installé dans le Nord-Est, il se rendit coupable de violences et de pillages, en conséquence de quoi il fut démis de ses fonctions un mois plus tard, au profit de Babati : « Babati l'archiviste ..., par les instructions qui lui ont été données, doit construire la muraille. Et pour ce qui te concerne, avec les hommes qui sont sous ton commandement, va creuser le fossé ! » (ll. 35–38). Tous deux devaient veiller à maintenir la paix dans ce territoire, à ne libérer la main-d'œuvre qu'une fois les travaux achevés et à informer le roi du bon déroulement de leur mission (ll. 39–44). Reprenant la formule laconique des mandements administratifs, la lettre s'achève par un « Urgent ! » (l. 45 a-ma-ru-kam) lapidaire.

Dans toutes ces occurrences, Babati est désigné par son titre le plus élevé, šadubba, bien que les sources dépeignent d'autres facettes de son activité. C'est d'ailleurs cette même dignité qu'invoque le fils de Babati sur son propre sceau à l'égard de son père[14], voulant ainsi privilégier la fonction la plus illustre dont il avait peut-être hérité.

Il faut cependant souligner que les lettres royales ne cherchent pas à refléter la réalité mais plutôt le prestige des protagonistes. La documentation administrative courante le présente sous un jour plus ordinaire, par exemple comme maškim, « donneur d'ordre »[15].

En outre, l'exploitation historique de cette documentation épistolaire littéraire est délicate car, comme on l'a dit, elle est issue du milieu scribal paléo-babylonien et présente de nombreux anachronismes, tant du point de vue de la grammaire que du contenu. La lettre de Šulgi à Išbi-Erra est encore plus douteuse, du fait de sa datation très tardive – à la fin de l'époque paléo-babylonienne – et de son origine géographique (Suse). La mention de Babati dans la correspondance de Šulgi, qui plus est dans

12 Edzard 1974: 22–3 n° I iii 14–9 (sum.)/16–9 (akk.); Michalowski 2011: 382, 385–6.

13 YBC 4672 et BM 54327, édités par Michalowski 1976: n° 18 et Michalowski 2011: n° 19. Sur les attributions de Šarrum-bani, voir Michalowski 1976: 46–56.

14 Pour l'interprétation de ces sceaux de présentation comme marque à la fois de l'autorité du roi et du rang élevé de son propriétaire, voir Winter 1987.

15 YOS 15 200, concernant la livraison de deux anneaux d'argent à un individu. Sur le sens de maškim dans les textes administratifs de Drehem, voir Kang 1972: 248–56.

la position éminente de šadubba, y est d'autant plus suspecte qu'il n'apparaît jamais dans les tablettes contemporaines de ce souverain. Les scribes qui ont produit ces deux textes ont manifestement utilisé la technique du pastiche, en mélangeant des matériaux historiques divers sans tenir compte de leur chronologie[16]. Il ne faut pourtant pas rejeter en bloc les informations fournies par ces sources car même si elles ne sont pas totalement fiables, elles s'appuient sur un fond historique vérifiable[17]. Ainsi Babati est-il connu par ailleurs, grâce à une documentation authentique et incontestable. On sait notamment qu'il se trouve bien dans la région du Nord-Est au début du règne de Šu-Sin, comme l'atteste l'apposition de son sceau sur un billet administratif retrouvé dans le palais d'Eshnunna[18]. Apparemment, il y séjourne dans le cadre de sa mission de surveillance frontalière, liée à ses compétences de gouverneur militaire de Maškan-šarrum. Il autorise une livraison de farine prélevée sur les réserves royales et destinée à un dignitaire de Ninive, en visite sur le territoire de l'empire avec son escorte d'une centaine d'hommes. Babati fait ainsi figure de représentant du pouvoir central à l'occasion de cette visite d'État d'un diplomate de Ninive, consécutive à la victoire militaire de Šu-Sin dans les territoires voisins. Derrière cet acte comptable anodin se cache en fait une opération politique visant à stabiliser la frontière Nord de l'empire. Les responsabilités de Babati dépassent donc de simples attributions administratives locales et empiètent largement sur la sphère étatique.

Qu'il soit paré de ses plus hautes fonctions et doté de mérites personnels remarquables dans la correspondance royale, montre à quel point le personnage a impressionné les lettrés de la période paléo-babylonienne, qui ont même recopié son sceau[19] sans toutefois reproduire fidèlement l'original. Le faussaire a en effet reconstitué *in extenso* l'itinéraire administratif de Babati, ajoutant par exemple ses fonctions de scribe ou de gouverneur d'Apiak qui ne figuraient pas dans la version d'époque sumérienne. L'objectif est clairement de constituer un document factice : l'auteur n'a pas forcément l'intention de faire passer son travail pour authentique et les interpolations qu'il insère sont autant de marques de sa propre érudition et de son admiration pour une grande figure de l'administration impériale.

C'est peut-être un procédé comparable qui est à l'œuvre dans la correspondance royale : la paraphrase des originaux, visant à parfaire l'éducation politique des hauts fonctionnaires ou des princes par la commémoration de célèbres devanciers, a pu évoluer en véritable production littéraire[20]. Pour autant, sa substance n'est ni narrati-

16 Tel est le cas pour l'exemplaire de Suse, considéré comme un pastiche par Michalowski 1980–1983: 57. Le même auteur doute de l'authenticité des faits rapportés dans la lettre d'Ur-DUN, cf. Michalowski 2011: 345.

17 Voir sur ce point les critiques contre la notion de corpus apocryphe développées par Hallo 2006.

18 Whiting 1976: 178–9.

19 Voir Walker 1983.

20 Pour cette interprétation, Cavigneaux 2007.

ve ni romanesque, et rappelle à certains égards l'ego-histoire chère à P. Nora[21], par la dimension historiographique – plus que pédagogique – de la démarche et la subjectivité assumée de l'auteur. Sans doute voulait-on souligner ainsi que Babati a toujours été un proche du pouvoir, ce que reflètent sa longue carrière[22] et sa glorieuse renommée.

2. Habduma-Dagan à l'époque de Mari

Entre les années 1810 et 1760, le royaume amorrite de Mari a joué un rôle politique d'une certaine importance dans le contexte international complexe qui marque cette période. La Mésopotamie se couvre d'une multitude de royaumes de tailles diverses, tous amorrites mais pourtant rivaux entre eux et organisés sur le modèle vassalique[23].

La conception du pouvoir politique à Mari est assez éloignée de la notion d'État. Le roi se comporte au contraire comme un chef de famille, agissant avec le royaume comme avec sa maisonnée. D'ailleurs, le palais est géré comme une grande maison et son personnel administratif est assimilé à une domesticité honorable. Entre la gestion d'un domaine privé et celle du palais royal, il n'y a pas une différence de nature mais plutôt une différence d'échelle[24].

Cette dimension fortement privée se ressent dans la nature des relations entre le roi et ses agents administratifs. Leur mission principale est l'information : ils doivent toujours rapporter au roi, et à lui seul, ce qu'ils ont appris. Ils prennent cet engagement solennellement, sous forme de serments collectifs faits devant le souverain, auquel ils sont donc attachés par un lien personnel très fort, semblable à celui qui préside aux rapports avec les vassaux et les autres grands rois amorrites. Les notions de fidélité et de loyauté sont des références constantes dans le cadre politique et administratif de la période amorrite[25].

Mari est un cas particulièrement intéressant car sa population est composée de nomades et de sédentaires. Ces deux groupes ne sont pas antagonistes mais complémentaires car quoiqu'ayant des modes de vie différents (agriculteurs *vs* pasteurs), ils se reconnaissent dans une origine bédouine commune.

Une conséquence remarquable du dimorphisme de la société mariote est la double organisation administrative du royaume. Les sédentaires sont soumis à une administration territoriale à la tête de laquelle est placé un gouverneur (*šapīṭum*) assisté d'un intendant (*abu bītim*) et d'un responsable du cadastre (*ša sikkatim*). Les nomades, qui se déplacent à la recherche des meilleures pâtures, y compris hors des frontières du royaume, sont rattachés à l'autorité d'un responsable spécifique, le chef

21 Nora 1987.

22 Il n'est pas exclu qu'on retrouve des textes documentant la présence de Babati dès le règne de Šulgi.

23 Sur l'histoire politique de Mari, voir Charpin & Ziegler 2003.

24 Voir Charpin 1996: 223 et n. 9.

25 Voir l'étude de Lafont 2001: 247–50.

des pâtures (*merhûm*), dont la compétence est géographiquement illimitée puisqu'elle couvre tous les lieux traversés par les pasteurs et leurs troupeaux. L'une de ses fonctions essentielles est d'ailleurs de conduire les grandes transhumances et de discuter avec les responsables locaux des modalités de passage et d'accès aux points d'eau. Il est aussi chargé de convoquer les nomades à l'armée en cas de guerre et prend parfois leur commandement au combat. Contrairement au gouverneur, dont les prérogatives s'exercent de manière continue, le chef des pâtures agit à la demande, lorsque son intervention apparaît nécessaire. Chaque institution se conforme ainsi au mode de vie des populations dont elle a la responsabilité.

Les deux fonctions de gouverneur et chef des pâtures ne sont pas incompatibles, comme le montre le cas de Habduma-Dagan, évoqué dans deux lettres datant du règne de Yasmah-Addu. Celui-ci fut placé – sans doute très jeune – sur le trône de Mari par son père Samsi-Addu, à la tête du Royaume de Haute Mésopotamie. Faute d'expérience et de goût pour le pouvoir politique, Yasmah-Addu fut souvent réprimandé par son père, qui lui reprochait sa paresse et son manque de clairvoyance, et fut sans doute astreint à rendre des comptes et à solliciter l'avis paternel avant de prendre une décision. La nomination de Habduma-Dagan en est un bon exemple : avant d'être recruté, sa candidature fut proposée à Samsi-Addu qui donna son accord en des termes élogieux.

Deux courriers furent adressés à Samsi-Addu, correspondant apparemment aux deux postes auxquels Habduma-Dagan fut nommé.

Dans un premier temps, il fut affecté à Tuttul comme gouverneur en remplacement d'un nommé Yašub-El :

> « Dis à Yasmah-Addu : ainsi parle Samsi-Addu ton père.
> Etant donné que Yašub-El, (l'homme) de Tuttul, est mort, tu m'as écrit pour installer à sa place Habduma-Dagan. Comment vois-tu l'affaire ? Ta tablette n'est pas explicite. Est-ce que tu comptes l'installer là-bas complètement et installeras-tu un autre responsable de service ? De toute façon, Habduma-Dagan convient à être nommé là-bas. C'est un homme de confiance. Il a pris son envol du côté du « Bureau de la viande » et, si je le considère, il n'a jamais commis de faute ou de manquement. Il est scrupuleux et de confiance. À l'heure actuelle, installe(-le) à Tuttul et tiens-lui ce langage : « Pourquoi habites-tu à Zibnatum parmi des familles sans avenir, sur un terroir caillouteux ? Réside à Tuttul même, là où tu pourras faire souche et créer une maisonnée. Le terrain labourable (y) est abondant : ce pays est comme le Šubartum. Le terrain labourable (y) est abondant. Vas-y résider. Installes-(y) une maison d'hommes et fais-y souche. Garde prospère pour son Seigneur ville et pays ! »
>
> Voilà le langage que tu dois lui tenir. Ôte-lui toute appréhension et installe-le à Tuttul. À ses côtés, place un intendant de confiance (et) un responsable du cadastre de confiance.

D'autre part, à Zibnatum, à la place de Habduma-Dagan, installe quelqu'un (pris) parmi les gens de cet endroit même, ou bien (pris) parmi les fonctionnaires du palais qui sont à ton service direct, ou bien encore une tierce personne de confiance »[26].

Cette lettre permet de reconstituer la carrière du nouveau gouverneur, à travers toutes les promotions qu'il a eues. Il débute comme chef de service au palais de Mari, plus précisément au Bureau de la viande où il était sans doute chargé de la gestion des stocks ; il dirige ensuite le centre provincial modeste de Zibnatum, dans la province de Saggaratum, avant d'être nommé gouverneur de Tuttul. Ce parcours progressif s'explique sans doute par l'origine familiale modeste de Habduma-Dagan, qui s'est élevé dans la hiérarchie grâce à ses compétences. Mais souvent, les dignitaires sont choisis parmi les notables locaux et directement nommés à des postes élevés, sans avoir à passer par les échelons intermédiaires.

On notera que Habduma-Dagan a commencé son cursus à Mari même et qu'il a ensuite été affecté à des postes plus éloignés. Contrairement à la règle actuelle pour les mutations dans l'administration, le mouvement des promotions va de la capitale vers la province. L'agent doit d'abord faire ses preuves sous la surveillance directe du palais royal, puis il reçoit des responsabilités plus importantes en province, où son activité est plus difficile à contrôler. Etre envoyé loin de Mari n'est donc pas une sanction mais au contraire une marque de confiance[27].

Le nouveau venu ne choisit pas sa propre équipe, qui lui est imposée par le gouvernement central. Il est assisté d'un intendant et d'un responsable du cadastre, et entouré d'employés subalternes dont la lettre ne dit rien mais qui devaient être recrutés sur place, avec peut-être l'assentiment du roi. Le texte ne détaille pas le contenu des fonctions du gouverneur, qui sont très vastes, incluant des attributions militaires, administratives et judiciaires. Il est particulièrement chargé des relations avec les habitants de sa province, doit surveiller les étrangers et renseigner les autorités centrales sur leurs activités. Il peut aussi réquisitionner la population pour des grands travaux ou des guerres ponctuelles et doit veiller au ravitaillement en cas de conflit armé.

Le passage vantant les avantages de la vie à Tuttul est très inhabituel : en principe, un fonctionnaire ne donne pas son avis sur son affectation. En outre, celle-ci semble être définitive ou au moins durable puisqu'il est offert à Habduma-Dagan de « créer sa maisonnée » à Tuttul ; or, la règle semble être plutôt la mobilité, pour assurer les besoins immédiats en personnel dans les diverses places du royaume, mais aussi pour garantir la fidélité des administrateurs au souverain. L'installation dans une région risque de faire prévaloir les intérêts privés au détriment de ceux de

26 Durand 1997: 160–1 n° 43.
27 Villard 2001: 113.

la royauté. La stratégie inverse proposée à Habduma-Dagan s'explique peut-être par l'emplacement géographique de Tuttul, située à la frontière du royaume et donc exposée aux attaques ennemies : le danger attaché à ce poste est ainsi compensé par la promotion qu'il représente[28].

On remarquera enfin que Samsi-Addu insiste sur les qualités personnelles du candidat, présenté comme loyal (« il n'a jamais commis de faute ou de manquement »), scrupuleux et digne de confiance. Il paraît être l'homme idéal pour le poste, combinant des compétences administratives reconnues avec une déontologie sans faille.

Une seconde lettre montre qu'il a aussi exercé la fonction de chef des pâtures (*merhûm*) en même temps que celle de gouverneur :

> « Dis à Yasmah-Addu : ainsi parle Samsi-Addu ton père.
> (…)
> Autre chose : tu m'as écrit à propos de la nomination de Habduma-Dagan, fils d'Aya-la-Sumu, à l'office de chef des pâtures. Comme tu me l'as écrit, il convient tout à fait à être nommé à ce poste. Qu'est-ce qu'un simple poste de gouverneur pour lui ? On croirait qu'il commande à une vaste région ! Il faut qu'il ait le commandement de Tuttul et exerce aussi la charge de chef des pâtures ! De la même façon que ses collègues ont de vastes territoires à commander, qu'il exerce le commandement à Tuttul ! Cela fera l'équivalent des territoires que ses collègues ont à commander »[29].

Le cumul des fonctions n'est pas fréquent et doit être dicté ici par les circonstances. Samsi-Addu semble considérer que la taille du territoire de Tuttul est insuffisante par rapport aux autres districts, ce qui pourrait placer Habduma-Dagan en position d'infériorité vis-à-vis de ses collègues. Pour lui assurer un niveau d'autorité comparable à celui des autres gouverneurs, il obtient donc l'office de chef des pâtures. L'argument est étonnant : il s'appuie sur des questions de préséance là où on attendrait des considérations sur l'efficacité administrative et la bonne gouvernance. La réponse du Grand roi semble motivée par la réaction probablement mitigée de l'intéressé face à la première offre d'un « simple poste de gouverneur ». C'est Habduma-Dagan lui-même qui a dû réclamer une position plus prestigieuse, sachant que sa mutation serait définitive et qu'il lui serait ensuite difficile d'obtenir une promotion. La description de la vie à Tuttul dans la lettre précédente est donc bien destinée à masquer tous les désagréments de cette affectation peu attractive, que doit corriger l'attribution d'une charge supplémentaire.

Il n'est pas certain que l'itinéraire de Habduma-Dagan soit représentatif de la carrière habituelle d'un haut dignitaire du royaume de Mari. Au contraire, chaque

28 Villard 2001: 114.
29 Durand 1998: 340 n° 639 (extrait).

cas semble être particulier, dépendant de l'origine familiale et ethnique au moins autant que des compétences politiques et administratives. Ainsi que l'a noté P. Villard, les lettres de Mari ne permettent pas de reconstituer un *cursus honorum* mais seulement des destins personnels[30].

3. Adad-šum-uṣur à l'époque néo-assyrienne

Le troisième volet de cette enquête se place au premier millénaire, à l'épogée de l'empire assyrien (VIIIe-VIIe s. av. J.-C.)

Le siège du pouvoir politique est désormais le palais royal, luxueuse résidence abritant la famille du souverain, son harem mais aussi les hauts fonctionnaires, les courtisans et le personnel domestique. L'administration palatiale est pléthorique et les fonctions sont parfois doublées à cause de la lourdeur des tâches.

À tous les échelons de l'administration – centrale, provinciale et locale – une confusion s'opère entre gestion impériale et gestion domaniale : le palais est un centre à la fois de gouvernement et d'administration du domaine du roi ; il en va de même dans les palais secondaires, c'est-à-dire dans les autres résidences royales, et dans les centres provinciaux.

Le régime présente les traits d'un absolutisme monarchique, en particulier sous les Sargonides[31] où la composition de l'administration dépend de la seule volonté royale. Les dignitaires sont donc révocables à tout moment. Les fonctionnaires jurent au roi fidélité et obéissance absolues, ce qui leur vaut les faveurs du pouvoir[32]. Au contraire, l'opposition réelle ou supposée est punie de mort. Cette pratique a instauré un climat de suspicion et de dénonciation dans l'entourage du roi. Pour éliminer un concurrent ou se venger d'un courtisan trop apprécié, il suffit de le faire passer pour un ennemi du pouvoir assyrien. Des clans se forment à l'intérieur de la cour, pour influer sur la nomination du successeur à un poste administratif important.

Un climat détestable s'instaure ainsi à la cour de Ninive, comme en témoignent les lettres au roi remplies de dénonciations, vraies ou fausses, mais aussi de protestations de fidélité de la part d'individus qui ont été accusés à tort ou craignent de l'être et prennent les devants pour faire cesser les racontars[33].

Dans cette atmosphère de suspicion, le souverain doit s'en remettre à la divination pour s'assurer de la fidélité de son personnel administratif, du moins pour ce qui concerne les postes les plus élevés. Le roi est donc entouré, voire cerné, d'un corps d'experts qui sont sa garde spirituelle : ils guettent dans les astres et les foies

30 Villard 2001: 113.

31 Derniers rois assyriens à partir de Sargon II (721 – 705).

32 Sur les serments du personnel politique et administratif à l'époque néo-assyrienne (*adê*), voir Parpola & Watanabe 1988.

33 Sur la correspondance des rois néo-assyriens, voir Parpola 1987, Lanfranchi & Parpola 1990, Fuchs & Parpola 2001, Luukko & Van Buylaere 2002, Dietrich 2003 et Reynolds 2003.

d'animaux des signes favorables ou défavorables. On mesure, grâce à ces textes du palais de Ninive[34], l'engrenage dans lequel s'enferme la royauté, obsédée par la crainte du complot et soumise à la surenchère constante de courtisans opportunistes.

C'est dans ce contexte que se place le texte ci-dessous, illustrant un cas de disgrâce à l'époque d'Assurbanipal (668 – 627).

La lettre a été écrite au tout début du règne d'Assurbanipal[35]. Son auteur est le chef des exorcistes Adad-šum-uṣur, un des grands lettrés de la cour qui appartient au groupe des experts composant la « garde spirituelle » du souverain, chargée de le protéger contre les mauvaises influences. Nommé à ce poste par le roi précédent Assarhaddon, il est reconduit par Assurbanipal son successeur suivant la procédure habituelle : à son avènement, les dignitaires et fonctionnaires en place remettent leur charge au roi, qui les leur restitue ou pas, selon son bon vouloir. Or, le fils d'Adad-šum-uṣur, Urad-Gula, a été évincé de la cour et n'a pas été reconduit dans ses fonctions. La lettre est donc destinée à le réhabiliter auprès du souverain. Elle correspond au genre des suppliques, si courantes dans de nombreux régimes monarchiques, et fournit un témoignage très intéressant sur les vicissitudes de la vie de courtisan.

> « Au roi mon Seigneur, de la part de ton serviteur Adad-šum-uṣur. Que la santé du roi mon seigneur soit bonne ! Que Nabu et Marduk bénissent grandement le roi mon Seigneur!
>
> Aššur, le roi des dieux, a prononcé le nom du roi mon Seigneur pour qu'il exerce la royauté en Assyrie. Šamaš et Adad, par leurs réponses oraculaires sans équivoque, ont donné confirmation au roi mon Seigneur, pour l'exercice de la royauté sur tous les pays.
>
> Le règne est bon : des jours de droiture, des années de justice, des pluies à profusion, des crues très abondantes, un cours des prix favorables ! Les dieux sont amicaux, la piété est répandue, les temples regorgent d'opulence, les grands dieux du ciel et de la terre ont été exaltés sous le règne du roi mon Seigneur. Les vieux dansent allègrement, les jeunes gens chantent, les femmes et les jeunes filles sont dans la joie et la jubilation. On épouse des femmes que l'on pourvoit d'anneaux précieux, on met au monde des fils et des filles, les naissances se déroulent bien. Celui qui était coupable et que l'on avait condamné à mort, le roi mon Seigneur lui a fait grâce de la vie ; celui qui était détenu depuis de nombreuses années, tu l'as libéré. Ceux qui étaient malades depuis longtemps ont retrouvé la santé. Les affamés ont été rassasiés, ceux qui étaient desséchés ont été oints, et les gens nus couverts d'un vêtement.

34 Voir notamment Parpola 1983 et Starr 1990.

35 Sur la datation précise de cette lettre, voir la proposition de Parpola 1983: 104 et les critiques de Villard 1994.

> Pourquoi Urad-Gula et moi-même, au milieu d'eux, serions-nous moroses et déprimés ? Or, le roi mon seigneur vient de témoigner à ses sujets son amour pour Ninive. Il a ainsi parlé aux chefs de famille : « Amenez-moi vos fils, afin qu'ils se tiennent devant moi ! » Urad-Gula est mon fils. Il devrait lui aussi se tenir avec eux dans l'entourage du roi mon Seigneur, afin que nous puissions avec tout le peuple nous réjouir, danser et bénir le roi mon Seigneur ! Mes yeux sont fixés sur le roi mon Seigneur. Mais ceux qui se tiennent dans le palais, tous ces gens-là ne m'aiment pas. Il n'y a personne parmi eux qui soit mon ami, pas un à qui je puisse faire tenir un présent, qui l'accepte de moi et intercède en ma faveur. Puisse le roi mon Seigneur prendre pitié de son serviteur, afin que parmi tous ses sujets, moi, je n'en vienne pas à périr ! Puissent ceux qui se réjouissent de mon malheur ne pas réaliser ce qu'ils désirent contre moi ! »[36].

Le premier paragraphe fait référence au mode de désignation du roi par Aššur, principal dieu assyrien, qui délègue son pouvoir au souverain.

En réalité, beaucoup d'intrigues entourent les successions royales car même si le principe dynastique est admis, ce n'est pas toujours l'aîné qui règne. Ainsi Assurbanipal était-il le cadet et fut-il désigné grâce au soutien de sa grand-mère Zakutu et au détriment de son frère Šamaš-šum-ukin, qui devint roi de Babylone[37].

Ce choix a été confirmé par des interrogations oraculaires, comme l'indiquent les références à Šamaš et Adad, patrons de la science divinatoire. Les dieux ont donné des réponses « sans équivoque » dit le texte, ce qui signifie qu'il y a eu plusieurs interrogations au cours de la procédure et qu'aucune n'a été négative ou douteuse[38]. Il est possible que cette étape ait abouti au changement de nom du prince, qui aurait reçu à cette occasion son nom de trône : Assurbanipal signifie en effet « (le dieu) Aššur a créé l'héritier » (*Aššur-bāni-apli*), ce qui paraît constituer une onomastique de circonstance[39]. L'allusion pourrait être aussi une manière de rappeler discrètement au roi qu'il a été soutenu par le milieu des experts en divination, auquel appartient l'expéditeur de la lettre. On voit par là le poids des influences de la cour dans les décisions politiques.

Le deuxième paragraphe consiste en une apologie du règne d'Assurbanipal et présente un tableau du « bon gouvernement », conséquence directe de la faveur divine.

36 Parpola 1993: 177–8 n° 226. Traduction récente par Foster 2005: 1017–8. Commentaires par Deller 1969 et Fales 1974.

37 Sur l'influence de la reine-mère Zakutu (= Naq'ia) dans la succession d'Assarhaddon, voir Melville 1999.

38 Sur les procédures oraculaires néo-assyriennes dans le domaine politique, voir Starr 1990.

39 Pour cette hypothèse, cf. Parpola 1983: 106.

On y retrouve les thèmes obligés du genre, dont certains sont communs à la littérature politique contemporaine : la longévité des sujets, la prospérité du pays[40], la justice, la richesse et la piété. Le bon roi est celui qui assure le bonheur de son peuple : jeunes et vieux s'épanouissent dans une société festive et insouciante ; les hommes sont assez riches pour offrir des bijoux à leurs femmes, lesquelles sont fécondes et vigoureuses. La référence aux « anneaux précieux » pourrait avoir un lien avec ce que les Lois médio-assyriennes appelent les *dumāqu*, litt. « ornements », remis par le mari à sa femme pour qu'elle en ait l'usage durant le mariage[41].

La notion de roi de justice est évoquée par deux allusions subtiles, l'une à la grâce et l'autre à la rémission des dettes. Ces deux piliers de la fonction royale sont très anciens et constituent la base de l'idéologie monarchique au deuxième millénaire.

Le pouvoir de ramener à la vie celui qui a été condamné à mort est attesté dans les sources paléo-babyloniennes à travers l'expression *imat ul iballuṭ*, « il mourra, il ne vivra pas ». Ainsi que l'a démontré R. Westbrook[42], cette forme n'est pas une redondance stylistique mais une description du droit de vie et de mort que détient le souverain sur ses sujets. La forme *imat* « il mourra », évoque l'exécution décidée par le tribunal. Cette sentence peut être annulée par la volonté du roi, qui seul peut « ressuciter » (*bulluṭum*, « faire vivre ») le mort juridique ; il arrive cependant que la gravité du crime interdise ce pardon, d'où la formule négative *ul iballuṭ* « il ne vivra pas ». La lettre d'Adad-šum-uṣur montre que cette prérogative royale, exclusive et exorbitante du droit commun, persiste au premier millénaire.

L'enfermement pour dettes est l'autre motif d'intervention du roi dans la vie juridique. On sait que les crises économiques et la pratique immodérée du crédit sont une cause majeure d'asservissement des individus, à partir du deuxième millénaire. Les souverains agissent ponctuellement pour atténuer provisoirement cette paupérisation endémique, en promulguant des édits qui annulent rétroactivement les dettes non-commerciales de l'année écoulée. Ces actes de « redressement » au sens propre (*mīšarum*) ont d'abord été connus pour le monde babylonien[43]. Ils sont désormais attestés en contexte assyrien au premier millénaire[44]. La supplique mentionne ces mesures de justice sociale en rappelant qu'Assurbanipal a libéré « celui qui était détenu depuis de nombreuses années ».

Les deux dernières phrases soulignent la fonction protectrice et nourricière du souverain : les malades guérissent, et les autres trouvent du travail comme l'indique

40 Voir la description de ces années heureuses dans le Prisme B d'Assurbanipal, édité par Piepkorn 1933: 28 ll. 22–38, et retravaillée par Parpola 1983: 104–5.

41 Cf. §§ 25–6 et 38 tabl. A Lois assyriennes ; pour l'interprétation juridique de ce terme, cf. van Praag 1945: 170–2 et Cardascia 1969: 153. Sur le terme *qudašāte* « boucles d'oreilles » (l. 19) en référence à un rite matrimonial, cf. Deller 1969: 53.

42 Westbrook 1997.

43 Voir l'édition et le commentaire des édits paléo-babyloniens par Kraus 1984, à compléter avec Charpin 1990.

44 Villard 2007.

la triple allusion finale à ceux qui avaient faim, étaient déssêchés et n'avaient pas de vêtements. Cette énumération rappelle, dans un style littéraire, les trois rations qui rémunèrent habituellement la main d'œuvre non qualifiée : l'orge, l'huile et la laine. P. Villard souligne cependant que le geste de vêtir celui qui est nu est associé à la proclamation d'un édit de rémission des dettes dans les inscriptions d'Assarhaddon[45].

Tout ce passage dépeint donc une société vivant dans l'opulence et la félicité. Le troisième paragraphe du texte marque une rupture de ton puisque, par contraste avec l'euphorie générale, Urad-Gula et son père sont « moroses et déprimés ». La raison qui en est donnée est d'ordre affectif : le roi a manifesté son « amour » aux habitants de Ninive, la capitale, mais il a oublié d'y associer son fidèle serviteur Adad-šum-uṣur. Les notables ont en effet été convoqués devant Assurbanipal pour lui présenter leurs fils afin qu'ils entrent à son service, littéralement qu'ils « se tiennent devant » le souverain. Urad-Gula n'a pas été choisi, et peut-être n'a-t-il même pas été convié. Ce manque de reconnaissance envers un allié du régime, qui s'est toujours montré loyal et n'a jamais démérité, est attribué par Adad-šum-uṣur à son isolement à la cour. Manifestement, la générosité du monarque bénéficie en priorité à celui qui a un intercesseur, un courtisan capable de faire valoir les qualités de son protégé. Naturellement, cette médiation n'est pas gratuite et il est d'usage d'offrir un cadeau à celui qui va plaider la cause d'un fils de famille auprès du roi. C'est même à cela que se reconnaît un « ami » dans les cercles politiques et c'est précisément ce qui manque à l'auteur de la lettre. Que le chef des exorcistes n'ait aucun soutien dans l'entourage royal signifie que ses anciens appuis ont disparu. À son avènement, Assurbanipal semble avoir renouvelé en profondeur le personnel politique et éliminé ceux dont il se méfiait. Adad-šum-uṣur n'a pas personnellement souffert de cette épuration puisqu'il a été reconduit, mais il se retrouve en position de faiblesse car il n'est pas assuré que son héritier lui succèdera au poste qu'il occupe. Le désaveu du fils affecte donc la réputation du père, lequel en est alors réduit à implorer directement le roi, ce qui est sans doute un peu humiliant vis-à-vis de ses collègues. Dans l'univers clos du palais qui se nourrit d'intrigues et de rumeurs, la disgrâce d'un prestigieux dignitaire est un affront. La seule issue est d'adresser au roi une supplique éblouissante de finesse et d'érudition. La mesquinerie des ragots qui ont provoqué le malheur d'une honorable famille n'en sera que plus évidente.

La lettre d'Adad-šum-uṣur apparaît ainsi comme un modèle du genre. La maîtrise des codes attendus dans ce type d'exercice est parfaite. Il n'est fait allusion nulle part aux compétences d'Urad-Gula, ni à la nature des critiques qui ont été répandues à son sujet. De tels arguments seraient indignes d'un grand intellectuel qui souhaite plaire au roi plutôt que le convaincre. Assurbanipal est instruit, cultivé et sensible à l'érudition. La bibliothèque qu'il a fait constituer pour son propre usage, distincte du fonds dynastique hérité de son grand-père Sennacherib, témoigne amplement de son

45 Villard 2007: 117.

goût pour les belles-lettres et la connaissance scientifique[46]. C'est donc sur ce terrain de l'érudition que le chef des exorcistes espère séduire son auguste destinataire. La mise en scène très théâtrale de son infortune rappelle la célèbre complainte du Juste souffrant – précurseur cassite du livre biblique de Job – dans laquelle le narrateur détaille tous les maux physiques et sociaux qu'il a dû affronter après une période de grande prospérité ; abandonné des dieux, du roi et même de ses esclaves, assailli par des maladies inconnues dont aucun expert ne peut le délivrer, il affronte la solitude et la souffrance sans comprendre la cause de cet accablement. Son calvaire ne s'achève que lorsque Marduk décide d'y mettre fin[47]. Adad-šum-uṣur décrit son sort en des termes semblables et attend le bon vouloir du souverain pour le sauver. Cette soumission totale à l'arbitraire royal manifeste la posture humble et résignée d'un personnage pourtant important, mais s'inscrit aussi dans le registre de la flatterie savante. Ainsi l'expéditeur de la lettre parvient-il à concilier son intérêt personnel avec les codes en vigueur à la cour.

En dépit de sa grande sagacité, Adad-šum-uṣur a échoué dans sa démarche. Assurbanipal a bien lu la lettre et l'a archivée dans sa bibliothèque, probablement parce qu'elle est exemplaire. Mais il n'a pas intégré Urad-Gula à la cour, malgré les tentatives réitérées de son père. Il faut croire que l'intelligence et les compétences du géniteur n'ont pas été transmises au rejeton, donnant ainsi un fondement aux médisances persistantes.

Les lettres sont, on le voit, un support d'expression très représentatif de la pratique administrative. Elles mettent l'accent sur des aspects quotidiens de l'activité des agents, mais documentent aussi les étapes de leur cursus et les aléas de leurs parcours. Elles révèlent les circuits décisionnaires, les enjeux des nominations aux postes importants, la variété des missions confiées à un officier et les incertitudes attachées à sa carrière. Grâce à la documentation épistolaire, l'administration cesse d'être une entité confuse et opaque, elle s'incarne dans des destins glorieux ou pathétiques.

46 Voir Villard 1997.
47 Pour une traduction récente, voir Foster 2005: 392–409.

« Garde ma lettre en témoignage » Le rôle de la correspondance dans le système juridique mésopotamien de la première moitié du deuxième millénaire av. n. è.*

Dominique Charpin (Paris)

La Mésopotamie des XXe–XVIIe siècles av. n. è. à laquelle est consacrée cette contribution est indubitablement l'héritière du troisième millénaire, tant du point de vue politique que culturel[1]. Elle se caractérise par une tension entre des mouvements de parcellisation, laissant place à des dizaines d'États, et un courant d'unification, qui a connu son apogée sous les rois de Babylone Hammu-rabi et Samsu-iluna[2] : durant un quart de siècle, entre 1763 et 1738, le territoire correspondant au centre et au sud de l'Irak actuel a été regroupé dans un ensemble politique unique, qui s'est ensuite assez rapidement décomposé. C'est en raison de cette brève phase unitaire sous l'égide de Babylone que l'ensemble de la période est décrite comme « paléo-babylonienne ». La place de l'écrit dans le droit mésopotamien s'est très nettement accrue à cette époque[3]. Il n'y avait pas alors d'archives publiques: les archives palatiales sont les archives de la Maison du roi, celles des temples reflètent seulement la gestion de ces grands organismes. La période paléo-babylonienne se caractérise avant tout par l'abondance des archives familiales. Elles comportent de très nombreux contrats, qu'il s'agisse de titres de propriété transmis de génération en génération avec les biens correspondants, ou de documents à durée limitée comme les prêts, les baux, etc., qui étaient régulièrement triés, les documents périmés étant mis au rebut. On y trouve également de nombreux procès, ou plus exactement « tablettes de non revendication » remises à celui qui l'emportait lors d'un procès (Dombradi

* Cette étude a été réalisée dans le cadre du projet « ARCHIBAB (Archives babyloniennes, XXe–XVIIe siècles) », financé pour 2008–2010 par l'ANR (Agence Nationale de la Recherche) au titre de l'appel d'offres « Corpus et outils de la recherche en sciences humaines et sociales ».

1 Pour le droit et la vie juridique au troisième millénaire, voir Wilcke 2007.

2 Pour une synthèse récente sur cette période, voir Charpin 2003. Plus complet: Charpin, Edzard & Stol 2004. Par convention, on utilisera ici la chronologie dite moyenne (Hammu-rabi: 1792–1750 av. n. è.).

3 Une bibliographie complète des quelque 31.000 documents d'archives paléo-babyloniens intégralement publiés est disponible sur le site www.archibab.fr, ou on trouvera également la liste des sigles utilisés dans cette contribution. Pour les sources écrites de la période paléo-babylonienne, voir la présentation et la bibliographie de Charpin 2004: 39–56 et 403–80.

1996). Mais ces archives comportent aussi de nombreuses lettres, qui forment également une part importante des archives découvertes dans les palais de la même époque[4]. Cette correspondance nous donne énormément d'information sur le droit et le système juridique[5]. Mais le genre littéraire de la lettre a aussi été utilisé en tant qu'instrument juridique. On étudiera d'abord la façon dont se sont développés à partir du formulaire standard de la lettre deux types spécifiques : les mandements (*letter orders*)[6] et les placets. On verra ensuite comment les lettres étaient présentées comme éléments de preuve par leurs auteurs. Pour finir, on analysera la façon dont les rois utilisaient la lettre pour communiquer leurs ordres et édits, ainsi que l'utilisation des rescrits royaux dans la jurisprudence.

1. Des lettres particulières

Le genre de la lettre a pris naissance en Mésopotamie au XXIVe siècle, mais il a connu un développement important au début du deuxième millénaire (Sallaberger 1999; Charpin 2007b; Charpin 2008: 161–92). Non seulement les lettres deviennent alors beaucoup plus nombreuses, mais leur longueur s'accroit et leur contenu se diversifie à l'extrême : à côté de la correspondance diplomatique et administrative, on dispose également de nombreuses lettres d'affaires mais aussi de missives à caractère privé. Même si les lettres n'ont pas un formulaire aussi rigide que les contrats rédigés à la même époque, on peut présenter quelques caractéristiques de la correspondance :

- la formule d'adresse est figée et remonte au temps où les messages n'étaient pas encore mis par écrit. Le début de la lettre est un discours de l'expéditeur au messager : « Dis à X ». Puis le messager s'adresse au destinataire : « ainsi (parle) Y. » La suite est le discours de l'expéditeur au destinataire;
- l'adresse est généralement suivie par une formule de bénédiction. Celle-ci, absente de la correspondance royale, est de règle dans les lettres échangées entre particuliers, même si elles ont un caractère officiel;

4 Plusieurs corpus sont consacrés à leur édition:
– la série des *Altbabylonische Briefe,* Leyde, 14 vol. depuis 1964 (2762 lettres dont 799 précédemment inédites, provenant essentiellement de collections acquises sur le marché des antiquités) ;
– les volumes et séries consacrés à l'édition d'archives issues de fouilles régulières. Le lot le plus important est celui des archives de Mari, éditées dans deux séries: *Archives royales de Mari* (Paris, 30 volumes depuis 1950) et *Florilegium Marianum* (=FM) (Paris, 11 volumes depuis 1991), avec au total 2536 lettres (sur un ensemble de 8667 textes intégralement publiés). On a également des lots plus restreints provenant surtout de Mésopotamie du nord (tell Rimah, Shemshara, etc.).

5 On pourra trouver quelques exemples significatifs dans Charpin 2000b. Voir aussi la recension très importante de Dombradi 1996 par Démare-Lafont (2003). De manière plus générale, voir Westbrook 2003.

6 Je remercie S. Démare-Lafont pour m'avoir suggéré « mandement » comme équivalent français de l'anglais « letter order ».

- il n'existe pas de formule finale obligée ;
- on doit également relever que les lettres ne sont en principe jamais situées dans le temps ni dans l'espace : le messager porteur de la tablette pouvait renseigner le destinataire sur ce point. Les exceptions concernent quelques lettres royales écrites dans des périodes particulièrement troublées ; même en ce cas, l'indication temporelle se limite généralement au mois et au jour, très rarement à l'année;
- les lettres étaient écrites sur des tablettes d'argile que l'on faisait sécher, puisqu'on recouvrait d'une mince pellicule d'argile. Cette enveloppe avait deux buts : garantir la confidentialité du contenu de la lettre et permettre l'authentification de son expéditeur, qui déroulait son sceau-cylindre sur toute la surface de l'enveloppe. On y inscrivait seulement le nom du destinataire, alors que sur les enveloppes des textes juridiques était recopié le texte de la tablette intérieure dans son intégralité.

Par rapport à ces normes, deux types de lettres présentent des divergences dues à leur statut juridique particulier : les mandements et les placets.

1.1. Les mandements

Les mandements (*letter ordrers*) sont généralement associés dans l'esprit des assyriologues à la période dite d'Ur III (IIIe dynastie d'Ur, XXIe siècle av. n. è.), mais on a continué d'en écrire à l'époque paléo-babylonienne. On a simplement une différence de proportion : à l'époque d'Ur III, ces billets forment l'essentiel de la correspondance qui a été retrouvée[7]. À l'époque paléo-babylonienne, il ne s'agit que d'une très faible proportion, ce qui explique que jusqu'à présent ce genre de documents n'ait pas reçu l'attention qu'il mérite.

Formellement, on a bien affaire à de la correspondance : l'adresse est généralement la même que dans une lettre. Parfois, le nom de l'expéditeur n'est pas noté, mais son sceau est déroulé sur la tablette elle-même (et pas sur l'enveloppe comme sur les lettres « normales »), ce qui permet de l'identifier[8]. Plus rarement, il arrive même que le nom du destinataire soit omis. Parmi les éléments qui distinguent ces billets des lettres « normales » on note l'absence de bénédictions après l'adresse.

7 Voir le corpus édité et commenté par Sollberger 1966; bibliographie complémentaire dans Lafont 1990. Voir en dernier lieu Michalowski 1993. On doit mettre de côté la correspondance royale, dont le statut est très discuté; elle n'est connue que par des copies postérieures et une partie au moins de ces lettres est apocryphe.

8 Rappelons qu'un sceau, à l'époque paléo-babylonienne, comporte presque toujours une légende. Celle-ci est le plus souvent tripartite, donnant le nom du propriétaire du sceau, celui de son père et le roi ou la divinité dont il se déclare serviteur (Charpin 1998). Parfois figure en tête le nom de la divinité ou du roi, suivi d'épithètes, le nom du propriétaire du sceau n'arrivant qu'à la fin (voi ci-dessous FM 3 113, cité note 13).

On note également le fait que ces documents sont souvent datés (mois, jour et année), alors que les lettres normalement ne le sont pas.

Un document de ce type permettait à l'expéditeur de donner un ordre, le plus souvent au bénéfice de la personne à qui il était remis. Celle-ci devait présenter le billet au(x) destinataire(s), qui devai(en)t exécuter l'ordre qu'il contenait. Un premier exemple le montre clairement[9] :

> « Aux différents maires de la rive. Le grain du palais doit aller à Larsa. Envoyez ville par ville devant lui une escorte, afin qu'on (le) fasse parvenir à bon port à Larsa. Mois ix, le 23, année où Rîm-Sîn (II) (est devenu) roi (= an 1). » Légende du sceau: « Nergal$^?$-[...], fils d'Apil-ilišu, serviteur du dieu Ilabrat ».

Le sens du texte est clair : il s'agit d'un billet émanant, d'après l'empreinte de sceau, d'un certain Nergal-[...]. Cette tablette devait être montrée aux maires des localités situées le long d'un cours d'eau par le responsable du convoi de bateaux chargés du grain qui devait parvenir à la capitale, en période d'insécurité et de famine. Nous ignorons malheureusement le statut de l'expéditeur de ce billet, manifestement une des plus hautes autorités du royaume de Larsa à cette époque.

Parfois, le nom du ou des destinataires est omis, comme dans ce mandement[10] :

> « Donnez au charpentier Apil-[...] 4 pins et 5 bottes de roseaux longs, qui conviennent pour (faire) les barreaux d'une fenêtre. Mois ix, le 5, année où Rîm-Sîn (II) (est devenu) roi (= an 1). » Légende du sceau: « Rîš-[...], fils d'Apil-ilišu, serviteur du dieu Lugal-nišu(?) ».

Dans la mesure où ce billet devait être remis, non pas à un messager, mais à l'intéressé, en l'occurrence le charpentier Apil-[...], celui-ci savait fort bien à qui il devait le présenter pour obtenir les matériaux dont il avait besoin. Dans un cas de ce genre, la conclusion est claire du point de vue de l'archivage : un tel billet était conservé par le destinataire, pour justifier la dépense qu'il avait effectuée en fonction de l'ordre reçu. C'est ce dont témoignent les archives du bureau de l'artisanat à Isin, où l'on trouve une étiquette de panier à tablette ainsi libellée[11] : « Documents scellés et lettres. » Les responsables conservaient donc ensemble les reçus scellés et les mandements du type de ceux qu'on a examinés ci-dessus. Manifestement, une personne qui recevait des biens contre remise d'un mandement ne devait pas sceller un reçu: les deux pratiques étaient mutuellement exclusives. C'est ce que confirme la décou-

9 AbB 10 67 (= OECT 15 43), repris avec commentaire sur la situation historique dans Charpin 2007a: 158–9.
10 OECT 15 56, édité et commenté dans Charpin 2007a: 160.
11 BIN 9 302: KIŠIB RA.A Ù.NA.A.DU_{11} ; voir le commentaire de Sollberger 1966: 2a. Pour ce lot d'archives, voir Van De Mieroop 1987.

verte, dans la salle 79 du palais de Mari, d'un lot de 107 tablettes relatives à des distributions d'huile pour les trois derniers mois de la première année de règne de Zimrî-Lîm[12]. Parmi ces documents figurent six mandements, comme celui-ci, émanant d'un haut fonctionnaire nommé Šub-nalû[13] :

> « Donne 1 litre d'huile pour frotter un bateau et les bains[14]. Mois d'*ebûrum* (xii), le 20. » Légende du sceau : « Zimrî-Lîm, roi fort, Šub-nalû, [...] ».

Le caractère parfois « mixte » de ce genre de documents apparaît à la lumière de billets retrouvés à Tell Rimah. On possède toute une série de lettres adressées par Ilî-Samas à Warad-šarrim[15]. Dans ce lot, on relève quatre mandements (n°s 283, 284, 286 et 288) : leur adresse est complète, ils ne comportent pas de date, ils sont consacrés à donner un ordre. Ils se différencient des autres lettres par le fait qu'ils sont scellés par l'expéditeur, comme celui-ci[16] :

> « Dis à Warad-šarrim : ainsi (parle) Ilî-Samas. Donne à Abdiya en personne 50 litres de grain selon la mesure de la taxe-*šibšum.* » Légende du sceau : « Ilî-Samas, fils de Iqqat-[...], serviteur de Pidha[...] ».

À l'époque paléo-babylonienne tardive, ce type de billet était décrit par le terme *ze'pum*[17], comme le montre ce texte[18] :

> « Dis à Sîn-imguranni : ainsi (parle) Damqi-ilîšu. Que Šamaš te fasse vivre ! En voyant mon billet (*ze'pî*), donne à Bêlšunu 120 litres de grain. » Légende du sceau : « Damqi-ilîšu, fils de Išgum-Irra, serviteur du dieu Nergal ».

Ce billet comporte une adresse et une bénédiction ; il n'est pas daté, mais il est scellé par l'expéditeur et il comporte un ordre. Le mot *ze'pum* n'est employé qu'à la fin de l'époque paléo-babylonienne, à partir du règne d'Ammi-ditana (1683 – 1647 av. n. è.). Il a été associé à des caractéristiques externes et internes très précises :

12 Duponchel 1997 (ci-dessous cité comme FM 3) ; pour la situation archéologique, voir p. 202.

13 FM 3, p. 254 n° 113. Les cinq autres billets sont les n°s 29, 86, 121, 126 et 128. Seul le n° 121 comprend le nom d'année; les autres sont simplement datés du mois et du jour.

14 Lit. « la maison du barbier » ; pour cette traduction, voir Durand 1997: 554 et 2000: 481 (« *hammam* »).

15 Dalley, Walker & Hawkins 1976: n°s 278–98. On a aussi retrouvé des lettres adressées au même Warad-šarrim par d'autres personnes (n°s 299–302). Ces documents ont été découverts sur l'escalier menant à la terrasse du temple (Dalley, Walker & Hawkins 1976: 195–202).

16 Dalley, Walker & Hawkins 1976: 283. Pour la légende du sceau, voir *ibid.*: pp. 248–9 n° 1.

17 Ce mot a suscité une importante bibliographie. Voir Finkelstein 1972: 2–6 et les références réunies par Edzard 1995: 142–3.

18 AUCT 4 86 (Sigrist 1990).

- une forme à peu près carrée, avec des angles arrondis[19], d'où l'absence de tranches au contraire des tablettes « classiques » ;
- le scribe n'a pas tracé de lignes, sauf à la fin du texte[20] ;
- un scellement n'apparait pas comme caractéristique ;
- il n'y a la plupart du temps ni adresse ni bénédiction ;
- le contenu est « an order or directive to the addressee to deliver some commodity to a third party (or to the sender), or to buy some object or commodity on the authority of the sender » (Finkelstein 1972: 5).

On voit donc qu'il a existé une tradition des « letter-order » durant toute l'époque paléo-babylonienne, qui a connu une évolution, mais qui constitue un cas à part au sein du genre des lettres. La place de ces billets dans la gestion administrative, étudiée ci-dessus à partir des archives du bureau de l'huile du palais de Mari, se retrouve un siècle plus tard dans les archives d'Ur-Utu à Sippar-Amnânum (Tell ed-Dēr). Un compte de bière est divisé en deux rubriques, récapitulées de la manière suivante[21] :

> « (…) 6 litres de bière, ayant fait l'objet à chaque fois d'un billet-*ze'pum* ; (…) x litres de bière pour 19 jours, ayant fait l'objet d'un autre billet-*ze'pum.* »

Ces *ze'pum* sont manifestement des billets du style « Donne à NP x litres de bière », sur le modèle de ce qu'on a vu plus haut. Ils étaient donc conservés par les responsables des magasins, qui s'y référaient lorsqu'ils rédigeaient un récapitulatif de dépenses.

1.2. Les placets

Une autre catégorie de textes qui ressemblent à des lettres, mais sont dépourvus d'adresse, est formée par ce que je propose d'appeler des placets. Au contraire des mandements, ils ne sont pas datés. Mais la différence principale tient à leur contenu : il ne s'agit pas d'ordre, mais au contraire d'une supplique, le contexte montrant qu'ils étaient destinés au souverain. L'un des plus significatifs est AbB 7 153[22] :

19 Ce que Finkelstein (1972: 5) appelait « "round" type ».

20 Voir par exemple la photo dans Saggs 1960: 5. Cette caractéristique a été notée pour la première fois par C. B. F. Walker, dans l'avant-propos de CT 52. Les lettres sont normalement lignées.

21 MHET 1/1 32: (4) 6 *qa* KAŠ.TA *ša* 1 *ze-eh-pí* ; (12) x KAŠ *ša* 19 ⸢*u*4⸣-[*mi*] *ša* ⸢*ša*⸣-*ni-im zé*-[*eh-pí*].

22 Ce texte était unique en son genre lorsqu'il a été publié (cf. Kraus 1977: 128 n° 153 note a), mais d'autres ont été publiés depuis (cf. notes 26 et 27). Traduction française et commentaire dans Charpin 2000b: 91–2 n° 47. Pour la datation de ce texte en l'an 28 de Samsu-iluna, voir Charpin 2000a: 202.

« Lorsque mon seigneur a levé la torche en or pour Sippar et a instauré le rétablissement de l'équité (*mîšarum*) pour Šamaš qui l'aime, que Tarîbatum, le chef des soldats (*šâpir rêdê*), a fait siéger à Sippar les juges de Sippar et de Babylone, qu'ils ont révisé les procès des gens de Sippar, ont "écouté" les tablettes d'achat des champs, maisons et ont brisé celles qui étaient invalidées par la *mîšarum*, 3 *sar* de terrain bâti à l'intérieur de Sippar-Yahrurum, acheté en fonction de son titre de propriété antérieur, ... dans l'année « Muraille de Kiš » (= Samsu-iluna 24), ce terrain, moi et mon adversaire ... Et les juges ... le contrat de vente ... comme ils avaient brisé la tablette ... (lacune d'une douzaine de lignes) Le lamentateur Gimillum ... la table de Šalim-ṭehhûšu ... Šalim-ṭehhûšu, le chef des barbiers, m'a réclamé ces [titres de propriété] et j'ai pris mes tablettes pour l'assemblée (*puhrum*). Rîš-Šamaš, le *wâšibum* de Sippar ; Kudiya, le *guzalûm* et Sîn-nâdin-šumi, le scribe du cadastre, ont examiné mes tablettes, les ont placées sous scellés et les ont fait porter à Šalim-ṭehhûšu dans sa maison pour qu'il les examine. Šalim-ṭehhûšu, le chef des barbiers, sans même écouter mes propos, a brisé mes tablettes dans la maison de son hôte. On m'a averti. En cachette, j'ai pris dans sa maison les morceaux de mes tablettes et je les ai montrés à Rîš-Šamaš, Kudiya et Sîn-nâdin-šumi, mais ils ont déclaré : « Que pouvons-nous dire au chef des barbiers ? ». C'est pourquoi je suis venu te trouver, toi, ô dieu : que mon seigneur rende un verdict dans le cas où on a brisé des tablettes en l'absence des juges et de l'intéressé ! Que tout Sippar voit que le faible ne peut pas être spolié par le fort devant mon seigneur ; le fort [...] pour spolier le faible ! »

Le style de ce document est particulièrement recherché, dans l'introduction et surtout dans l'exorde. Cette dernière fait clairement allusion à l'idéologie royale de la justice, le plaideur allant jusqu'à s'adresser au roi comme à une divinité[23]. Nous ignorons de quelle manière une telle supplique était portée à la connaissance du souverain. Dans ses lettres à ses délégués à Larsa, Sîn-iddinam ou Šamaš-hâzir, Hammu-rabi indique toujours : « Un tel m'a appris ceci », sans qu'on puisse savoir si la personne spoliée a pu avoir un contact personnel avec le roi. À Mari, l'idéologie voulait que le roi soit accessible à tous. Le dieu Addu d'Alep le rappela à Zimrî-Lîm par l'intermédiaire d'un prophète[24] :

« Écoute cette seule parole de moi ! Lorsque quelqu'un qui aura un procès en appellera à toi en te disant : "On m'a fait du tort", tiens-toi debout et rends-lui jugement ; réponds-lui droitement. Voilà ce que je désire de toi. »

23 Sur la divinisation royale, voir récemment le recueil édité par N. Brisch (2008); cf. aussi Charpin sous presse.

24 FM 7 38: 6'-11' ; voir Durand 2002: 135.

Cependant, un certain nombre de lettres des archives de Mari montrent que les personnes en difficulté comptaient sur l'intervention en leur faveur d'un proche du roi[25].

Il existe un autre exemple de placet retrouvé dans les archives d'Ur-Utu à Tell ed-Dēr, concernant un procès opposant cet individu à ses frères à propos du partage de l'héritage paternel[26]. Il est intéressant de constater que le document a été retrouvé chez le plaideur, et non chez son destinataire. Ce cas permet de poser la question : n'avons-nous pas affaire à des copies, dans lesquelles seul le corps de la supplique a été reproduit, en omettant l'adresse ? C'est ce que la comparaison avec d'autres suppliques permet de supposer. On a en effet retrouvé à Mari une lettre écrite par un scribe à l'avènement de Zimrî-Lîm : désireux de retrouver un poste, ce lettré, soucieux de montrer son talent, rédigea sa lettre non seulement en akkadien, mais aussi en sumérien[27]. Il prolongeait une tradition bien attestée à la cour de Larsa, notamment par la lettre de la prêtresse Nin-šata-pada au roi Rîm-Sîn[28]. Dans les suppliques de ce type, l'adresse prend une place extraordinaire, étant parfois triple, le nom du roi destinataire étant accompagné à chaque fois par un grand nombre d'épithètes. On possède également des lettres du même genre adressées à des divinités[29] : la question se pose de savoir si les suppliques au roi s'inspiraient de celles qu'on adressait aux divinités, — ou si c'est le contraire.

2. Les lettres comme instrument de la preuve

Le rôle de l'écrit dans la vie juridique à l'époque paléo-babylonienne est peu à peu devenu très important[30]. Lors d'un procès, les juges demandaient en général que les parties fournissent à l'appui de leurs affirmations des témoins (*šîbum*) ou une tablette[31]. Il n'était pas rare qu'ils procèdent à la lecture de celle-ci. Or les exemples sont nombreux où un correspondant demande explicitement au destinataire de conserver sa lettre pour lui servir de témoin[32] : « Conserve mon billet en témoignage pour moi (*ana šîbûtiya*). » On peut gloser ces demandes ainsi: ma tablette parlera pour moi, grâce à elle je serai à nouveau entendu, elle témoignera de mes propos. Il apparaît clairement que l'expression *ana šîbûtim*, littéralement « en témoignage », doit être

25 Voir par exemple ARM 26/2 344.

26 Di 1194, publié par Janssen 1992: 22–6; voir Charpin 2000b: 104–5 n° 62.

27 Charpin 1992; copie par Guichard 1997; voir en dernier lieu Durand 1997 n° 22 et Foster 2005: 221–3.

28 Edition la plus récente par Brisch 2007: 245–61.

29 Voir par exemple Ni. 13088, publiée par Kraus 1983. Voir d'autres exemples réunis et traduits par Foster 2005: 215–20.

30 Voir Charpin 2008, chapitre 4: « Le geste, la parole et l'écrit dans la vie juridique » (version en anglais dans Charpin 2010b, chapitre 3). Voir également Boyer 1965 et plus récemment Cardascia 1995, ainsi que Kienast 1996.

31 E. Dombradi a noté que l'apparition de textes écrits comme preuve n'est pas antérieure au règne de Hammu-rabi (1996: 338 § 446).

32 *ze-eh-pí a-na ši-bu-ti-ia ki-i-il* AbB 12 130: 11 ou 12 194. Nombreuses autres références sont réunies par Kraus 1985: 142–3 et CAD Š/1 p. 401a.

traduite par « comme preuve ». Une lettre de Šamaš-hâzir le montre[33] : « Et Šamaš-nâṣir m'a apporté sa tablette comme preuve (*ana šîbûtim*). » Dans certains cas, l'expression est renforcée[34] : « Tu conserveras ma présente tablette chez Lu-Enlila comme élément de vérification (*qîpum*) de mon affaire et comme preuve de mon affaire. »

La terminologie employée dans les contextes judiciaires est intéressante à analyser de près : on « écoute » (*šemûm*) une tablette, qui a une « bouche » (*pûm*). Les écrits étaient donc considérés en quelque sorte comme une « parole figée »[35]. Dans ce contexte, on comprend qu'une lettre ait pu servir de témoin. Kraus avait observé cette « personnification » de la tablette, mais avait refusé d'aller plus loin[36]. Or il apparaît clairement que pour les Mésopotamiens, les tablettes étaient considérées comme vivantes. On pouvait les « tuer » (*dâkum*[37]) et même les « ressusciter » (*bulluṭum*) quand elles étaient perdues[38]. On voit donc qu'il n'y a pas lieu d'opposer preuve testimoniale et preuve écrite: lorsque l'écrit se développa, les Mésopotamiens assimilèrent les tablettes à des témoins, pourvus d'une bouche et qu'il était possible d'écouter[39].

On doit cependant observer que dans les procès que nous connaissons, les seuls textes apportés devant les juges sont des contrats, jamais des lettres[40]. Il peut s'agir d'un hasard dans la conservation des textes. Il est toutefois vraisemblable que c'est davantage au niveau de la dissuasion que les lettres étaient utilisées[41]. C'est ce que confirme le fait que dans certains cas, le contexte de l'expression « garder en témoignage » n'est pas judiciaire, mais politique. Ainsi, Zû-Hadnim écrivit-il au roi de Mari pour le prévenir des risques de révolte dans son district. Il suggéra au roi de venir en personne apaiser la population. Il termina sa lettre ainsi[42] :

33 AbB 9 19: (23) *ù* [d]UTU-*na-ṣi-ir a-na ši-bu-tim* (24) *ṭup-pa-šu ú-ša-bi-lam*.

34 AbB 10 148: (32) [*a-n*]*a qí-ip a-wa-ti-ia* (33) *ù ši-bu-ut a-wa-ti-ia* (34) *ṭup-pí an-ni-a-am ma-har* LÚ.[d]EN.LÍL.LÁ (35) *ta-na-aṣ-ṣa-ra-am*. Commentaire du terme *qîpum* par Kraus 1985: 142, qui a eu raison de reprocher aux dictionnaires de n'avoir pas reconnu ce sens.

35 Bien entendu, les Mésopotamiens ne méconnaissaient pas la différence entre l'oral et l'écrit, comme le montre la courante opposition entre *ina pîm* « par oral » (lit. « par la bouche ») et *ina ṭuppim* « par écrit » (lit. « par tablette »); voir par exemple Dalley, Walker & Hawkins 1976 n° 121: ll 10–1.

36 « Von einer spekulativen Rekonstruktion des Gedankenganges, der zu dieser Personifizierung von Tafeln a. a. geführt haben könnte, sieht Vf. ab » (Kraus 1985: 142).

37 À ma connaissance, l'expression n'est utilisée que dans des textes paléo-assyriens (Veenhof 1987).

38 Voir le cas étudié dans Charpin 1986: 133–5 (CT 47 63) ; version anglaise revue dans Charpin 2010b (chapitre 5; voir en particulier la note 48).

39 Je remercie S. Démare-Lafont, dont les observations lors de la discussion qui a suivi mon exposé à Rome m'ont permis de mieux formuler mon point de vue.

40 Voir les listes de Dombradi 1996: 338 § 446 et 447.

41 Il y a sans doute ici une différence avec l'emploi des lettres par les marchands assyriens de Cappadoce. Voir Michel 2008: 134.

42 Inédit A.3119: (24) *a-nu-um-ma a-wa-tam ša a-mu-ru* (25) *a-na ṣe-er be-li-ia aš-ta-ap-ra-am* (26) *be-lí ša e-pé-ši-šu li-pu-úš* (27) *ṭup-pí an-né-em a-na ši-bu-ut* (28) *a-wa-ti-ia* (29) *i-na* [gi]*pí-ša-an qa-tim* (30) *ša be-lí-ia lu-ú na-ṣi-*⸢*ir*⸣. Ce texte doit paraître dans mon ouvrage *La correspondance à*

> « À présent, je viens d'écrire à mon seigneur l'affaire que j'ai constatée : que mon seigneur fasse ce qu'il y a lieu de faire. Que ma présente tablette soit conservée dans le coffre portatif de mon seigneur en témoignage de mon affaire ! »

3. Ordres, édits et rescrits royaux

L'écrit a joué un rôle considérable dans l'administration de la justice par le roi. Bien entendu, on pense immédiatement au Code de Hammu-rabi[43]. Cependant, la valeur symbolique forte de ce monument, et de quelques autres comparables, ne doit pas occulter d'autres pratiques qui jouaient dans la réalité un rôle plus important. La lettre a souvent été un instrument utilisé par le roi pour communiquer ses ordres, parfois même pour faire connaître un édit qu'il avait promulgué. C'est également par des rescrits qu'il complétait les lacunes de la législation.

3.1. Les ordres royaux

Les ordres royaux étaient le plus souvent communiqués sous forme de lettre (Charpin 2012). Je me limiterai ici à quelques exemples, qu'on pourrait aisément multiplier.

La gestion du domaine royal était déléguée à des « fonctionnaires », qui recevaient constamment des lettres de ce genre[44] :

> « Au sujet du champ de Sîn-gimlanni qu'il détient dans le terrain entre deux cours d'eau, en voyant ma présente lettre (*unnedukkûm*), donne à Idnatum le champ de Sîn-gimlanni, autant qu'il y en a dans le terrain entre deux cours d'eau ».

Des lettres royales permettaient à des personnes chargées d'une mission de se présenter sans problème aux autorités locales[45] :

> « Je vous attendrai à Al-Aha-nûta avec un gendarme (ou : des gendarmes) du roi ainsi que des lettres (*unnedukkûm*) du roi, comme quoi jusqu'à Larsa personne ne doit mettre d'obstacle devant vous. »

l'époque amorrite. Écriture, acheminement et lecture des lettres d'après les archives royales de Mari, en préparation. Un autre cas similaire est rapporté dans l'inédit A.1231 (*ibid.*).

43 La bibliographie sur le Code de Hammu-rabi et les autres textes du même genre est considérable. On me permettra de renvoyer à Charpin 2005 ; version revue et augmentée (en anglais) dans Charpin 2010b, chapitre 6.

44 AbB 13 2: *aš-šum* A.ŠÀ-*lim ša* NP *ša i-na bé-e-ri-tim ṣa-ab-tu un-ne-du-uk-ki i-na a-ma-ri-ka* A.ŠÀ NP *ma-la i-na bé-e-ri-i-tim i-ba-aš-šu-ú a-na* NP_2 *i-di-i*[*n*].

45 AbB 9 112: *qá-du-um re-di-i šar-ri-im ù un-*<*ne*>*-du-uk-ka-at šar-ri-im ša a-di* NG *ma-am-ma a-na p*[*a*]*-ni-ku-nu la pa-ra-ki-im i-na* NG *r*[*i-i*]*š-k*[*u*]*-nu ú-ka-al*.

Un membre de l'entourage du souverain annonçait parfois l'envoi d'un ordre royal en résumant ce que devait être son contenu[46] : « Une tablette (*ṭuppum*) du roi te parviendra et Ilšu-ibni et Gimillum devront examiner la maison de Ur-Utu. »

3.2. Les édits royaux

L'avènement des rois était marqué par des mesures de remises des arriérés et des dettes, qui pouvaient également être prises par le souverain plus tard dans son règne, lorsque des conditions économiques défavorables les rendaient à nouveau nécessaires[47]. Une lettre du roi Yasmah-Addu adressée à son père mentionne un décret par lequel les dettes de la région du Suhûm devaient être remises[48] :

> « Les gens du Suhûm sont dans une grande famine. Il faut absolument que j'aille les trouver (lacune). Il faut que je les sauve pour que ceux de leurs frères qui s'étaient enfuis, l'ayant appris, reviennent au pays. Voilà le résultat de mes réflexions. Maintenant, je vais leur remettre le grain qu'ils ont emprunté, intérêt compris. Voilà Père informé ! En outre, voilà que j'envoie un message : les responsables des localités (*sugâgum*) du Suhûm vont se rassembler : je leur proclamerai mon édit (*šipṭum*) et je les apaiserai. »

On voit donc que le décret (*šipṭum*) devait être proclamé par le roi devant les intéressés réunis[49]. Certaines remises individuelles ne donnaient pas lieu à un document écrit, d'où parfois l'embarras des responsables[50] ; il arrivait aussi que le roi écrive simplement une lettre[51]. Mais dans un autre cas, on voit que le décret doit donner lieu à la rédaction d'une tablette spécifique, dite *ṭuppi isiktim*. C'est ce que montre une lettre du gouverneur Samu-Ila au roi Yasmah-Addu[52] : « Au sujet de l'*andurârum* pour laquelle mon seigneur a pris un décret (*šipṭum*) et pour laquelle une tablette de protocole (*ṭuppi isikti*) de l'*andurârum* a été rédigée (...). » On n'a malheureusement jusqu'à présent pas repéré de texte de ce genre dans les archives de Mari.

C'est le royaume de Babylone qui nous permet de voir au mieux la relation entre les lettres et les édits royaux. On possède ainsi une lettre écrite par Samsu-iluna au tout début de son règne[53] :

46 Di 1194: *ṭup-pí* LUGAL *il-li-ka-kum-ma* é NP NP$_2$ *ù* NP$_3$ *im-ma-ru* (inédit cité par Janssen 1992: 22–6).

47 Voir en général Charpin 1990b ; version révisée (en anglais) de cette étude dans Charpin 2010b, chapitre 7.

48 ARM 4 16 (= Durand 2000 n° 1049).

49 Pour le terme *šipṭum* et ses dérivés, voir Charpin 1991.

50 Voir la lettre de Sammêtar ARM 2 138 (= Durand 2000 n° 1050).

51 Voir la lettre de Samsî-Addu ARM 1 80 (= Durand 2000 n° 1048).

52 M.14033 (= Durand 2000 n° 1082), éditée dans Charpin 1990a: 266–7. Voir également M.5499 (= Durand 2000 n° 1083), éditée dans Charpin 1990a: 268.

53 TCL 17 76 ; voir en dernier lieu la réédition de ce texte dans Veenhof 2005: n° 130 (avec bibliographie antérieure).

> « À Etel-pî-Marduk, dis : ainsi (parle) Samsu-iluna. Le roi mon père est ma[lade?]. Afin de m'asseoir sur le trône de mon père devant Marduk et afin de fortifier les tributaires (*nâši biltim*), j'ai remis l'arriéré des bergers, des cultivateurs et des équarrisseurs. J'ai brisé la tablette de dette du soldat-*rêdûm*, du soldat-*bâ'irum* et du simple sujet (*muškênum*). J'ai institué le "redressement" (*mîšarum*) dans le pays. Dans le pays, le gouverneur ne devra pas user de mesure coercitive à l'encontre de la maison d'un soldat-*rêdum*, d'un soldat-*bâ'irum* ou d'un simple sujet (*muškênum*) quel qu'il soit. Dès que tu verras ma tablette, toi et les Anciens du pays que tu gouvernes, montez et qu'on vous voie près de moi ! »

Ce texte est très nettement une lettre « classique », dans laquelle le roi nouvellement installé sur le trône indique à un gouverneur de province l'essentiel du contenu de l'édit de *mîšarum* qu'il vient de prendre[54]. Nous possédons par ailleurs le texte de cet édit et d'autres du même type, postérieurs. Celui de Samsu-iluna n'est connu que par deux fragments[55] ; le texte le plus complet date de l'avènement du roi Ammi-ṣaduqa (1646)[56].

Récemment, ce dossier a été enrichi par un document originaire de Harrâdum, l'actuel Khirbet ed-Diniye[57]. Cette petite localité du Moyen-Euphrate irakien a livré des archives retrouvées *in situ*, qui datent des derniers rois de la première dynastie de Babylone (de Samsu-iluna à Ammi-ṣaduqa)[58]. L'un des documents les plus intéressants est le texte n° 11. Selon son éditeur, « ce document comportait une tablette et une enveloppe reproduisant le texte de celle-ci et portant le déroulement du sceau d'un personnage probablement de statut officiel, car se réclamant d'Ammi-ditana. Le texte semble pourtant relever aussi du style épistolaire ». Vu les usages paléo-babyloniens, il serait très curieux que l'enveloppe d'une lettre comporte la copie complète du texte. L'examen de la légende du sceau permet cependant une autre explication. Je propose de reconnaître dans cette empreinte le sceau d'Ammi-ditana en tant que prince héritier, en lisant [59]:

> « [Abi-e]šu[h], [roi] fort, [roi] de Sumer et d'Ak[kad], [à Am]mi-dita[na], [son héritier b]ien-aimé, [a do]nné (ce sceau). »

54 Il s'agit là d'un résumé, et non d'une citation. Pour un exemple de citation de l'édit de Samsu-iluna dans une lettre, voir Charpin 2000b: 195–6.

55 Kraus 1965, repris dans Kraus 1984: 154–60 ; plus récemment, Hallo 1995.

56 Voir l'étude très complète de Kraus 1984.

57 Je résume ici les conclusions de mon étude Charpin 2010a.

58 Les textes ont été publiés dans Joannès 2006 (ci-dessous *Haradum II*).

59 (1) [*a-bi-e*]-*šu*-[*uh*] (2) [lugal] kal-ga (3) [lugal] ki-en-gi ki-[uri] (4) [*am*]-*mi-di-ta*-[*na*] (5) [ibila ki]-ág-gá-[ni(-ir)] (6) [in]-na-an-[ba].

A priori, l'attribution du sceau à Ammi-ditana doit le faire faire considérer comme l'autorité d'où émane le texte. Du coup, le rapprochement opéré par F. Joannès entre les l. 4'-7' du fragment B et l'édit d'Ammi-ṣaduqa[60] prend un relief tout particulier. Le texte *Haradum II* 11 est malheureusement très mal conservé, mais il me semble qu'il pourrait s'agir d'un édit qu'Ammi-ditana proclama immédiatement après son avènement au sujet de la situation économique délicate du Suhûm. Le document commence sans adresse par des attendus sur la situation particulière de la ville de Harrâdum (tablette fragment A) :

> « [Les ...] de Harrâdum qui sont dépourvus de tout et résident à l'intérieur du pays, – [j'écr]is afin qu'ils reviennent dans leur ville et qu'ils résident dans leurs demeures habituelles. »

Suit un texte de valeur plus générale qui est presque mot pour mot celui de l'Édit d'Ammi-ṣaduqa (tablette fragment B). Je propose de lire :

> « Concernant [les arriérés] de l'argent du prélèvement-*miksum*, du grain du prélèvement-*šibšum* et du grain du *bamâtum*, personne [ne devra élever de réclamation contre] leurs [maisonnées] ».

Le texte donne enfin la conséquence de cette mesure (enveloppe) : « Ils devront revenir à Harrâdu et résider dans leurs habitations habituelles. » Je ne pense pas que l'on ait ici une lettre d'Ammi-ditana comparable à celle que Samsu-iluna envoya au gouverneur Etel-pî-Marduk pour annoncer la proclamation de l'édit de *mîšarum* de son avènement[61] : cela n'expliquerait en effet pas que le texte du document figure aussi sur l'enveloppe[62]. Il faut imaginer plutôt un texte de statut officiel, ce que explique d'ailleurs sa présence dans le « bâtiment 1 » : celui-ci n'est autre que le principal sanctuaire de Harrâdum, le temple d'Adad. Il est clair que le texte des édits en notre possession ne consiste qu'en des copies : nous ne possédons pas d'« original ». Le document *Haradum II* 11 pourait nous donner une idée de leur forme : l'absence d'adresse (au début de la tablette, sinon sur l'enveloppe) et le fait que le texte soit recopié intégralement sur l'enveloppe montrent bien qu'il ne s'agit pas exactement d'une lettre, malgré l'usage de la première personne.

60 *Haradum II*, p. 55 ; il s'agit du § 14 selon Kraus 1984: 178–9.

61 TCL 17 76 (cf. ci-dessus).

62 Rappelons que dans les usages paléo-babyloniens, les enveloppes de lettres ne comportent que le nom du destinataire (*ana* NP « a NP »), en plus du déroulement du sceau de l'expéditeur. En revanche, les enveloppes des textes juridiques comportent le plus souvent la copie intégrale du texte de la tablette intérieure (avec parfois des variantes); on trouve plus rarement un simple résumé.

3.3. Les rescrits

Un dernier cas doit être traité : celui des lettres royales ayant acquis une valeur législative, ce qu'on doit appeler un rescrit (S. Lafont 1997). Une lettre du roi Samsu-iluna (1749 – 1712) adressée à de nombreuses autorités de Sippar, contient la réponse à deux cas qui lui ont été soumis. Les responsables des religieuses-*nadîtum* vouées au dieu Šamaš de Sippar avaient alerté le roi sur deux problèmes. Il s'agissait d'abord de la situation des jeunes filles que leur famille faisait entrer dans le cloître de Sippar comme religieuses-*nadîtum* sans leur donner de moyens de subsistance convenables. La seconde question était de savoir si un créancier pouvait saisir les biens d'une *nadîtum* dont le père était insolvable. Voici la traduction de ce texte[63] :

> « Dis à Sîn-nâṣir, Nûratum, Sîn-iddinam, au *kârum* de Sippar et aux juges de Sippar-Amnânum, à Awîl-Nabium, à Sîn-iddinam, aux administrateurs-*šangûm*, aux juges, aux chefs des temples, aux chefs des religieuses-*nadîtum*, aux [...] des juges et aux portiers de la porte du cloître de Sippar-Yahrurum : ainsi (parle) Samsu-iluna.
>
> (Exposé du premier cas :)
> Les [chefs des *nadîtum* de] Šamaš de Sippar m'ont appris ceci : "Les gens de Sippar ont fait entrer leurs filles dans le cloître, mais ne les ont pas pourvues de moyens de subsistance : elles ont eu faim et on les a nourries au grenier de notre seigneur. Or les gens de Sippar continent à faire entrer leurs filles dans le cloître". Voilà ce qu'ils m'ont appris.
>
> (Directive royale :)
> Si une *nadîtum* n'est pas pourvue, j'ai ordonné qu'on ne la fasse pas entrer dans le cloître. Et une *nadîtum* que père et frères n'ont pas pourvue de moyens de subsistance et pour laquelle ils n'ont pas écrit de tablettes et qui habite dans le cloître, j'ai ordonné de faire pression sur son père et ses frères pour qu'ils écrivent une tablette et la fassent entrer dans le cloître. Et quoi qu'il donne à sa fille, qu'il le confie en présence de Sîn-nâṣir, Nûratum, Sîn-iddinam, du *kârum* de Sippar et des juges de Sippar-Amnânum, d'Awîl-Nabium, Sîn-iddinam, des *šangûm*, des juges, des chefs des temples, des chefs des religieuses-*nadîtum*, des ... des juges et des portiers de la porte du cloître de Sippar-Yahrurum, qu'il écrive pour elle une tablette et qu'il la fasse entrer dans le cloître.
>
> (Exposé du second cas :)
> Ils m'ont en outre appris ceci : "Le juge Awîl-Sîn a une créance d'argent au débit de Mâr-Šamaš, un homme de Sippar. Du fait que ce dernier n'a pas remboursé, il a saisi Mâr-Šamaš en disant : 'Si tu gardes tes biens (i.e. refuses

63 Elle repose sur l'édition de Janssen 1991; voir déjà Charpin 2000b: 86–8 n °43.

de les vendre pour me rembourser) et que je ne reçois rien, je prendrai l'esclave de ta fille *nadîtum* de Šamaš qui habite dans le cloître'. Voilà ce qu'il lui a dit". Voilà ce qu'ils m'ont appris.

(Directive royale :)
Une religieuse-*nadîtum* de Šamaš à qui son père et ses frères ont fourni de quoi vivre et à qui ils ont écrit une tablette (i.e. qu'ils se sont engagés par écrit à entretenir sa vie durant), et qui habite le cloître, n'est pas responsable des dettes et du service-*ilkum* de la maison de son père et de ses frères. Son père et ses frères [accompliront] leur service-*ilkum* et [...]. Un créancier qui saisirait une *nadîtum* de Šamaš à propos des dettes ou de l'*ilkum* de la maison de son père et de ses frères, cet homme est un ennemi de Šamaš !

(Colophon :)
Copie d'une tablette de Samsu-iluna [...] déposée dans la maison du/des ju[ge(s)] du cloître. »

Formellement, cette lettre constitue la réponse à deux cas précis. Mais on peut voir qu'il s'agit de plus que cela. Il faut d'abord remarquer la façon dont le roi rédigea sa lettre. Ainsi, dans le second cas, au lieu de dire : « Le juge Awîl-Sîn n'a pas le droit de saisir l'esclave de la fille-*nadîtum* de Mâr-Šamaš », il formula de manière anonyme une règle ayant une portée générale[64]. Ce seront ensuite les autorités locales qui devaient la mettre en application. Le style même du passage, rédigé de façon casuisitique, évoque très clairement l'apodose d'un paragraphe de « code de lois ». On notera aussi que le roi élargit le cas : il n'était question que de dettes, pas de service-*ilkum*, dans la lettre des responsables de religieuses-*nadîtum*. On remarque qu'il s'agit de situations qui ne sont pas traitées dans le Code de Hammu-rabi. Mais celui-ci ne fit jamais l'objet de « réédition revue et augmentée » : les nombreuses copies que nous en possédons, pendant un millénaire, sont pratiquement *ne varietur*. Cependant, cette lettre de Samsu-iluna a été conservée en plusieurs exemplaires ; des copies se trouvaient des décennies plus tard à la fois dans le temple du dieu Šamaš de Sippar-Amnânum et « dans la maison du/des ju[ge(s)] du cloître » à Sippar-Yahrurum[65]. Cela montre bien qu'un tel rescrit avait conservé une valeur au-delà des circonstances initiales de sa rédaction ; la forme qui lui avait été donnée dès le départ prévoyait clairement cette fonction.

64 Il y a sur ce point une évolution depuis Hammu-rabi. Dans un cas analogue (AbB 13 22), ce roi donna une décision qui « reste limitée au cas particulier soumis au souverain, mais la formulation tend cependant vers l'énoncé de principe: "Que Tarībum, qui a pris la part successorale de son fils, paye l'argent selon les termes mêmes de sa tablette scellée" » (Demare-Lafont 2003: 656): le nom propre est ici conservé dans la décision de Hammu-rabi, au contraire du rescrit de Samsu-iluna.

65 Pour le détail, voir Janssen 1991, et Veenhof 1997–2000: 57–8.

Conclusion

On voit donc comment la forme très souple de la lettre a pu être adaptée à des usages juridiques très divers, un ou plusieurs de ses éléments caractéristiques pouvant être omis (comme l'adresse ou l'enveloppe), tandis que d'autres pouvaient être ajoutés (comme la date). L'archivage de ces différents genres de textes répondait à chaque fois à des règles particulières.

Middle Assyrian Summonses: The Epistolary Format in Judicial Procedures[1]

Eva Cancik-Kirschbaum (Berlin)

1 Introduction

The paper discusses a small group of texts from late 13th century BCE Assur, which make use of the epistolary format and at the same time have the character of a legal document. These legal summonses constitute a formal subgenre in its own right. The aim of this article is to delineate the characteristics of this 'genre' as well as its function within Middle Assyrian legal administration.

Among the cuneiform textual sources from the Ancient Near East letters take a prominent place. As a means of communication they were used in institutional as well as in individual contexts and frequently kept in archives. As a written textual genre the "letter" emerges after the middle of the third millenium and since that time the letters became commonly used within all sectors of script-based society.[2] Besides the mundane usage of letters it is important to note that the epistolary format became a literary genre in its own right, resulting in the composition of letters to and from gods as well as to fictitious letters from kings and heroes. The number of epistolary texts that have come down to us varies regionally and chronologically, depending last but not least on the casualities of archaeological findings. During the second millennium, the use of letters is broadly attested. Thus for instance, the actual documentation of the *Old Assyrian period* (19th and 18th cent. BCE), consists almost exclusively of thousands of letters, the correspondence of the merchants conducting the trade between the city of Assur on the Tigris and Central Anatolia. The contemporary *Old Babylonian period* provides us with letters of all kind from kings and governors, merchants and scholars, spies and officials, but also the correspondence within families. A fine example for the role of letters in international contacts is provided by the Late Bronze Age correspondence in cuneiform found in Tell-el-Amarna in Egypt attesting to the dynamic exchange of letters of the Egyptian Phar-

1 This paper has been written in the context of "Political governance and governed space" of the EC 264 TOPOI "The Formation and Transformation of Space and Knowlegde in Ancient Civilizations". I am very grateful to S. Démare-Lafont, H. Freydank and C. Johnson for their comments on earlier drafts of this paper. It goes without saying that what follows is my responsibility alone.

2 A useful overview as regards the general outline of lettered documents in cuneiform sources is given by Borger 1975: §§ 46–59 (60 = reports).

aoh with the rulers of the established great powers in the Near East, namely Hatti, Mitanni and Babylonia, but also with a newcomer on the international political scene, the king of the land of Assur.

Assyria appears as an autonomously acting political entity in the 14th century BCE. Centered on the old city of Assur on the Tigris, but with a nucleus in the East-Tigridian region of Ninive and Arbela, the kingdom rapidly expanded and reached a first maximum of territorial extension in the 13th century: having incorporated several formerly independent policies, the Middle Assyrian empire encompassed Upper Mesopotamia from the Euphrates in the West to the ranges of the Zagros in the East, from the foothills of the Taurus in the North to the borders of the Babylonian plain in the south (temporarily even Babylon was part of the first Assyrian empire). After a period of political and economic instability a second peak is reached towards the end of the 12th century, when Assyria starts a new expansive phase, which comes to an end in the 11th century BCE. A continuous process of gradual transformation does not bring an end to the Middle Assyrian empire, but leads into a phase of endogenous solidification, from which in the first millennium the Neo Assyrian empire was built. Compared to the periods mentioned above, the textual documentation from the *Middle Assyrian Period* is rather scarce. The main bulk of textual sources was found during excavations in the capital city Assur at the beginning of the 20th century AD, whereas during the last decades several provincial centers have also yielded texts, covering, however, only short timespans of some 30 years. Besides royal inscriptions[3] and a considerable number of scholarly, religious and literary texts, most texts pertain to the sector of state administration.[4] Currently some 300 letters are known and amongst the broad variety of themes and topics, legal matters and judicial affairs do play a certain role.

*

In 1933 Erich Ebeling published under the general heading "Aus den Archiven von Uruk und Assur" three texts found during the German excavations in the ruins of the royal residence and capital Assur, which he dubbed "gerichtliche Ladungen".[5] A common feature of these texts is the use of the "letter" genre as a judicial documentary format in the sense of "*Rechts-Urkunde*". The cuneiform tablets in question were published in handcopy by Otto Schroeder in the series "Keilschrifttexte aus Assur Verschiedenen Inhalts" as KAV 168, KAV 169 and KAV 201.[6] They were found together with some fifty-eight tablets and fragments in a broken jar near the

3 See Grayson 1987.

4 See Pedersén 1998: 2.3. The distinction between a 'private' sector versus an institutional sector is not so clear, as it may appear from the fact that some of the archives have been found in 'private houses'.

5 Ebeling 1933: 34–6. See also in Weidner 1939–1941: esp. 111–7.

6 H. Freydank 2004: Nr. 86 provides new handcopies of KAV 169 and of KAV 201 (1997: 114) and MARV V, Nr. 88.

remnants of the royal storehouses north of the Tabira-Gate.[7] They date from the 13th century BC and – as the situation of storage in ancient times indicates – were part of the same archive.[8] In the 1970s two more texts were published, both likewise stemming from Assur.[9] Since part of the finds from the German excavations in Assur are housed at the *İstanbul Arkeoloji Müzeleri* some more texts of the same type can be found under the cuneiform material stored there.[10] If the once reported number of 11 more documents in Istanbul[11] is correct, this would add up to 16 texts. Recently, two texts from Istanbul have been dealt with by Veysel Donbaz. In this context, the author makes reference to at least four more letters of the same type "dealing with court proceedings mainly concerning animal theft", without giving any further specification.[12] The group of Middle Assyrian legal summonses thus consists of at least 11, maybe 16 extant texts, 7 of them published so far. For one more text (n° 4) at least the general coordinates are known.

The following table summarizes the key details of the tablets:[13]

7 The situation of the excavation in bB6I is reported by Andrae 1907: 16. The reasons for the attribution of differing findspot numbers remain obscure. According to Pedersén's calculation from the excavation inventories and the numbers assigned to the pieces during the excavation (see above note 4), the original number could have amounted to 60 texts and fragments.
The building complex itself was identified in 1913 by Andrae (1913: 140) as 'Poternen', due to its position near the city wall. Ernst Weidner (1939–1941) proposed, on the basis of his analysis of the textual documentation, that the building was functional in the state organisation. For the storehouse see the meticulous compilation of material by Llop-Radua 2005.

8 This archive, also known as the « Archive of Ubru », is registered as **M 8** « Archive at the northwest fortification with vaulted passages », in Pedersén 1985: 82–8. Several texts from this archive have been published in KAJ, KAV and elsewhere. Hitherto unpublished texts from M8 were edited in handcopies by Llop-Raduà 2009 in connection with the "Assur-Projekt: Aufarbeitung der Funde aus den Deutschen Grabungen in Assur".

9 Freydank 1976: Nr. 13 (VS 19, 13 = MARV I 13); Hall 1983. This text, formerly in the Erlenmeyer collection, certainly originates from Assur.

10 The allocation of the tablets has been laid out by Weidner 1939–1941: 111–2.

11 Hall 1983: note 3. Hall claims that two more letters pertain to the same type, VS 19 (= MARV I), 15 and VS 19 (= MARV I), 71. These, however, are a letter order (MARV I 15) and a letter report (MARV I 71) respectively.

12 A.133 and A.748, s. Donbaz 2004 nrs. 1 and 2 (with autographies on p. 77).

13 The heading **n°** refers to the number of the text in this article. – The heading **ALA** refers to the list of texts given by Pedersén 1985. – The heading Assur-Photo refers to the photographs taken during the excavation.

Table 1:

n°	ed.-sigle	Mus.-Inv.	Excav.-Nr.	ALA	Assur-Photo	Sealing
(1)	KAV 169=MARV V 86	VAT 8748	Ass11018p	M8, 47	2058/59	-
(2)	VS 19, 13=MARV I 13	VAT 16374	Ass11018q	M8, 48	2056/57	x
(3)	FS Grayson 2	A.748	Ass11017c	M8, 13	2047/48	x
(4)	-	A.988+	Ass11017o+q	M8, 24	2052/53	?
(5)	KAV 201=MARV V 88	VAT 8745	Ass11019c	M8, 59	2060/61	-
(6)	FS Grayson 1	A.133	Ass11017n	M8, 23	2049/50	x
(7)	Hall 1	Ex-Erlenm.	Ass 11017v	M8, 28	2049/50	-
(8)	KAV 168	VAT 8752	Ass11019a	M8, 57	2060/61	x

All tablets show the outward appearance of a typical Middle Assyrian letter: the tablet is of square to oblong vertical shape, and – depending on the length of the text – inscribed on both sides. The texts open with the usual introduction, giving the names of sender and addressee. In Middle Assyrian correspondence the formulae used in the introduction are defined by the relationship that exists between the sender and the receiver.[14] Consequently, one can infer from the type of formulary used in all legal summonses that the sender of the letter, named first, generally occupied a higher rank than the addressee, named in second place – a feature which is hardly surprising given the functional situation of the document (see below esp. n° 5, 6, 7).

In several cases the persons mentioned are known also from other contexts and their position can be verified by external evidence. This will become apparent when the functional setting of the texts will be investigated. All texts are dated, usually giving month, day and the name of the eponym in office. The occasional exception, with a reduced date formula and giving only the day, is attested in text n° 7. Table 2 provides a summary on dating and the main personalities involved:

14 See Cancik-Kirschbaum 1996: 50–62.

Table 2:

n°	Sigle	Dating	T-N year	Sender	Addressee	Plaintiff
(1)	KAV 169 = MARV V 86	12. Allanātu, Aššur-nādin-apli	7	Aššur-amranni	Ubru	Aššur-apla-ēreš
(2)	VS 19,13	19. Šasarāte, Abattu	10 or 11	Aššur-amranni	Ubru	Aššur-apla-ēreš
(3)	A.748	18. Tag		Sîn-lušallim-šarra	Ubru	Aššur-apla-ēreš
(4)	A.988+	*unknown*	*unknown*	Aššur-amranni	Ubru	Aššur-apla-ēreš
(5)	KAV 201 = MARV V 88	4. Kuzallu, Abattu	10 or 11	Kaṣru	Ubru	Aššur-bēl-apli
(6)	A.133	26. Kuzallu, Abattu S. d. Adad-šuma-lēšir	11	Naram-Aššur-libūr	Ubru	Aššur-bēl-apli
(7)	Erlenm.	24. Sîn, Abattu	10 or 11	Uṣur-namkūr-šarri	Šalipīja	Adad-x-x
(8)	KAV 168	25. Šasarāte, Aššur-da''ān	12	Mušabši-Adad	Munabittu	Urad-Šerū'a

Usually Middle-Assyrian letters are provided with an envelope, as to preserve the secrecy of correspondence. On the envelope were written the names of addressee and sender. While the letter itself usually saw no further verification, the envelope was sealed with the sender's seal. However, as the envelope had to be broken to have access to the actual letters, they were only rarely kept together with the documents in the archives. Although a considerable amount of fragments of envelopes reportedly have been found together with the letters, and some are even shown on the photographic documentation from the excavation, unfortunately, as regards the group treated here, no envelopes have been positively identified as yet.[15] But one may safely assume, that all texts were originally configured in the usual way, that is in a sealed clay envelope.

15 Weidner (1939–41: 112) notes "Briefe, zum Teil kuvertiert"; Pedersén, 1985: 85 reports several preserved case fragments, without further specification.

2 The Texts[16]

N° 1) KAV 169 [17]

To Ubru speak, thus Aššur-amranni:

Aššur-apla-ēreš approached me (as follows:) "I am neither in debt nor a criminal! (However), he {i.e. Ubru, E.C.K.} raised a claim against me". I sent you a letter! Why didn't you come (and) make your case? If I herewith sent you a second tablet – take your witnesses and everything that goes into making your case! Come, make your case! If you do not come, I will send bailiffs to you, in order to capture you, they will seize you!

Month of Allanātu, 24th day, eponymy of Aššur-nādin-apli.

N° 2) VS 19, 13 [18]

To Ubru speak, thus Aššur-amranni:

Aššur-apla-ēreš approached me (as follows:) "I am neither in debt <nor a criminal>![19] Nevertheless he has raised claims against me!" Take your witnesses and everything that goes into making your case and come! Make your case!

Month of Šasarāte, 19th day, eponymy of Abattu.

N° 3) A.748 [20]

To Ubru speak, thus Sîn-lušallim-šarra:

Aššur-apla-ēreš approached me (with the following words) "I am neither in debt nor a criminal! Nevertheless he raised claims against me!" Take your witnesses and everything that goes into making your claim, come and make your case!

Day 18.

16 Transliterations are given at the end of the paper, photographs courtesy of the "Assur-Projekt" (dir. J. Renger). Cf. pl. 1–4.

17 Studies and remarks: Ebeling 1933: 36; Weidner 1939–41: 117; Deller 1984b: 228; Jacob 2003: 186–7 (text without collation!).

18 Weidner 1939–41: 113; Jacob 2003: 185–7.

19 The second part of the formula *u lā sarrāku* has probably been omitted, but see below p. 70.

20 Studies and remarks by Weidner 1939–1941: 117 n. 21; Pedersén 1985: 87 M8 Nr. 13, Donbaz 2004: 70–1, 77 (Text 2).

N° 4) A.988+

The two "Sammel-Aufnahmen" taken during excavation show obverse (2053) and reverse (2052) of the text, whereas the fragment of the upper right edge of the tablet is given with the obverse on 2052, and with the reverse on 2053. From the photo it becomes clear that the letter concerns the affairs of Aššur-amranni. Since the date formula is not visible on the photo, it is impossible to assign a placement within the chronological sequence of the other letters.

N° 5) KAV 201 [21]

> To Ubru speak, thus Kaṣru:
>
> Aššur-bēl-apli approached me (as follows:) "I am neither in debt nor a criminal! (However,) he {i.e. Ubru} raised a claim against me". Before me you shall answer (the accusation). It is not yours to impose (anything on him). And (although) his claim is released, you did not release your claim against him.[22] (However, if) you don't renounce the claim against him – take your witnesses (and) everything that goes into making your case, come and make your case!
>
> Month of Kuzallu, 4th day, eponymy of Abattu.

N° 6) A.133 [23]

> "To Ubru speak, thus Narām-Aššur-libūr:
>
> Aššur-bēl-apli approached me (as follows:) "I am neither in debt nor a criminal! One female <donkey> and one female mule ten years ago(???) he took".
>
> Take your witnesses and everything that goes into making your claim, come and make your case!
>
> Month of Kuzallu, 26th day, eponymy of Abattu, son of Adad-šuma-lēšir.

21 Ebeling 1933: 35–6; Kraus 1936: 108; Weidner 1939–41: 113; Deller 1984b: 228; Freydank 1997: 110–4.

22 The extreme brevity compromises our understanding of the text. A somewhat different perspective could be achieved if one accepts an interpretation suggested by Freydank (1997), who discussed the expression *bitqī batāqu*. According to Freydank's interpretation, lines 15–6 are an order directed towards the addressee. Accordingly, Freydank gave the following translation: "Folgendermaßen (habe ich gesprochen): Seine Vollstreckungen gib frei!" (loc. cit. p. 111). In a recent discussion of the passage Freydank agreed on the modification: "Du wirst vor mir Rede und Antwort stehen, (und gesetzt,) es gibt kein Fordern, das Du gefordert hast: Dann ist Dir nichts auferlegt, und (?) das ihm Abgeforderte gib frei! (Gesetzt), Du gibst das ihm Abgeforderte nicht frei, so …" (letter 27.8.2008).

23 Weidner 1939–41: 113 sub 3, 117 sub 21; Frankena 1956: 141; Donbaz 2004: 68–70, 77 (Text 1).

N° 7) Erlenmayer [24]

To Šallipīja say, thus Uṣur-namkūr-šarri:

Adad-nērārī[25], the chariot builder approached me (as follows:) "One female mule / donkey-mare together with its offspring (?) he took with him – (saying) ‚That donkey-mare is Sutean and it is..?.. (unclear). – But the donkey-mare is not Sutean, she is homebred.[26] She belongs to my house. I went to him (saying) ‚Bring my donkeys!' – (whence he said) 'They ran away; they are not here!' But today I saw one/a/the donkey-mare; from the hand of an Assyrian I took (her)". He {Adad-nērārī, E.C.K.} showed the donkey-mare to me {Uṣur-namkūr-šarri, E.C.K.). Take your witnesses (and) everything that goes into making your claim, come and make your case!

Month of Sîn, 24th day, eponymy of Abattu.

N° 8) KAV 168 [27]

To Munabittu say, thus Mušabši-Adad:

Urad-Šerūa approached me (as follows:) "In Aššur the (=my?) house has been robbed. The thieves have divided the missing objects in the house of Munabittu!" Take the men, who divided the things in your house, and all the objects, everything, no matter how small, your witnesses and everything that goes into making your claim and come! If you do not bring the people and all the objects you will be stripped off (your property)![28]

Month of Šasarāte, 25th day, eponymy of Aššur-da''ān.

24 Edited by Hall 1983. It is highly probable that Weidner (1939–1941: 114 sub 13) cites the first lines of this letter (Hall already pointed to the identical address, loc.cit. 78). The excavation photos 2049 and 2050 show the obverse and reverse of the letter. Weidner states that he quoted from the photo. How the letter found its way into the Erlenmayer collection remains a mystery.

25 The personal name is not very frequent and since the 13th century BC pertains to the royal onomasticon. Thus it is somewhat doubtful whether the reading is indeed correct (Hall 1983).

26 As meaning of *umzarḫu* has been proposed: "freed" ("freigelassen", AHW s.v.), "native" (Deller 1984a) and homebred (CAD U/W 156 s.v. u. b.). A text from Tell Chuēra, published by St. Jacob in his *Die mittelassyrischen Texte aus Tell Chuēra in Nordost-Syrien* (Wiesbaden 2009), Nr. 7, helps to understand the differentiation made in the legal text under discussion here. It becomes clear that mules and horses raised by pastoral nomads were called "Sutean" or "Shubarean", whereas "homebred" refers to animals raised by settled inhabitants of a town.

27 Studies and remarks by Ebeling 1933: 35; Weidner 1939–1941: 113; Saporetti 1978–79: 83.

28 This expression remains obscure: a root *nṭp* seems difficult, but so does *edēpu* (as suggested by CAD s.v. n. 2. AHW I 186 s.v. e./N Präs. "weggeblasen werden").

3 Common Features and Overall Structure of the Legal Summonses

Integrated in the formal frame of a letter, the texts are characterised by a mixture of descriptive and prescriptive text, as well as direct and indirect speech referring to former letters or citing oral speech. The sender of the letter is always an Assyrian state official, whose function might be described as that of an arbitrator, although a precise title of office is never given. A certain Aššur-amranni acts as an arbitrator in the affair Aššur-apla-ēreš contra Ubru and so does Sîn-lušallim-šarra. The case Aššur-bēl-apli contra Ubru is also worked on by two different arbitrators, Kaṣru and Narām-Aššur-libūr. A third case is directed by Uṣur-namkūr-šarri, and the affairs of Urad-Šerū'a are followed by a certain Mušabši-Adad. The arbitrator obviously has the authority to summon any individual to court by means of a written document.

It is not very clear what exactly triggered such a procedure. But from the text one might infer that someone claims to be a victim of false accusation, an unlawful action or some other kind of illegal act that was committed by the letter's addressee. Altogether three parties are involved: 1. the plaintiff, contradicting a previous action that he considers unjust; 2. the defendant and addressee of the letter, who acted against the plaintiff; 3. the arbitrator and sender of the letter, who summons the parties to a convocation. This convocation must be understood as an orally performed trial, as in every letter the addressee is asked to reply to the situation in the presence of the sender; never explicitly stated, the presence of the plaintiff must be taken for granted.

After the usual greeting, the case is introduced by naming the plaintiff in question: PN *imtaḫranni* "So-and-so approached me ...". This formula – using the verb *maḫāru* – refers to the formal appeal to an official with judicial powers, the usual way to bring about a legal case in Assyria.

The accusation of the plaintiff refers to legal proceedings that obviously had involved the defendant and had taken place earlier. Since he is now requested to contest the legitimacy of that earlier enactment, he usually gives the following tripartite (A+B+C) formal statement:

[A] *lā ḫābulāku (u)*	"I am neither in debt
[B] *lā sarrāku (u)*	nor a criminal,
[C] *bitqīja ibtataq*	(nevertheless) he has brought / raised a legal claim against me".[29]

29 This formula has been subject to intensive discussion. As for the rendering of *lā ḫābulāku u lā sarāku*, the conventional translation "I am not a traitor nor a thief" has led to a general misjudgement as concerns the preceding situation. So, for example, Pedersén (1985: 85) noted that the texts deal with "arrested men ... who claim to be unjustly detained". *De facto* all cases deal with special scenarios following real, fictious, legal or illegal imposition of debts on an individual, against whom 'claims' are brought forward by creditors. As regards the two elements A + B, we follow the translation proposed by Deller 1984b: 230f.

It is the third element (C) which informs us about the relationship of the plaintiff with the addressee of the letter and actual defendant: it is he, the addressee, who obviously raised claims on behalf of the actual plaintiff, who – on the other hand – is contesting these claims by appealing to a judicial authority. This official then issues a legal summons to meet the defendant. Indeed, the sender always seems to act from an official position – although probably not as a **judge**, since the term *dajjānu* "judge" is not used in the context of the legal summonses. However, the individuals under discussion here occupied high ranking positions in the Middle Assyrian state organisation and thus their decisions seem to have a binding force on the parties involved in the legal case. Although the Akkadian term *bātiqānu* "entitled person" itself is never used in the text, this must have been the addressee's position towards the plaintiff in the foregoing legal procedure.[30]

Texts n° 1, 3 and 5 exhibit the complete formula A+B+C, whereas n° 2 combines A + C, and n° 6 A + B respectively. These variations may rather be due to the individual situation than to a formal lapse by the recording scribe. In n° 7 and 8 only element A is present. In the case of n° 8 this most probably is to be explained by the somewhat curious account of the initial case: here evidently the action of laying hands on the property is described as robbery – from the perspective of the plaintiff: things were taken from the house of the actual plaintiff within the course of a legal action – a situation laid out more clearly by n° 6, where two animals were taken away. The same constellation appears in n° 7, a letter that also exhibits several individual features to be discussed later.

Equally formal is the closing formula *šēbutēka u mimma ša ana dabābīka ibaššiūni/illukuni leqe'a alka ina dinika dubbu* "Take your witnesses and everything that goes into making your case, come and make you case", which all texts (n° 1, 2, 3, 5, 6, 7, 8) show. Occasionally additional remarks follow: text n° 8 explicitly orders the claimant to present the objects and people involved in the case, in combination with a threat of sanctions ("If you do not bring the persons and all the objects you will be stripped off (your property)!") This additional clause fits nicely into the somewhat strange declaration in the text. Text n° 1 on the other hand has "If you do not come, I will send bailiffs to you, in order to capture you, they will seize you!", clearly referring to the earlier failure of the addressee to appear in the same case.

The introductory and closing formulae attest to the legal character of the document – no further legitimation is warranted – as texts n° 2 and 3 show. Here the self-referential character is a mark not only of letters as a genre, but also of ongoing legal affairs. Text n° 5 is the only document that specifies the objects of the action – not to be mistaken for the cause of action (that is the legitimacy of claim). On the other hand, at least two texts document a more complex situation: n° 1 shows that the conduct of these affairs could involve multiple letters sent to assemble the litigants

30 For *bātiqānu* and *bitqi batāqu* see Cancik-Kirschbaum forthcoming.

in court. N° 6 makes it clear that one possible result of such an arbitration in court was an oral declaration stating the release of all claims. Moreover, the same letter shows that such a declaration did not always put an end to the affair: in this case the result is another legal summons, sent by the judicial supervisor. And, last but not least, one has to account for the possibility that the formal opening allowed for a certain variation, depending probably on type and status of action.

A hypothetical reconstruction of the procedure would have to account for at least five steps:

1. Originary legal act of party **D** (defendant) versus party **P** (plaintiff), leading to the seizure of goods in the possession of **P**. The basis of the legal act is a claim by **D** against **P,** that brings the former in the state of a *bātiqānu*. Party **P** contests the lawfulness of this claim and the actions following from it.
2. Party **P** approaches an arbitrator **A**, and makes his accusations.
3. Arbitrator **A** takes legal action against party **D** by sending him a letter, which summons **D** as a defendant to trial. **D** is asked to eventually bring witnesses resp. objects pertaining to the case.
4. Party **P** and Party **D** meet and negotiate in presence of the arbitrator.
5. Decision.

While steps 1 to 3 can be inferred from the textual sources, i.e. the summonses, it is not clear whether steps 4 and 5 led to a written form.

4 Chronological Setting

The chronological layout of the texts is based on external as well as on internal parameters, the most prominent feature being the date-formula of the single document, which allows for a general ordering of the texts. However, given that the sequence of the eponyms during the Middle Assyrian period is still under discussion, most of the eponyms can only very generally be fixed within a given period of time.[31] Hence the order based on the calendrical datings has to be considered somewhat hypothetical and to be tested against the sequence of events as given in the texts themselves.

Principally, all texts were written during the reign of one king, namely Tukultī-Ninurta I, who reigned from 1233 to 1197 BC (according to the corrected Assyrian chronology). Within this time frame the texts seem to cover quite a short period, that is, some years during the second third of his reign. According to the current (altogether hypothetical) reconstructed order,[32] the earliest eponymy recorded is that in

31 Due to the absence of an original eponym list covering the timespan from Post-Old-Assyrian to Late Middle Assyrian the relative order and the chronological correlation of the individual *līmu* relies on combinatory methods. General information on Middle Assyrian Eponyms: Saporetti 1979; Freydank 1991; Freydank 2000. As regards the reign of Tukultī-Ninurta I, the period under consideration in this article, cf. Röllig 2004; Freydank 2005: 47–8; Freydank 2009: 75–7; Cancik 2012.

32 Freydank 2005: esp. 49ff. See also Cancik 2012: 39–51, for the reconstructed sequence see esp. p. 41 and 42 with Tableau A.

text n° 1, namely Aššur-nādin-apli, who is a "son of the king" and who kept the office early in the reign of Tukultī-Ninurta I, eventually to be placed in year 7. Four texts are dated by the name of a certain Abattu. The fact that one of them is specified by giving his father's name, Adad-šuma-lēšir, points to the problem that there were at least two eponyms of the same name. And indeed in this case the situation is extremely difficult to resolve, since these two probably served in direct succession during the years 10 and 11 of Tukultī-Ninurta I: first Abattu, son of Adad-šamšī, followed by Abattu, son of Adad-šumu-lēšir. According to the patronym, n° 6 can be assigned with certainity to the 11th year. Whether n° 5 – dated some 22 days earlier in the same month – relates to the same year is not clear. The attribution of the remaining two texts to either of the two eponyms named Abattu has to be left open for the moment.[33]

Yet, taking into account the perspective of the contents referred to in the letters, another problem as to the chronological sequence arises. Four letters pertain to litigations which involve Aššur-apla-ēreš and Ubru, thus forming a small dossier. The actual ordering at least produces a gap of three years between the oldest text (n°1) and the next one, n° 2 – suggesting that these two men were at odds over several years. If indeed texts n°1 and 2 concern the same case, then they should be placed in reverse order, text n° 2 being the first summons, referred to in text n°1 ll.9–10 "I sent you a letter". Consequently, this would call into question not only the position of the eponymate of Aššur-nadin-apli in year 7 of Tukultī-Ninurta I, but even its placement *before* the two eponymates assigned to an Abattu. Aššur-nādin-apli then has to be placed after the second Abattu eponymate. Since the content of the text n° 3 is only partially known, and the sequence of eponyms following Abattu II (for external reasons)[34] seems to be quite stable, a definite decision seems difficult. Hence, for the time being the order will be kept as it is, assigning thus to the dossier of Aššur-apla-ēreš and Ubru a time span of perhaps 3 years.

Lastly, the eponymy of Aššur-da''ān (son of Ikkaru) marks the latest of the texts n° 8, written during the 12th year of Tukultī-Ninurta I. Text n° 3 is assigned to only a day (without month-name or year), which usually means that it was written in direct connection with another more elaborately dated text. But as the contents of the texts from Istanbul remain unpublished, no hypothesis can be put forward safely.

5 Social Setting

Looking at the persons involved, the identity respectively of the plaintiff and the defendant allow for further systematization. Most prominent are the affairs of Mr. *Ubru*, who seems to have been quite busy in raising claims against his co-citizens.

33 See already on this problem Weidner 1939–1941: 113. Weidner assigned all texts to one and the same Abattu.

34 See note 31.

No less than six letters refer to his affairs, of which four have been initiated against him by Aššur-apla-ēreš (n° 1–4), and two by a certain Aššur-bēl-apli (n° 5+6).

The litigation of Aššur-apla-ēreš was conducted by two different officials – Aššur-amranni, who oversaw the case(s) alluded to in text n° 1, 2 and 4, and Sîn-lušallim-šarra, who was responsible for the situation reported in n° 3. It has been noted that the three, even four of the aforementioned texts might relate to the same case – given the identity of all persons involved (arbitrating official – plaintiff – defendant), but this conflicts somewhat with the chronology obtained from the dating (see above, section 4). Probably the same affair is mentioned in a letter (not a legal summons) written 3 months later in the context of withholding cattle.[35]

The accusations of Aššur-bēl-apli are treated in the texts n° 5 and n° 6. Although here also allusion is made to an ongoing case (n° 5), there seems to be no direct connection between the situation referred to in text n° 5. Rather, these two texts show by their datings that at least here Abattu from text n° 4 has to be identified with Abattu I (son of Adad-šamšī), and cannot be identical with Abattu II, son of Adad-šumu-lēšir of text n° 6. Thus the two letters might stem from two different years. This inference is supported by the fact that these two letters were sent by two different officials, namely Kaṣru and Narām-Aššur-libūr.

The remaining letters n° 7 and n° 8 are quite different in their contents as well as the individuals involved. Like n° 6, letter n° 7 treats the removal of animals from the household of the plaintiff. The texts lack the usual introductory formula in parts B+C, but instead have a long statement on the contested situation. Like n° 6, the number of animals taken away is given. Leaving the analysis of the extant legal situation aside, what follows is a detailed recitation of the arguments exchanged between the plaintiff and the actual defendant. This description is extraordinary insofar as it is given as a sequence of oral speeches: not only citing the utterances of the plaintiff before the judge, but also referring to the arguments exchanged between the two parties on an earlier occasion. The last text n° 8, stands apart as it partly lacks the introductory legislation-formulae.

What about the various individuals appearing in the texts? Most of them are well known from other parts of Assyrian state administration. Among the acting officials, the senders of the letters, we find Uṣur-namkūr-šarri, a high-ranking courtier at the king's court, and Aššur-amranni, member of an old family from the city of Assur, regularly participating in the office of eponym. The name of Kaṣru is attested in at least three more texts from Assur.[36] Sîn-lušallim-šarra and Narām-Aššur-libūr have interesting names, rather typical for a certain group of highly loyal people in the service of the king.[37] As regards the plaintiffs – Aššur-apla-ēreš is most probably a

35 The letter pertains to the Ubru-Archive M8. The text (AO 19.227) was edited by Aynard & Durand 1980: 3–5 as n° 1, without reference to the group of legal summons discussed in this paper.

36 See Freydank 1991: 55f ad VAT 16380.

37 For Narām-Aššur-libūrs activities as attested in the texts from Kār-Tukultī-Ninurta cf. MARV IV p. 35 s.v.

member of the prominent family of Nusku-aḫā-iddina[38]; Aššur-bēl-apli is, apart from the letter mentioned above, not attested elsewhere, but Urad-Šerū'a is a merchant and diplomat, stemming from an old Assur-family, attested at least for three generations.[39] And lastly, among the men challenged for raising claims against others, Ubru himself is the most prominent person of the archive M8, where all texts concerning him have been found.[40] Together with his brothers Ištar-ēreš and Qibi-Aššur, he is responsible for large numbers of forced laborers in the service of the king, involved mainly in the production and transfer of large quantities of grain and bricks etc. Munnabittu, despite his somewhat simple name, occupied various positions of high responisbility during the reign of Tukultī-Ninurta I. No information can be found about Šalipīja (perhaps = Šallim-pi-Ea).

This short survey on the individuals involved shows that all are members of the Assyrian elite, belonging more or less to the same social group, some of them even being colleagues. This means that claim and contest is settled within the peer-group, the king is not involved in persona. The Middle Assyrian Laws make no reference to this special legal procedure, the mode of which can be deduced from the legal administrative documents discussed here.

6 The Summons as a Legal Document

The epistolary form adds more or less automatically an important feature, namely the envelope as a protective and authoritative element. Envelopes constitute an important feature of legal documents in general, as the technical term "Hüllentafel" suggests. To document the intactness and thus validity of a contract (an inheritance document or the like), the text was recorded not only on the tablet, but also on the envelope. In a contested case the envelope was broken and the correctness of the document could be verified. The envelope thus served a double goal: not only to protect the document, but also to authorise its content. In the case of ordinary letters, authorization was provided by sealing the envelope, with the tablet itself never being sealed. At this point however, we must note a major difference vis-à-vis the legal summonses: in contrast to ordinary Middle Assyrian letters, some of the legal summonses show traces of a sealing on the tablet itself, this being always the seal of the sender of the letter.[41] This feature clearly differentiates the legal summonses from regular letters and makes them more naturally at home in the genre of legal documents, which always show one or more sealings, depending on the type of text. On the other hand the summonses completely lack another qualitative hallmark of

38 = Nusku-apla-uṣur, cf. OMA I, 104.

39 Attested acitvities in the archive M10, cf. Postgate 1988.

40 A short overview regarding Ubru was already given by Weidner 1939–1941: 117 sub *Up-ru*. See also Jacob 2003: 185–187.

41 This certainly is the case in texts n° 2, 5 and 6. As regards n°1 and 8 Dr. B. Feller kindly assures me that the tablets show no traces of sealing.

legal texts, that is: name and signatures of witnesses, testifying to both the formal correctness and veracity of the recorded facts and legal actions. However, it is clear that the legal summons in the epistolary format functions as a legal document in its own right, fusing characteristic features of the genre 'letter', such as address, differing states of narration, and a self-referential character, with elements common to legal documents, such as sealing and formulae declaring the current state of legal activity. Within this framework there is room for variation regarding the finer details of the basic situation, as well as the individual circumstances of a given case.

7 The 'Sitz-im-Leben' of the Epistolary Legal Summonses

Although not all of the biographies of the people involved in these texts can be clearly fleshed out, most of them are wealthy, important people. However, none of them is given a title or function.[42] This raises an interesting question regarding the group of 'legal summonses': on the one hand formal uniformity of the texts, their number and the shared knowledge of their associated procedures, suggest a well-established instrument of Middle Assyrian legal custom. On the other hand, the accumulation of evidence during a relatively short period of time during the reign of Tukultī-Ninurta I points to a more short-lived legal device that developed in the face of a specific socio-economic situation during that time.

The background always seems to be a situation where somebody in his function as an official of the Assyrian state claims rights against a third party. This claim is connected with the personal situation of the third party, who has experienced indebtedness or other serious loss of property. Obviously the claims laid on goods or property were then contested by the plaintiff. Thus a letter was sent in order to open legal proceedings, where the plaintiff and the *bātiqānu* were to confront one another directly. No documents describing the results of such arbitration have been identified so far, but at least one text makes allusion to a similar situation.[43]

In this particular case a decision of the king himself led to a complete cancellation of debts and thus annulment of existing claims! The text, a royal edict, was published as MARV IV 151 by Helmut Freydank.[44] The king grants, as a personal favor (*rimuttu*), to a certain Aššur-tišamme security against further reclamation, saying: "The creditors, to whom Aššur-tišamme, the son of Šamaš-aḫa-iddina is liable, they took everything – whether referring to a title or referring to a pledge. They have

42 Thus Jacob's classification (2003: 188) as a 'judge' (dayyānu) is based on modern assumptions, not on textual evidence.

43 It is not clear whether KAJ 294 (written out a century before) might represent the result of such an arbitration.

44 Partly treated by the same author (Freydank 1997). In his collection of Middle Assyrian attestations of the term *rimuttu*, Llop refers (2003: 126 tabl. 2) to *ṭuppu* "tablet" as the royal *rimuttu* in Freydank 2001: 151. However, what the king granted to Aššur-tišamme is the remission of the inherited debts (as written out apparently in a legal document).

no further claims against Aššur-nādin-apli, his son. Nobody has the right to bring forward a claim which has been made, or an object which has been given as a pledge." The text dates from around the same period as the legal summonses discussed here, that is, from a chronological point of view, this type of situation seems to be quite frequent, at least at that moment in time. Whether the accumulation of evidence under the reign of Tukultī-Ninurta I is due to the uneven distribution of sources is difficult to say at the moment. Nevertheless it is quite striking that similar texts from other well documented phases of the empire, such as the times of Adad-nērārī I, Shalmaneser I or Tiglath-pileser I, are lacking. Even more so as a genre, this type of legal summonses does not occur in Neo-Assyrian times. Similar cases seem to have been solved by means of differently composed documents, although always with legal proceedings in the background.[45]

The Middle Assyrian legal summonses in epistolary form thus constitute a very specific form of litigation, probably developed on account of a given socio-economic change in society. It shows how flexibly established genres such as the ordinary 'letter' could be adapted to the needs of newly arising problems, transforming them into a sort of legal document. The most striking phenomenon, the high degree of 'orality' in these texts not only points to the largely oral procedure of judicial legislation even at that time, but might also explain why the 'letter' was chosen as the formal framework, namely because it allowed for a detailed description of the case.

Appendix – Transliterations of the texts[46]

N° 1)

a-na ^{m}*Ub-ri*
qí-bi-ma
um-⌜*ma*⌝ ⌜^{md}⌝*A-šur*-IGI-*ni-ma*

---

^{md}*A-šur*-DUMU.UŠ-KAM
im-taḫ-ra-a-ni
ma-a la ḫab-bu-la-ku
ù la sa-ra$^{!}$*-ku bi*[47]*-it-*[*qí-i*]*a* ⌜*ib-ta-*<<*ta*>>*táq*⌝ * (on the reverse)
na-aš-pi-ir-ti
ul-te-bi-la-ku
a-na i-ni
la ta-li-ka
i+na di-ni-ka

45 Deller 1984b: pl. 24–5; Jas 1996; Kataja 1987 (with reference to ADD 680, ABL 1024, ADD 1139).

46 For photographs of the texts see plates 1-4, courtesy of the "Assur-Projekt" (dir. J. Renger).

47 BI seems to have been written over the top of another sign, probably I.

la ta-ad-bu-ub
šum-ma ša-ni-tam
ṭup-pi ul-te-bi-[*lak-ku*]
še-bu- ⸢*te-ka ù mi-im-ma*⸣
⸢*ša a-na da-ba-bi-ka*⸣
⸢*il-lu-ku-ú-ni*⸣
⸢*lé-qe-a al-ka*⸣
i+na d[*i-ni-ka dub-u*]*b-bu*
šum-ma l[*a ta-li-k*]*a*
a-na ṣ[*a-ba-t*]*i-ka* ERÍN^{MEŠ}
al- ⸢*tap-ra*⸣ -[*ku*]
i-ṣa- ⸢*bu-tu-ka*⸣
^{ITI}*Al-la-* ⸢*na-tu* UD-24^{KÁM}⸣
li-mu ^{md}*A-šur*-SUM-DUMU.UŠ

N° 2)

a-na ^{m}*Ub-ri*
qí-bi-ma
um-ma ^{md}*A-šur-am-ra-ni-ma*

^{md}*A-šur*-DUMU.UŠ-KAM
im-taḫ-ra-a-ni
ma-a la-a ḫa-bu-la-ku
bi-it-qi-ja
ib-ta-//ta//[48]*-táq*
še-bu-te-ka
ù mi-im-ma
ša a-na da-ba-bi-ka
i-ba-ši-ú-ni
le-qe-a
al-ka i+na di-ni-ka
du-ub-bu

^{ITI}*Ša-sa-ra-a-te* UD-19^{KÁM}
li-mu A-bat-tu

N° 3)

a-na ^{m}*Ub-ri*
qí-bi-ma

48 The scribe erroneously wrote TA twice.

um-ma ^{md}*30-lu-ša-lim*-LUGAL

---

^{md}*A-šur*-DUMU.UŠ-KAM
im-taḫ-ra-ni
ma-a la ḫa-bu-la-ku
la-a sa-ar-ra-ku
bi-it-qi-ja
ib-ta-ta-aq
še-bu-te-ka
ù mi-im-ma
ša a-na da-ba-bi-ka-ni
le-qe-a
al-ka i-na de-ni-ka
du-bu

UD-18^{KÁM}

N° 4) act. situation of text unknown, unpublished so far, gen. information from the excav. Photographs (Ass 2053 obv. /Ass 2052 rev.).

N° 5)

a-na ^{m}*Ub-r*[*i*]
qí-bi-m[*a*]
um-ma ^{m}*Kaṣ-ru-ma*

---

^{md}*A-šur*-EN-DUMU.UŠ
im-taḫ-ra-a-ni

---

ma-a la-a ḫa-bu-la-ku //ù/
ù la-a sa$^{!}$*-ra-a-ku*
ù bi-it-qi$^{!}$*-ja*
ib$^{!}$[49]*-ta-ta-aq*
a-na pa-ni-ja
ta-du-bu-ub
ša[50] *la-a ba-ta-qa*
ta-ab-tu-qu-ú-ni
la-a i-mi-id-ka
⌜*ù?*⌝ *bi-it-qi-šu*

49 The sign looks more like an AL with a supplementary vertical.
50 Reading according to collation of the original.

ú-še-er
bi-it-qi-šu
la-a tu-še-er
še-bu-ti-ka mi-im-ma
ša a-na da-ba-bi-ka
⌜*i*⌝-*lu-ku-ú-ni*
le!-*qe-a al*!-*ka*
i+na di-ni-ka
du-ub-bu
^{ITI}*Ku-za*[*l-lu*]
UD-4^{KÁM} *li-mu*
{^{m}}*A-bat-tu-ma*

N° 6)

a-na U-bri
qí-bi-ma
um-ma Na-ra-am-^{d}*A-šur-li-bur-ma*

---

^{md}*A-šur*-EN-DUMU.UŠ
im-ta-aḫ-ra-ni
ma-a la ḫa-bu-la-ku
ù la sa-ra-ku
1 MÍ 1 EME$_{5}$ *ša* ANŠE^{MEŠ}
iš-tu 10 MU^{MEŠ}
il-te-qe
še-bu-te-ka
ù mi-im-ma
ša a-na da-ba-bi-ka
i-lu-ku-ú-ni
le-qe-a al-ka
a-na di-ni-ka du-bu

---

^{ITI}*Ku-zal-lu* UD-26^{KÁM}
li-mu ^{m}*A-bat-tu*
DUMU 10-MU-*le-šìr*

N° 7)

a-na ^{m}*Ša-li-pi-ia*[51]

51 Hall 1983: 78 follows Saporetti's proposal in regarding Šallipīja as a non-Akkadian name. But one

qí-bi-ma
um-ma ^{m}PAP-*nam-kur*-LUGAL-*ma*

---

^{md}IM-DUḪ.ERÍN ^{LÚ}NAGAR ^{GIŠ}GIGIR
im-taḫ-ra-an-ni
ma-a 1 EME$_{5}$ *ša* ANŠE
a-di 3 ANŠE^{MEŠ} *ṣi-it lìb-bi-ša*
uṣ-ṣa-bi-it il-te-šu
ma-a EME$_{5}$ *su-ti-tu*
ši-i-it
u ⸢*x ḫu sa-at*⸣
ma-a EME$_{5}$ *la-su-ti-a-at*
ma-a EME$_{5}$ *um-za-ar-ḫu*
ša É-*ti-ia ši-i-it*
ma-a at-ta-al-ka-áš-šu
ma-a ANŠE^{MEŠ}-*ia bi-la*
ma-a ḫal-qu ma-a la-áš-šu
ma-a u$_{4}$-*ma* 1 EME$_{5}$ *a-ta-mar*
i+na ŠU *áš-šu-ra-ie-e aṣ-ṣa-bat*
EME$_{5}$ *uk-tal-li-ma-an-ni*
še-bu-te-ka mi-im-ma
ša a-na da-ba-bi-ka
il-lu-ku-ni le-qe-a
al-ka ı-na dı-nı-ka
du-ub-bu
$^{\text{ITI d}}$*Sîn* UD-24^{KÁM}
li-mu ^{m}*A-bat-tu-ma*

N° 8)

a-na ^{m}*Mu-na-bi-it-te*
qí-bi-ma
um-ma ^{m}*Mu-šab-ši*-^{d}IM-*ma*

---

^{m}ÌR$^{!}$[52]-^{d}*Še-ru-a*
im-taḫ-ra-an-ni
ma-a i+na URU.ŠÀ-*bi*.URU
É *ḫa-mu-uṣ ú-nu-ti*

might also take it as an abbreviation of the very common Assyrian name *Šallim-pī-Ea*.
52 Text shows clearly DUMU.

ḫa-li-iq-<Rasur *-te-*>*ta*
i+na É ^{m}*Mu-na-bi-te sa-ru-tu*
iz-zu-zu ERÍN^{MEŠ}
ša ú-nu-ta
i+na É*-ka*
i-zu-zu-ni
ù ú-nu-ta gab-ba
mi-im-ma lu la i-ma-ṭi
še-bu-te-ka ù mi-im-ma
ša a-na da-ba-bi-ka
il-lu-ku-ni le-qe-a
al-ka šum-ma ERÍN^{MEŠ}
ù ú-nu-ta gab-ba
la-a ta-tab-la at-ta
i+na ŠÀ*-be ta-an-ni-ṭi-ip*
^{ITI}*Ša-sa-ra-te* U$_4$-25^{KÁM}
li-mu ^{m}*A-šur-da-a-an*

The Use (and Abuse) of Letters in the Speeches of the Attic Orators

Paola Ceccarelli (Durham)

1 Introduction

It has often been argued that the transition from the fifth to the fourth century constitutes a watershed in terms of literacy (at least in an Athenian context), and specifically in terms of interest in, and preservation of, documents. Starting with the late fifth century, documents and references to laws are cited in the speeches of the Attic orators as part of the evidence. A compelling case has been made for the earlier existence in Athens of archives of some kind, and more generally for a fairly widespread use of writing already in the fifth century;[1] the fact remains that references to documents, both on stone and 'archival' ones, begin towards the end of the fifth century, and thicken in the fourth century. What of a specific type of written document, the letter?

In discussions of the respective roles of orality and literacy in Greek culture and society, letters have played a marginal role, if they have been at all considered. This is probably the consequence of an objective fact, the relative scarcity of letters in archaic and classical Greece. A comparison with the ancient Near East makes the peculiarity of the Greek situation clear: while letters constitute an extremely important part of the overall written documentary corpus that we have from the Near East, they are a very small percentage of the overall written material from archaic and classical Greece. The loss of documents written on perishable material may, at least in part, account for this difference. Yet, it is a generally accepted fact that until the late fifth century in Greece the letter is not codified as a genre: the extant letters do not show traces of standard introductory and closing epistolary formulae, but appear to be simply the written version of an oral message, sent by an individual who cannot (or does not want to) use his voice. Nor is there yet a specific word for 'letter': the terminology is still in flux.[2] This means that the loss of documents written mainly on perishable materials, as letters would have been, cannot be the only explanation for the late appearance and reduced presence of letters in archaic and early classical Greece. Only with the fourth century does letter-writing impose itself; interestingly,

1 E.g., Sickinger 1999 for the archives; Pébarthe 2006 for literacy (against the more traditional vision of Harris 1989 and Thomas 1989). For the debate inasmuch as it concerns law, Faraguna 2007.

2 For the development of letter-writing and its connotations see Harris 1989: 88–9; Lewis 1996: 143–8; Rosenmeyer 2001: 19–35 (introductory sketch, definition), 45–60 (in the historians) and 61–97 (in tragedy); Ceccarelli 2005a and b. For early letters on lead see now Eidinow & Taylor 2010.

the form 'letter' covers now a wide number of different categories that include private letters, official letters, and long 'literary' letters such as philosophical treatises, encomia or apologics.[3]

It has however recently been claimed that from the mid-fifth century onwards the 'letter' was one of the accepted, usual instruments for communicating at a distance. Thus, in a discussion of the letters mentioned by the orators in the course of their speeches, Pébarthe remarks, "dans cette deuxième moitié du cinquième siècle, la correspondance écrite est banale".[4] Some texts may seem to bear this assertion out: thus, a passage from the Apollodoran speech *Against Timotheus*, delivered at some time in the late 360s, but referring here to the situation of Athens in the year 373 BC, may be understood as presenting oral messages and letters in parallel, as the two ways in which information concerning the army could be conveyed home: publicly, through a report in the assembly; and privately, through letters by each individual to his family.[5]

And yet, a very different assessment has been made by Sian Lewis, who suggests that "personal communication through writing letters never became common in Classical Greece".[6] A look at the practicalities of sending a letter in the ancient Greek world helps understand why: in the world of ancient *poleis*, there was no 'royal service', as in Persia, nor were there messengers in the service of kings, as was the case with Macedon; for official communication, the *poleis* had groups of couriers (*hemerodromoi* or *dromokerykes*) who would cover all the distance, and at this point, the message might just as well be transmitted orally, but for specific details difficult to remember. For private communications, one had to rely on individual travelers to bring over the message, or send a slave. As for diplomatic communications, Lewis' point that heralds, if captured, would probably not be tortured to force them to deliver information – heralds in theory were sacred –, while a letter, once intercepted, would betray whatever plans were being made, is a good one.[7]

We shall see in a moment that letters were indeed a relatively common instrument of communication, possibly already in the fifth, and certainly from the fourth

3 Sykutris 1931. Reed (1997) discusses the connections between epistolary and rhetorical practices.

4 Pébarthe 2006: 81–4 and 86, who bases this claim on a disputable analysis of early 'letters' on ceramic and lead from Athens, and on Antiphon 5.53–6, discussed below.

5 ([Dem.] 49.13 "those who came from the army were reporting before the assembly (ἀπαγγελλόντων ἐν τῷ δήμῳ) the distress and need that existed, and at the same time individuals kept receiving word/letters from their relatives and friends (δι᾽ ἐπιστολῶν ἑκάστου πυνθανομένου παρὰ τῶν οἰκείων καὶ ἐπιτηδείων) telling of their plight". Note however that δι᾽ ἐπιστολῶν is ambiguous: while Gernet for Budé translates "connaissaient la situation par des lettres de parents et d'amis", A.T Murray, in his Loeb translation, assumes it to mean "through messages", since he translates: "kept receiving word". The problem is the ambiguity inherent in ἐπιστέλλω / ἐπιστολή; but on the whole by the fourth century BC ἐπιστολή seems indeed to mean letter (rather than "injunction" or oral message).

6 Lewis 1996: 142; resulting, in her eyes, from the fact that "the letter was never trustworthy enough" (p. 152).

7 Lewis 1996: 148. On couriers, see Matthews 1974; Klauck 2006: 60–5; Muir 2008: 11–2.

century onwards; but it is important to differentiate between public and private communication, and between types of letters and occasions, while at the same time bearing in mind the generic and socio-political context within which a reference to a letter is made. This is why I have chosen to look at letters, their uses, typology, and perception, within a homogeneous corpus, the symbouleutic and forensic speeches of the Attic orators.[8] These speeches are located, in many ways, at the interface of orality and writing: they were delivered orally, and were meant to give the impression of being composed on the spur of the moment, but were in most cases prepared. Yet the documents within the speeches were read out by a clerk, and this shift from the orator to the clerk, creating a break, will have enhanced the written status of the documents.[9] Letters too are very close to oral communication: according to ancient epistolary theory, a letter is a (formalized) speech, in which the person of the sender is very markedly present.[10] It may not be an accident that the first collection of 'literary letters' is probably that of Lysias; and that in the work of Isocrates there is no clear-cut distinction between speech and epistle.[11]

In what follows, the focus will be mainly on the letters read out, or alluded to, in the speeches of the early logographers (Antiphon, Andocides, Lysias and Isaeus), of Demosthenes, and of Aeschines; but I shall occasionally contrast the mentions and uses made of letters in the speeches with that of other types of documents, in order to highlight the specificity of letter-writing in respect to other forms of writing.[12] After others, Thomas has stressed the gradual 'encroachment' of writing in legal contexts throughout the fourth century, highlighting three aspects of this process: written contracts gradually appear alongside the use of witnesses in the sphere of business; written testimony replaces oral testimony (a change that most scholars agree had taken place by c. 380 BC); and a written plea (a γραφή) replaces the oral plea in the preliminary hearing (the ἀνάκρισις). Thus at least from the end of the first quar-

8 I follow the traditional dating of the various speeches, as it is enough for my argument if the speeches discussed belong to the fourth century BC; for the same reason I do not discuss their authenticity.

9 See, for instance, Nicolai 2004: 20: "l'intersezione fra oralità e scrittura nell'oratoria è continua". Nicolai (2004: 22–3) makes however also the important point that early prose deliberately takes its distances from spoken language; imitation of spoken, everyday language is something that begins later, with Lysias, and that will reach its climax with Demosthenes.

10 So in Demetrius *De Eloc.* 223, a letter is one half of a dialogue; on the projection of the persona of the sender in letter-writing and on the sense of *parousia*, of presence, thus created, see Stirewalt 1993: 4–5.

11 Lysias: Blass 1887: (I) 422–3, accepting the authenticity of the majority of the letters. Isocrates: Too 1995: 195–9; Livingstone 2001: 5–8; Nicolai 2004: 118–27.

12 I have looked at all passages in which the word *epistole* appears. I also discuss most instances where some form of written note passing between two persons is mentioned, whether designated as *gramma/grammata* or denoted by means of a verb of writing; a note of acknowledgement has however a different status from that of a letter as it is simply a written record of something also orally agreed upon between the involved parties.

ter of the fourth century, written documentation has become a central element in the construction of a speech.[13] What of letters?

2 Antiphon, Andocides, Lysias, Isaeus

Writing and written documents make a slow and gradual entrance in the law-courts. Thus, it is no surprise to find that no laws or decrees are cited in any of the fifteen extant speeches of Antiphon, although a number of witnesses are called in. There are however two references to the writing of a message. The first, from the speech *On the murder of Herodes,* delivered probably c. 420 (at any rate between 420 and 412 BC), is a staple of all discussions of the perception of letters in Athens. Here is the text:

> "The prosecution further allege that they discovered on board a note (γραμματείδιον εὑρεῖν ἐν τῷ πλοίῳ, ..., ὡς ἀποκτείναιμι) stating that I had killed Herodes, which I had intended to send to Lycinus. But what need had I to send a note, when the bearer himself was my accomplice? Not only would he, as one of the murderers, have told the story more clearly in his own words, but it would have been quite unnecessary to conceal the message from him, and it is essentially messages which cannot be disclosed to the bearer that are sent in writing. 54. Then again, an extensive message would have had to be written down, as its length would have prevented the bearer remembering it. But this one was brief enough to deliver—"The man is dead". Moreover, bear in mind that the note contradicted the slave tortured, and the slave the note. The slave stated under torture that he had committed the murder himself, whereas the note when opened revealed the fact that I was the murderer. 55. Which are we to believe? The prosecution discovered the note on board only during a second search, not during their first one; they had not hit on the idea at the time. It was not until the first witness had said nothing to incriminate me when tortured that they dropped the note in the boat, in order to have that, if nothing else, as a ground for accusing me. 56. Then, once the note had been read and the second witness, when tortured, persisted in disagreeing with the note, it was impossible to spirit away the message read from it. Needless to say, had the prosecution supposed that they would induce the slave to lie about me immediately, they would never have

13 Thomas 1989: 41–4. On the use of written documents and witnesses' statements (oral and later written) as evidence in Athenian courts see further Bonner 1905: 46–53; Harrison 1971: 133–54; Mirhady 1996: 128–9; Sickinger 1999; Thür 2005. An excellent discussion of the role played by writing in the trial in Faraguna 2007. Carey (1994) shows how these written documents could still be manipulated. In what follows, the translations of the texts of the orators will be based on: K.J. Maidment, *Minor Attic orators: Antiphon, Andocides*, Cambridge, Mass. and London 1941; C.A. Vince and J.H Vince (1926), J.H. Vince (1930), A.T. Murray (1939), N.W. De Witt and N.J. De Vitt (1949), *Demosthenes. Orations*, I-VII, Cambridge Mass. and London; C.D. Adams, *Aeschines*, Cambridge Mass. and London, 1919; J.O. Burtt, *Minor Attic Orators* II, Cambridge Mass. and London, 1962.

> devised the message contained in the note. Call me witnesses to confirm these facts". (Antiph. 5.53–6)

This passage shows that the fact of sending a written note, a letter, was not in itself extraordinary: the prosecution must have produced the note with the rest of the evidence. However, what Antiphon makes of this note is very interesting. The fact that he accuses the prosecution of having forged the letter (tragic examples, such as the *Palamedes* of Euripides, were a much discussed topic at the time, as shown by Alcidamas' treatment of the story) is not an argument against the use of letters in long-distance communications – the readiness to attempt a forgery might almost be interpreted in the opposite sense. But the defendant makes two important points about letters: the first and most important one is that written messages are necessary only when one does not want the bearer to learn the content of the message. This reminds one of a number of letters in Herodotus and Thucydides (in particular, the story of Pausanias' correspondence with Xerxes, Thuc. 1.132.5): written notes containing private information, 'letters', are suspect, dangerous documents.[14] Would the orator have risked making such a point, if writing letters had been common practice among the judges? The second point is that the only other reason for writing letters is when the message is excessively long, too much to be remembered; and this clearly was not the case with the *grammateidion*. Antiphon may have added this because he felt that his first point alone might not have been convincing; his statement shows at any rate that a letter is not envisaged as anything more than a message couched in writing, and to be used only if other reasons (length, secrecy) make the oral transmission difficult.

Thus, while letters have a place in the world of long-distance traders, these documents are not free from suspicion. Another passage in Antiphon's corpus confirms this, from his *Prosecution of a stepmother for poisoning*, another forensic speech, delivered at some point between 420 and 411 BC. Here the prosecution, in the final peroration, affirms that victims of murder, if they have the time, summon friends and relatives and tell them who the murderers are, charging them to take vengeance; but if this is not possible, they make a statement in writing, call the slaves as witnesses, and reveal the murderers to them. The speaker adds that his father revealed the facts to him, young though he was, and 'laid his charge upon him (ἐπέστειλεν), not on his slaves'.[15] A chiastic structure is clearly at work here, in which the writing and showing to the slaves corresponds to the showing and 'transmitting' to the son (interestingly, ἐπιστέλλω can be used for oral or written messages); the second procedure is supposed to be the best one. The defence had certainly stressed the ig-

14 A point highlighted by Harris 1989: 88–9 (see also 78); see also, on treacherous letters, Rosenmeyer 2001: 45–55.

15 Ant. 1. 30: ἐὰν δὲ τούτων ἁμαρτάνωσι, <u>γράμματα γράφουσι</u>, καὶ οἰκέτας τοὺς σφετέρους αὐτῶν ἐπικαλοῦνται μάρτυρας, καὶ <u>δηλοῦσιν</u> ὑφ ' ὧν απόλλυνται. Κἀκεῖνος ἐμοὶ νέῳ ἔτι ὄντι ταῦτα <u>ἐδήλωσε</u> καὶ <u>ἐπέστειλεν</u>, ὦ ἄνδρες, οὐ τοῖς ἑαυτοῦ δούλοις.

norance of the slaves concerning the facts, and possibly also the absence of any written indication on the part of the dead man as to the culpability of the stepmother. The prosecution counters this by emphasizing the status of the son, and by using a term that substitutes for the missing written statement. There is thus here a sense that a written accusation might have some weight; but it is only a vague intimation, quickly countered. But for these two instances, no written documents are part of the argument in Antiphon's speeches.

Andocides marks a difference in respect to Antiphon, inasmuch as he quotes a number of documents: two decrees and three laws (besides numerous references to specific decrees), along with three lists of names, in his forensic speech *On the Mysteries* (delivered 399 BC); and a decree in his assembly speech *On his return* (dated before 403, probably delivered around 408 BC).[16] There is however no mention of letters in any of his speeches. Similarly, while various categories of documents are mentioned in Isaeus (mainly laws, but also decrees and written depositions), there is no reference, among the various pieces of evidence, to letters.[17]

A letter appears in one early speech of the *Corpus Lysiacum*, the *For Polystratus*, dated to ca. 410 BC: the defendant asks the jury to consider (σκέψασθε) a letter (ἐπιστολήν) of his father, meant to show that his father was a loyal citizen (Lys. 20.27) – but the letter is not read, the content is simply summarized, while the weight of the argument is carried by witnesses. Letters are also mentioned, but again not read out, in the speech *On the property of Aristophanes* (387 BC): ἐπιστολαί (messages, and not necessarily all of them written ones) sent by his father from Cyprus were one of the reasons why Aristophanes decided to go there and join Conon. Here too, no weight at all is laid on the ἐπιστολαί (whose status, to repeat, is not necessarily that of written messages), and immediately the speaker calls on a witness, Eunomus, to attest the truth of what he has affirmed (Lys. 19.23). The scarcity of letters in Lysias is to be set against a background of relatively frequent references to (and quotes *in extenso* from) decrees, laws, and other documents;[18] but if letters are infrequent, no particular connotations are attached to letter-writing.

16 Respectively And. 1.77; 1.83 (decrees) 1.85; 1.87; 1.96 (laws); and And. 2.23.

17 A law on adoption in the *On the estate of Menecles* (2.16); laws in the *On the estate of Pyrrhus* (3.53), along with a number of written depositions; laws regulating the right of inheritance in the *On the estate of Hagnias* (11.11 and 22); decrees in the speech *On the estate of Philoktemon* (6.50), along with a number of written depositions.

18 Lysias quotes a number of decrees in his *Against Agoratus* (13.22,28,35,50,55,59,71); another decree in the speech *Against Andocides* (6.24); three laws in the *On the murder of Eratosthenes* (1.28,30,31); a law in the *For the soldier* (9.8); a high number of laws in the *Against Theomnestus 1* (10.9,14,16, and 17,18,19), two of which are again referred to in the *Against Theomnestus 2* (11.3 and 6: in this speech, the emphasis is on the wording of the laws, hence the number of quotes); laws are also read out in the *Against Alcibiades 1* (14.5 and 8; the speech closes with a request to read, one after the other, the laws, the oaths, and the charge, 14.47). Other documents are also read out: thus, in the speech *On the property of Aristophanes*, an inventory of bronze plates (19.28) and the record of public service of the father of the appellant (19.58).

We reach at this point the second quarter of the fourth century, the moment in which, even according to the most conservative estimates, the orators begin to make an ample use of documents. In this connection, Thomas has pointed at Aeschines' (and in a smaller measure at Demosthenes') 'innovative' use of written documents, in particular decrees and laws.[19] What of letters?

3 Demosthenes

Letters are treated rather differently in the forensic and in the political speeches. A handful of references to letters occur, alongside references to decrees, laws, and wills, in some of Demosthenes' forensic speeches. The letters he refers to in this context were for the most part composed to impart information, or to convey a recommendation. A ready example is in the speech *Against Polycles* (transmitted in the *corpus Demosthenicum*, but written by Apollodorus, and delivered at some point between 360 and 358 BC): the speaker, who was at the moment of the events serving as trierarch, mentions sending a subordinate, a certain Euktemon, with money and letters to friends of his father ([Dem.] 50.18). Letters from relatives are again mentioned later in the speech ([Dem.] 50. 62). Similarly, the speech Against Nicostratus, delivered sometime after 368/7 BC, shows that Apollodorus probably used a letter (the Greek has ἐπιστέλλω without further precisions) to communicate with Nicostratus when he had to leave in a hurry ([Dem.] 53.5); and it is clear that Nicostratus, when captured and sold as a slave in Aegina, used both letters and messengers to inform his brother of what had happened and of his actual situation ([Dem.] 53.6).[20]

But letters are also vehicles for intrigue: in the same *Against Polycles*, the speaker recalls the arrival of a dispatch-boat with a messenger and letters (50.46), that turn out to have been sent by Callistratus (the well-known Athenian politician from Aphidna) to Timomachus (the *strategos* in charge). This testifies to the use of written correspondence, but letters were in this case necessary, as Callistratus was at the moment an exile. More importantly, Callistratus' is a 'secretive' letter, according to Apollodorus part of a ploy to have Callistratus illegally transported on board his trireme – when he learnt of the content of the letter from a sailor who had overheard slaves talking, Apollodorus refused to continue on the mission.

19 Thomas 1989: 69–72 and 83–93. A list of all documents read out would take too much space; to give just an example each, in Demosthenes' *Against Meidias*, the following documents are read out: five laws (8,10,47,94,113); seven witnesses' statements (22,82,93,107,121,168,174); an oracle (52–3). In Aeschines' *Against Timarchos*, laws are read out *in extenso* four times (at 12,16,21 and 35); witnesses' statements six times (50,66,68,101,105 and 116); the copy of an agreement (ἀντίγραφα συνθηκῶν) once (116); the orator asks three times that the *grammateus* read passages of the *Iliad* (148–50). Mirhady (2000) stresses the importance attributed by Demosthenes to written proofs (be they from witnesses or other).

20 On the use of letters in an emergency see also Harris 1989: 5f. (the letters of Achillodorus and Lesis). Cf., e.g., Eidinow & Taylor 2010.

Something more on the status of the letter as document can be gathered from Demosthenes' oration 38, *Against Nausimachus and Xenopeithes*, probably written around 346 BC: here, the speaker stresses the unlikelihood that a written message (the Greek says *grammata*, which may mean a letter, but is not specific) may succeed in enforcing a request for payment:

> "Now is there any man so silly as voluntarily to pay money to one not entitled to it, who demanded it by letter, when he had for so long a time evaded payment to the rightful owners?" (ἔστιν οὖν οὕτω τις ἀνθρώπων ἄτοπος, ὥσθ ' ἃ τοὺς κυρίους διεκρούσατο μὴ καταθεῖναι τοσοῦτον χρόνον, ταῦτα τῷ μὴ κυρίῳ πέμψαντι γράμμαθ ' ἑκὼν ἀποδοῦναι;)(Dem. 38.12).

Finally, two other speeches illustrate the milieu in which letters were mainly used: that of the long-distance traders. Thus in the (possibly Demosthenic) speech *Against Phormio*, dated 327/6 BC, the speaker mentions having given Phormio letters for his commercial partners in the Bosphorus:

> When he went, then, to Bosporus, having letters (ἐπιστολάς) from me, which I had given him to deliver to my slave, who was spending the winter there, and to a partner of mine—in which letter I had stated (γράψας ἐν τῇ ἐπιστολῇ) the sum which I had lent and the security, and bade them, as soon as the goods should be unshipped, to inspect them and keep an eye on them—the fellow did not deliver to them the letters (ἐπιστολάς) which he had received from me, in order that they might know nothing of what he was doing (Dem. 34.8).

The letters had been sent to warn the slave and the commercial partner of the claimant of the need to personally check the actions of Phormio (and the speech insists throughout on the lack of witnesses). Phormio's failure to deliver these letters is then repeatedly used by the speaker to discredit his character.[21] The use of letters by merchants is also a conspicuous feature of the speech *Against Dionysodorus,* delivered some time after 323/2 BC: the dealings of Dionysodorus are contextualised within a

21 Dem. 34.28-9: "You did not bring as a witness my slave who was in Bosporus or my partner, nor did you deliver to them the letters (τὰς ἐπιστολάς) which we gave into your charge, and in which were written instructions (ἐν αἷς ἐγέγραπτο) that they should keep close watch on you in whatever you might do! Why, men of Athens, what is there which a man of this stamp is not capable of doing, who, after receiving letters (γράμματα λαβών) did not deliver them in due and proper course?", and again 34.32: "Yes, he says, for the agreement bade me pay the cash to the shipowner. But it did not prevent you from summoning witnesses, or from delivering the letters!" (Ἡ γὰρ συγγραφή με, φησί, τῷ ναυκλήρῳ ἐκέλευεν ἀποδοῦναι τὸ χρυσίον. μάρτυρας δέ γ ' οὐκ ἐκώλυεν παρακαλεῖν, οὐδὲ τὰς ἐπιστολὰς ἀποδοῦναι). Mercantile cases (*dikai emporikai*) such as this one followed a special procedure: the prosecution had to be based on a written contract, whose terms had not been adhered to by some of the contracting parties. Cf. MacDowell 2004: 13.

description of the workings of the grain market, in which retailers manipulate the price of the grain by sending letters to merchants in Egypt, informing them of the fluctuations of the price and allowing them to decide whether to ship the grain to Athens or elsewhere.[22] This is what the speaker claims happened, against the contract that had been agreed: Dionysodorus sent a man with a letter to Rhodes (τὰ γράμματα τὰ παρὰ τούτου ἀποσταλέντα, 56.10), informing his partner that the price of the grain in Athens was low, with the result that the merchants sold the grain in Rhodes.

As for Demosthenes' political orations, they refer to two main types of letters: official royal letters, most of them from Philip II of Macedon; and the official reports that Athenian *strategoi* or ambassadors would send to the *polis* while away on a campaign or a mission. Concerning the latter, the speech *On the false embassy* shows that these reports were discussed collectively, for according to Demosthenes, his colleagues in the embassy voted against sending a dispatch he had written, and chose to write a different one, which they sent to Athens.[23] Thus, these are letters, but by no means private, exclusive communication. In the speech *Against Aristocrates* (352 BC), letters from the *strategoi* Iphicrates and Timotheus to the Athenians are read as evidence against Charidemus (23.151–2), together with a decree and a witness' statement; in the same speech, a (deceptive) letter of Charidemus to Athens – or rather, as Demosthenes specifies, to his friend Cephisodotus, but meant for the Athenians – is also brought forward as evidence (23.153–6), as well as other letters from Athenian magistrates of cities in the Thracian Chersonese (23.156–62).[24] Such reports make it clear that from the fourth century onwards letter-writing was integrated among the administrative practices of the Athenian *polis*, at least for what concerned internal communication (i.e., between Athenians). The famous letter of Nicias in Thucydides provides the earliest example of this, and the length to which Thucydides goes to explain Nicias' decision shows that the practice cannot have been usual; but there are also references to such reports in Xenophon and in fourth century honorific inscriptions.[25]

22 [Dem.] 56.8: "Then those who remained here would send letters to those abroad (ἔπεμπον γράμματα οἱ ἐπιδημοῦντες τοῖς ἀποδημοῦσιν) advising them of the prevailing prices, so that if grain were dear in your market, they might bring it here, and if the price should fall, they might put in to some other port. This was the chief reason, men of the jury, why the price of grain advanced; it was due to such letters and conspiracies (ἐκ τῶν τοιούτων ἐπιστολῶν καὶ συνεργιῶν)". See also on this practice Harris 1989: 122–3.

23 Dem. 19.174: τὴν μὲν γραφεῖσαν ἐπιστολὴν ὑπ ' ἐμοῦ πρὸς ὑμᾶς ἀπεψηφίσαντο μὴ πέμπειν, αὐτοὶ δ ' οὐδ ' ὁτιοῦν ὑγιὲς γράψαντες ἔπεμψαν.

24 A discussion of the events, their chronology and the letters in Heskel 1997: 54–9.

25 Thuc. 7.10–5 (on which see Harris 1989: 78; Nicolai 2004: 119; Ceccarelli 2005a: 349–50; and the different opinion of Pébarthe 2006: 291–3, for whom Nicias' letter reflects common practice); Xen. 1.7.4 and 1.7.17 (Arginusae); decrees: Rhodes 1972: 43 n. 7, Ceccarelli 2005a: 357–9, Pébarthe 2006: 293 n. 17.

However, the bulk of references to letters in the *corpus Demosthenicum* concerns royal letters. This is not surprising, as letters are the usual means through which monarchs communicate their decisions to functionaries and cities, within their kingdom, but also outside.[26] Philip II of Macedon, Alexander, and after them the Hellenistic kings made an ample use of letters; but it is interesting to find that the Thracian kings already made a fairly ample use of this means of communication. Thus, in his *Against Aristocrates*, Demosthenes mentions two letters of Cotys to the Athenians, one written when Cotys was in difficulties (probably around 362 BC), the other when he felt secure, in late 361– early 360 BC, and contrasts them sharply: "I will read to you the letter which Cotys sent at the time of the revolt of Miltocythes, and also that which, when the whole kingdom was his, he sent to Timomachus before seizing your outposts. Letters" (Dem. 23.115).[27] Other letters by Cersobleptes and the Thracian kings are read out to the assembly to show the unreliability of Charidemus (23.178). Just as is at times the case for the other documents used by the orators, embedded letters often carry a meaning that goes beyond the literal import of the letter itself, and are used to give strength to the argument.[28]

Most references to letters in the political speeches of Demosthenes concern Philip. The orator may limit himself to an allusion, or may ask that the text of the letter be read (in a few cases, the text of short letters, whose authenticity is uncertain, has been incorporated in the speeches); a longer, self-standing letter of Philip, probably authentic, has also been transmitted in the *corpus Demosthenicum* alongside the *Reply to Philip*.[29] Of course, the number of references to letters of Philip is much higher than the number of letters actually sent, since Demosthenes and Aeschines more than once refer to the same letters:[30] references to royal documents are exploited by Demosthenes as part of a rhetorical strategy, as weapons of psychological persuasion.

The *First Philippic* is a case in point: Rowe has stressed the central role played by imagery connected with letter- and decree-writing in the speech (delivered in

26 See Welles 1934; Bertrand 1985; Lewis 1996; Ceccarelli 2005a. Philip, in the letter preserved in the *corpus Demosthenicum*, states more than once that he sent letters: e.g., at the opening of the speech, in 12.2, where he also complains of the rupture of privacy: "When Nicias, my herald, was kidnapped from my territory, you not only failed to bring the law-breakers to justice, but you kept the victim a prisoner for ten months, and the letters from me, of which he was the bearer, you read before your Assembly (ἃς δ ᾽ ἔφερε παρ ᾽ ἡμῶν ἐπιστολάς, ἀνέγνωτ ᾽ ἐπὶ τοῦ βήματος)". Further letters are mentioned in 12.22.

27 The Athenian general Timomachus failed in the war against Cotys in 361/0 BC and preferred exile to condemnation. See on the events and on the date of the letters Heskel 1997: 81–3 and 88–91.

28 Carey (1994) provides an excellent discussion of the role played by written documents (not letters though), and of the possibilities for manipulating them.

29 The authenticity of this letter ([Dem]. Or. 12), whose dramatic date is 339 BC, has been disputed with some attributing it to Anaximenes; but see most recently Gauger 2000: 73 ('wohl echt') and 306 n. 20. The *Reply* (Or. 11, probably non-Demosthenic) answers to another letter of Philip; on the historical context, see Harris 1995: 75–6.

30 List of the actual letters of Philip in Gauger 2000: 45.

352/1 BC). According to Rowe, Demosthenes here pursues an 'inversion strategy', and builds a *mundus perversus* out of the opposition between action on the one hand, and hearing, talking, writing, sitting on the other.[31] Thus real troops belonging to the *polis* are contrasted to the thousands of mercenaries and to the 'letterary forces' (ἐπιστολιμαίους ταύτας δυνάμεις), forces on paper, typical of the Athenian democracy (Dem. 4.19); in the following paragraph, Demosthenes pursues his theme by remarking that "thinking everything insufficient, you adopt the mightiest measures in decrees; but when it comes to action you fail to do the slightest" (πάντ' ἐλάττω νομίζοντες εἶναι τοῦ δέοντος, καὶ τὰ μέγιστ' ἐν τοῖς ψηφίσμασιν αἱρούμενοι, ἐπὶ τῷ πράττειν οὐδὲ τὰ μικρὰ ποιεῖτε, Dem. 4.20). Letters and decrees, and their opposite, action, are brought together ten paragraphs later, when Demosthenes exhorts the Athenians to vote for his proposal:

> "When you give your votes, pass the proposals, if you approve them, so that you may fight Philip not only with decrees and dispatches, but with deeds also". (ἐπειδὰν δ' ἐπιχειροτονῆτε τὰς γνώμας, ἂν ὑμῖν ἀρέσκῃ, χειροτονήσετε, ἵνα μὴ μόνον ἐν τοῖς ψηφίσμασι καὶ ταῖς ἐπιστολαῖς πολεμῆτε Φιλίππῳ, ἀλλὰ καὶ τοῖς ἔργοις.) (Dem. 4.30).

It is worth noting that here, letters are on the side of inaction and of the *polis* (Athens), rather than on the side of the king; only when they are royal, letters correspond to action (in Demosthenes' presentation). Key terms such as 'decrees', 'letters', 'hopes' are repeated throughout the speech, in combination with other key terms such as 'Philip', 'triremes', 'forces', and with the notions of enforcement, or conversely of emptiness and inaction;[32] 'straight', tyrannical letters surface as well, with the mention of hybristic ἐπιστολάς ('letters/orders') sent by Philip to the Euboeans (Dem. 4. 37–8: 'Meanwhile Philip has the effrontery to send such letters as these to the Euboeans', ὁ δ' εἰς τοῦθ' ὕβρεως ἐλήλυθεν ὥστ' ἐπιστέλλειν Εὐβοεῦσιν ἤδη τοιαύτας ἐπιστολάς). The letter is read; Demosthenes wryly comments: 'Most of what has been read, Athenians, is unfortunately true—possibly, however, not pleasant to listen to'.[33]

Similarly, there are numerous references to two letters of Philip in the pseudo-Demosthenic *De Halonneso* (342 BC). The speech was written as an answer to a letter by Philip proposing a settlement through arbitration of the ownership of the island, so references to this letter and to an earlier one, 'still to be seen in the

31 Rowe 1968; see also Mader 2006, for the contrast *psephisma*/action. I single out those elements of the 'topsy-turvy' Athenian world created by Demosthenes that pertain to letters.

32 As in 4.44–5; see Rowe 1968: 365–7. Mader 2006 extends this strategy to all Philippic speeches.

33 Is there something in the fact that the manuscripts indicate the reading of one letter only, against the plural of Demosthenes' reference? Could the discrepancy be interpreted in the sense of a conscious 'tragic' choice on the part of Demosthenes of the plural *epistolas* (the term is always found in the plural in tragedy)? This would fit in well with Rowe's 1968 overall argument.

bouleuterion' (ἥ ἐστι νῦν ἐν τῷ βουλευτηρίῳ), are not surprising.[34] Particularly interesting is however the beginning of the speech, for there, for a moment, in the opening sentence, the 'letter-form' chosen by Philip is pitted against the free discussion of the assembly:

> "For it would be monstrous if the freedom of utterance which is the privilege of this platform should be stifled by dispatches from him". (δεινὸν γὰρ ἂν εἴη, εἰ τὴν ἐπὶ τοῦ βήματος παρρησίαν αἱ παρ' ἐκείνου πεμπόμεναι ἐπιστολαὶ ἀνέλοιεν) (Dem. 7.1).

The same picture emerges from the speech *On the false embassy* (343 BC). One letter of Philip is here at the centre of the attention, the one allegedly composed with the help of Aeschines: reference to it is made for the first time in 19.36, the letter is read out at 19.38. Here we find a positive evaluation of writing—or at any rate, a shrewd appreciation of the respective merits of written and oral reports: for according to Demosthenes, in the letter Philip took upon himself the failure of the ambassadors to do what they had been charged of doing, a gesture for which there was no danger that he would be punished;

> "On the other hand, all the matters in which he was trying to cheat you and overreach you were left for Aeschines to report by word of mouth (οὗτος ἀπήγγειλεν), so that you might never have it in your power to incriminate Philip or throw any blame on him, as the assertions were not to be found in the letter or in any other direct communication of his (μήτ' ἐν ἐπιστολῇ μήτ' ἄλλοθι μηδαμοῦ τῶν παρ' ἐκείνου τούτων ἐνόντων)" (Dem. 19.38).[35]

Writing—in this case, official letters—is presented as a powerful means of fixing people to their statements. Demosthenes follows this up with the reading of excerpts from an earlier letter of Philip (19.40), from which it appears that Philip had committed himself, once a peace was reached and if there would be an alliance, to couch down in writing what great benefits he would confer to the *polis*.[36] Clearly Demosthenes is here reading more into Philip's letter than there ever was, and manipulating the writing with his words; clearly also, whatever the power of written words, Philip could and would back out of anything he might not have found con-

34 Letters are mentioned in *De Halonneso* 1; 18–21; 27; 29; 32; 33–4; 41; 45; 46.

35 The entire passage (Dem. 19.37–8) is built on the complementary roles played by Philip (ἐκεῖνος) and Aeschines (οὗτος); but the conclusion of the passage presents the two as accomplices, with the letter forming the ideal medium: "Read to them the letter, which this one wrote, but that one sent (λέγε δ' αὐτοῖς αὐτὴν τὴν ἐπιστολήν, ἣν ἔγραψε μὲν οὗτος, ἔπεμψε δ' ἐκεῖνος.)".

36 19.41: πρὶν μὲν εἰρήνης τυχεῖν, εἰ καὶ συμμαχία προσγένοιτ' αὐτῷ, γράψειν ὡμολόγει ἡλίκα τὴν πόλιν εὖ ποιήσει. ἐπειδὴ δ' ἀμφότερ' αὐτῷ γέγονεν, οὐκ εἰδέναι φησὶ τί ἂν ποιῶν χαρίσαιτο. On the vague character of these promises, see Harris 1995: 64–5, and on the historical background of the whole affair, Harris 1995.

venient. Philip of course sent also ambassadors to Athens (in Elaphebolion 346 BC, before the peace of Philocrates was ratified, or also in 343 BC, when Pytho of Byzantium and other ambassadors from the allies came, to announce the king's willingness to revise the terms of the peace of Philocrates), and he could remain evasive in his letters as much as through his ambassadors;[37] but while such embassies can only be 'remembered', the reading out of a letter is a dramatic moment, invested with a sense of the presence of the sender (if only because the document is read by a person different from the orator, by a clerk), a pause in the speech. This strategy Demosthenes pursues at some length; it must consequently have had some rhetorical credibility. Thus slightly later in the speech (19.44–5), the first letter, as well as the words of Philip's ambassadors (ἐκ τοῦ μὴ τοὺς παρὰ τοῦ Φιλίππου πρέσβεις ταῦτα λέγειν μηδὲ τὴν ἐπιστολὴν τὴν Φιλίππου), are contrasted with the words of Aeschines, and the latter is found a liar. Two further letters of Philip II are also read out in the Assembly, inviting the Athenians to join him in his campaign in Phokis: but that was not, says Demosthenes, Philip's real intention, and the ambassadors played along with him (19.51–2). Letters of Philip are mentioned or read out and discussed along these lines quite a few other times in the *On the false embassy* (for instance, in 19.187 they are pitted against the πρόχειρος λόγος, the 'easy phrase' of those who affirm that Philip is in fact a benefactor).[38] It is in a sense the very number of references to letters of Philip that support Demosthenes' claim of his heavy handed intervention in Athenian (and Greek) affairs, by showing how forceful the king's presence is in Athenian public affairs.

Letters from Philip are also mentioned in the *On the Chersonese* (341 BC) and in the *Third Philippic* (341 BC);[39] in the latter, a contrast is drawn between the writings (and the actions) of Philip, and the inactivity of the Greeks, who "see and hear all this, and yet [we] do not send embassies to one another and express [our] indignation". This theme is picked up in other speeches: the contrast between the inactivity of the Athenians and the energy (inclusive of letter-writing) of Philip reappears for instance in the *Reply to the letter of Philip*.[40]

Five letters from Philip are read out in the *On the Crown* (held in 330 BC, a long time after the events);[41] of these two are particularly interesting, inasmuch as

37 On the embassy of 343, see Harris 1995: 110–2.

38 See also 19.161, where a letter from Philip is 'sandwiched' between three decrees, with the purpose of showing that the embassy did not accomplish what it had been asked to do; and 19.316–7, where, at the close of the oration, Demosthenes returns to the issue of Aeschines' complicity in Philip's letter.

39 Dem. 8.16; 9.27.

40 Dem. 11.17: "He always takes a personal share in the hardships and dangers of the campaign, never neglects a chance, never wastes any season of the year; while we—for the truth must out—sit here idle; we are always hanging back and passing resolutions and haunting the market-place to learn the latest news. Yet what more startling news could there be than that a Macedonian should insult Athenians, daring to send us such a letter as you have heard read a moment ago?".

41 Dem. 18.39; 18.73 (mention of) and 77–8 (actual letter); 18.156–7; 18.166 and 167 (to the Thebans).

through their position they highlight the fact that the decree is the standard method used by the Greek cities for interstate communication, while kings use letters. These letters, directed one to Athens and one to Thebes, are Philip's response to two decrees of the Athenians (18. 164–7). Later in the speech, other letters of Philip are read to the public (18.218); the text of these is not given (they had been sent to the Peloponnesians – Demosthenes might possibly have heard a report of them, or even have gotten hold of a copy of them, but they would hardly have been preserved in Athens); again, interestingly, Demosthenes presents this latest outburst of epistolary activity on the part of Philip as a result of the many decrees moved by himself:

> "The situation was reversed ... But indeed, what sort of language Philip gave vent to at that time, and how seriously he was discomposed, you shall learn from letters sent by him to Peloponnesus. Please take and read them, that the jury may learn the real effect of my perseverance, of my journeys and hardships, and of that profusion of decrees at which Aeschines was just now scoffing ...". ('Αλλὰ μὴν οἵας τότ ' ἀφίει φωνὰς ὁ Φίλιππος καὶ ἐν οἵαις ἦν ταραχαῖς ἐπὶ τούτοις, ἐκ τῶν ἐπιστολῶν τῶν ἐκείνου μαθήσεσθε ὧν εἰς Πελοπόννησον ἔπεμπεν. καί μοι λέγε ταύτας λαβών, ἵν ' εἰδῆτε, ἡ ἐμὴ συνέχεια καὶ πλάνοι καὶ ταλαιπωρίαι καὶ τὰ πολλὰ ψηφίσμαθ ' ἃ νῦν οὗτος διέσυρεν, τί ἀπειργάσατο...; 221: Read the letters of Philip" (Λέγε τὰς ἐπιστολὰς τὰς τοῦ Φιλίππου) (Dem. 18.218–221).

We have come almost full circle from the picture drawn in the *First Philippic*; democratic decrees are now the reason for royal discomfort, and for epistolary royal communication. What comes out clearly from this is the role played by rhetorical construction in the use of these 'documents'.

4. Aeschines

Two of the three extant speeches of Aeschines contain frequent references to letters and letter-writing; not coincidentally, these are the two speeches that have to do more directly with Demosthenes. Aeschines opens his speech *On the false embassy* (delivered in 343 BC, as an answer to Demosthenes' attack), with a summary of what he had said to Philip at the time of the first embassy (346 BC); this he ends by saying that he then produced for Philip as proof of what he had said "the letters of the persons in question, the decrees of the *demos*, and the text of the truce concluded by Callisthenes" with Perdiccas in 363 BC.[42] It is unclear what letters exactly Aeschines is referring to in this context; these must be relatively ancient documents, going back some twenty years in time, involving Macedonian kings, such as Amyntas, and members of the Macedonian royal house (Eurydice), but also possibly

42 Aeschin. 2.31: καὶ πάντων ὧν εἴποιμι μάρτυρας τὰς ἐκείνων ἐπιστολὰς παρειχόμην καὶ τὰ ψηφίσματα τοῦ δήμου καὶ τὰς Καλλισθένους ἀνοχάς. On the first embassy see Harris 1995: 50–70.

Athenian generals such as Iphicrates. In this case, Aeschines could have found the letters in the Metroon; they were anyway used to impress Philip, not the Assembly.

Aeschines goes on to recount how, on their return to Athens, the embassy gave a short oral report to the *boule*, and handed in a letter sent by Philip (2.45); and how, when the embassy then gave a report to the Assembly, this same letter was read, on the request of Demosthenes, together with the decree according to which the embassy had been sent. Later in the speech, when discussion has moved to the second embassy, Aeschines has a clerk read a letter (ἐπιστολή) sent by Chares to the Athenians, informing them that Cersobleptes had lost his kingdom and that Philip had taken Hieron Oros (Aeschin. 2.90). This is again an instance of the use of letters for internal communication between *strategoi* on campaign and the *polis*. The letter is however used here not for its content, but in order to mount a chronological argument: the fact that the information contained in the letter reached Athens on the twenty-fifth of Elaphebolion serves to exculpate Aeschines from the accusation of having delayed bringing help to Cersobleptes: the *boule* decreed that the ambassadors should set out to receive the oaths on Mounichion third, well after the fall of Cersobleptes.[43] (Incidentally, we learn that dispatches could travel at a remarkable speed: the letter announced that Hieron Oros was taken on the 24th of Elaphebolion; it reached Athens on the 25th of the same month!).

A few paragraphs later in this same speech, Aeschines defends himself from the accusation of having written for Philip the letter that the latter sent to Athens (Aeschin. 2.124–5). Again, it is not the content that is – for the moment – at issue, but the fact that Aeschines supposedly would have helped Philip in writing it. This accusation gives Aeschines the opportunity to mention quite a few persons (Leosthenes, Philip himself, and Pytho of Byzantium) who would have been perfectly able of writing such a letter, without any need of himself being involved in the affair. Interestingly, the ability in letter writing is linked to ability in public speech: so in the case of Leosthenes, "competent to write a clever letter—a man whom some do not hesitate to rank next to Callistratus of Aphidna as an able orator (ὁ μὲν γὰρ Λεωσθένης,...δυνατὸς ἦν ἐπιδεξίως ἐπιστολὴν γράψαι, ὃν οὐκ ὀκνοῦσί τινες ἀποφαίνεσθαι μετὰ Καλλίστρατον τὸν ᾿Αφιδναῖον τῶν ἄλλων μάλιστα εἰπεῖν δύνασθαι)", so in the case of Philip, "against whom Demosthenes was not able to hold his own when he tried to speak in your behalf". The only one of the group whose ability in writing letters is not paralleled by ability in speaking is the otherwise little known Pytho, "a man who takes pride in his ability as a writer (ὁ Βυζάντιος Πύθων, ἄνθρωπος ἐπὶ τῷ γράφειν μέγα φρονῶν)"; there may be a

43 On Aeschines' innovative use of letters and more generally of documents not for their content, but for their 'archival' value, for the dates they contain, see Thomas 1989: 69–71.

negative connotation in this remark—the man was a student of Isocrates, hence the connection with writing rather than speech, and he had gone over to Macedon.[44]

The letter in question is cited a few paragraphs later—and if we are to trust Aeschines' summary of it, and the rhetorical question asked of the audience at the end, it must have been a fairly plain and matter-of-fact one, in nothing different from other messages of Philip.[45]

Another letter, this time by the Athenian general Proxenus, is mentioned next, when Aeschines undertakes to show that the Phocians, even before he was elected ambassador, had turned towards Philip.[46] A letter by Proxenus, in which he stated that the Phocians had refused to hand over to him the posts, had been read in the assembly, Aeschines recalls, just on the day in which the Athenians were deliberating on the peace (Aeschin. 2.134); on the same day, the heralds of the Mysteries had announced the refusal by the Phocians of the sacred truce. Now Aeschines names as evidence for his argument the two heralds of the mysteries, the letter of Proxenus, and the testimony of the envoys sent by Proxenus to the Phocians. The wording here shows that the letter and the witnesses serve two different purposes:

> "To prove that I am speaking the truth, please call the heralds of the truce, and the envoys Callicrates and Metagenes, whom Proxenus our general sent to the Phocians, and let the letter of Proxenus be read. TESTIMONY. LETTER. You have heard, fellow citizens, the dates from the public archives being read out (τῶν χρόνων παραναγιγνωσκομένων ἐκ τῶν δημοσίων γραμμάτων), and you have heard the witnesses, who further testify that before I was elected ambassador, Phalaecus the Phocian tyrant distrusted us and the Lacedaemonians as well, but put his trust in Philip" (Aeschin. 2.134–5).

The letter is necessary here as evidence for the date, while the witnesses attest to the main point at issue. A further letter of Philip, in which he calls the Athenians to join against the Thebans, and relating to an incident later on in Skirophorion of 346 BC, is mentioned in 2.137. In this speech, thus, letters appear to figure mainly as ele-

44 A student of Isocrates, he was in Pella in 346 and may have played a role in the negotiations that led to the Peace of Philocrates; he certainly came to Athens in 343 BC as a representative of Philip to renegotiate the Peace of Philocrates. See *RE* 'Python' 4. On this passage see Harris 1995: 10, as well as Carey 2000: 135 and 139.

45 Aeschin. 2.128–9: "Take this letter (ἐπιστολήν), which Philip sent. It clearly must be full of deception for the city, this letter we spent the entire night writing (ἠγρυπνοῦμεν γράφοντες). LETTER. You hear, gentlemen, that he says 'I gave my oath to your ambassadors', and has written (γέγραφε) the names of those of his allies who were present, both the names of the representatives themselves and of their states; and he says he will send to you (ἀποστελεῖν φησι) those of his allies who were not there in time. Does it seem to you that it would have been beyond Philip's ability to write (γράψαι) that in the daytime (μεθ ' ἡμέραν), and without my help?".

46 On the historical background of the affair, see Harris 1995: 53–4.

ments of the case, and not as rhetorical weapons: Aeschines carefully builds his defence around dates and facts that he extracts from documents.[47]

The other speech in which letters figure, alongside other types of documents, is the *Against Ctesiphon* (delivered in 330 BC). But the way they are used here is very different from the *On the false embassy*. Twice, letters are mentioned in connection with the Persian king: they function as markers of his insolence, and in both instances they are used to underline a change in the balance of power. The first passage in which letters appear defines the power of Xerxes in terms of digging a channel through the Athos, bridging the Hellespont, and daring to write in his letters "that he was lord of all men from the rising of the sun unto its setting", and then contrasts this power with the actual situation of the Great King. The second reference functions in a similar way: the power of the King (Artaxerxes III) is encapsulated in his daring to write 'a most insolent and barbarous letter, in which everything was expressed in the most ill-mannered terms', and in which the king refused to give any gold to the Athenians; the reversal is made manifest by the initiative of that same king, in need of allies, to send to Athens 300 talents, which the city wisely did not accept (but part of which, Aeschines continues, Demosthenes embezzled).[48]

Letters are also used to subtly incriminate, or at least discredit, Demosthenes: thus, Aeschines suggests that Demosthenes sent a letter to Alexander (γράμματα πέμψας, 3.162) through the mediation of a young, beautiful boy, and thus reconciled himself with the Macedonian king. The implication is that both instruments of communication (the letter and the messenger) are similarly disreputable. More importantly, letters are symbolic of double playing, of hidden contacts: a few paragraphs later, Aeschines affirms that before the battle of Issus, when the situation was unclear and looking not too favourable for Alexander, "there was not room enough in the city to contain your odious demonstrations and the letters that you carried around, dangling them from your fingers" (τὴν δὲ σὴν ἀηδίαν ἡ πόλις οὐκ ἐχώρει καὶ τὰς ἐπιστολὰς ἃς ἐξηρτημένος ἐκ τῶν δακτύλων περιῄεις, 3.164), although even then Demosthenes did not dare to take any action. The image is brilliant: Demosthenes is portrayed as showing off the letters (i.e. his contacts) to the city; but these letters do not have any referent, they are not mentioned in any other part of the speech; their only purpose is to show Demosthenes being in secret, private contact with a number of similarly private, powerful and secretive persons (such as the

47 See further Thomas 1989: 69–71.

48 Aeschin. 3.132: οὐχ ὁ μὲν τῶν Περσῶν βασιλεύς, ὁ τὸν ῎Αθω διορύξας, ὁ τὸν Ἑλλήσποντον ζεύξας, ὁ γῆν καὶ ὕδωρ τοὺς Ἕλληνας αἰτῶν, ὁ τολμῶν ἐν ταῖς ἐπιστολαῖς γράφειν, ὅτι δεσπότης ἐστὶν ἁπάντων ἀνθρώπων ἀφ᾽ ἡλίου ἀνιόντος μέχρι δυομένου, νῦν οὐ περὶ τοῦ κύριος ἑτέρων εἶναι διαγωνίζεται, ἀλλ ᾽ ἤδη περὶ τῆς τοῦ σώματος σωτηρίας; and 3.238: κατέπεμψε τῷ δήμῳ καὶ μάλα ὑβριστικὴν καὶ βάρβαρον ἐπιστολὴν ἐν ᾗ τά τε δὴ ἄλλα καὶ μάλ᾽ ἀπαιδεύτως διελέχθη, καὶ ἐπὶ τελευτῆς ἐνέγραψεν, "ἐγώ", φησίν, "ὑμῖν χρυσίον οὐ δώσω: μή με αἰτεῖτε: οὐ γὰρ λήψεσθε".

Persian king, or Alexander himself). This image must have struck a deep chord: the connection between Demosthenes and unsavoury letters will reappear in the speech that Dinarchus wrote against Demosthenes for the trial of 323 BC. Here, however, the letters are mentioned in connection with events that took place slightly later (the revolt against the Macedonian control coordinated by King Agis III of Sparta, between 333 and 331 BC):

> "In that hour—for I need not dwell on other crises—what was the behaviour of this Demosthenes who had the power to give advice and make proposals (ὁ τοῦ συμβουλεῦσαι καὶ γράψαι κύριος), who will shortly tell you that he hates our present circumstances? On these matters, Demosthenes, did you offer any proposal (ἔγραψάς τι), any advice? Did you contribute money? Were you of the smallest value to the men safeguarding us all? Not the least; you went round suborning speechwriters; writing a letter at home, and defiling the city's honour, he walked about dangling it from his finger ends, living in luxury during the city's misfortunes, travelling down the road to the Piraeus in a litter and reproaching the needy for their poverty" (ἀλλὰ περιῄεις κατασκευάζων λογοποιούς, καὶ παρ᾽αὑτῷ γράφων ἐπιστολήν, καὶ καταισχύνων τὴν τῆς πόλεως δόξαν, ἐκ τῶν δακτύλων ἀναψάμενος περιεπορεύετο, τρυφῶν ἐν τοῖς τῆς πόλεως κακοῖς, καὶ ἐπὶ φορείου κατακομιζόμενος τὴν εἰς Πειραιᾶ ὁδόν, καὶ τὰς τῶν πενήτων ἀπορίας ὀνειδίζων) (Din. I 35–6).

The similarity in the wording makes it clear that Dinarchus had here in mind Aeschines; again, there is much that is unclear or simply allusive slander in this passage. Particularly puzzling is the "letter at home" allegedly written by Demosthenes: Dinarchus here seems to be accusing Demosthenes of moving frequently and in an unnecessarily luxurious way between his houses in the Piraeus and his house in the city, and of doing this while holding in a conspicuous way a letter written by himself, so as to give the impression of being in touch with events and powerful persons much more than was actually the case.[49] It may not be an accident if the only other (rather cryptic) reference to letters in what we have of Dinarchus (admittedly not much) also comes from his *Against Demosthenes*: in 1.27 the orator asks a clerk to read a Theban decree, to cite the evidence, and to read the letters. It is impossible to

49 The connection between Din. 1.36 and Aeschines' description has always been noticed (e.g., Worthington 1999: 153), but no commentator addresses the question of what Dinarchus may have meant with the letter written at home, and why walking with it defiled the city's honor. The emotional (rather than technical) import of the passage, and for that matter of the entire speech, is well brought out by Nouhaud 1990: XII, who points out that the speech was a deuterology, whose main purpose was not to argue, but rather to excite the anger of the citizens. For a reconstruction of this period see, e.g., Cawkwell 1969.

know to what this exactly refers; Nouhaud's suggestion that this refers to some written communication between Demosthenes and the Thebans is plausible.[50]

The image of epistolary exchanges taking place in the last days of Athenian independence will shape the later tradition. Plutarch, *Demosthenes* 20.4–5, mentions letters sent by the king of Persia to his satraps, with orders to supply Demosthenes with money, something that afterwards would have come to the knowledge of Alexander, "by certain letters of Demosthenes which he found at Sardis", and by other papers of the Persian officers, accounting for the large sums which had been given him.[51] According to the same Plutarch (*Demosthenes* 23.2), after the death of Philip, in 335 BC, the orator sent letters to the Persian officers of the King, inviting them to attack Alexander. More interestingly, when pursued by the Macedonians until the temple of Poseidon at Calauria, Demosthenes obtained from Archias (his pursuer) some time to 'write a letter home' (μικρὸν οὖν επίσχες, ὅμως ἐπιστείλω τι τοῖς οἴκοι, Plut. *Dem.* 29.3); now according to the version of the otherwise unknown Pappus, whose work was used by Hermippus (as cited in Plut. *Dem.* 30.1), when Demosthenes fell by the altar because of the poison he had taken a scroll was found, with the beginning of a letter, "Demosthenes to Antipater", and nothing more—would this have been the letter home? Fittingly, vengeance for Demosthenes overtook Demades in the form of a letter of his addressed to Perdiccas, in which he suggested that Perdiccas should free the Greeks from Antipater; when found, the letter excited the anger of Cassander, who had Demades (and his son Demeas) executed (Plut. *Dem.* 31.3).[52] The epistolary activity ascribed by the ancients to both Demosthenes and Aeschines (six letters of Demosthenes have been preserved, whose authenticity is discussed; twelve letters have survived under Aeschines' name, none of them authentic) fits the picture extremely well.[53]

To go back to Aeschines: the next mention of letters in the *Against Ctesiphon* concerns letters forged by Demosthenes to gain advantage over Aeschines himself:

> "I say nothing of forged letters ('Επιστολὰς δὲ σιγῶ ψευδεῖς) and the arrest of spies, and torture applied on groundless charges, on your assertion that I with certain persons was seeking a revolution" (Aeschin. 3.225).

50 Nouhaud 1990: 58, followed by Worthington 1999: 148.

51 A piece of information known only from this passage.

52 In Diodorus 18.48.2 'letters' (in the plural) by Demades to Perdiccas are found in the royal archives by Antipater (not Cassander); Plutarch, *Phocion* 30.9–10 has a slightly different version, in which the addressee of Demades' letter is Antigonus.

53 On Demosthenes' letters see Goldstein 1968. Nine of the twelve letters ascribed to Aeschines were known to Photius (*Bibl.* 61) as 'the Nine muses' (the speeches were 'the three Graces'), and may have been composed in Rhodes in the mid-second century BC; the others were added later. See Martin & Budé 1928: 121–2, with Goldstein 1968: 265–6.

Indeed, Aeschines does not say anything else of these forged letters, and we may suppose that the Assembly did not know more about them than we do; they figure here simply to complete the picture of a man using all means at his disposal to reach his goal. Obviously, none of these documents is—or can be—read as evidence. And this applies also to the last mention of letters in this speech, a passage particularly important in the richness of its detail. Here is the text:

> "Does it not seem to you to be an outrage if the *bouleuterion* and the people are coming to be ignored, while the letters and the ambassadors come to private houses, sent not by ordinary men, but by the first men of Asia and Europe? And deeds the legal penalty for which is death, these deeds certain men do not deny, but acknowledge them before the people; and they read their letters to one another comparing them. And some of them ask you to look into their faces as being guardians of the democracy, and others call for rewards as being saviours of the state. But the people, discouraged by what they have experienced, as though in very dotage or declared of unsound mind, lay claim only to the name of democracy, and have surrendered the substance to others. And so you go home from the meetings of your assembly, not as from a deliberative session, but as from some picnic, where you have been given the leavings as your share".
>
> (ἢ οὐ δεινὸν ὑμῖν εἶναι δοκεῖ, εἰ τὸ μὲν βουλευτήριον καὶ ὁ δῆμος παροράται, αἱ δ ' ἐπιστολαὶ καὶ αἱ πρεσβεῖαι ἀφικνοῦνται εἰς ἰδιωτικὰς οἰκίας, οὐ παρὰ τῶν τυχόντων ἀνθρώπων, ἀλλὰ παρὰ τῶν πρωτευόντων ἐν τῇ 'Ασίᾳ καὶ τῇ Εὐρώπῃ; καὶ ἐφ ' οἷς ἐστιν ἐκ τῶν νόμων ζημία θάνατος, ταῦτά τινες οὐκ ἐξαρνοῦνται πράττειν, ἀλλ' ὁμολογοῦσιν ἐν τῷ δήμῳ, καὶ τὰς ἐπιστολὰς ἀλλήλοις παραναγιγνώσκουσιν παρακελεύονται δ' οἱ μὲν βλέπειν εἰς τὰ ἑαυτῶν πρόσωπα ὡς φύλακες τῆς δημοκρατίας, ἕτεροι δ ' αἰτοῦσι δωρεὰς ὡς σωτῆρες τῆς πόλεως ὄντες. ὁ δὲ δῆμος ἐκ τῆς ἀθυμίας τῶν συμβεβηκότων ὥσπερ παραγεγηρακὼς ἢ παρανοίας ἑαλωκώς, αὐτὸ μόνον τοὔνομα τῆς δημοκρατίας περιποιεῖται, τῶν δ ' ἔργων ἑτέροις παρακεχώρηκεν. ἔπειτ' ἀπέρχεσθε ἐκ τῶν ἐκκλησιῶν οὐ βουλευσάμενοι, ἀλλ' ὥσπερ ἐκ τῶν ἐράνων, τὰ περιόντα νειμάμενοι) (Aeschin. 3. 250–1).

The exchange of letters is seen as destructive of democracy.[54]

In the two speeches by Aeschines in which letters are mentioned, then, two different strategies are at work. In the *On the false embassy*, a few 'normal' letters, the dispatches of the Athenian *strategoi*, are mentioned, and actually read; but it is not their content that matters. The letters are used for their date, in order to build a

54 See, along these lines, already Lewis 1996: 148.

chronologically sound argument. Otherwise, as in the *Against Ctesiphon*, letters are in Aeschines associated with foreign rulers (Philip, the Macedonians, or the Persian kings) and with private, unsavoury dealings, that are undermining the democracy. This time again it is not the content that matters – most of these letters are probably non-existent; the very existence of a correspondence is deemed sufficient to provoke the anger of the people. In the public arena, the act of writing (or of receiving) letters can be used as a weapon against the opponent – all the more easily if the letters in questions are not read.

5. Conclusion

The evidence on the use of letters from the speeches of the orators has to be considered in both qualitative and quantitative terms; it is also important to distinguish between public and private letters (and public and private speeches). To begin with the quantitative aspect: in comparison with other documents, such as decrees, laws, contracts, and also witnesses' statements, very few letters are mentioned, let alone read.[55] However, if we move to the qualitative level, it transpires from forensic speeches that letters were indeed relatively frequent in private dealings, especially among merchants engaged in maritime trade; it is also to be expected that in a context of litigation quite a few of these letters should be 'deceptive' ones. In general, letters appear to have been used in all sort of private occasions. So why was evidence from letters not used more? The reason must surely be that while all other documents (obviously decrees and laws; but also testaments, contracts, and statements by witnesses) would be accepted as technically correct, since written in presence of witnesses, the same would not have applied to private letters. The issue of preservation probably also plays a role: letters simply transmitting a message, a tip, some instructions or a request, would not have been preserved. And if the letter did not exist anymore, if its evidentiary value was moreover doubtful, mention of it might have been made *en passant*, but it would not have made much sense to spend time on it.

Letters are quoted more frequently in symbouleutic speeches, because official letters would be kept in an archive – it would thus be possible to make use of them at a later occasion, while their authenticity would not be open to doubt; moreover, even if the letter did not anymore exist, capital might be made out of a mention of it in a way that was impossible in forensic speeches. A qualitative analysis shows that letters were used for public service, in the form of reports sent by generals or embassies to their own polis; but the greatest letter-writers by far are the Thracian kings,

55 For the distinction in artistic and non-artistic 'proofs', see Ar. *Rhet.* 1355b35, with Carey 1994; and for the distinction of 'non-artistic proofs' in νόμοι, μάρτυρες, συνθῆκαι, βάσανοι, ὅρκοι see Ar. *Rhet.* 1375a24f. Laws here must include decrees, while the agreements will comprise all other written documents. After 380 BC, witnesses make a written deposition to be read out in the law-court without any possibility of modifying it or 'cross-examining' the witness. For the role of the witness, see Harrison 1971: 133–54; Bonner 1905, and a further important discussion in Todd 1990; Thür 2005.

Philip of Macedon and the king of Persia. References to letters from them are concentrated in a few important speeches; the letters are used as documents of a policy, as archival documents permitting an exact dating of events, or also simply to show, by the sheer number of references to them, the heavy-handed intrusion of a foreign power into the city's affairs. In this context, the act of writing letters (and at times the act of writing tout court) can be used as a weapon against the opponent;[56] this is particularly true when letters having implications for the entire community are privately written by common citizens.[57] Letter-writing appears thus as something that belongs to the private domain; when it moves into the public space, it has to be kept under control.

56 Thus, even in the advanced fourth century Demosthenes can reproach to Aeschines his former activity as *hypogrammateus* (Dem. 19.200), or insult him as a *grammatokyphon*, someone who is hunched over records (Dem. 18.209): Thomas 1989: 71.

57 On the connection between *rhetores* and epistolarity, and on comedy's take on this, see Ceccarelli 2004. Mirko Canevaro, Michele Faraguna and Edward Harris read a draft version of this paper, and improved it greatly; I am responsible for all remaining errors.

Were there Business Agents in Classical Greece? The Evidence of Some Lead Letters

Edward M. Harris (Durham)

I

Regulations regarding commerce in modern states provide a vast array of legal arrangements to help those in business cooperate with each other. Modern law codes contain thousands of complex rules about contracts, employment, mortgage, sale, the trading of securities, methods of accounting and corporations. The economy of ancient Greece was far less complex than that of the modern world, but the Athenians and other Greeks also created various legal relationships and provided mechanisms to resolve disputes arising from these relationships in order to facilitate trade and commerce. The Athenians in particular recognized and enforced several different types of contracts: sale (*prasis*, *ônê*), hire/lease (*misthosis*), deposit (*parakatatheke*), partnership (*koinonia*), loan (*daneion*).[1] Athenian law also provided two forms of accessory contracts: real security (*apotimema*) and personal security (*engye*).[2] But the Athenians did not develop modern notions of juristic personality and invent the concepts of the private corporation and corporate liability.[3]

Roman law went further than Athenian Law in some respects and formulated an elaborate classification of contracts.[4] Where the Athenians operated with a rough and ready set of contracts, Roman Law divided contracts into four categories (*re*, *consensu*, *litteris*, *verbis*) and devised a set of rules for each type of contract. Yet despite its relative sophistication, Roman law never developed the notion of agency, by which "if an agent enters into a contract on behalf of his principal with a third party, he creates rights and duties directly between principal and third party, and himself incurs neither".[5] In the first century BCE the jurist Mucius Scaevola laid down the principle "no one can legally bind someone else through compact, arrangement or covenant". Gaius (*Institutes* 3.103) states "Moreover, a stipulation is ineffective if we

1 For the different types of contracts recognized and enforced in Athenian courts see Knopf 2005.

2 On real security in Athenian Law see Harris 2006: 163–240. For the special arrangement devised for security in maritime loans see Harris 2006: 241–8. On personal security see Partsch 1909.

3 On the absence of the notion of corporation see Harris 2006: 241–2 with the bibliography cited there. On the liability of groups in Athenian law see most recently Ismard 2007, who comes to the conclusion that groups did not possess legal personality.

4 For the classification in Classical Roman Law see Gai. 3.89–162.

5 Nicholas 1962: 201. Cf. Crook 1967: 206–7; Aubert 1994: 40–1.

take a stipulation that something is to be given to someone other than the head of our family" (*Praeterea inutilis est stipulatio, si ei dari stipulemur, cuius iuri subiecti non sumus*).[6]

To a certain extent, the Romans were able to get along without the legal concept of agency because many of the functions performed by business agents in modern economies could be carried out by other means. For instance, a master could buy property through his slaves or his children who had not been emancipated. According to Gaius (2.86) "Acquisitions come to us not only by our own acts, but also through those whom we hold in *potestas*". A slave could thus pay a seller for an item, and his master would thus gain ownership without being present or giving his explicit consent.[7] A master could also give his slave or unemancipated child a *peculium* and grant him the power to carry on business with it.[8] These practices enabled masters to carry on business over long distances and to profit from the economic activities of their slaves and sons without their direct involvement.[9]

Even though Roman law never developed the concept of agency, J.P. Wilson, following B. Bravo, claims to have found evidence for business agents operating during the Archaic and Classical periods in several lead letters found in Berezan, Olbia, Pech-Maho and Emporion.[10] E. Cohen has also claimed that "Athenian law (…) was able easily to give legal effect through representatives, even to commitments that might not be undertaken directly by principals" and that Athenians utilized "Agency as a Legal Mechanism".[11] Part II shows that none of the literary sources analyzed by E. Cohen provides any evidence for the existence of business agents, then explains why there was no need to develop the concept of agency and how the functions performed by business agents in the modern economy were carried out by other means in the ancient Greek economy. Part III begins with some methodological remarks about the use of lead letters as evidence for ancient business practices. The rest of Part III shows that these letters contain no evidence for the existence of business agents and that the economic arrangements described in these letters are better understood in terms of other practices well attested in the literary sources. Part IV contains some brief observations about the role played by letters in the ancient Greek economy.

6 Cf. D. 45.1.38.17 (Ulpian).

7 On the acquisition of property through those *in potestate* see Kirschenbaum 1987: 7–30.

8 For the rules about the *peculium* see Kirschenbaum 1987: 31–88.

9 The *actio institoria* permitted free business managers to carry out various transactions, but these were not agents in the modern sense. On this action see Aubert 1994.

10 Wilson 1997–1998; Bravo 1977.

11 Cohen 1992: 98–101.

II

Much of the literary evidence about commerce in Classical Greece comes from speeches delivered at trials in fourth-century Athens. The main advantage of this source is that the litigants who delivered the speeches provide a detailed narrative of the events that gave rise to the dispute and describe the nature of the relationships among the people involved in the dispute. Even though it is often difficult to know whether or not a litigant is telling the truth about these events, the nature of the relationships must have been familiar to the judges who heard the case.[12] Once we have understood the various kinds of legal and informal relationships linking those engaged in commerce, we will be in a better position to analyze the evidence provided by the lead letters.

E. Cohen claims to have found evidence for the existence of business agents in Classical Athens in ten passages from forensic orations. Even though Cohen believes that "the legal acceptability of acting through agents facilitated the operation of *trapezai* by non-Athenians", he does not identify the specific Greek word that is the precise equivalent of the modern term "business agent" and provides no evidence that the Athenians formulated any legal regulations concerning agency. Nor does he demonstrate that Athenian law recognized agreements contracted between agents and third parties as binding on principals.[13] To prove the existence of this "remarkable legal innovation", therefore, Cohen lists ten pairs of individuals who he alleges acted as agents and their principals.[14] Unsuspecting readers might think that this collection of evidence lends ample support to his thesis, but none of these individuals are connected by the legal relationship of agent and principal. Although all these men are cooperating in one way or another, in no case is one creating rights and duties for the other in the latter's absence.

1. Cohen's first example is Pythodorus who acted on behalf of Pasion (Isoc. 17.33–4). The plaintiff in Isocrates' *Trapeziticus* states that Pythodorus "says and does all things for Pasion". But what did Pythodorus actually do for Pasion? Cohen does not say, but the plaintiff is quite forthright. He accuses him of opening the voting urns in the previous year and taking out the ballots with the names of those nominated by the Council to act as judges at the City Dionysia. The plaintiff next charges him with forging a small document left with a foreigner and bribing his slaves. Yet such activities, that could not be lawfully carried out by Pasion himself, would likewise hardly be a legitimate undertaking of an agent.

12 On forensic speeches as historical evidence see Harris 1995: 7–16.

13 The standard Athenian rule about contracts (see for example Dem. 56.2) that only those transactions concluded between willing parties were legally binding would appear to exclude the possibility.

14 Cohen 1992: 98–101.

Whatever one's views of business ethics, the relationship between Pasion and Pythodorus is not one of agency.

2. Cohen's next example is Archestratus (Isoc. 17.42–3). Cohen claims that Archestratus acted as an agent for Pasion in providing a pledge of personal security for the plaintiff in Isocrates' *Trapeziticus*. The situation described in the speech is as follows: the plaintiff had lent money on the security of a ship, which was denounced by the procedure of *phasis* as contraband since it allegedly belonged to a man from Delos. When the speaker denied the charge and asked that the ship be allowed to sail, he drew suspicion and was accused of a serious crime, probably treason or collusion with the enemy. The plaintiff claims that the Council, which was ready to execute him without trial, was convinced to allow him to provide sureties to guarantee his appearance in court (Isoc. 17.42). When one of the plaintiff's friends declined to act as surety, Pasion provided (παρέσχεν) Archestratus, "a man from the bank" as surety for the sum of seven talents. The relationship between Archestratus and Pasion is a little murky: both appear to have had an interest in the bank.[15] But all that the plaintiff says is that Archestratus became his surety. The plaintiff does not state that Pasion made a contract with him that was binding on Archestratus. The verb need indicate nothing more than that Pasion introduced Archestratus to the plaintiff. In the phrase where the actual contract is mentioned, there are only two parties, the plaintiff and Archestratus. Pasion has no involvement in the legal relationship, which is certainly not concluded for his benefit.

3. According to Cohen "Pasion also used the citizen Agyrrhius (of Kollytos) as a confidential representative in litigational matters". The evidence is again drawn from Isocrates' *Trapeziticus* (17.31–2). The case involves money allegedly deposited in the bank of Pasion by the plaintiff. When Pasion denied that the plaintiff had deposited any money in his bank, the latter went and asked the former to turn over his slave Cittus, who knew about the loan, so that he could have him questioned under torture. The plaintiff then claims that Pasion hid Cittus away to prevent him from providing evidence, but Pasion retorts by charging that the plaintiff was the one who had taken Cittus and demanded that he return the slave to his master (Isoc. 17.11–2). Menexenus later found Cittus and seized him. This time Pasion allegedly claimed that Cittus was a free man. Menexenus then forced Pasion to provide surety for the sum of seven talents before the Polemarch.

   Menexenus grew so angry at this treatment that he brought a charge of slander against Pasion (21). Eager to reach a settlement, Pasion sent Agyrrhius to ask the plaintiff to drop his charge or to end his dispute with him. Once more nothing in the passage indicates that Pasion gave Agyrrhius the power to con-

15 On their relationship see Trevett 1992: 18.

clude an agreement on his behalf. Agyrrhius was merely interceding for Pasion and communicating his willingness to negotiate with the plaintiff and Menexenus. Nor is anything said about Agyrrhius making a contract with the plaintiff or Menexenus.

4. To show that "citizen-bankers appear to have acted through or with other persons" Cohen adduces the example of the pair Antidorus of Phaleron and Aristolochus, who performed six liturgies together.[16] Cohen follows Davies' suggestion and thinks that "the two seem to have functioned much as joint venturers in the banking business". Yet he notes that Antidorus appears to have avoided losing his fortune when Aristolochus fell on hard times and concludes that the former "was probably not liable for the *trapeza*'s debts and therefore was not an actual partner in Aristolochus' bank". Even if we assume that Davies' ingenious suggestion about their cooperation in banking is correct, the relationship between joint venturers, each of whom owns shares in an enterprise, is quite different from that between agent and principal, where the former makes contracts that create rights and duties for the latter.[17] There is no evidence that one man was acting as an agent for the other.

5. Cohen notes that "Stephanos was dispatched to represent a banker's interest at Byzantium (Dem. 45.64)". In this passage Apollodorus reports that Stephanus became a close friend of Phormio. When the Byzantines seized Phormio's ships, Stephanus went to their city and spoke on his behalf against the people of Calchedon. Stephanus is described by Apollodorus as a *presbeutes*, "ambassador" or "envoy".[18] This might mean that Stephanus was elected or appointed as an envoy by the Athenians and sent to Byzantium to ask for the release of Phormio's ships. He was thus similar to the actor Aristodemus, who was sent by the Assembly to request the release of Athenians captured by Philip of Macedon after the conquest of Olynthus (Aeschin. 2.15–16). Or he may be using the term in an informal sense ("personal envoy"). But Apollodorus does not say that Stephanus had the power to conclude agreements that would bind Phormio or that he made such agreements. His mission was clearly to persuade the Byzantines to allow Phormio's ships to leave their city, nothing more. He went to present Phormio's case as his advocate, not to make contracts as his agent, and the case involved rights of ownership.[19]

16 For the evidence of their relationship and the suggestion that they were joint owners of a bank see Davies 1971: 35–6 and 60–1.

17 For joint ownership of property in Athenian law see Biscardi 1999: 23–74.

18 Murray (1939) translates this term with the word "agent", but, as I hope this essay makes clear, the term is anachronistic and inaccurate.

19 One should note that the *presbeutes* of a *polis* did not normally have the power to make treaties that were binding on that *polis*; treaties had to be approved by the Assembly of the *polis*, whose officials

6. Cohen next observes how "the money-lending Dêmôn sent Aristophôn to Kephallênia to resolve a commercial maritime dispute (Dem. 32.10–12)". Demo had lent money to Protus so the latter could buy grain in Sicily. Protus had this grain transported to Athens in a ship owned by Hegestratus. On its return voyage, the ship ran into difficulties (caused according to Demo by Hegestratus acting in concent with Zenothemis) and had to put in at Cephallenia. Here some men from Massalia told the authorities that the ship should proceed to their city since the owner and those who lent money on the ship resided there. Demo responded by sending Aristophon to Cephallonia as his *presbeutes* or "envoy". Aristophon thus appears to have played a role similar to that of Stephanus for Phormio: he went to a foreign city to defend the interests of an associate. Demo does not say what Aristophon said to the authorities, but he must have requested that they order the ship to continue its voyage to Athens, because it arrived there soon afterwards.[20]

7. Cohen's next example of an agent is Demosthenes, who was used by Phormio "to speak for him in an important bank-related litigation". In this case Phormio had been sued by Apollodorus, who claimed that certain deposits in his bank belonged to him (Dem. 36). Phormio was not a good speaker so at his trial he had Demosthenes speak for him as his *synegoros* (Dem. 36.1). But a *synegoros* merely spoke on behalf of a plaintiff, an accuser, or a defendant; he did not make contracts for him. The role of the *synegoros* was to present a litigant's case; he had no power beyond that. A *synegoros* was certainly not an agent: his task was to speak in court, not to carry on business for someone else.[21]

8. Cohen believes that agency "might also resolve the otherwise disabling incapacity of a slave-banker (or any other non-Athenian) to foreclose on security for a loan provided in the form of Attic land" and cites the example of Phormio when Pasion leased him his bank (Dem. 36.6).[22] This case requires some explanation. As a metic, Phormio could not own land in Attica. As a result, he could not seize any land that had been pledged as security for a loan. When Pasion leased him his bank, Phormio discovered that although most of the loans were unsecured, several were secured by real estate in Attica. The former category posed no problem, for if the borrowers refused to repay, he could prosecute them before

then swore the oaths that ratified it. See de Ste. Croix 1963. For the rare exceptions to this rule see Harris 2000: 487–95.

20 This can be inferred from the narrative and from the parallel to Stephanus' mission. Demo probably does not want to say that Aristophon succeeded in his objective since Aristophon later sided with his opponents. He wanted to undermine his credibility.

21 For the role of the *synegoros* see Rubinstein 2000.

22 I draw on my analysis of the arrangement in Harris 2006: 343.

the Polemarch. But if those who had borrowed on real security defaulted, Phormio was barred from foreclosing on their property, for that would make him the owner of land in Attica. To overcome this legal hurdle, Pasion, the owner of the bank, had all the secured loans transferred to his account. Phormio could thus go ahead and administer the loans, that is, collect interest payments and recover the principal, but if one of the debtors were to default, Pasion could step in and seize the property pledged as security.

The relationship between Phormio and Pasion is that of lessee and lessor, not agent and principal. By having the loans, secured by land in Attica, transferred to his account, Phormio was merely taking direct responsibility for these loans. Nothing in the speech suggests that Phormio was acting as Pasion's agent; he was not making contracts with third parties on his behalf and creating rights and duties for him without incurring any himself. On the contrary, Phormio was assuming the rights of creditor in the case of the secured loans.

9. The next two examples also involve persons involved in banking. Cohen observes how "Pasion, while still a slave, had developed a relationship of the highest trust" with Archestratus (Dem. 36.44). The passage cited by Cohen does not specify how Pasion gained this trust, but it is irrelevant to the issue of free persons working as agents because Pasion was a slave at the time.

10. Cohen's final example of a legal relationship between an agent and a principal is the connection between Phormio and Timosthenes (Dem. 49.31). Apollodorus, who delivered the speech *Against Timotheus,* describes Timosthenes as a friend and partner of Phormio (ἐπιτήδειος ... καὶ κοινωνός).[23] He recounts how when Timosthenes left Athens on a trading voyage he entrusted to Phormio, who was in charge of Pasion's bank (Dem. 49.17,60), several items including two Lycian bowls. When Timosthenes returned and asked for his property to be returned, it was discovered that they had been given to Timotheus, who had not given them back. Pasion therefore persuaded Timosthenes to accept payment for their value and added this figure to the debts already owed by Timotheus to the bank (Dem. 49.32). Once again there is no indication that Phormio is acting as Timosthenes' agent. Timosthenes merely gives Phormio some movables to be deposited in Pasion's bank. There is a contractual relationship between Timosthenes and Pasion, but it is one of deposit *(parakatatheke)*, not agency. Apollodorus calls Phormio the "partner" (κοινωνός) of Timosthenes, but here too the relationship is contractual (*koinonia*).

There were two main reasons why the Athenians and other Greek *poleis* did not develop the concept of agency. First, the level of economic development (especially

23 Davies (1971: 431–2) suggests that this indicates that Phormion was manumitted by this time.

the organization of production) did not require such a practice.[24] Business agents become necessary only when the level of technology becomes more advanced or the units of production in private hands become larger and more complex. In the modern economy the demands of technology necessitate the cooperation of hundreds, if not thousands of workers, and management. Corporations must employ agents who can act on their behalf in their relations with suppliers and sellers at various levels. The economy of ancient Greece was far less complex. Although there was a considerable amount of horizontal specialization in the economy of some Greek *poleis*, there was little vertical specialization. For the most part, production was carried out by households or individuals working with a few associates or slave labour. In some cases sons might help fathers in pursuing family business interests (see for example Isocrates 17.4). This type of economy did not require numerous business agents. The arrangements found in the passages examined in this section (partnership, joint-ownership, lease/hire) and other informal relationships were sufficient to enable individuals to carry on trade.

The second reason is that slaves could act on behalf of their masters and thus fulfil some of the functions performed by business agents in modern economies. Slaves might live apart from their masters (*choris oikountes*) and produce goods that they sold in the market. They would then pay their masters a portion (*apophora*) of the proceeds from these transactions (Aeschines 1.97; Andocides 1.38; [Xenophon] *Ath. Pol.* 1.10–12). These slaves must have had the capacity to buy and sell and to make other contracts. But these contracts were the responsibility of their masters because slaves had no right to initiate legal proceedings.[25] For instance, when Epicrates bought the slave Midas from Athenogenes, he was held responsible for the debts contracted by Midas for his perfume shop (Hyperides *Athenogenes* 4–10). Midas was clearly working on his own and buying, selling, and borrowing without the direct involvement of his master. Thus the Greeks, like the Romans, did not require the concept of agency because their laws about slaves permitted them to make contracts on their behalf.

III

Before examining the documents preserved on lead tablets a few words are necessary about the differences between these texts and the literary sources. Most of the evidence studied so far comes from speeches written for delivery in court before judges who did not have first-hand knowledge of the events that gave rise to the case before them. The litigant composing the speech therefore needed to explain the background to the case and the relationships among the various persons involved in

24 This analysis draws on the findings of Harris 2002 and the analysis of Harris 2006: 143–62.

25 See Hyp. *Ath.* 6.22 with Harrison 1968: 175 and MacDowell 1978: 82. Both Bravo (1977: 1) and Wilson (1997–1998: 47) are aware of this practice.

the dispute. Letters are very different. The sender was writing only for the addressee, who presumably was familiar with the sender's position and general circumstances. Both men understood the nature of the relationship binding them; the sender does not have to explain it to the addressee. As a result, scholars analyzing these texts must supply the background information and provide a context for the information contained in it. But this task is fraught with difficulties and risks becoming little more than speculation about events for which there is no actual evidence. Above all one must interpret the statements found in these texts in terms of social and economic practices attested in the contemporary world. What one must not do is attempt to explain the situations that prompted the senders to write these letters in terms of practices and concepts without secure parallels in ancient Greece, then turn around and claim that these documents provide evidence for these practices and concepts. In this case, one must not assume that the documents can only be understood by assuming that the sender and addressee were linked as agent and principle. That would be to explain *ignotum per ignotius*.

The first document is a letter dated to around 500 BCE (*SEG* 26.845). I have presented the text in the Appendix and give a translation:

> O Protagoras, your father sends you (a letter). He is being wronged by Matasys because he is enslaving him and has deprived him of his cargo (or cargo-ship). Go to Anaxagoras and explain (the situation) because he (Matasys) claims that he (Achillodorus) is the slave of Anaxagoras and says: "Anaxagoras has my property and slaves, male and female, and houses". But he (Achillodorus) shouts aloud and says that there is nothing (i.e. no dispute) between himself and Matasys. But whatever is going on between Matasys and Anaxagoras they themselves know among themselves. Tell this to Anaxagoras and his wife. He (Achillodorus) sends you other (instructions). Your mother and brothers who are in Arbinati take into the city. Euneros himself going to him (Achillodorus) will come immediately.
>
> Verso
>
> The lead (letter) of Achillodorus to his son and Anaxagoras.

There is general agreement about the situation described by Achillodorus. Matasys has seized Achillodorus as his slave and deprived him of his *phortegesion*, a word that means either cargo or cargo-ship.[26] Achillodorus asserts that he is being treated unjustly by Matasys, but presents the latter's reasons for seizing him and his property: "Anaxagoras has my property, both my male and female slaves and my houses" (lines 5–6). Matasys claims that Anaxagoras has wrongly taken his property and therefore believes that he is entitled to take Anaxagoras' property in return. As several scholars have noted, Matasys may be exercising his right of reprisal

26 For a summary of the debate about the meaning of *phortegesion* see Wilson 1997–1998: 36, n. 37.

(*sulân*).[27] According to this practice, if a citizen of one *polis* had a dispute with a citizen of another *polis*, he could seize the property of the latter either as compensation or as a way of forcing the other party to come to a settlement. Alternatively, Anaxagoras may have failed to pay a debt or other obligation to Matasys, who is now distraining on his property (*enechyrasia*).[28] Because Matasys believes that Achillodorus is the slave of Anaxagoras, Matasys has seized him (lines 4–5).[29] Because the property of the slave belongs to the master of the slave, Matasys also thinks that he has the right to take Achillodorus' ship or cargo.[30]

That is reported by Achillodorus to be Matasys' side of the story. As is usual in disputes of this type, there was another side to the story. Although Matasys believes that the seizure is justified, Achillodorus disagrees. He gives two reasons for his view. First "he says that there is nothing between him and Matasys" (lines 7–8). This should mean that he had no legal dispute with Matasys. Matasys therefore has no legal grounds for seizing his property. If Achillodorus had unjustly taken the property of Matasys, the latter would have been justified in seizing his property, but this is not the case. Second, "he says that he is free and there is no dispute between himself and Matasys" (lines 8–9). If Achillodorus were the slave of Anaxagoras, Matasys would be justified in seizing him and his property in compensation for any wrong to him done by Anaxagoras, but this too is not the case. Because Achillodorus is free, Matasys has no right to distrain on him and his property as part of his dispute with Anaxagoras. Finally, Achillodorus disclaims all knowledge of any dispute between Matasys and Anaxagoras. As far as Achillodorus is concerned, he is *hors d'affaire*.

There are thus two versions of the situation. It is possible that neither version is correct, but in the absence of other evidence we have no means of evaluating the reliability of each story. On the other hand, Matasys' version does confirm part of our analysis. Achillodorus is clearly operating on his own and at a distance from Anaxagoras. Hence his need to write a letter to Anaxagoras when trouble arises. In Matasys' opinion Achillodorus is a slave carrying goods on behalf of his master. If he is being sent abroad to sell these goods and return to Anaxagoras with the proceeds, he is acting just like the Athenian slaves who acted on their masters' behalf. Matasys was familiar with the practice of slaves acting as agents for their masters

27 The most extensive treatment of this practice remains Bravo 1980. For a recent summary with bibliography see Lintott 2004.

28 For the practice at Athens see Finley 1952: 222–3 with [Pl.] *Axiochus* 367b; Ar. *Nub*. 239–41; Ar. *Eccl.* 565–7; Dem. 24.197; Aeschin. 3.21; *IG* II^2 2492, lines 7–9. For an example from Hellenistic Asia Minor see Harris 2008: 81–3.

29 Cf. Lintott 2004: 342: "The implication is that if he had been a slave, the procedure would not necessarily have been unjust".

30 For a parallel see the Attic Stelai (*IG* I^3 426). Aristarchus, the leather-worker, has his property confiscated by the *poletai* (lines 24–39), when he is seized and sold by the *poletai* as the property of his master Adeimantus, son of Leucolophidos, of Skambonidai (lines 10–22).

and assumed that this was Achillodorus' relationship with Anaxagoras. Thus we can explain Matasys' version of the situation in terms of practices attested elsewhere in the contemporary Greek world.

But Achillodorus claims that he is not a slave, has no knowledge of Anaxagoras' dealings with Matasys, and implicitly denies any connection between himself and Anaxagoras. Yet Wilson follows Bravo and argues that Achillodorus was an agent of Anaxagoras on the grounds that Achillodorus does not explicitly deny "qu'il existe des rapports entre lui et Anaxagoras". and because there must be some connection between the two men for Achillodorus to be writing to Anaxagoras.[31]

One can however easily explain why Achillodorus is sending a letter to Anaxagoras without assuming that the former is the agent of the latter. Matasys is claiming that Achillodorus is the slave of Anaxagoras, but Achillodorus denies this and says that he is free (line 8). But it is one thing to assert his freedom, another to prove it. Thus Achillodorus needs someone to confront Matasys and provide testimony about Achillodorus' true status. The person who is in the best position to know whether or not Achillodorus is the slave of Anaxagoras is naturally Anaxagoras. That is why Achillodorus writes to him in the obvious expectation that he will either come to tell Matasys the truth, dispatch a messenger to deliver his statement, or send a letter. Achillodorus is asking Anaxagoras in effect to "take him away to freedom", a practice well attested in Classical Athens.[32] Such an explanation dispenses with any unnecessary hypothesis about the existence of free business agents and makes sense of the letter's contents in terms of a practice known from contemporary sources.

The letter of Achillodorus was not sent to conduct business but to summon help in an emergency. In this respect it resembles the letter sent by the slave Lesis found in the Athenian Agora (*SEG* 50.276).[33] Lesis was entrusted to a man in a foundry and was badly mistreated. He sent the letter to his mother and a man named Xenocles asking them to intercede with his masters and to rescue him in the same way that Achillodorus asks Protagoras to help him. If we can accept Protagoras' version of events, the situations are different (Protagoras is free while Lesis is a slave), but

31 Gauthier (1982: 567) plausibly suggests that Achillodorus was "un citoyen - peut-être un voisin ou un ami" of Anaxagoras. Wilson (1997–1998: 37) rejects this proposal because "Matasys' seizure of Achillodorus, and in particular of the *phortegesion*, only seems to make sense if it is of direct significance to Anaxagoras". He then follows Bravo's speculation (for which there is no evidence) that Achillodorus was "trading on Anaxagoras' behalf". This argument ignores Matasys' reason for seizing Achillodorus and his goods (he was the slave of Anaxagoras, not his agent). It also ignores Achillodorus' statement that he has nothing to do with any dispute between Anaxagoras and Matasys, which by implication means that he has no legal relationship with Achillodorus.

32 See Aeschin. 1.62–3 and [Dem.] 59.4–5 with Zelnick-Abramowitz 2005: 292–300.

33 For the *editio princeps* see Jordan 2000 with the analysis of Harris 2006: 271–9 (= Harris: 2004).

the purpose of the two letters is essentially the same, that is, to ask the addressee to help in rescuing the sender.[34]

Wilson also claims to find evidence for business agents in a letter found at the ancient city of Olbia and dated to around 500 BCE. I present a translation of this letter here and give the recent text of M. Dana in the Appendix (*SEG* 54.694).

> Translation[35]
> "Apatorios to Leanax. I have had the goods seized by Heracleides, the son of Eotheris. It is in your power that I not lose the goods. For I stated that the goods are yours, and Meno stated that you entrusted them to him and all the other things you entrusted to him. He also stated that your goods are in my possession. If you should give the records (*diphtheria*) to Heracleides and Thathaie, [your goods will be recovered?]. For these men are saying that they shall return whatever of yours they are holding. The total amount seized is (worth) 27 staters. Concerning the slaves of Thymoleos [.... to Eu?]thymios: as far as I am concerned, I do not know if it will go well".

The basic situation is fairly clear. Apatorios had possession of goods belonging to Leanax. These goods have been seized by Heracleides. Apatorios does not indicate the grounds for the seizure, but from what is known about the practice of reprisal (*sulân*) Heracleides must have had some grievance against one of the people associated with Apatorios. He therefore seized the goods either by way of compensation or as a means of forcing the person who wronged him to come to a settlement. It is possible that Heracleides had a quarrel with Thymoleos and seized all the goods in Apatorios' possession, both the slaves of Thymoleos and the goods of Leanax. Apatorios is therefore confident that he can recover the goods of Leanax when he can prove that they belong to him, but is less optimistic about getting back the slaves of Thymoleos.

But what are the relationships linking Leanax, Apatorios, and Meno? Wilson suggests that "It could be that Apatorios was a business agent, responsible for buying and selling goods on behalf of Leanax—the exact nature of the goods is unclear, and he may be talking about the domestic slaves—which would explain how he

34 Cf. Trapp 2003: 6: "the Berezan letter itself (...) seems to show (...) that sending a message by this particular means is a measure for emergencies only". One could also compare the letter Iphigeneia gives to Pylades to deliver to Orestes (Eur. *IT* 727–92). Cf. Rosenmeyer 2001:79: "the letter functions as rescuer". A letter written on a potsherd from the Athenian Agora dated to the end of the fifth century BCE may also fall into this category (Lang 1976: 9, no. B9). The sender is a person named Sosineos, who appears to be in prison (ἐν δεσμῷ), and the addressee is named Glaukos. Sosineos may be asking Glaukos to help him get out of prison.

35 I have used the text given by Dana (2004) presented in the Appendix. My translation follows her French translation closely and differs from that of Wilson (1997–1998: 38) in a few places. Wilson used a text provided by Dr. A. W. Johnston.

came to be in possession of goods that he himself admits belong to Leanax".[36] Nothing in the letter compels us to view Apatorius as the agent of Leanax. All that the letter indicates is that Apatorios was carrying goods belonging to Leanax and is now trying to recover them. Nowhere is it stated or implied that Apatorios had the power to enter into legal relationships with third parties, thus creating rights and duties for Leanax. And what about Menon to whom the goods belonging to Leanax have been entrusted? Wilson does not discuss his role.

Is there another possible way of explaining the relationships linking the three men without resorting to the anachronistic concept of business agent? To begin with, we can probably assume that neither Apatorios nor Menon is the slave of Leanax. In that case, they would have been considered property and like the goods of Leanax have also been subject to seizure just as Achillodorus was. But unlike Achillodorus Apatorios does not ask for help from Leanax in securing his release from Heracleides.

A possible parallel can be found in a transaction described by Apollodorus in his speech *Against Timotheus* ([Dem.] 49.60–1).[37] According to Apollodorus Timotheus introduced Philondas, a Megarian living in Athens as a metic, to his father Phormio. Apollodorus describes Philondas as one who "helped" or "did favours for Timotheus" (ὑπηρετοῦντα). Amyntas, the Macedonian king, had given Timotheus a shipment of timber. Philondas was instructed to travel to Macedonia, pick up the timber, and bring it back to Athens. At Timotheus' request, Phormio agreed to give Philondas money to pay the freight for the timber after his return to Athens. Philondas went to Macedonia in the archonship of Asteius (373/2) and returned in the next year (372/1). As previously agreed, Phormio turned over the money to Philondas, who paid the freight. Philondas then brought the shipment to Timotheus' house where it was used in construction. Philondas was not acting as an agent for Timotheus because he was not creating rights and duties for Timotheus with any third parties. The gift of the timber was made directly to Timotheus, and the agreement to pay the shipowner for the freight was made between Timotheus and Phormio.[38]

The arrangement involving Timotheus, Philondas and the shipowner suggests a possible parallel for the relationships linking Leanax, Menon, and Apatorios. Just as Timotheus entrusted the timber received from Amyntas to Philondas for transport to Athens, Leanax entrusted his goods to Menon (lines 3–4) probably for transport abroad. The only difference here is that Leanax appears to have entrusted the goods to Menon for transport abroad whereas Timotheus had Philondas bring the timber from Macedonia to his house in the Piraeus. Then just as Philondas placed the tim-

36 Wilson 1997–1998: 38, followed by Dana 2004: 12 ("Apatorios, vraisemblablement l'agent commercial de Léanax").

37 For the date of the speech see Harris 2006: 355–64.

38 Timotheus appears to have denied that he asked Phormio to pay the money to Philondas from his account. At the proceeding before the public arbitrator, Timotheus claimed that Philondas bought the timber for purposes of trade and sold it in Athens.

ber entrusted to him in the vessel of the ship-owner, Menon could have placed the goods entrusted to him in a ship owned by Apatorios. It is possible that Menon could also have loaded the goods on wagons belonging to Apatorios, but given the difficulties and expense of land transport, this alternative is quite unlikely. When Apatorios' ship was at sea with Meno on board or after it arrived in a foreign port, the cargo was seized by Heracleides. At this point, Meno declared that the goods were not subject to seizure because they belonged to Leanax, and Apatorios wrote to Leanax to send them proof so that they could recover the goods.

This scenario is only a hypothesis, but it has several advantages over Wilson's suggestion. First, it accounts for the role of Meno, whom Wilson does not discuss. Second, it explains how the goods came into the possession of Apatorios even though they were not entrusted to him directly by Leanax. Third, it suggests that Leanax need not have been transporting his goods abroad for trade, but may have simply been sending them to a friend or relative as Amyntas was sending the timber to Timotheus as a gift. Fourth, and most important, it provides a way of understanding the relationships linking the three men without resorting to the anachronistic concept of agency but in terms of an arrangement well attested in the ancient sources. Once again, the letter is sent in an emergency with the aim of informing Leanax about the situation. The letter does not serve to create a legal relationship between the sender and the addressee, but only to convey information about goods owned by the addressee.

Wilson also claims to find evidence for the activity of agent-traders in a document found at Pech-Maho (*SEG* 38.1036), a small settlement near the modern city of Narbonne in the south of France. The translation and interpretation of lines 3–5 of the document are still disputed, but the rest of the text presents fewer problems. For the purposes of this essay, the most important questions are the nature of the document and the relationships among the various participants in the transaction recorded in it.[39] First, there is no reason to believe this is a letter.[40] On the verso of the two letters just examined, there is the name of the sender followed by the person(s) to whom the letter is addressed. The first line of the Berezan letter gives the name of the addressee in the vocative, then reveals that the document is a letter by next phrase: "Your father sends (ἐπιστέλλε) to you (i.e. a letter)". In the first line of the Olbia letter the name of the sender appears in the nominative, the name of the addressees in the dative, and one naturally supplies a verb of sending to give the sense "Apatorios sends Leanax a letter". On the verso of the Pech-Maho text, all that is found is a single name (Ἥρων ὁ Ἴλιος). As Faraguna has observed, the structure of the Pech-Maho inscription resembles that of documents recording sales, in which the

39 My analysis of this document is much indebted to the perceptive remarks of Faraguna 2002: 247–52.
40 Thus Vinogradov 1998: 166–70.

names of the buyer(s) and seller(s) are given, and the amount paid.[41] The language of this document suggests however that this is a private document, not one drawn up by an official for deposit in a public archive.[42] First, there is no indication of the date by eponymous magistrate. Second, there is no mention of any tax or fee paid to a public body.[43] Third, the document is authenticated by private witnesses instead of a public official.

The relationship of the payments recorded in lines 3–6 to the payments described in lines 1–12 remains the subject of debate, but the nature of the transaction is clearly a sale. The buyer has paid a deposit to initiate the agreement (lines 6–7, 10),[44] then paid the balance (line 11). The document appears to indicate that the *arrhabon* was paid "where the boats are moored" (ὄκο τἀκάτια ὀρμίζεται) and that the seller received the final payment "on the river" (ἔλαβεν ἐν τῶι ποταμῶι). The reason for the different places of payment may have to do with the nature of the transaction and the rights and duties incurred by a contract of sale. In the laws of the Greek *poleis* the seller had to provide a warranty against latent defects. This meant that if a defect appeared in the item sold at some time after the transfer of ownership, the seller was liable for the damage incurred by the buyer, or the buyer could return the item to the seller and demand reimbursement of the purchase price.[45] The most serious latent defect in a ship was the presence of leaks in the hull. To protect the seller, therefore, the final payment took place on the ship "in the river" so that all present could see that there were no leaks in the hull at the time of conveyance. If leaks were later found in the hull, and the buyer claimed that they were present when the ship was sold, the buyer could use the document to prove that the boat was in good shape at the time of sale and that the leaks must have appeared later (possibly due to the negligence of the buyer). If this explanation is correct, it reinforces the view that the aim of the document is to record a sale and to set forth the rights and duties of the two parties in the transaction.

There is no reason to "imagine Heron as one of several working for a man who kept records of all their dealings in this manner; in other words, the third party in this case would have been Heron's boss. Heron would then be an agent-trader: an individual who traded on behalf of another individual, using this man's capital to finance his activity".[46] There is no indication in the letter that the buyer is acquiring

41 For parallels see Lambert 1997: 18–9; Faraguna 2000.

42 Faraguna makes the attractive suggestion that the document was given to one of the witnesses for safe-keeping and adduces the parallel of a similar arrangment described in the Hebrew Scriptures (*Jeremiah* 32.9–15).

43 As is found for example in the *Rationes Centesimarum*. For the *hekatostai* paid in these inscriptions, see Lambert 1997: 269–76.

44 I find attractive the suggestion of Chadwick 1990 that the ἀρραβών and the ἐγγυητήριον are identical.

45 On warranty against latent defects see Pringsheim 1950: 472–97. The document may also have helped the buyer to secure warranty of title. On this aspect of sale see Pringsheim 1950: 429–72.

46 Wilson 1997–1998: 45.

the boat with borrowed money or that either of the parties were acting on behalf of someone else. The claim that Heron is "agent-trader" is mere speculation, and it is possible to make sense out of the document without any such hypothesis.

The documents preserved on lead tablets are valuable evidence for the ancient Greek economy. As Wilson rightly observes, they call into question Hasebroek's stereotype of the "illiterate trader". These letters show that by the early fifth century BCE traders were capable of communicating over distances to provide information or convey instructions. But they do not provide any evidence for the existence of business agents. That is an anachronistic concept in the context of Archaic and Classical Greece.

IV

The use of letters in economic activity during the late Archaic and Classical periods was very restricted. Letters appear to have served three main functions in commerce. First, as we have seen in Part II, letters were sent in an emergency to ask for help.[47] The letters by Apatorios and Leanax fall into this category. Second, a letter may be sent to make requests or issue orders to slaves and business partners. The Demosthenic speech *Against Phormio* provides an example of this use of letters. Chrysippus, the plaintiff in this commercial suit, has made a loan of twenty minai to Phormio, a merchant, on the condition that he use the money to buy goods to be transported and sold in the Crimean Bosporus. Phormio also promised to use the money from the sale of these goods to purchase more goods for transport back to Athens (Dem. 34.6–7). When Phormio left Athens, Chrysippus gave him a letter to deliver to his slave (παιδί) and his business partner (κοινωνῷ), instructing them to inspect the goods after they were unloaded at the Bosporus and to keep an eye on them.

There are several lead letters that give instructions about commercial matters to the addressee. The letter may be written by someone in the countryside to an addressee in the city asking him to purchase items in the market and to have them sent. A letter found at Chaidari near Daphni in Attica and dated to the fourth century BCE provides an example of this type:

Side A

> "Mnesiergos bids greetings and good health to the people at home; he says that he too is like that. Dispatch a covering, if you please, sheepskins or goatskins, the cheapest possible and not shaped into cloaks, and shoe-soles; I will pay when I get the chance".

47 For the use of a letter to request help in an emergency see Th. 1.137 (Themistocles to the King of Persia).

Side B

"Take to the earthenware pottery and give to Nausias or Thrasycles or his son".

(*SIG*[3] 1259, adapted from Trapp)

The sender, Mnesiergos, asks the addressee to purchase items and to take them to Nausias or Thrasycles or his son, who will either bring them to him or keep them until he can come to fetch them. If "to the earthenware pottery" is a reference to the potters' district (cf. Ar. *Lys*. 557–8), Mnesiergos intended to send the letter to the city where the items were to be purchased. "Those at home" would appear to be his own family; there is no reason to think that he is sending this letter to a business agent. If the addressee were the agent of Mnesiergus, he would have the agent make the purchase from the seller on his behalf and the agent would tell the seller that Mnesiergus would pay him back. In this letter however the addressee is to make the purchase, and the sender is to pay the addressee.

Alternatively the writer may send a letter to someone who is abroad with a request to purchase items in a foreign market and to have them shipped to him. A letter found at Torone in Sithonia provides an example of this kind of request (*SEG* 43.488). The writer was abroad, possibly in Mende, a city in the neighbouring Pallene, and asks the addressee to buy some wood for him and to convey it by ship.[48]

> "[ca. 4 letters]tos sends greetings to Tegeas. I am unable to buy wood in M[ende (?).] So you dispatch some to me immediately if you have a boat, buying seven talents if it is possible [from X.] Let him not provide you with any fewer at all, preferably [of ......]; but if not, [......]. And if you do this, you will be doing us a favour. Complete purchase within seven days or I shall put a stop (sc. to the arrangement). Farewell (?)".
>
> (trans. Jordan)

The letter indicates nothing about the relationship between the sender and the recipient: Tegeas could have been a friend or a business partner or, less likely, his slave.[49] Although the sender does not promise payment, there is no reason to assume that Tegeas would not have asked to be repaid. A fragmentary letter found in the marketplace of Olbia may contain similar instructions (*SEG* 48.1011). The letter appears to mention iron (σιδήρος), Lydian plates (line A: κάνδολ[ον ?) and woad, a plant producing a dark blue dye (line A1: ἰσάτιν). The letter may also contain a promise to re-

48 For the *editio princeps* see Henry 1991.

49 It is unlikely that the addressee is a slave because the sender would have resorted to another kind of threat if his slave failed to obey his orders.

pay the addressee (line B3: [- - μὴ ἀπο]διδῶ and line B5: ἀπ]οδῶσεν). Another letter found near Olbia dated to the second half of the fourth century BCE states that Nicophanas, the son of Adrastos, has given a horse to Zopyrion and asks him to return it to him in the city (*SEG* 42.711).[50] A letter found at Kerkinitis on the Black Sea and dated to around 400 BCE is written by another man named Apatorios and sent to a certain Neomenios (*SEG* 37.665). The sender instructs the addressee to ship dried fish and perch to his house and to take care of his cows.[51] A letter found at Gorgippea, another city on the Black Sea, asks the addressee to give an axe to his slave and possibly to perform some tasks for the harvest (*SEG* 47.1175).[52]

A letter found at Emporion (*SEG* 37.838) is very fragmentary but may also fall into the category of business letters.[53] The letter is probably to be dated near 500 BCE.[54] The letter appears to address someone in another city called Saiganthe, which has been identified with ancient Saguntum,[55] and to give instructions about items to be purchased and possibly about shipping these goods to him. Wilson proposes two alternative explanations for the relationship between the sender and the addressee: "One has to suspect that there is an employer-employee relationship here, perhaps even master-slave; that the receiver of the letter was an agent for the sender". As the passage from *Against Phormio* shows, it is possible that this letter and the others giving instructions were addressed to slaves or business partners, but there is no reason to think there was an "employee-employer relationship" or that the addressee was an agent. In no case does the sender ask the addressee to conclude a contract on his behalf with a third party.

The third function of letters in commercial matters was to send information about prices from one place to another. None of the lead letters preserved afford an example of this practice; the only evidence comes from a Demosthenic oration *Against Dionysodorus* ([Dem.] 56). In this speech the plaintiff Dareius accuses the defendant Dionysodorus of plotting with Cleomenes, the ruler of Egypt, to manipulate the price of grain in the Eastern Mediterranean. He claims that Dionysodorus was part of a network that received news about prices in different ports, then would ship grain to the port where the prices were the highest. It is impossible to evaluate the charge because Dareius provides no evidence to support it, but there is no reason to doubt that merchants used letters in this way. Merchants therefore used letters to obtain information about prices, which could help them to make rational economic

50 For the text and references to earlier discussions see Dana 2007: 79–81.

51 For the text, translation and references to earlier discussions see Dana 2007: 83–5.

52 For the text, translation and references to earlier discussions see Dana 2007: 89–90.

53 For the *editio princeps* see Sanmarti-Grego & Santiago 1987. For a subsequent discussion see Sanmarti & Santiago 1988a and 1988b; Santiago 1990a; Santiago 1990b; Velaza 1992; Santiago 1993; Slings 1994.

54 See Slings 1994.

55 Santiago 1990a: 80.

decisions and to maximize profits by finding the best prices for their goods.[56] A merchant could therefore use communication by letter to gain a commercial advantage over rivals who did not have access to this information.

Though private letters could help merchants to convey instructions to partners and slaves, they do not appear to have played any role as legal documents in Classical Athens. In commercial suits, litigants use the testimony of witnesses or written contracts to prove that an obligation exists.[57] The use of the letter-form for recording contracts would have to await the development of the *cheirographon* in Ptolemaic Egypt during the second century BCE.[58]

Appendix

Documents on Lead Tablets from Berezan, Olbia, Emporion and Pech-Maho

*I. Lead Letter from Berezan (*SEG *26.845) Text from Bravo (1974) and Wilson (1997–1998):*

῏Ω Πρωταγόρη, ὁ πατήρ τοι ἐπιστέλλε. ἀδικε͂ται
ὑπὸ Ματάσυος, δολο͂ται γάρ μιγ καὶ το͂
φορτηγεσίο ἀπεστέρεσεν. ἐλθὼμ παρ᾽ ᾽Αναξαγόρην
ἀπήγησαι, φησὶ γὰρ αὐτὸν ᾽Αναξαγόρεω
δο͂λον ε͂ναι μυθεόμενος· τᾶμ᾽ ᾽Ανα‹ξα›γόρης ἔχε,
καὶ δόλος καὶ δόλας κοἰκίας. ὁ δὲ ἀναβῶι τε
καὶ οὔ φησιν ε͂ναι οὐδὲν ἐωυτῶί τε καὶ Ματάσ‹υι›
καί φησιν ε͂ναι ἐλεόθερος καὶ οὐδὲν ε͂ναι ἐωυτ‹ῶι›
καὶ Ματάσ‹υι. Μα›τάσυ‹ι› δὲ τί αὐτῶι κἀναξαγόρη αὐτοὶ
οἴδασι κατὰ σφᾶς αὐτός. ταῦτ᾽ ᾽Αναξαγόρη λέγεν
καὶ τῆ γυναικί. ἕτερα δέ τοι ἐπιστέλλε. τὴν μητέρα
καὶ τὸς ἀδε‹λ›φεὺς ‹ο›ἵ ἐσ‹σ›ιν ἐν᾽Αρβινάτηισιν ἄγεν ἐς τὴμ πόλιν,
αὐτὸς δὲ Εὔνεορος ἐλθὼμ παρά μίν θύωρα καταβήσεται.

Verso

᾽Αχιλλοδώρο τὸ μολί-
βδιον παρὰ τὸμ παῖδα
κἀναξαγόρην

56 For the use of letters to send information about prices in Roman Egypt see for example P.Oxy. XXXI 2601.

57 Witnesses: Dem. 49.33,41,61. Written contract: Dem. 34.7; 35.9; [Dem.] 56.6.

58 On the *cheirographon* see most recently Yiftach-Firanko 2008.

*II. Text of Lead Letter from Apatorios to Leanax, c. 500 BCE (*SEG *54.694) (Text from Dana 2004):*

Λήνακτι ᾿Απατόριος Ⱶ ⁝ τὰ χρήματα σισύλημαι ὑπ᾿ ᾿Ηρακ-
λείδεω το͂ Ε[ὀ]θήριος ⁝ κατὰ δύναμιν τὴν σὴν ⁝ μὴ ἀπολέ-
σω τὰ χρήματα ⁝ τὰ γὰρ χρ[ήμ]ατα σὰ ἐφάμην ε͂ναι ⁝ καὶ Μένω-
ν ⁝ ἔφατό ⁝ σε ἐπ[ι]θε͂ναι ἑωυτῶι ⁝ καὶ [ἄ]‹λ›λα ὅσα σὺ αὐτῶι ἐπέ-
θηκας καὶ π[ρὸ]ς ἔφατο Ⱶ {σ᾿} ἐμοὶ σὰ τὰ χρήματα ἐνῆν ⁝ ἰὰν ἐπιθε-
ίης διφθέρια π[ρὸς] ᾿Ηρακλείδην καὶ Θαθαίην ⁝ τὰ χρήματα σ-
έο Υ̣Σ̣ ọπό[σα ? – ca. 4 –] Ⱶ ἐκε͂νοι γάρ φασιṿ ⁝ ὅ τι σὸν ἔχοσιν ἀποδώ-
[σεν] τὸ συλη[θὲν ὅλ]ον ἑπτὰ καὶ εἴκοσιν στατῆρες. vacat
[Τι ? θε]λήσες ; περὶ τῶν οἰκιητέων Θυμώλεω (sic)
[- - ca. 10–11 - - Εὀ]θυμίωι αὐτῶι μοι οὐκ οἶδα ἢν {ε} γένηται εὄ

*III. Document Found on Lead Tablet at Pech-Maho (*SEG *38.1036) (Text from Wilson 1997–1998):*

ἀκάτι[ον] ἐπρίατο [.] πρι[-- παρὰ τῶν] vacat
᾿Εμποριτέων. ἐπρίατό τε [-----] vacat
ἐμοὶ μετέδωκε τὤμυσυ τ[ρίτο] ἡ[μι]οκταν-
ιο. τρίτον ἡμιεκτάνιον ἔδωκα ἀριθμῶ-
ι καὶ ἐγγυητήριον τρίτην αὐτὸς καὶ κε-
ἰν ' ἔλαβεν ἐν τῶι ποταμῶι. τὸν ἀρρα-
βῶν᾿ ἀνέδωκα ὄκο τἀκάτια ὁρμίζεται.
μάρτυρ(ες) Βασιγγερος καὶ Βλερυας καὶ
Γολ[.]βιυρ καὶ Σεδεγων. ο[ὗ]τοι μάρτ-
vacat υρες εὖτε τὸν ἀρραβῶν᾿ ἀνέδωκα
vacat εὖτε δὲ ἀπέδωκα τὸ χρῆμα τρίτον
vacat [ἡμ]ιοκτάνι[ο]ν, [.]αυαρυας, Ναλβε[..]ν.

Verso

῞Ηρων ὁ ῞Ιιος.

Greek Letters on Stone

James Sickinger (Tallahassee)

Among the distinctive features of the Greek epigraphical record of the Hellenistic period is the appearance of the official letter. By "official" I mean letters produced and sent by a state official or organ of government in the course of conducting state business. The best known examples are, of course, the inscribed royal letters of the Hellenistic kingdoms, many of which were collected and ably discussed by C.B. Welles (1934) over 75 years ago. Those letters address a wide range of matters, but they regularly convey decisions of Hellenistic monarchs on issues brought to them by individual subjects or by *poleis* under their control. Some royal letters respond to very specific issues affecting only a particular city or region; others are more general and apply to all subjects and *poleis* within a kingdom. But as a whole the corpus stands out for its newness. Official letters are unrepresented in Greek inscriptions of earlier periods, and their appearance in Hellenistic times requires some explanation.

On a general level this innovation in epigraphic practice reflects the changed nature of politics and diplomacy in the Hellenistic period, when Greek *poleis* no longer exercised complete control over their domestic and external affairs, and when the decisions of kings and queens, often transmitted via letters, possessed an authority unparalleled in earlier periods.[1] But the emergence of inscribed, official letters also has relevance to the role of writing in the Greek world and to the ideological uses of the written word. J.-M. Bertrand (1990), for example, has drawn attention to differences in language between decrees and letters as forms of political communication. He notes how each type of document reflects and suits the form of government that produced it: decrees embodied the collective decision-making of the *polis* while letters were more appropriate to the personal nature of royal government. P. Ceccarelli (2005a) has similarly emphasized the connection between official letters and autocratic government. But she also observes that some Greek *poleis* were employing letters for official communications already in the fifth century BC, and that even in the Hellenistic period kings were not the only ones to rely on epistolary communications: letters were closely associated with and favoured by monarchic governments, but they were not exclusively royal, and some *poleis* also resorted to the letter form.

1 For a general discussion of official Greek letters, including their growing importance in the Hellenistic period, see now Muir 2009: 83–116; Stirewalt 1993: 6–10.

This paper seeks to continue discussion of the role of letters in Greek culture by examining the development of letter writing for official purposes, and by setting the appearance of official letters in inscriptions within the context of that development. Although Greek *poleis* did not routinely display official letters in public until late in the fourth century, some had made use of letters for diplomatic and administrative purposes for more than a century, as Ceccarelli has noted. Failure to publish these texts permanently on stone or some other medium was the result not of a failure to recognize the utility of letters as a form of communication but of the epigraphic practice of individual *poleis*. The decision of *poleis* to start publishing letters in the Hellenistic period reflects the growing importance of kingship, which had traditionally relied on letters as a tool of official communication, but it also betrays an acceptance of the new role that letters had won in *polis* life; cities, after all, and not kings were often responsible for engraving and displaying royal letters on stone. This acceptance is further manifested in a greater use of letters by the *poleis* themselves, some of which adopted the epistolary form as a form of communication. Just how far this acceptance went remains to be seen.

Letters enjoyed a long history in the Greek world. The earliest attested instance is probably the folded *pinax* carried by Bellerophon from Argos to Lykia and mentioned in book six of Homer's *Iliad* (6.168–81), although the passage hardly reflects Greek practice of Homer's times.[2] Any sort of letter writing remains poorly attested until the fifth century, and even then references to letters, public or private, are fairly infrequent.[3] Letters written by Phaedra, Iphigeneia and other characters in fifth-century Greek tragedies may suggest that private correspondence was on the rise, but recourse to letters by state officials or other public bodies is not as well documented. Even so, the *Histories* of Herodotus suggest that Greek *poleis* were familiar with their diplomatic potential in the late archaic period, a usage already hinted at in the Homeric letter of Bellerophon. The Samian tyrant Polycrates is said to have corresponded with the Egyptian pharaoh Amasis in the 520s (Hdt. 3.41–3), but Achaemenid practices in the Persian empire were probably more influential. Persian satraps maintained secretaries to handle their correspondence (Hdt. 3.128), and Persian kings and their subordinates routinely issued commands and maintained contact with one another through letters. Thus, Darius wrote to Magabyzos ordering him to expel the Paionians from their territory and to bring them to him (Hdt. 5.14), and the Persian Bagaios carried to Sardis letters purporting to come from Darius (Hdt. 3.120). Secrecy, intrigue, and betrayal regularly underlie these and other stories that involve written correspondence, and these themes dominate the image of letters found in fifth-century Greek litera-

2 For a discussion of the passage and its implications see Kirk 1990: 181–2, and Rosenmeyer 2001: 39–44.

3 For an overview see Harris 1989: 55–6, 78, 88–9; cf. also Rosenmeyer 2001: 24, "Even in the classical era ... letters did not become commonplace".

ture.[4] But the tales also reflect an environment in which letters were a standard means for Persian officials to communicate with one another and with their subjects.

More important from the Greek perspective, Greek tyrants and aristocrats were active participants in written correspondence. Herodotus describes letters sent by the Milesian Histaios to leading Persians at Sardis to stir up rebellion (6.4), and the exiled Spartan king Demaratos wrote from Persia to the Spartans to inform them of Xerxes' planned invasion (7.239). Even the Greeks Aristagoras and Histaios corresponded by letter with one another and with others as they planned the Ionian revolt (5.35.2–3; 6.4). Intrigue and deception also characterize these epistolary exchanges, and they too contribute to the literary image of writing as a tool of trickery and deceit. But they also betoken familiarity with the use of written messages among the Greek elite, especially those who had interactions with the Persian empire.

Greek elites continued to correspond by letter after the Persian Wars. Exchanges in the 470s and 460s between the Spartan regent Pausanias and Xerxes, and between the Athenian Themistocles and the satrap Artaxerxes, as reported by Thucydides (1.128–32; 1.137.4), point to persistent epistolary contact between Greeks living on the edges of the Persian empire and their Persian counterparts; even if the texts quoted by Thucydides are not authentic, the exchanges are consistent with the earlier letters mentioned by Herodotus.[5] To be sure, reports of letters between Greek and Persian elites are lacking for nearly the next fifty years, but an event early in the Peloponnesian War shows that written correspondence had not disappeared. In 426 the Athenians captured at Eion a Persian named Artaphernes who was conveying letters from the Persian king to the Spartans (Thuc. 4.50.1–2). The letters were written in Assyrian and the Athenians subsequently had them translated and read aloud at Athens. Thucydides does not make it clear whether the Spartans themselves had been communicating earlier with Xerxes in writing; he states only that Xerxes complained of previous Spartan ambassadors who said different things (4.50.2). Even so, the case is significant. Correspondence between Greeks and Persians early in the fifth century had involved Persians and individual members of the Greek elite. But Thucydides implies that Xerxes' letter was addressed to the Spartans. Official correspondence now involved not only individuals but entire Greek communities.

The role of Sparta and individual Spartans in these written exchanges of the fifth century also stands out because it runs counter to a stereotype that characterizes the Spartan as an illiterate, or at best semi-literate, people with little use for the written word. E. Millender (2001), however, has shown that this image is more a representation of Athenian attitudes towards Sparta than reflection of actual Spartan practice; the written word and use of official letters were established features of Spartan ad-

4 For a discussion of these themes in Herodotean letters see especially Rosenmeyer 2001: 45–54 and Ceccarelli 2005b; cf. also Steiner 1994: 149–54; Lewis 1996: 142–6.

5 On the letters mentioned by Thucydides see Rosenmeyer 2001: 54–60; Longo 1978.

ministrative practice.[6] Thus, Thucydides relates that in the 470s the Spartans sent out a herald to the regent Pausanias ordering him to return to Sparta from the Troad and answer charges against him (Thuc. 1.131). That message was sent by means of a *skytale*. The exact form and function of this object remain the subject of debate, but it was certainly a medium by which Spartan authorities sent written messages, possibly cryptic, to officials in the field.[7] Thucydides mentions other written messages sent by the ephors in the 470s (Thuc. 1.131.1), and by the end of the Peloponnesian War the Spartans appear to have regularly transmitted orders in writing to their officers in the field; those same officers also sent written reports back home.[8] Nor was written correspondence limited to the kings or ephors: the title of the vice-admiral of the Spartan navy was *epistoleus*, the "letter writer", a clear sign that written correspondence was among this official's chief duties.[9]

Athens, by contrast and in spite of its reputation as the center of Greek learning and culture, displays remarkably little evidence for the use of letters or written messages by state officials before the late fifth century. Whether this silence reflects contemporary reality or simply ignores a wider use of written communication is difficult to say. Interaction between Athens and Persia on both the military and diplomatic levels continued well after the Persian Wars, and the establishment and expansion of the Delian League increased the frequency and volume of Athens' contacts with other Greek states; but letters addressed to or from the Athenian *demos* are nowhere mentioned. Historical and epigraphical sources that depict dealings between the Athenians and member-states of the Delian League mention heralds and other officials, and their work sometimes involved recourse to written documents.[10] But the exchange of letters between Athens and members of the Delian League is nowhere attested.

Written communication between Athens and Athenian officials abroad is also poorly attested. The best known and most frequently cited example is the letter sent by Nicias from Sicily describing the plight of the Athenian force on that island in the winter of 414/3.[11] It is the first Athenian letter mentioned by Thucydides, who says that Nicias chose to write it because he feared his emissaries might misrepresent his words, forget his instructions, or otherwise alter his report to pander to the masses

6 On Spartan literacy see also Cartledge 1978; Boring 1979.

7 On the *skytale* see also Xen. *Hell.* 3.3.8–9; 5.2.34, 37; Plut. *Lys.* 19. On its form and use see especially Kelly 1985, and Millender 2001: 142.

8 Letters of ephors to Pausanias: Thuc. 1.131; letters sent to Spartan generals: Thuc. 8.45.1; letters between individual Spartans and Spartan admirals: Thuc. 8.33.3, 8.99.1; report to Sparta from commanders: Thuc. 8.38.4; 8.39.3; Xen. *Hell.* 1.1.23. For a further discussion of Spartan epistolary practice see Ceccarelli 2005a: 365–8.

9 Xen. *Hell.* 2.17; 4.8.11; 5.1.5, Plut. *Lys.* 7; Pollux 1.95; on the title see especially Pritchett 1974: 45–6.

10 See Pébarthe 2006: 300–10, for a discussion of the written texts deployed in the administration of Athens' fifth-century empire; cf. also Sickinger 2007.

11 Thuc. 7.10–5; for a discussion see especially Ceccarelli 2005a: 349–50; cf. also Longo 1978: 530–1; Harris 1989: 78; Lewis 1996: 151; Rosenmeyer 2001: 57–60; Pébarthe 2006: 292.

(Thuc. 7.8–10). Thucydides' account suggests that writing a letter was unusual for a general on campaign, but the opening words of the letter that he reports have Nicias state that he had kept the Athenians apprised of developments in Sicily in other ἐπιστολαί, the term normally used for letters (7.11.1). The word may simply mean "messages" in this passage and refer to earlier oral reports sent by Nicias, but a fragment of the comic poet Eupolis suggests that generals were already sending written reports of their activities back to Athens at least a decade earlier.[12] That fragment is addressed to Cleon and hails him as the first to have addressed the word χαίρειν, "Greetings", to the city (Eupolis F 331 K-A). Later sources explain the reference in terms of a letter sent by Cleon that announced his capture of the Spartans on Sphacteria in 425; some say that Cleon was the first to have attached this salutation to a letter, although others reject that claim and describe it simply as standard practice.[13] Whatever the truth of the assertion that Cleon was responsible for innovation in epistolary practice, none of the sources express surprise that a general might report on his activities in a letter to the Council or the Assembly, and generals might have been sending letters recounting their activities far more often than our sources reveal.

The practice is attested with greater frequency later. The victorious generals at Arginusai reported their victory in 406 with a letter to the Council, and Xenophon does not hint at any novelty in this practice.[14] In the fourth century Demosthenes has read out written messages sent by the generals Iphikrates, Timotheos, and Chares, while Aeschines too mentions a letter of Chares announcing Philip's capture of Kersebleptes and the fall of Hieron Oros, as well as another from the general Proxenos reporting the failure of the Phokians to hand over their outposts in 346.[15] Inscriptions too offer relevant evidence: a decree of 347/6 renewing an Athenian treaty with Mytilene mentions a letter sent to Athens by the Athenian general Phaidros.[16] Nor were generals the only officials to engage in written exchanges with the *demos*: Demosthenes mentions several letters that he and others ambassadors composed when serving as envoys abroad.[17]

Interstate communication also saw a growing use of letters in the fourth century. Persian kings continued to write to Greek *poleis* by means of letters, but so too did other rulers.[18] An Athenian decree of 368 granting citizenship to Dionysios of Syracuse mentions a letter sent by the Sicilian tyrant that addressed the rebuilding of a temple and the terms of the King's Peace. Another decree honouring the Bosporan

12 For *epistolai* meaning verbal messages see Gomme, Andrewes & Dover 1970: 385.

13 Lucian *Pro Lapsu* 3; schol. Ar. *Clouds* 609a; schol. Ar. *Plutus* 322; *Suda* s.v. χαίρειν. For a more detailed discussion see Ceccarelli 2005a: 353–6; cf. also Lewis 1996: 150; Pébarthe 2006: 292.

14 Xen. *Hell.* 1.7.1–7,17; cf. also Diod. Sic. 13.101, with Lewis 1996: 151–2.

15 Dem. 23.115,151,183; Aeschin. 2.90,134.

16 *IG* II^2 213, lines 6–9; other decrees may also allude to written dispatches from generals: see *IG* II^2 110, lines 187, 408, and Pritchett 1974: 47.

17 Dem. 18.211–2; 19.174.

18 Examples of Persian letters include Xen. *Hell.* 5.1.30–2; 7.1.39; cf. also 1.4.3.

kings Spartokos and Pairisades was similarly enacted in response to a letter from them, and Demosthenes mentions in the speech *Against Aristokrates* letters to Athens from the Thracian kings Kotys, Kersebleptes, and Berisades.[19] Even Olympias sent letters to Athens as queen of Molossos, complaining of Athenian activity at the sanctuary of Zeus at Dodona in 331 (Hyp. 3(Eux.).25). But by far the most prolific writer was Philip II of Macedon. The speeches of Aeschines and Demosthenes preserve numerous references to and quotations from his correspondence with the Athenians throughout the 340s and early 330s. His letters contained everything from promises of peace and alliance with Athens, to offers to renegotiate the terms of the Peace of Philokrates, to complaints about Athenian behaviour.[20] Nor were the Athenians the only recipients of his letters. Demosthenes cites epistles sent by Philip to the Euboians, Thebans, and the cities of the Peloponnese.[21] The scattered and fragmentary nature of our evidence makes it difficult to quantify the frequency with which Greek *poleis* sent or received official letters, and it would be ill-advised either to exaggerate or to downplay their numbers.[22] What is clear is that, whatever the frequency of correspondence, Greek diplomatic and administrative practice was deeply familiar with the letter form by the middle of the fourth century.

And yet Greek cities did not fully exploit letters as tools for communicating official business. Kings and tyrants sent letters to Greek *poleis* to explain their intentions, register complaints, and gain information. By contrast, *poleis* did not communicate with other *poleis* in writing but preferred instead to deal with other communities through envoys and ambassadors who delivered oral messages. Some envoys might cite documents to support their positions: Aeschines, for example, relates how he read out to Philip a Pan-Hellenic decree asserting Athenian control over Amphipolis.[23] But the *polis* itself expressed its views and decisions by means of decrees or through other documents.[24] A similar contrast underlies the use of letters in the internal administration of the *polis*. Individual officials operating abroad sometimes sent written reports in the form of letters to their governments at home, but city-states and their governments did not respond in kind; as was the case with diplomatic correspondence, so too in communicating with its own officials, *poleis* tended to issue either verbal instructions or written orders in the form of decrees. Even in the service of the *polis*, the letter primarily remained a form of personal communication, one that cities knew as recipients but seldom as senders. The Spartans, as

19 *IG* II^2 103, lines 8–13; *IG* II^2 212, lines 8–10; Dem. 23.151; cf. also Dem. 23.115,159,174,178.

20 Letters from Philip are mentioned or read out at Aeschin. 2.45,50,124–5,129 and in Dem. 2.6; 7.1; 8.17; 9.16,27; 11; 18.39,77,166,221; 19.38,40,51,161. A detailed study of this correspondence would be welcome.

21 Dem. 4.37; 18.156,167,221.

22 For differing views see Hornblower 1987: 39–40; Lewis 1996: 149–50.

23 Aeschin. 2.32.

24 See especially the discussion of Bertrand 1990: 101–6.

usual, were an exception: ephors acting on behalf of the Spartan *polis* wrote to officials abroad throughout the fifth and into the fourth century.[25] But that practice is probably more indicative of the broad powers exercised by Spartan officials; if officials from other city-states dispatched letters on behalf of their city-states in a similar manner, those letters have left virtually no traces in our sources.[26]

However widespread the circulation of officials letters may have been, their role and significance in *polis* affairs appears to have been relatively minor, at least when compared to other types of official documents that also served as tools for executing state business. Letters were useful as practical tools to convey information but they lacked any real political significance or meaning. This relative insignificance is reinforced by their absence from the corpus of Greek inscriptions of the archaic and classical periods: not a single official letter is represented among the surviving inscriptions on stone before the middle of the fourth century. The numbers of documents published by different city-states of course varied, but certain types of texts predominate among those that survive: laws and decrees enacted by citizen assemblies or other bodies; treaties and agreements with other *poleis*; and financial accounts of monies and state property handled by civic or sacred officials. The motives for publishing different documents also varied, but one feature was common to almost all those that were inscribed: their contents were of a general and enduring value. The Greeks did not publish decisions of purely temporary or ephemeral import; they reserved publication on stone for texts with more lasting meaning and significance. That is not to say that all documents with long-term value were inscribed and publicly displayed; publication on stone or other durable media was highly selective. But only texts that had a lasting meaning or significance found themselves monumentalized in the form of a stone inscription.[27] The official letters that circulated in Greek *poleis* before the late fourth century lacked such enduring value. The reports sent by generals or ambassadors were generally simple; they might include proposals for the future, as did the letter of Nicias, but they lacked the authority to compel action; only a formal decision by the *demos* or one of its organs had that effect and would merit publication on stone. Letters and written communications from foreign rulers were similarly deficient as tools of political authority. Persian and Macedonian kings could communicate their wishes and desires to Greek *poleis*, but cities were not bound to obey or act on them. Proposals made by foreign rulers still

25 Thuc. 1.131.1; 8.45.1; Xen. *Hell.* 3.3.9; Plut. *Lys.* 19.4; *Ages.* 10.5.

26 A letter from Philip to the Thebans and preserved in Demosthenes' speech *On the Crown* purports to reply to a letter sent by the Thebans to Philip (Dem. 18.167). But the surrounding context makes no allusion to a Theban written message, and the letter in which the reference itself appears is itself spurious.

27 The motives that spurred recording documents on stone are complex and the bibliography increasingly long; see especially Pébarthe 2006: 243–89; cf. also Sickinger 2009; Liddell 2007: 78–83, 160–74, 182–98; Rhodes 2001: 139–41; Hedrick 1999; Lewis 1996: 127–42; Thomas 1992: 84–8; Linders 1992.

required ratification by citizen assemblies, and *poleis* published those ratified agreements in the form of treaties, not royal letters or edicts.[28]

The rise of Macedonia as a major player in the international politics of the Greek world in the fourth century, however, had the effect of raising the status of the letter in Greek political life. As Philip and later Alexander gained control over the *poleis* of Greece, city-states had to reckon increasingly with royal decisions that often affected their internal affairs. And as kings often expressed those decisions through letters, as had been the traditional practice in the Near East, royal letters gained increasing authority, and eventually the number of letters inscribed on stone also grew. That development, however, was not immediate, and more than a generation passed before Greek cities accepted this new role for epistolary communications and began to publish royal letters in permanent form. A few inscriptions from the reigns of Philip and Alexander, to be sure, have been identified as letters and survive. But several of these prove to be problematic when interpreted as letters, and their relevance to understanding the development of the political significance of official letters is correspondingly limited.

Consider the earliest Greek inscription identified as an official letter. It comes from Oleveni in the Former Yugoslav Republic of Macedonia and commemorates a victory by Philip and a group of individuals called *katlestai* (κατλεσταί) over the Dardanians; Hatzopoulos dates it to 345.[29] The stone is damaged and its opening lines are illegible, but the preserved text includes instructions for setting up the document "in the most conspicuous place" (ἀνάθετε ἐν τῶ[ι] ἐπιφανεστάτωι τόπωι, lines 6–7). It concludes by mentioning the *katlestai* who with Philip defeated the Dardanians (lines 9–14). The contents are otherwise unrecoverable, but the document may have described honours or awards granted by Philip to the *katlestai*. The identification of the text as a letter depends primarily on its use of the second person imperative (line 6), and on the fact that royal letters of the Hellenistic period mention similar types of grants.[30] Some features of the text, however, make this identification less than certain and argue against seeing the inscription as a precursor of the inscribed royal letters better known from the Hellenistic period. The date of the inscription is not secure, and some scholars have assigned it to 206 during the reign of Philip V, when royal letters were common tools of diplomatic and administrative practice.[31] The identity of the *katlestai* is equally uncertain; they may have been a unit within the Macedonian army or a separate ethnic group, but in either case the author of the letter may have been dealing with his own subjects or close allies. Most important, the

28 The King's Peace of 386 offers a good example: it was transmitted from the Persian King Artaxerxes to the Greeks as an edict or rescript (Xen. *Hell.* 5.1.30–1), but its published versions are described as συνθῆκαι, "treaties" or "agreements" (Isoc. 4.180; 12.107).

29 *IG* XI.2.2.1 (= Hatzopoulos 1996, II, no. 5). For the date see Hatzopoulos 1995.

30 Hatzopolous 1996, II, no. 10 (Beroia); Welles 1934: nos. 16,51.

31 See Papazoglou 1998–1999 and Arena 2003, both of whom put the letter in 206.

inscription was found on the margins of the Macedonian kingdom and on the periphery of the Greek world; Philip's use of the letter (if that is what it is) to grant rewards and its publication on stone need not reflect practices or attitudes current in contemporary Greek *poleis*.

The epistolary character of other inscriptions from the reign of Alexander is similarly problematic. One inscription from Philippi dates to 330 and preserves a document regulating cultivation of the city's territory. It appears to settle some sort of land dispute and cites Alexander as its authority; a second document inscribed on the opposite side of the same *stele* defines that territory more precisely.[32] The stone is badly damaged, but editors restore the opening line of the first document to make it a letter, either from Alexander himself or from his ambassadors who are reporting a decision made by him. The line making the document a letter, however, is entirely restored, and even if that restoration is correct, the relationship of Philippi to the Macedonian kingdom makes it difficult to take practices attested there as representative of the Greek world in general. Another inscription from the island of Chios that dates from the 330s is also problematic. It preserves what appears to be a ruling of Alexander concerning problems that arose on the island after a period of unrest, confiscations of property, and the return of exiles brought about by his campaigns.[33] The document is sometimes described as a letter, but its text consists of instructions expressed with infinitives. The first person, a characteristic of letters, is absent, as are a salutation and farewell, also standard features; the text reads more like an order or edict. Only the prescript, which declares that the text is "From King Alexander to the *demos* of the Chians" (παρὰ βασιλέως Ἀλε[ξάνρδ]ου Χίω[ν τῶι] δήμωι) suggest that the text could be a letter, but those words need not have formed part of the original document; they may simply identify the source of the document, not its form.[34] Another inscribed document from Chios and found on the same stone as the preceding has better claims to epistolary status.[35] Its opening lines are lost, but the preserved sections use the first person and include a personal request from the sender for special treatment of a certain Alkimachos, who is described as "my friend" (ἐμός τε φίλος) and someone who was (as restored) "eager" (πρόθυμος) toward the Chian people. These features are more personal than those expected in a royal edict, and they find parallels in similar petitions for favours in royal letters of the Hellenistic period.[36]

Other documents recognizable as letters do not appear in the epigraphic record of the reign of Alexander, and official letters sent by his successor kings only start to ap-

32 *SEG* 34.664 = Hatzopoulos 1996, II, no. 6; for a discussion see Vatin 1985; Missitzis 1985; Hatzopoulos 1997.

33 See Rhodes & Osborne 2003: no. 84A; Heisserer 1980: 79–95.

34 Heisserer, who calls the inscription a "letter" in his chapter title, suggests (1980: 92 n. 31) on the basis of Alexander's title that it may be more accurate to label it a *diagramma*.

35 Rhodes & Osborne 2003, no. 84B; Heisserer 1980: 96–117.

36 For a similar recommendation for a king's friend see Welles 1934: no. 45.

pear in inscriptions at the end of the fourth century.[37] The reasons for this delay are not entirely clear. There is no question that Alexander and his immediate successors corresponded with Greek cities through letters. Foremost among these was one that conveyed the Exiles' Decree of 324, by which Alexander ordered the *poleis* of Greece to accept the return of their exiled citizens (Diod. 18.8.3–4). Other letters mentioned in our sources include a request to the Athenians to send triremes (Plut. *Phoc.* 21.1), another to the Plataians announcing his desire to rebuild their city (Plut. *Alex.* 34.1), and still another to the Greeks in general announcing the abolition of tyrannies and their right to live under their own laws (Plut. *Alex.* 34.1). Undoubtedly there were others, but they have not left any trace among the surviving inscriptions on stone. Why?

Some, like Alexander's request to the Athenians for triremes, were probably simple administrative pronouncements that lacked the enduring value characteristic of the documents the Greeks normally chose to publish on stone. Others, however, like the one pronouncing Exiles' Decree or the letter granting the Greeks their autonomy, had broader implications, and the failure or refusal to inscribe them is striking and calls for some explanation, especially in light of later practice. Their autocratic tone may have been a factor. Self-government had characterized *polis* politics for over three centuries, and orders issued by Alexander, in whatever form, that interfered with the internal affairs of a city were at odds with principles that had long governed *polis* life. Moreover, the manner in which Alexander conveyed his decisions to Greek cities may have offended. An anecdote preserved in Plutarch's *Life of Phocion* relates that Alexander dropped his use of the word χαίρειν from the start of his letters, except in ones written to Antipater and Phocion (Plut. *Phoc.* 17.6). The historicity of the detail is irrelevant; but it points to a belief that some of Alexander's written communications lacked the conventions, courtesies, and formalities that characterized the typical letter form.[38] If that was the case, the growing number of inscribed royal letters in the late fourth century and early third century may point to an awareness on the part of Hellenistic kings that the conventional letter, as opposed to the impersonal order, was more appropriate for dealing with Greek cities.

37 Two other inscriptions from the reign of Alexander are sometimes cited as examples of his letters. One (Rhodes & Osborne 2003: no. 82) preserves a series of documents from Eresos related to the punishment of tyrants. These refer to a *diagrapha* ("edict") of Alexander and include a document issued by Philip Arrhidaios (γ, lines 21–8); but this latter document lacks a formal greeting and closing. A second inscription (Rhodes & Osborne 2003, no. 86B) comes from Priene and records a settlement arbitrated by Alexander between the citizens of Priene and their neighbors. But it too lacks a formal salutation and reads more like an edict; moreover, it may not have been published until the third century (Sherwin-White 1985), long after Alexander's reign and when publication of royal letters was becoming more common.

38 According to Diodoros (18.56.3), Alexander and Philip regularly issued orders in the form of *diagrammata*, "edicts" or "ordinances". It may be that the two types of documents—letters and royal orders—were not sharply distinguished. For attempts to distinguish between them see Ehrenberg 1930 and Welles 1938.

The surviving royal letters consist largely of correspondence between kings, other dynasts, and their agents on the one hand and Greek cities on the other. Length varies from a single line to several thousand words but most include a salutation, often including the word χαίρειν, that identifies both sender and recipient; a body that announces a decision or provides specific instructions on a topic or both; and a closing word of farewell.[39] Content and subject matter also vary, but most fall into a few broad categories, ones similar to those that characterize the documents published on stone by Greek *poleis*. Indeed, in the hands of Hellenistic monarchs, letters achieved a political status in *polis* affairs that previously had been reserved for laws and decrees. That Greek cities were willing to publish them is testimony to their skill at adapting the epistolary form to a new political reality.

In some letters kings take on the functions of *nomothetai* or *nomographoi* and issue cities new laws addressing citizenship, legal procedure, and property rights. One of the earliest surviving royal letters on stone consists of Antigonos' regulations for the synoecism of Teos and Lebedos; in it, he promulgates a series of rules that will affect the distribution of property in the new settlement, rules of citizenship, pending lawsuits, and city revenues. Antigonos also provides for the passage of new laws, which he himself will vet (Welles 1934, no. 3). A century later Philip V wrote to the city of Larissa and instructed its citizens to change their requirements for citizenship so as to increase the city's population (*IG* IX.2 517 = *SIG*^{3} 543). And a second-century inscription from Pergamon records a letter from an unknown ruler dealing with allotments of land, maintenance of temples, and the disposition of property for a military colony, all areas previously administered by civic laws and decrees.[40]

Letters also served as a medium through which rulers could grant rewards and privileges to cities or individuals who supported them, in much the same way that Greek *poleis* bestowed honorary titles or awards of land, citizenship, and other privileges upon their benefactors with decrees. Some letters make gifts to individuals, like the grant of land from Antiochos I to Aristodikides, one of his friends.[41] Others offer grants to entire cities, like a letter of the 190s from Laodike, wife and sister of Antiochos III to the city of Iasos. In it Laodike announces the creation of an endowment of grain for the city, the sale of which was to be used to pay for the dowries of daughters of poorer citizens.[42] Just as common were letters bestowing titles and less tangible privileges, like grants of freedom, autonomy, and immunity from

39 Welles 1934: xliii-xlv remains indispensable for the discussion of the format and conventions of royal letters; cf. also Ma 1999: 183.

40 Welles 1934: nos. 51. See also the letter of Antiochos III to Zeuxis regarding the foundation of a colony and quoted by Josephus *AJ* 12.148–53. For earlier examples of laws and decrees regulating new settlements see the Athenian decree establishing a colony at Brea (*IG* I^3 46) and a Lokrian law on property and inheritance (*IG* IX.1^2 609).

41 Welles 1934: nos. 10–3; cf. Welles 1934: no. 45, a letter of Seleukos IV granting citizenship and a statue to Aristolochos, a supporter of Antiochos III.

42 *IIasos* 4, lines 1–32; for a discussion of the gift see also Ma 1999: 180–1.

various forms of taxation (*ateleia*). Thus, Antiochos I granted autonomy and freedom from taxes to the people of Erythrai in return for the loyalty they had displayed to him (Welles 1934, no. 15). Eumenes of Pergamon in a similar way wrote to the citizens of Pergamon to praise their retiring generals and report his decision to crown them for the services (Welles 1934, no. 23). Also frequent are letters announcing royal grants of *asylia* to cities and sanctuaries, and others that recognize the special, "crowned" status of games and festivals.[43]

Letters also supplied a suitable medium for kings to intervene in the religious affairs of Greek and other subject cities. An inscription from Beroia dating from 248 preserves three letters from Demetrios II, at that time co-regent with his father Antigonos, that themselves respond to troubles encountered by the priests of a sanctuary of Herakles (*SIG*^{3} 459 = Hatzopoulos 1996, II, no. 8). In the first Demetrios orders revenues reserved for use of the sanctuary but misappropriated by secular officials to be returned to the sanctuary. The second letter apparently responds to a surplus of dedications offered by manumitted slaves in the sanctuary and permits horns and *skyphoi* to be dedicated in the future, and not *phialai* as had been past practice. In the third letter Demetrios grants the priests of Herakles freedom from the same taxes as the priests of Asklepios, a type of exemption granted in other royal letters (Welles 1934, nos. 47, 64). Similar intervention in religious affairs appears in a dossier of letters from Labraunda in Asia Minor. One of the earliest documents in the collection, dated to c. 240, comes from Seleukos and responds to a complaint brought by Korris, priest of Zeus Labraundos, that the Mylasians were taking revenues from the land but not using them to finance sacrifices at the sanctuary.[44] Seleukos informed Olympichos, his governor in the region, that he found the claims of Korris justified. But in a subsequent letter Olympichos reports to the Mylasians that Korris had lied, and he restores to them their rights to the sanctuary (*ILabraunda* 3). The situation changed yet again, and in a letter dated c. 220 Olympichos restored the sanctuary to the Mylasians and announced his intention to write to Philip V, who now controlled the area. A letter from Philip followed, confirming the decision of Olympichos and Mylasian control of the sanctuary (*ILabraunda* 4, 5).

These and other letters modified constitutional and legal rules, granted awards to royal friends and benefactors, and intervened in the religious affairs of the cities to which they were sent. These were subjects that Greek *poleis* had traditionally regulated internally through their own legislation, and the degree to which Hellenistic kings interfered in the civic affairs of the *poleis* under their control finds little precedent in earlier periods. And yet the inscriptions show no signs of resentment or hostility, and the impetus for publishing royal correspondence often came not from kings or royal officials but from the recipients themselves, the very communities into whose

43 *Asylia*: Welles 1934: nos. 25–8, 35, 50, 64; crowned games: Welles 1934: nos. 31–4.

44 *ILabraunda* 1; for a discussion of the entire dossier see Dignas 2002: 59–69 and Crampa 1969: 86–96.

affairs kings intruded. Senders of royal letters seldom make explicit instructions for permanent display of their letters; instead, recipients often took the initiative to have correspondence inscribed and displayed on stone. So, for example, the letters of Philip V to Larissa regarding new citizens contain no provisions ordering their terms to be inscribed on stone. Instructions for publication appear only in a decree enacted by the Larissans themselves and inscribed below a second letter (*IG* IX.2 517 = *SIG*³ 543). That decree prescribes that both letters of Philip, along with two decrees of the Larissans, should be displayed on two *stelai* set up in different sanctuaries (lines 41–6). Similarly, the letter of Laodike to Iasos establishing an endowment for dowries for the daughters of poor citizens includes no provision ordering its inscribing. The letter is followed on the stone by a decree of Iasos granting honours to both Antiochos and Laodike; its closing sections are missing, but it is not too risky too assume that they carried instructions ordering publication of both the decree and Laodike's letter.[45]

Several motives will have compelled Greek communities to publish these epistolary orders, however much they may have infringed their autonomy.[46] Many of the provisions conveyed in royal letters impacted their political, religious, or economic affairs, in the same way as their own laws and decrees, and that importance made them deserving of permanent display and visibility. Inscribing royal letters on stone made their provisions accessible to those most affected by them. In some instances publication of letters also provided visible, tangible proof that a city or individual had received the benefits, material or otherwise, that they claimed to have received. But the form of the royal letter itself may also have played some role in the decision to publish individual ones on stone. Philip and Alexander are said to have governed the Greek cities through *diagrammata*, royal edicts or ordinances (Diod. 18.56.3); by the early third century Hellenistic kings appear to have preferred to govern and interact with Greek cities principally through letters. Letters were less oppressive than the royal edict or *diagramma*, and their use by Hellenistic monarchs allowed Greeks to act as if the orders they received were part of an exchange and dialogue, as opposed to orders issued from on high.[47]

Other factors also contributed to the publication of royal correspondence. A letter of Antiochos III dating from 193 and surviving in several copies calls for the appointment of priestesses for the cult of Laodike throughout the kingdom (Welles 1934, no. 36). Antiochos also instructs the recipients to publish copies of his letter on *stelai* "in the most conspicuous places, so that both now and in the future our esteem toward our sister in these matters may be visible to all" (lines 33–8). Publication, that is, was intended not only to preserve a record of his decision to create a new office, but also to advertise his goodwill to his sister; the inscription was an in-

45 *IIasos* 4, lines 1–32 (letter of Laodike); *IIasos* 4, lines 33–50 (decree of Iasos).

46 See also Ceccarelli 2005a: 363, noting that decisions to publish letters must be understood in the context of the "epigraphical habit" of Greek cities.

47 See Ma 1999: esp. 179–242 for further elaboration of these points.

strument to exhibit his generosity just as much as her piety or the establishment of a new cult office. A similar desire for self-promotion is suggested by a petition of the priests of Isis at Philae in Egypt (*IPhilae* 19). They wrote to Ptolemy VIII and the queens Kleopatra II and III in the second half of the second century to request relief from government officials who were exploiting their sanctuary for its hospitality. But they also requested permission to set up a *stele* that would record the generosity of the rulers, so that "your kindness would remain in memory for all time" (lines 39–40). The statement appeals to the royal family's desire for eternal commemoration of their beneficence, so publication of the letters served not only to publicize Ptolemy's decision to grant the priests their request, but also to provide physical and lasting reminder of the king's generosity and goodwill.

Thus far I have focused on the letters sent by Hellenistic rulers, but it will be useful to conclude with some final observations on another feature of epistolary practice in the Hellenistic period, namely the growing use of letters by Greek cities. Greeks *poleis* and their officials had communicated with one another and with foreign states with letters in the classical period, but the role of official letters was limited in *polis* affairs and they never attained anywhere near the political significance of their inscribed, royal counterparts of the Hellenistic period. During the third century, however, letters sent by *poleis* or their officials begin to appear in Greek inscriptions.[48] It is tempting to attribute this development to the influence of royal correspondence, and some of the letters sent and inscribed by Greek *poleis* share features with those dispatched by kings, dynasts, and their agents. But *polis* letters are more limited in scope. Unlike royal letters, which transmit announcements and decisions with a potentially significant impact on the lives of their recipients, *polis* letters generally fail to convey information of much substance or import. Many function as simple covering letters used to introduce other documents, usually decrees, whose contents recorded decisions of real importance.

This type is well illustrated in an inscription of the middle of the third century from Delos. Its text begins with a letter from the *polis* of Thessalonike addressed to the council and *demos* of the Delians (*IG* XI.4 1053 = Hatzopoulos 1996, II, no. 50). It relates that Boulon, an envoy from Delos, had delivered to the Thessalonikans decrees in which the Delians honoured Admetos son of Bokros of Thessalonike, and that he had also reported the contents of those decrees to the city's assembly. The letter continues by stating that the citizens of Thessalonike welcomed what the Delians had decided, and that they were appending a copy of their own decree in which they granted everything requested by the Delians. The letter supplies no clues as to the nature of those requests; they are, however, made clear in the text of the decree that follows. It

48 For a more detailed discussion of *polis* letters in the Hellenistic period see Ceccarelli 2005a: 363–8.

relates that, among other things, the Thessalonikans had agreed to make space in their agora for one of two statues voted by the Delians for Admetos.

A similar covering letter appears in an inscription recording an arbitration award made by the Milesians in a land dispute involving Sparta and Messene and published at Olympia (*IvO* 52, lines 29–40). The letter is addressed to the magistrates of Elis from the *prytaneis* and other officials of Miletos. It was written in response to a Messenian request that a copy of the arbitration award, which went in their favour, be sent to Olympia for publication, and it informs the Elians that a sealed copy of the award is attached to the letter. Here too the letter conveys no meaningful information and simply explains how the arbitration award found its way to Olympia. An even shorter cover letter appears in an inscription from Delphi dating from the early first century (*FDelph* 3.2.48). It is addressed from the archons of Delphi to the *technitai* of Dionysos at Athens, and it states simply that a copy of their reply to the *technitai* is attached below, "so that you may know it" (lines 1–2). The reply, which is cast in the form of a decree, follows and specifies the rights and privileges awarded to the Dionysiac artisans.

Some inscribed letters, however, do more than introduce or accompany other documents. These convey decisions of individual *poleis* and point to the more substantive usage of the epistolary form familiar from contemporary royal letters. One group comes from Teos and includes several letters recording grants of *asylia*. Greek *poleis* typically awarded *asylia*, inviolability, to sanctuaries and other cities through decrees, and inscriptions from Teos and other cities record numerous enactments of this sort (Rigsby 1996). Kings, however, typically made such grants via letters.[49] But a small number of cities from Crete also recognized Teian *asylia* through letters. One from the Cretan city of Kydonia addresses itself to the council and *demos* of the Teians and starts by explaining that it was written in reply to a Teian embassy that brought a decree, one that presumably requested the award of *asylia* (Rigsby 1996, no. 139). There follows praise of the ambassadors and then the Kydonian response announcing their grant. The text retains its letter format throughout and concludes with the word "farewell". Letters awarding *asylia* to Teos from other Cretan cities follow a similar pattern. [50] Still other Cretan *poleis* used letters to report honors granted to foreign benefactors or to request just treatment of their citizens.[51]

How and why these *poleis* adopted the letter as a means of interstate communication cannot be readily explained, but whatever the reasons, instances of *polis* letters

49 For a royal grant of *asylia* to Teos see Rigsby 1996, no. 135; cf. also royal grants of *asylia* to other cities expressed in letters (Rigsby 1996, nos. 7,8,9,10, etc.).

50 Rigsby 1996: no. 137 (Polyrrhenia); 141 (Sybrita); 144 (Hierpytna); 154 (Aptera).

51 *IC* II xvi 2 (Knossians to Coans) and *IC* IV168 (Gortynians to Coans) both record honors granted to a Coan doctor for his services. In *IC* II v 19 (=*SIG*[3] 622B), the *kosmoi* and *polis* of Axos wrote to the Aitolians, with whom they had shared citizenship, asking that the descendants of an Axian citizen be granted all the rights due to him.

illustrate that the epistolary form was not incompatible with *polis* government. An official letter could record and disseminate the political decision of a community in much the same way as a decree. It is tempting to see in the adoption of the letter form by Hellenistic *poleis* a final stage in development of the letter as a tool for administrative and political communication. From its earliest uses in the fifth century as a medium for receiving communications from kings or state officials stationed abroad, the functions of the letter had expanded so that now, in the Hellenistic period, they were suited for decisions and communications of far greater political weight. The letter was no longer a strictly personal form of communication but could be used and exploited both by kings and cities as they carried out their business.

But caution is in order. The cities that sent and published the surviving letters were geographically limited in scope; virtually all of them are found on the island of Crete. They were also characterized by governments in which state officials were extremely powerful and less democratic than many of their counterparts.[52] More important, some *polis* letters simply repeat the substance of decrees that had been enacted by their senders. One letter from Polyrrhenia on Crete to Teos describes a Teian embassy that had visited the city and then announces that the *kosmoi* and the *polis* itself had decreed to give that embassy an answer; they had decided to declare the city of Teos and its territory sacred and inviolable (Rigsby 1996, no. 137, lines 7–11). The letter in this case serves as a simple tool for transmitting the decision of the *polis* that had taken the form of a decree; it differs from a covering letter only insofar as it incorporates the decree into its text, as opposed to introducing it as a separate document. The distinction is inconsequential.

The form and nature of the *polis* letters of the Hellenistic period merit more attention, but their limited geographical scope and their apparent function as covering letters for decisions enacted as decrees raise some doubts about the compatibility of the letter format with *polis* society. The *polis* had gradually expanded the role of letters for communicating state business over the course of its history, but even in the Hellenistic period epistolary communications had their limits. Hellenistic monarchs eventually found the letter format a useful medium for conducting business with Greek *poleis*, and Greek cities were willing to accept and even advertise these epistolary communications, as their frequent publication on stone show, perhaps because the letter form was far less autocratic than the simple royal order or edict. Some Hellenistic cities also sought to expand the epistolary form to communicate with state officials and other *poleis*, but that experiment was not widespread. Why that was cannot be determined, but it may be that the associations of the letter with monarchy and autocratic government were too challenging to overcome.

52 See Ceccarelli 2005a: 363–5; note that Spartan letters are also known in the Hellenistic period (Ceccarelli 2005a: 365–8).

Briefe als Rechtsurkunden
Zu einigen aramäischen Briefen des Aršames

Ingo Kottsieper (Göttingen/Münster)

Das trockene Klima Ägyptens hat nicht nur eine große Zahl ägyptischer Dokumente bewahrt, sondern auch ein umfangreiches Korpus aramäischer Zeugnisse aus der Perserzeit, darunter viele Briefe.[1] Ihre formale Gestaltung zeigt beträchtliche Variationsmöglichkeiten, wobei die gewählten Formelemente in Korrelation zum Zweck des Schreibens und zum sozialen Status des Absenders und Adressaten stehen.[2]

Eine eigenständige Gruppe dieser Briefe bilden die Schreiben des Satrapen Aršames (A6.2–13), die durchweg auf Leder geschrieben wurden. Die einzige Ausnahme ist der Papyrusbrief A6.2. Dieser Unterschied im Schreibmaterial spiegelt die verschiedenen Abfassungsorte der Briefe wider: A6.2, eine Anweisung für die Reparatur eines Bootes, wurde in Ägypten geschrieben, wo Aršames nur zeitweise anwesend war, während die anderen Briefe aus Babylonien (oder Susa; Driver 1954: 5–6) stammen, wo sich Aršames normalerweise aufhielt, Papyrus als Schreibstoff aber ungebräuchlich war (Kottsieper 2004: 330).

Die nicht aus Ägypten stammenden Briefe lassen sich wiederum in zwei Gruppen teilen. So enden die Briefe A6.8–13 jeweils mit der Notiz *PN_1 yd' ṭ'm' znh PN_2 spr'* „PN_1 kennt diese Anordnung. PN_2 ist der ‚Schreiber'", während in A6.3–7 diese Angaben fehlen. Dagegen weist diese Gruppe nach der in allen Briefen des Aršames obligatorischen Adresszeile *mn 'ršm 'l PN* „Von Aršames an PN" noch die Grußformel *šlm wšrrt šgy' hwšrt lk* „Viele (Wünsche für) Wohlergehen und Bestand habe ich (hiermit) dir gesandt", die in A6.8–13 nicht begegnet.

Der „ägyptische" Brief des Aršames (A6.2) bietet eine Variante zur Gruppe der Briefe ohne Grußformel, aber mit der Angabe zweier am Vorgang beteiligter Personen am Ende des Briefes. So fehlt auch hier die Grußformel. Dafür findet sich in Z. 23 die zweiteilige Aussage *'nny spr' b'l ṭ'm nbw'qb ktb* „'Anani, der Schreiber,

1 Die heutige Standardausgabe der Texte wurde von B. Porten und A. Yardeni (1986–1999 = TAD A-D) vorgelegt. Für die Texte vgl. jetzt auch Schwiderski 2004. Im Folgenden werden die Texte nach TAD nur unter Angabe des Bandes (A-D) und der Textnummer zitiert. Die auf Papyrus oder Leder geschriebenen Briefe sind in TAD A (vgl. auch in D, S. 150) zusammengestellt, dazu kommen in D 1–32 noch fragmentarisch erhaltene Briefstücke. Auf Ostraka geschriebene Briefe sind in D 7.1–57 gesammelt; weitere Briefe auf Tonscherben finden sich jetzt auch in der Edition der Sammlung von Clermont-Ganneau, Lozachmeur 2006.

2 Vgl. die detaillierte Analyse bei Schwiderski 2000: 91–240.

als/ist ein ‚Herr der Anordnung'. Nabuʿaqab hat geschrieben/schreiben lassen".[3] Von besonderer Bedeutung ist, dass beide Teile jeweils von einer anderen Hand stammen.[4] Damit liegt die Annahme nahe, dass es sich bei diesen beiden Zusätzen um Autographen der jeweils genannten Personen handelt, die damit den Inhalt des Schreibens gegengezeichnet haben.

Einige Beobachtungen und pragmatische Überlegungen bestätigen diese Annahme:

1. Die beiden Zusätze folgen ohne Absatz in der letzten Zeile des eigentlichen Brieftextes (Z. 23) und erscheinen somit einerseits als direkte Fortsetzung des Briefkorpus, andererseits grenzen sie den eigentlichen Text nach hinten hin ab.
2. Die Außenadresse ist in derselben Handschrift wie der Haupttext des Briefes geschrieben worden, d.h. der Schreiber selber hat den Brief nach seiner Fertigstellung gefaltet und adressiert.[5]
3. Unter der eigentlichen Adresszeile (Z. 27: *mn ʾršm zy bmṣ[ryn ʿl wḥprʿmḥy]* „Von Aršames, der in Ägy[pten (weilt), an Waḥpremaḥi.]") findet sich hier eine weitere Zeile (28) in derselben Handschrift, die den „Schreiber" Nabuʿaqab und das Ausstellungsdatum verzeichnet: *nbwʿqb sprʾ b XIII [l]ṭbt šnt XII dryw[hwš mlkʾ]* „Nabuʿaqab, der ‚Schreiber'. Am 13[.]Tebet des 12. Jahres des [Königs] Dari[us]".
4. In Z. 24–25 folgen nach einem deutlichen Zeilenumbruch[6] auf den Brief zwei weitere Notizen: Eine längere aramäische, deren Handschrift weder dem Brieftext noch den Zusätzen in Z. 23 entspricht, und in Z. 25 nur durch ein kleines *vacat* getrennt die demotische Notiz *sẖ Sꜣ-sbk* „Sasobek hat geschrieben". Da die zum Teil unlesbare aramäische Notiz mit dem Namen des Adressaten, Waḥpremaḥi, beginnt und in Z. 25 mit *kzy šym ṭʿm xxxl ktb* endet, was möglicherweise mit „wie es als Anordnung bestimmt ist. XXX hat geschrieben" zu

3 Vgl. dazu weiter unten.

4 Vgl. schon Sachau 1911: 48; Cowley 1923: 97; die Annahme, dass *ʿnny sprʾ bʿl ṭʿm* von derselben Hand stamme wie der Haupttext und nur *nbwʿqb ktb* von einer anderen (so Arnold 1912: 24–5; Schwiderski 2000: 207, vgl. auch 188.190; auch Porten 1996: 121, Anm. 74–5 hält diese offenkundig für möglich) ist offenkundig falsch, wenn auch die Abzeichnung von A. Yardeni in TAD A (S. 97) auf den ersten Blick diesen Eindruck erweckt. Die ausgezeichneten, bei Sachau als Pl. 8–9 zu findenden Aufnahmen zeigen deutliche Unterschiede in der Schrift: Unübersehbar ist, dass die ʿAnani-Notiz mit einem anderen Stift und/oder Stifthaltung geschrieben wurde, was sich darin ausdrückt, dass insbesondere die schräg von oben rechts nach unten links verlaufenden Striche deutlich schmaler ausfallen. So sind die linken Aufstriche der *n*'s in *ʿnny* im Gegensatz zu den entsprechenden Strichen in den *n*'s des Haupttextes nur sehr schmale Striche, deren Ansatz an dem Hauptstrich unübersehbar ist und die deutlich höher hinauf ragen, als es sonst meist der Fall ist. Das *y* ist merkwürdig weit von *ʿnn* abgesetzt, das *r* von *sprʾ* besteht nur aus sehr dünnen Strichen. Schließlich ist das *ṭ* von *ṭʿm* nahezu 50% breiter als die übrigen *ṭ*'s in diesem Text und auch das *m* desselben Wortes fällt nahezu um 50% höher aus, ist aber wiederum nur mit sehr mageren Strichen geschrieben.

5 Zu diesem Vorgang vgl. Porten 1980: 43, 47–8.

6 Z. 23 endet knapp 4 cm vor dem eigentlichen Zeilenende.

> übersetzen ist, dürfte hier eine Ausführungsnotiz von Seiten des Adressaten vorliegen, die wahrscheinlich zum Inhalt hat, dass eine entsprechende Anweisung „wie es als Anordnung bestimmt ist“ an die ägpytischen Schiffsbauer weitergeleitet wurde. Offenkundig wurde diese Anweisung entsprechend in Demotisch verfasst und von Sasobek niedergeschrieben, der dies durch seine eigenhändige Notiz bestätigt. Entsprechend dürfte in „XXX hat geschrieben“ die Nennung desjenigen zu sehen sein, der die aramäische Bearbeitungsnotiz verfasst hat, die deutlich durch einen Zeilenumbruch vom vorangehenden Text abgesetzt ist.[7]

Diese Beobachtungen lassen folgende Schlüsse zu: Die Tatsache, dass die Zusätze in Z. 23 unmittelbar an den eigentlichen Brieftext anschließen und von anderen Händen stammen als die graphisch deutlich abgesetzte Ausführungsnotiz in Z. 24–25 lässt erkennen, dass sie nicht zu der Ausführungsnotiz gehören, sondern offenkundig schon bei der Abfassung des Briefes und vor seiner Adressierung eingefügt wurden. Da die Schrift der äußeren Adressierung sich in keiner Weise von der des Haupttextes unterscheidet, hat sie derselbe Schreiber mit derselben Feder und Tinte angebracht, was bedeutet, dass der Brief wohl unmittelbar nach seiner Abfassung auch für den Versand fertiggemacht wurde. So wird man davon ausgehen können, dass die beiden Schreiber der Zusätze in Z. 23 bei der Abfassung des Briefes zugegen waren oder ihnen das Schriftstück direkt danach zur Gegenzeichnung vorgelegt worden ist.

Dies bedeutet aber, dass mit *nbwʿqb ktb* nicht gemeint sein kann, dass Nabuʿaqab der Schreiber des Briefes war[8] – warum sollte eine andere (!) Person diese Information, die nebenbei bei einem Brief auch recht unüblich wäre, zu diesem Zeitpunkt, an dem der Schreiber ja noch zugegen war oder nach dem er unmittelbar noch einmal als Schreiber der Adresse tätig wurde, eigenhändig nachgetragen haben?[9] Dazu kommt,

7 Dies bleibt jedoch angesichts des unklaren Textes nur eine Vermutung. Dagegen vermutet Cowley (1923: 97) Waḥpremaḥi in dem Schreiber der Notiz (vgl. auch Grelot 1972: 294), während Porten (1968: 57) auch einen Sekretär des Waḥpremaḥi für möglich hält; vgl. auch die zurückhaltenden Erwägungen bei Sachau 1911: 49.

8 So die meisten Bearbeiter, vgl. Sachau 1911: 48; Grelot 1972: 293; Porten 1968: 56; TAD; dagegen kritisch Cowley 1923: 97: „If this means that he was the copying clerk, it is strange, as the hand is again different“.

9 Schwiderski (2000: 207) argumentiert, dass dies nötig geworden sei, da „möglicherweise … durch die doppelte Verwendung von ספרא, in Z. 23 bezogen auf ʿAnanja sowie in Z. 28 (nach außen hin sichtbarer Teil) bezogen auf Nabuʿaqab, auch für den damaligen Kontext eine gewisse Uneindeutigkeit entstanden, die dann durch die Hinzufügung des eindeutigen כתב (‚er schrieb <diesen Brief>‘) beseitigt wurde“. Abgesehen davon, dass eine Unklarheit über die Person des aktuellen Schreibers in einem Brief niemanden gestört hätte, da solche Informationen normalerweise sowieso nicht geboten wurden, übersieht Schwiderski hier dreierlei: a) *spr* „Schreiber“ ist eine Amtsbezeichnung und hat nichts damit zu tun, ob eine als *sprʾ* bezeichnete Person auch der Schreibende war. Dass entsprechend in einem Schreiben gleich mehrere „Schreiber“ erwähnt werden, würde keinen Adressaten verwirren – man vergleich allein A6.1, einem Schreiben, das unter anderem von den Schreibern (pl.!) zweier

dass entsprechende Schreibernotizen, die aber nur in Rechtstexten üblich sind, sonst stets ausdrücklich auch das Schreiben mit *spr' zk/znh* anführen.[10]

Damit stellt sich die Frage, was mit *ktb* in der Phrase *nbw'qb ktb* gemeint sein kann. Arnold (1912: 25) hat hierzu unter zurückhaltender Zustimmung von Cowley (1923: 97) die ebenfalls eigenhändige Zeugenangabe *ktb mḥsyh bkᵖy | npšh* „Machseja hat es mit seiner eigenen Hand geschrieben" (B2.7.17–18) verglichen. Wenn diese Deutung auch durchaus möglich ist, so bliebe bei ihr im Gegensatz zu ʿAnani (s.u.) die eigentliche Funktion Nabuʿaqabs unklar, in der er den Brief eigenhändig unterzeichnet.

Ein Blick in die Rechtsurkunden eröffnet aber eine andere Deutungsmöglichkeit: *ktb* bezeichnet dort einerseits in der Formel *ktb PN spr' zk/znh* das konkrete Schreiben des Dokuments, begegnet aber in den Außenaufschriften derselben Dokumente in der Formel *spr X zy ktb* PN_1 *l*PN_2 in der Konnotation „ausfertigen, schreiben lassen": „Urkunde über X, die PN_1 für PN_2 hat schreiben lassen". Wenn nun Nabuʿaqab in der Adressierung als „Schreiber" (*spr*) bezeichnet wird und in einer anderen – und wohl eigener – Handschrift als der, die den Brief zu Papyrus gebracht hat, als der bezeichnet wird, der „geschrieben hat", so zeigt sich hier die Funktion eines „Schreibers": Er war offenkundig für die Abfassung bzw. Formulierung solcher Schreiben zuständig, was aber nicht unbedingt bedeuten muss, dass er sie auch eigenhändig schrieb. Damit zeichnete er als derjenige, der das Schreiben schreiben ließ – d. h. wohl diktierte oder seine Formulierungen vorgab –, und nicht als der eigentlich Schreibende für den Inhalt des Schreibens verantwortlich.

Das Amt des Schreibers umfasste aber nicht nur die Abfassung solcher Schreiben. So wird mit ʿAnani vorher ein anderer Schreiber genannt, dessen Funktion im vorliegenden Fall aber dann ebenso eindeutig bestimmt wird, wie die des „Schreibers" Nabuʿaqab: ʿAnani fungiert hier als ein „‚Herr' einer Anordnung". Die Tatsache, dass *bʿl ṭʿm* undeterminiert ist, zeigt, dass damit keine feststehende Amts-, sondern eine Funktionsbezeichnung vorliegt.[11] *bʿl ṭʿm* ist also keine Apposition zu

Provinzen stammt. b) Wie oben ausgeführt, wurde die Erwähnung des „Schreibers" Nabuʿaqab in Z. 28 wohl erst bei der Aufrollung des Briefes vom Schreiber selbst hinzugefügt (und war danach nicht sichtbar!) – die Unklarheit hätte sich, wenn überhaupt, also erst nach dem Öffnen des Briefes ergeben können. Es spricht aber nichts dafür, dass erst die Adressaten die Notiz in Z. 23 nachgetragen haben. c) Da, wie auch Schwiderski annimmt, der „Schreiber" ʿAnani mit einer eindeutigen anderen Funktionsbezeichnung im Hinblick auf diesen Brief versehen wird (s.u.), würde man kaum auf den Gedanken kommen, dass er hier auch als Schreibender angeführt wird. Nabuʿaqab wird aber im Adressbereich nur als „Schreiber" bezeichnet und wäre damit der einzige Kandidat für denjenigen, der den Brief realiter geschrieben hat. Es ist also kein Grund zu erkennen, warum eine zweite Person in diesem Schreiben an dieser Stelle die Information nachgetragen haben sollte, dass Nabuʿaqab der Schreibende gewesen war.

10 Z.B. B1.1.17; B2.1.15; B2.2.16–7; B2.3.25; B2.4.16; B2.6.37; B2.7.16–7; B2.8.11; B2.9.16.

11 Das hat offenbar schon Cowley (1923) gesehen, der entsprechend den Ausdruck recht frei mit

ʿAnani, sondern entweder Prädikat ("ʿAnani ist ein ‚Herr' der Anordnung") oder hat adverbial-funktionale Bedeutung in einem elliptischen Satz ("ʿAnani (unterzeichnet) als ein ‚Herr der Anordnung'").

Das Fehlen der Determination zeigt aber noch mehr. Offensichtlich konnte es in einem solchen Kontext nicht nur einen, sondern mehrere „Herren der Anordnung" geben – andernfalls wäre der „Herr der Anordnung" ja sachlich determiniert (es gibt nur einen!) und man würde dann auch bei einer funktionalen Aussage die determinierte Form *bʿl ṭʿmʾ* „der Herr der Anordnung" oder sogar *bʿl ṭʿmʾ znh* „der Herr dieser Anordnung" erwarten. Dies erhellt auch eine neubabylonische Urkunde (BM 74554) aus dem Jahr 486 v. Chr., in der die Ausgabe von Getreide auf Geheiß des Satrapen von Babylon und Transeuphratene und zweier Beamter beurkundet wird, die als LÚ *si-pi-ri* EN *ṭè-e-mu* auftreten. Schon der Erstherausgeber des Textes verwies auf die hier behandelten Briefe des Aršames: „The organization implicit in the Babylonian text can be understood as a counterpart of the situation found in the Arsames correspondence and the Elephantine documents. The men entitled 'scribe' and 'chancellor' were supervisors in the satrap's administrative and executive services" (Stolper 1989: 300). Es dürfte aber wohl kaum zu bezweifeln sein, dass die Phrase *PN* LÚ *si-pi-ri* EN *ṭè-e-mu* ohne verbindendes *u/ù* analog zu *PN sprʾ* (= LÚ *si-pi-ri*) *bʿl ṭʿm* (= EN *ṭè-e-mu*) zu verstehen ist. Mithin bringt der Text zum Ausdruck, dass die in ihm dokumentierte Ausgabe von Getreide nicht nur „gemäß der Anweisung des Gouverneurs von Babylon und Transeuphratene" durchgeführt worden ist, sondern dies auch eine Anweisung „des ‚Schreibers' Liblut̩, Bruder des Adadibni, als[12] ein ‚Herr der Anordnung', und des ‚Schreibers' Gadalama, Sohn des Banna-Ea, als ein ‚Herr der Anordnung'" gewesen war. Der Text darf damit als Beleg dafür gelten, dass bei einem solchen Verwaltungsakt mehrere „Schreiber" involviert sein konnten und dass offenkundig Verwaltungsbeamte, die mit einem solchen Vorgang befasst waren, mit der Funktionsbezeichnung *bʿl ṭʿm* bezeichnet wurden, die mithin keinen Amtstitel darstellt.[13] Dem entspricht, dass auch die übrigen (neuassyrischen

„drafted the order" (91) übersetzt und dazu erklärt: „ ‚author of the order'. He drew it up for approval by Arsames …". (93); vgl. auch Schwiderski 2000: 190.

12 Die jeweils prädikative Übersetzung mit „<ist>" bei Schwiderski (2000: 192) sprengt das Satzgefüge und ist daher nicht überzeugend.

13 Zu diesem Ergebnis kommt, wenn auch nicht auf exakt demselben Weg, auch Schwiderski 2000: 190–3, 358; vgl. auch Anm. 11. Die ältere Forschung nahm dagegen ausgehend von Esra 4.8–9,17 in *bʿl ṭʿm* grundsätzlich einen Amtstitel an (vgl. z.B. Sachau 1911: 49; Porten 1968: 55–8, dort in Anm. 108 weitere Vorschläge, welches Amt hier gemeint sein könne; Dion 1982: 79), was dann z.B. auch bei Stolper (1989: 299–300) und Heltzer (1992: 60) zu Überlegungen führten, wo dieses Amt in der Verwaltungshierarchie einzuordnen wäre. Man sollte aber mit Schwiderski (2000: 358) den umgekehrten Weg gehen: Ausgehend von den Primärquellen der erhaltenen Briefe und Dokumente dürfte dann in der Sekundärquelle Esra 4 der undeterminierte Funktionsbegriff *bʿl ṭʿm* aus der achämenidischen Verwaltungssprache auch in den Erzähltext übernommen worden sein.

und babylonischen) Belege für die akkadische Entprechung *bēl ṭēmu* damit einen in einer Sache Beauftragten oder mit den Interessen oder Belangen eines anderen Befassten bezeichnen, den Ausdruck aber nicht als Amtstitel belegen.[14]

Da nun derjenige, der (neben anderen) mit einer Anordnung befasst ist, natürlich diese kennt, entspricht die Bezeichnung ʿAnanis als *bʿl ṭʿm* „Herr der Anordnung" sachlich völlig der Aussage in den „babylonischen" Briefen des Arsames, dass ein namentlich genannter Beamter „diese Anordnung kennt". Und wenn von der zweiten Person dann jeweils ausgesagt wird, dass sie „der Schreiber" war, womit *sprʾ* hier als Prädikat und nicht, wie bei ʿAnani, als appositionelle Titelangabe begegnet, so entspricht dies wohl der Tätigkeit des „Schreibers" Nabuʿaqab, der für die Abfassung des Briefes zuständig war.[15]

Zu diesen Briefen des Aršames ist der demotische Brief P.Berlin inv. 13540 aus dem Jahr 492 v. Chr. als eine weitere Parallele zu stellen. Dieses Schreiben des Satrapen Pherendates an die Chnum-Priesterschaft über die Einsetzung eines Lesonis ist, wie Vleeming (1981) und Hughes (1984: 77–84) nachgewiesen haben, „a literal translation from an Aramaic original draft" (Hughes 1984: 77).[16] An seinem Ende findet sich in Z. 8f. folgende Notiz: „Satibara ke|nnt diesen Befehl. Peftuauneit ist es, der diesen Brief geschrieben hat. Geschrieben von Wahibre im Jahr 20, 29. Chojak". Abgesehen von der Schreibernotiz über Wahibre, die sich aber eindeutig auf den Schreiber des demotischen Teils bezieht (Hughes 1984: 83–4) entspricht dieser Schluss nahezu exakt den Angaben der aramäischen Briefe. So ist die Notiz über Satibara „a precise translation" (Hughes 1984: 83) von *ydʿ ṭʿmʾ znh*. Wenn man auch fragen darf, ob die Aussage über Peftuauneit eine exakte Parallele zu dem prädikativen *sprʾ* in den „babylonischen" Briefen des Aršames,[17] eine freiere Interpretation der *ktb*-Aussage wie in B6.2 oder aber Zeuge einer weiteren Variante dieser Aussage ist, so ist es doch deutlich, dass hier in jedem Fall die entsprechende

14 Vgl. Stolper 1989: 300–2; CAD Ṭ, 97a. Dies trifft wohl auch für CT 53 391.6 (= SAA XVI 6.6; Luukko & Van Buylaere 2002: 8) zu, auch wenn dort mit EN *ṭe-e-[mì-ia* von einem „particular official in permanent service" (Stolper 1989: 301) die Rede ist. Dieser wird aber dort nicht mit Titel genannt, sondern im Kontext seiner Funktion, sich um die Angelegenheit des Absenders zu kümmern, in der er eben auch seine Briefe öffnete. Dass *bʿl ṭʿm* als *Amtstitel* nicht dem akkadischen Gebrauch von *bēl ṭēmu* entsprechen würde, hat auch schon Kaufman (1974: 109 Anm. 390) betont.

15 Natürlich konnte ein solcher „Schreiber" das Schreiben auch selber schreiben. Möglicherweise war dies bei den „babylonischen" Briefen des Aršames der Fall, wofür die Beobachtung sprechen könnte, dass die unterschiedliche Handschrift von A6.8 einerseits und A6.9–13 andererseits mit den unterschiedlichen „Schreiber"-Angaben in diesen Texten (A6.8: ʾAḥpepi :: AA6.9–13: Rašta) korrelieren. Aber es ist auch nicht auszuschließen, dass den „Schreibern" jeweils eine Hilfskraft zugeordnet war, die die eigentliche Schreibarbeit verrichteten.

16 Der Text wurde von Spiegelberg (1928: 605–6) publiziert und ist jetzt auch in der Demotischen Textdatenbank der Akademie für Sprache und Literatur über das Portal „Thesaurus Linguae Aegyptiae" der Berlin-Brandenburgischen Akademie der Wissenschaften (http://aaew.bbaw.de/tla/index.html) online zugänglich. Die hier gebotene Übersetzung lehnt sich an die dort gegebene an.

17 So Hughes 1984: 83; dafür spricht die Nominalisierung der Aussage mit determiniertem Partizip.

Aussage über den Schreiber vorliegt, der für die konkrete Abfassung des Schreibens zuständig ist. Angesichts dieser Parallelen ist es nicht verwunderlich, dass auch dieser Brief ohne Grußformel am Beginn abgefasst wurde.

Dass sich somit eine Parallele zu diesen Formelementen in einigen Briefen des Aršames schon aus der Zeit des Pherendates finden lässt und dass diese Formelemente offenkundig in ihrer konkreten Ausformung zwischen der babylonischen und ägyptischen Kanzlei des Aršames variieren konnten, zeigt, dass dies keine lokale Eigenart einer bestimmten Kanzleitradition ist, sondern die besprochenen Elemente allgemein zu entsprechenden Briefen eines Satrapen gehören. Dies beantwortet aber noch nicht die Frage nach ihrer genauen Funktion. Diese erhellt sich aber aus einem Vergleich mit den Schreiben des Aršames, die diese Elemente nicht aufweisen. Es handelt sich dabei um die „babylonischen" Briefe auf Leder A6.3–5 und A6.7,[18] von denen A6.3 und A6.5 sicher, A6.4 wahrscheinlich[19] an Artavant, A6.7 aber an Artahant adressiert sind.[20] All diesen Briefen ist nicht nur das Fehlen der Namensnennungen am Ende gemeinsam, sondern sie weisen alle am Anfang die oben erwähnte Grußformel auf, die ihrerseits in der anderen Gruppe fehlt. Von besonderer Bedeutung ist dabei, dass die Handschrift von A6.3–4 völlig der von A6.8 entspricht und mithin von demselben Schreiber (Aḥpepi?, vgl. Anm. 15) und aus derselben Kanzlei stammen. Dies belegt wiederum, dass die Wahl der Formelemente weder mit einer speziellen Kanzlei- noch mit einer besonderen Schreibertradition korreliert und von daher erklärt werden könnte.

A6.4 informiert seinen Adressaten, dass dem Psamšek, dem Beauftragten des Aršames für dessen ägyptische Domänen, ein früheres Lehen seines Vaters auf Beschluss des Königs und Aršames übertragen worden war und dementsprechend Psamšek ermächtigt sein soll, das Lehen dort in Ägypten zu übernehmen (Z. 4: *psmšk brh šlyṭ yhwy lmnšʾ dšnʾ zky tmh bm[ṣ]ryn*).

A6.3 und A6.5 fordern Artavant auf, in jeweils einem zu Beginn der Briefe geschilderten Fall eine bestimmte Anordnung (*ṭʿm*) ergehen zu lassen (*ʾnt šm ṭʿm*, A6.3.7; A6.5.3). Dabei handelt es sich in A6.3 um einen Rechtsfall zwischen dem schon erwähnten Psamšek und den früheren Bediensteten seines Vaters, die offenkundig die Gelegenheit des Wechsels zu dessen Sohn nutzten, diesen zu berauben und zu fliehen. Diesen Fall will Psamšek vor Artavant mit dem Ziel bringen, eine Bestrafung als Anordnung durchzusetzen, wofür Psamšek um Beistand bei seinem

18 A6.6 ist zu zerstört, um hier behandelt zu werden.

19 Vom Namen des Adressaten ist in A6.4.1 nur *ʾr[xxx]t* erhalten. Da der Brief wie A6.3 über eine Angelegenheit des Psamšek, des Sohnes des ʿAḥḥapi, handelt, ist eine Identifizierung des Adressaten mit Artavant (*ʾrtwnt*), die schon Driver (1954: 13) vorgeschlagen hat, gut möglich. Dafür spricht auch, dass die Lesung *ʾrtwnt* perfekt zu der Lücke passt, während die Lesung *ʾrthnt*, die Driver auch nicht ausschließen wollte, deutlich zu lang wäre.

20 Driver (1954: 11.18 + 1957: 38.51) geht davon aus, dass Artahant lediglich eine andere Schreibung für Artavant und damit die Adressaten letztlich identisch sind.

Herrn Aršames gebeten hat. So zitiert das Schreiben in Z. 5–6 ein entsprechendes Schreiben des Psamšek an Aršames mit den Worten: „Jetzt: wenn es meinem Herrn gefällt, so möge an Artavant gesandt werden, [dass (hinsichtlich) jener Bediensteten, die] | ich vor ihn bringen werde, die Leibesstrafe, die ich für sie als Anordnung verfüge, an ihnen vollstreckt wird".[21] *ṭʿm* bezeichnet hier also eine juridische Strafanordnung, die von dem Herrn der Bediensteten zwar angeordnet, deren Vollstreckung aber offenkundig noch der offiziellen Ratifizierung durch die lokal zuständige Behörde bedarf, wobei diese Ratifizierung ebenfalls ein *ṭʿm* ist: „Verfüge als Anordnung über die Leibesstrafe, die Psamšek für sie als Anordnung zur Vollstreckung verfügt, (dass) diese an ihnen vollstreckt werde". (Z. 7–8)[22] Aršames nutzt zwar hier seine Macht als Satrap, um in ein schwebendes Verfahren einzugreifen, der eigentliche juridische Akt wird aber von Artavant durchgeführt.

Auch in A6.5 fordert Aršames Artavant dazu auf, eine Anordnung zu verfügen (Z. 3: *ʾnt šm ṭ[ʿ]m*), aber der Text ist so stark beschädigt, dass der Kontext nicht deutlich wird.

Aber auch mit A6.7 greift Aršames in einen juridischen Konflikt zugunsten seiner eigenen Untergebenen ein, die im Rahmen der ägyptischen Revolte unter dem Verdacht festgesetzt wurden, dass sie sich den Aufständigen angeschlossen hätten. In Z. 8–9 bittet Aršames Artahant, dass dieser die Anordnung (*ṭʿm*) verfüge, dass sie nicht bestraft, sondern freigelassen werden: „Jetzt: Wenn es dir als gut erscheint, dann möge von dir eine Anordnung erlassen werden, dass niemand | jenem Parijama und seinen Genossen etwas Böses antue. Sie mögen entlassen werden".[23]

Artavant und Artahant fungieren beide – sofern sie nicht sogar identisch sind – als eine Art Richter in Ägypten, der Aršames nicht direkt untergeben ist. Aršames kann zwar seinen Einfluss als Satrap geltend machen und sie auffordern beziehungsweise höflich bitten, eine rechtskräftige Anordnung oder einen Entscheid (*ṭʿm*) zugunsten seiner, Aršames' Entourage zu erlassen, aber diese Briefe sind offenkundig selbst keine rechtsverbindlichen Anordnungen, also offenbar keine *ṭʿmn*.

Hingegen werden, wie die oben behandelten Namensnennungen zeigen, die Inhalte der Briefe der anderen Gruppe entweder ausdrücklich als *ṭʿm* bezeichnet, oder aber ein Beamter, der mit dem Fall vertraut ist, als *bʿl ṭʿm* („Herr der Anordnung").

A6.11 ist dabei eine eindeutige Rechtsentscheidung, die Aršames fällt. So hat sich einer seiner Untergebenen an ihn mit der Klage gewandt, dass ein Erblehen seines Vaters nach den Unruhen nicht auf ihn, den Sohn, übertragen wurde (Z. 1–3). Aršames trifft nun in Z. 3–6 die Anordnung, dass, wenn sich der Fall so verhält, wie der Beschwerdeführer es ausgeführt hat und über das Lehen auch nicht mittlerweile

21 *kʿn hn ʿl mrʾy ṭb yštlḥ ʿl ʾrtwnt [kzy ʿbdyʾ ʾlk zy] | ʾhqrb qdmwhy srwšytʾ zy ʾnh ʾšym lhm ṭʿm ytʿbd lhm*

22 *ʾnt šm ṭʿm srwš[yt]ʾ zy psmšk y[šym] | lhm ṭʿm lmʿbd zky ytʿbd lhm*

23 *kʿn hn ʿlyk kwt ṭb mnk ytšm ṭʿm kzy ʾyš mndʿm bʾyš lʾ | yʿbd lpyrmʾ zk wknwth yštbqw*

anderweitig verfügt wurde, es dem Kläger notariell[24] übergeben werden soll. Dabei wird bei dieser Anordnung einerseits analog zu einem kasuistischen Rechtssatz die geforderte Voraussetzung für die Entscheidung (es verhält sich so, wie der Klagende angibt und das Land ist nicht anderweitig vergeben) mit *hn* eingeleitet, andererseits aber die Folgerung analog zu einer Rechtsurkunde mit Perfekt eingeführt: *hn knm hw k ... ʾnh ... yhbt lpṭswry* „Wenn sich dies wie … (verhält), dann habe ich (hiermit) … dem Peṭosiri gegeben".[25]

Auch mit A6.13 reagiert Aršames auf eine Klage eines Dritten: Aršames hatte Varuvahja eine Domäne offenbar zur Nutznießung überlassen, aber der Verwalter dieser Domäne liefert aus dieser nichts an Varuvahya ab. So bittet Varuvahja nun Aršames darum, seine Verwaltung anzuhalten, eine entsprechende Anweisung an den Verwalter der Domäne zu geben, was Aršames mit dem Schreiben durchführt. Dabei ist bezeichnend, dass die lokalen Anweisungen an den Verwalter der Domäne durch die Verwaltungsbeamten des Aršames – also die Ausführungsanweisungen – nicht als *ṭʿm*, sondern als *hndrz* bezeichnet werden. *hndrz* bezeichnet also in diesem Schreiben eine Handlungsanweisung, die auf einem *ṭʿm* beruht, wobei der *ṭʿm* von demjenigen gegeben wird, der als Oberherr über die Domänen das Bestimmungsrecht über diese hat. *ṭʿm* ist mithin hier die Rechtsgrundlage, auf der die Untergebenen ein *hndrz* erlassen können – und der Brief letztlich eine Urkunde, mit der diese das Recht (und die Pflicht) dazu gegenüber dem säumigen Verwalter nachweisen können.

Der rechtliche Hintergrund dieser Schreiben wird auch in A6.8 und 10 deutlich. Beide Schreiben sind jeweils eine Strafandrohung gegen widerspenstige (A6.8) oder säumige (A6.10) Untergebene des Aršames, die formelhaft mit *kn ydyʿ yhwh/y lk hn <Fallbeschreibung> ḥs(y)n tštʾl(wn) wgst ptgm ytʿbd lk* „So wird/sei dir (hiermit) bekannt: Wenn <Fallbeschreibung>, dann wirst du/werdet ihr streng befragt werden und ein Strafurteil (?) wird gegen dich verfügt/an dir vollstreckt" zum Ausdruck gebracht wird (A6.8,3–4; A6.10,8–10). Der juridische Charakter wird durch die Formelhaftigkeit des gesamten Ausdruckes deutlich, die mit der kasuistischen Formulierung *hn* … Impf. „Wenn … dann …" beginnt, die sich ähnlich schon in A6.11 fand. Die in A6.8 und 10 jeweils identische Apodosis ist offenkundig eine Formel der zeitgenössischen Rechtssprache, deren genaue Bedeutung uns Heutigen entgeht. Der erste Teil scheint jedoch darauf zu verweisen, dass der Beschuldigte sich einem Gerichtsverfahren zu unterziehen hat, dem dann eine Verurteilung zu einer Strafe folgt. Da *gst ptgm* wörtlich „Böses der Nachricht/des Wortes" bedeutet, ist hier wahrscheinlich an eine Verurteilung zu einer empfindlichen Strafe gedacht, wobei *ytʿbd lk* entweder im Sinne von „(ein Strafurteil) wird in Bezug auf dich gemacht = verfügt" oder in Analogie zu *srwšytʾ* ... *ytʿbd lhm* „eine Leibesstrafe wird an ihnen

24 Dies dürfte der Sinn von *ʾntm hḥwwhy* „Ihr sollt (es) ihm anzeigen" sein (Z. 5).

25 Vgl. z.B. die Einleitung der Überschreibung einer Immobilie in B2.3.3: *ʾnh yhbt lky* „Ich habe dir (hiermit) gegeben …".

vollstreckt" (A6.3.6 + 7–8) dahingehend zu interpretieren ist, dass sie schon die Vollstreckung des Strafurteils im Blick hat.[26] Man wird jedenfalls kaum fehlgehen, dass Aršames den Adressaten mit dieser Formel ein geordnetes Strafverfahren gegen sie androht.[27] Und es dürfte wohl auch kaum zu bezweifeln sein, dass Schreiben wie den vorliegenden in einem solchen Rechtsverfahren eine bedeutsame Rolle zukommen konnten, belegen sie doch eindeutig, dass die Adressaten über ihre Pflichten und über die Folgen einer Pflichtvergessenheit informiert waren.[28] So werden in beiden Dokumenten (A6.8.2–3; A6.10.5–8) die entsprechenden Pflichten der Adressaten sogar noch einmal *expressis verbis* wiederholt, wobei in A6.10 Aršames sogar ausdrücklich ein früheres Schreiben zitiert. Damit liefern die Schreiben alle Informationen, die bei einem möglichen kommenden Prozess in dieser Sache relevant wären.

Die übrigen drei Schreiben (A6.2; A6.9; A6.12) schaffen jeweils die rechtliche Grundlage dafür, dass ihre Adressaten auf Kosten des Aršames Aufträge ausführen oder den Übermittler des Briefes mit genau spezifizierten Rationen versorgen können. So referiert A6.2 detailliert die Materialien, die für eine bestimmte Bootsreparatur vor Ort ermittelt wurden. Diese Liste wird Aršames mit der Bitte mitgeteilt, dass man sie ausgeben möge, so dass die Reparatur *kzy šym ṭʿm* „wie als Anordnung gegeben" ausgeführt werden kann. Aršames' Antwort besteht dann lediglich in der Einwilligung, dass die Adressaten entsprechend dem, was die Finanzbeauftragten gemäß dem, was als Anordnung gegeben wurde, sagen, verfahren sollen. Mithin berechtigt dieses Schreiben die Adressaten, die Kosten für die Materialien zu finanzieren, wobei die detaillierte Aufführung der Materialien zeigt, dass hier nicht eine

26 Vgl. zu abweichenden Deutungen von *gst ptgm* die Angaben bei Hoftijzer & Jongeling 1995: 230 (s.v. gst_1). Dass die Befragung der Pflichtvergessenen lediglich zu einem „adverse word", „reprimand" (Driver 1957: 50–1), „a harsh word" (TAD) oder einem „Verweis" (Kottsieper 2006: 366, 369) führen soll, wie die Mehrheit der Bearbeiter annimmt, erscheint dann doch etwas schwach zu sein.

27 Zur hier vorgeschlagenen Deutung vgl. auch Greenfield 1982: 9–10, der aber allein auf Grund des Kontextes davon ausgeht, dass beide Teile der Apodosis „may best be understood as saying the same thing twice: 'you will be severely punished' " (9). Wenn auch in Dan 4.14 *šʾlh* im *parallelismus membrorum* zu *ptgm* in Bezug auf ein Strafhandeln begegnet (Greenfield 1982: 10), so bedeutet dies doch nicht zwingend, dass dort *šʾlh* im Sinne von „Strafe" und hier *šʾl* im Sinne von „strafen" vorliegt. In Dan 4 bezeichnet *šʾlh* wie *ptgm* eine Art Urteil, das durch ein Gremium (Wächter/Heiligen) ergangen ist, wobei der Text offenkundig auf Begriffe der Rechtssprache zurückgreift, ohne selbst ein Rechtsdokument zu sein. Am einfachsten lässt sich die Sachlage damit erklären, dass die *šʾl* Gt im Sinne von „verhört/angehört werden" ursprünglich nur die Anhörung der Parteien bezeichnet, aber dann, da dies ja einen wesentlichen Aspekt eines geordneten Rechtsverfahrens ausmacht, auch ein solches Verfahren allgemein konnotieren konnte. Durch die Verbindung mit *gst ptgm* wird dann ein solches Verfahren als ein Rechtsakt gekennzeichnet, der zu einem Strafurteil führt. Dan 4.14 nimmt diese Rechtsterminologie auf, wobei die Parallelisierung von *ptgm* und *šʾlh* wahrscheinlich zum Ausdruck bringen soll, dass das zuvor angekündigte Vorgehen einem Urteil in einem Rechtsverfahren entspricht und nicht einfach einen Willkürakt darstellt.

28 Dies kommt auch in der Einleitung der Strafandrohung zum Ausdruck: *kn ydyʿ yhwh/y lk* „So wird/sei dir (hiermit) bekannt:", die ihr Pendant in dem demotischen Text P.Berlin inv. 13540.8 hat und dort nach der Anordnung des Satrapen steht; vgl. Anm. 30.

informelle Einwilligung vorliegt, sondern eine verbindliche und konkrete Zusage. Ähnlich weist A6.13 die Verwaltung in Ägypten an, einem namentlich genannten Bildhauer die für Künstler üblichen Rationen auszugeben und ihn dafür eine Reiterstatue anfertigen zu lassen.

Dass ein solches Schreiben wie eine Rechtsurkunde dazu dienen kann, dass sein Besitzer Ansprüche geltend machen kann, zeigt dann deutlich A6.9. In diesem Schreiben, das sich an die Verwalter in den Orten wendet, die als Stationen auf der Strecke zwischen Babylonien und Ägypten liegen, werden diese angewiesen, Naḥtḥor, dem Beauftragten des Aršames, genau spezifizierte Rationen – und nur diese! – auszugeben. Da das Schreiben an mehrere Adressaten in unterschiedlichen Orten adressiert war, konnte es nicht bei den Adressaten verbleiben, sondern wurde offenkundig von dem Beauftragten des Aršames jeweils vorgezeigt, um damit seinen Anspruch auf die Rationen zu belegen – entsprechend war es auch nie verschlossen und gesiegelt gewesen und wurde schließlich auch in Ägpyten wohl im Archiv des Naḥtḥor aufbewahrt.[29]

Mithin haben die Schreiben, die neben dem „Schreiber" auch eine mit dem als *ṭʿm* bezeichneten Inhalt vertraute Person bezeichnen, zwar durchaus unterschiedliche Inhalte, aber durchweg eine rechtliche Bedeutung.[30] So können sie als Dokumente dienen, die demjenigen, der sie in Händen hält, das Recht bestätigen, gewisse Rationen zu erhalten (A6.2) oder aus dem Besitz des Aršames auszugeben (A6.9; A6.12). Oder sie autorisieren die Adressaten, ihrerseits eine Verfügung zu erlassen (A6.13). Andererseits können sie auch als eine Art Klageandrohung dienen, die zugleich alle Elemente enthält, die Berechtigung dieser Klage auch zu belegen (A6.8; A6.10). Und schließlich können sie Entscheidungen des Aršames in rechtlich umstrittenen Fällen mitteilen (A6.11). In diesem Sinne können diese Schreiben funktional als Rechtsdokumente angesprochen werden, während die übrigen Schreiben des Aršames, die zum Teil von denselben Schreibern stammen, diesen Aspekt nicht aufweisen. Sie können sich zwar mit Rechtsfällen beschäftigen, aber sind in keiner

29 Die Schreiben A6.3–A6.16 gehören zu einer Gruppe von Dokumenten, die 1933 in Ägypten zusammen mit einer Ledertasche und acht Bullen erworben wurden (Driver 1954: 1–2). Dabei tragen sieben der Bullen eindeutig das Siegel des Aršames. Die Schreiben A6.9–16 sind an Naḥtḥor adressiert (A6.10–3) oder stammen von ihm (A6.14–6) oder erwähnen ihn (A6.6+9). Sein Vorgänger war wohl Psamšek, der in A6.3–4+8 eine Rolle spielt. Dies spricht dafür, dass dieses Konvolut an Briefen zum Archiv des Naḥtḥor gehörte, in dem auch Briefe, die sich mit seinem Vorgänger beschäftigten, Eingang gefunden haben; vgl. schon Driver 1954: 3.

30 Dies dürfte auch für das nur demotisch erhaltenen Schreiben des Pherendates P.Berlin inv. 13540 gelten, in dem der Satrap die Voraussetzungen darlegt, die jemand für die Wahl zum Lesonis mitbringen muss. Anlass des Briefes ist dabei, dass die Chnum-Priesterschaft Pherendates einige Kandidaten vorgeschlagen haben, die nicht diesen Voraussetzungen entsprachen. Somit klärt das Schreiben, das sich dabei gleich zweimal auf einen Erlass des Dareios beruft (Z. 5+7), offenkundig rechtsverbindlich diese Frage, wobei die Darlegung mit der Formel endet, dass dies den Adressaten bekannt sein möge. Diese hat ihr Pendant in A6.8 und 10 hat und soll wohl zum Ausdruck bringen soll, dass der Adressat sich nicht (mehr) auf Unwissenheit berufen kann (vgl. Anm. 28).

Weise verbindlich oder können auch nicht als Nachweis eines Rechtsanspruches dienen.

Der Brauch, solche Schreiben mit der Nennung des „Schreibers" und einer mit dem Vorgang vertrauten Person zu versehen, dafür aber die Grußformel wegzulassen, korreliert folglich mit der Rechtsverbindlichkeit der Schreiben. Dabei handelt es sich offenkundig nicht darum, dass auf diese Weise offizielle Schreiben von informellen in dem Sinne unterschieden werden,[31] dass in offiziellen Schreiben der „Dienstweg" vom Auftraggeber Aršames bis zum „Schreiber" angegeben wird und so die maßgeblichen Verantwortlichen genannt werden.[32] Dagegen spricht die vorherrschende Formulierung „PN kennt diese Anordnung". Mithin ist hinsichtlich dieser Person nicht irgendeine konkrete Funktion im Prozedere der Abfassung von Bedeutung, sondern ausdrücklich nur die Tatsache, dass sie darüber informiert ist. Die genannte Person kann also ebenso wie der zuständige „Schreiber" Auskunft geben, wenn eine andere Person die Korrektheit oder die Relevanz des Schreibens in Frage stellt – sie kann mithin als eine Art Zeuge für die rechtlich relevanten Vorgänge dienen, die die Briefe dokumentieren. Dem entspricht auch die abweichende Formulierung in A6.2, wo das undeterminierte *bʿl ṭʿm* an das undeterminierte *šhd* „(als/ist) Zeuge" in Zeugenangaben von Rechtsdokumenten erinnert[33] – und erklärt zugleich, warum in diesem Schreiben dieser *bʿl ṭʿm* und der „Schreiber", der hier nicht der Schreibende ist, den Brief eigenhändig unterzeichnen: Dies findet sich auch vielfach bei den Zeugenangaben in Rechtsdokumenten. Wenn diese Angaben lediglich dazu dienen würden, das korrekte Prozedere innerhalb der Kanzlei zu dokumentieren, wäre dies überflüssig gewesen. Aber offenkundig wurden zumindest in der ägyptischen Kanzlei des Aršames diese Angaben also ein persönliches Zeugnis der Beteiligten verstanden, mit denen sie bezeugen, dass sie mit dem Vorgang entweder als eine Art Zeuge oder als „Schreiber" vertraut sind.

Dass diese Angaben damit eine rechtlich relevante Funktion haben, die mit dem rechtlich relevanten Inhalt der Schreiben korreliert, erklärt vielleicht auch die Tatsache, dass auch die Unterschriften in A6.2 unmittelbar hinter das letzte Wort des Textes gesetzt wurden. Das Verfahren, diese abschließenden Angaben unmittelbar auf den Text folgen zu lassen, macht es unmöglich, dem Text noch irgendetwas hinzuzufügen, womit *de facto* die Integrität und auch die Vollständigkeit des

31 In der Literatur zu den verschiedenen Formelementen aramäischer Briefe wird immer wieder hinsichtlich dieser Besonderheiten darauf verwiesen, dass es sich hier um (semi-)offizielle Briefe handele, vgl. z.B. Fitzmyer 1979: 191, 194; Schwiderski 2000: 187.

32 So schon Driver 1954: 8: „this designation … probably means not merely that the person so described is aware of the order but that he is charged with the responsibility for issuing it and perhaps also of seeing to the execution of it". Da *ydʿ* jedoch schlicht „(er)kennen, wissen" heißt, ist diese Annahme schon philologisch nicht zu halten.

33 Vgl. B2.1.16–9; B2.2.17–21; B2.3.29–34; B2.4.17–22; B2.6.39; B2.7.19; B2.9.17–8; B2.11.16; B3.3.15; B3.4.23–4; B3.6.17; B3.10.23–6; B3.11.18–20; B3.12.34; B3.13.13–4; B6.3.15; B6.4.9–10; D6.25.8–10(?).

Schreibens gesichert wird. Es ist unwahrscheinlich, dass dieser Effekt nicht intendiert war – notwendig wurde er aber nur, wenn das Schreiben rechtsverbindlich sein sollte.

Man wird also annehmen dürfen, dass durch die Nennung einer Person, die mit dem Vorgang vertraut ist und ihn daher kennt und für die Richtigkeit einstehen kann, und des für die Ausfertigung des Briefes zuständigen Schreibers die Briefe eine belastbare Rechtskraft beziehungsweise -verbindlichkeit bekamen, so dass sie wie Rechtsdokumente herangezogen werden konnten – etwa, um die Rechtmäßigkeit einer Zahlung oder einer Forderung nach Rationen zu belegen. Da sie aber als Briefe die unterschiedlichsten Inhalte transportieren konnten, waren sie auch als prozesstaugliche Strafandrohungen dazu geeignet, bei Insubordination Untergebene mit der Androhung rechtlicher Konsequenzen abzumahnen.

Im Hintergrund dieser Praxis steht wohl der in elamischen Kanzleien gut belegte Brauch, bei Schreiben hochrangiger Beamter am Ende den Schreiber zu nennen und danach entweder den, der den Beurkundungsbefehl erteilt hat (z.B. PF [= Hallock 1969] 1792; PF 1793; Hinz & Koch 1987: 825, s.v. *li-iš-da*), oder den, von dem er (der Schreiber) die *du-(um)-me* erhalten hat (z.B. PT [= Cameron 1948] 1; PF 1794), wobei das Wort am ehesten im Sinne von „Konzept, Entwurf" zu verstehen ist (Hinz & Koch 1987: 360).[34] Zuweilen können beide Angaben auch nebeneinander auftreten (z.B. PF 1819).[35] Es liegt auf der Hand, dass *diese* Angaben den Dienstweg in der Kanzlei wiedergeben, auf dem die Schreiben entstanden sind. Dabei handelt es sich sowohl um Briefe, die die Ausgabe von Gütern anordnen, als auch um Empfangsquittungen seitens des hohen Beamten – also beides Textarten, die ebenfalls rechtliche Bedeutung haben. Auffällig ist zudem, dass die Briefe auch keine Grußformel aufweisen. Im Gegensatz dazu finden sich Grußformeln in anderen Briefen, die mehr informativen Charakter haben und in denen dann die Angaben über Schreiber und Mittelsmänner fehlen (z.B. PF 1832, 1857–1860, 2070). Auf der anderen Seite konnten aber auch Anweisungsbriefe ohne die Nennung der Mittelsmänner – aber auch ohne Grußformel – abgefasst werden (z.B. PF 1833–1836), wobei sogar Anordnungen von offenbar demselben Beamten vorliegen, die teils mit (PT 68), teils aber ohne diese Angaben verfasst sind (PT 75).

Da diese Elemente im wesentlichen bei Schreiben hoher Beamter begegnen (Hallock 1969: 24) und den Dienstweg in der Kanzlei widerspiegeln, dürfte ihr ursprünglicher Zweck darin gelegen haben, gerade bei größeren Kanzleien die jeweils Verantwortlichen für diese rechtlich relevanten Texte zu benennen, zumal kaum davon ausgegangen werden kann, dass die hohen Beamten, in deren Namen die Schreiben verfasst wurden, über diese einzelnen Transaktionen persönlich informiert waren. Dass dabei auch hier schon der Gedanke eine Rolle gespielt hat, durch die Nennung

34 Auf diese Verbindung hat schon Hinz (1971: 310) aufmerksam gemacht.

35 Vgl, auch die Übersicht bei Hallock 1969: 24, 51–2.

der involvierten Beamten es zu ermöglichen, die Gültigkeit der Anweisung nachzuprüfen, zeigt sich darin, dass vereinzelt auch in diesem Korpus schon die Formulierung auftaucht, dass eine gewisse Person über den Vorgang informiert sei (PF 1790.27–28). Die Gültigkeit des Schreibens war aber bei diesen Texten, die auf Tontafeln geschrieben und daher permanent gesiegelt waren, auch durch das Siegel gewährleistet.

Hier liegt nun ein wesentlicher Unterschied zu den rechtlich relevanten Briefen auf Leder oder Papyrus: Zwar wurden auch diese vor Versendung gesiegelt, aber das Siegel musste entfernt werden, wenn der Brief gelesen wurde. Und das Schreiben A6.9, in dem Aršames die Verwalter mehrerer Güter anweist, Naḥtḥor auf seiner Reise nach Ägypten zu versorgen, war überhaupt nicht gesiegelt, da es von Naḥtḥor von vornherein an mehreren Orten präsentiert werden musste. Damit entfiel für diese Schreiben die Möglichkeit, dass ihre Korrektheit und damit rechtliche Gültigkeit durch ein permanentes Siegel gewährleistet werden konnte. Mithin musste dies auf anderem Wege gesichert werden. Offenkundig besann man sich dabei der Praxis der elamischen Kanzleien im Osten und adaptierte deren Vorgehen. Dass diese Angaben aber in den Leder- und Papyrusbriefen in erster Linie dazu dienten, die Korrektheit der Anweisung zu sichern bzw. nachprüfbar zu machen, schlug sich darin nieder, dass der Aspekt der Information über den korrekten Dienstweg zugunsten der Nennung einer Person, die mit der Anordnung inhaltlich vertraut war und daher die Sachlage bezeugen konnte, in den Hintergrund trat.

The Evolution and Use of Demotic Contracts in Epistolary Form

Mark Depauw (Leuven)

Summary

Demotic legal documents, from the earliest examples in the 7th century BC until the latest contracts and letters in the 3rd century AD, sometimes use the format and formulae of letters instead of more traditional and more typical forms. Many less formal deeds have therefore often been called 'contracts in epistolary form', although the distinction between the various categories has often been far from clear-cut.

By looking at the characteristics of formal and informal contracts and comparing these with the typical structure of letters, however, strict criteria such as the place of the date at the beginning or end of the text can be established. When these are applied, 'contracts in epistolary form' turn out to be exceptional up to the second half of the 2nd century BC. Most of the alleged early examples are clearly narrow type informal contracts with very limited epistolary features.

The new style of contracts that emerges around 125 BC seems to emphasize the principle of autography at the expense of witnesses: most of them are written by the first party in his own hand or explicitly state that they were inked by a third party at the first party's request. The prevalence of autograph subscriptions under other, more formal contracts also increases around the same time, and similar developments can be observed in the Greek contracts from the same period, once again underlining the need to study both traditions at the same time.

1. Introduction

In my book on Demotic epistolography, I have – with the 4th–6th century AD treatise Ἐπιστολιμαῖοι Χαρακτῆρες – defined letters as messages sent between spatially separated correspondents.[1] By concentrating on the purpose of bridging physical distance between people, letters 'stricto sensu' could thus conveniently be distinguished from contracts, which in Demotic are also phrased as declarations from one party to the other and hence are intrinsically likely to resemble letters. But the contracts were normally drawn up with both parties present and, unlike letters, would have been written even in the presence of the addressee.

1 Depauw 2006: 3–5.

As I did note in another chapter of the same book,[2] however, distinguishing letters from contracts can occasionally still be quite problematic, because of the flexibility of the epistolary genre. People wanting to document obligations from one party to another could employ the format and formulae which had become typical for letters. It is the genesis and development of this category of 'letters with contractual value' or 'contracts in epistolary style' that I would like to examine in more detail in this paper.

This study is part of a broader research project 'The formal evolution of Demotic deeds against the social background of the hellenization of Egypt in the Graeco-Roman period. A typological study', initially sponsored by the Fund for Scientific Research (Flanders) and from 2005 onwards integrated into 'Multilingualism and Multiculturalism in Graeco-Roman Egypt', sponsored by a Kovalevskaja Award of the Alexander von Humboldt Foundation. For this project I created a database of 744 reasonably well-preserved published Demotic contracts, from the very beginning (644 BC) until the very end (3rd century AD), concentrating on their form.

2. Contracts in Epistolary Style: Definitions and Problems

The position of the so-called contracts in epistolary style is schematically presented in Table 1: documents which take the form of a letter (dimensions and formulaic framework) but whose contents are those of a contract (recording legally binding obligations). There is no in-between category of documents which take the form of a contract, but have epistolary contents. Only the flexibility of the epistolary format allowed it to be used for more formal purposes, in opposition to the rigidity of the contractual format.

Table 1. Between Letters and Contracts: the Contents and Format of Contracts in Epistolary Style:

'Real' letters	Contracts in epistolary style	'Real' contracts
not legally binding, informal contents	legally binding, formal contents	legally binding, formal contents
epistolary format (physical dimensions, framework formulae)	epistolary format (physical dimensions, framework formulae)	contractual format (physical dimensions, framework formulae)

To determine what form a contract should take to be called 'epistolary', I will first give a survey of the formal characteristics of letters and contracts respectively, as they have been described in earlier literature.

2 Depauw 2006: 317–21.

2.1 Letters

Demotic letters are written on a piece of papyrus cut from a papyrus roll, often preserving its width (also called the height of the papyrus). In the 'broad format', typical for the early Demotic or early Ptolemaic period, the width (being the distance between either end on the horizontal axis, parallel to the writing) far exceeds the height of the letter, with relatively few long lines as a result. In the 'high format' letters, on the other hand, the height far exceeds the width and the text is written in many short lines.[3] There are various typical introductory formulae which evolve over time, but amongst the most common ones are *ḫrw A m-bȝḥ B* 'the voice of A before B' or *A smȝʿ r B (m-bȝḥ G)* 'A greets B (before the god G)'. A relative late-comer is *A pȝ nty ḏd (n B)* 'A is the one who says to B'. Most letters have some form of courtesy, either at the beginning or at the end of the letter. The standard closing formula consists of the signature of the scribe and a date. Most letters seem to be written by the sender himself. After folding and sealing the letter an exterior address can be added to guide the messenger towards his destination.[4]

2.2 Contracts

In Demotic, traditionally a distinction is made between notary contracts on the one hand and 'contracts in epistolary style' on the other hand.

2.2.1 Notary Contracts

The archetypical Demotic contracts are among Demotists generally known as *sẖ* or 'notary-contracts', because they were written by the notary (*monographos*) or at least on his authority. They start with the regnal year *ḥȝ.t-sp*, often calligraphically written and mentioning the name of the ruling pharaoh, and after 290 BC often also referring to the eponymous priests; they introduce the parties by *ḏd A n B* 'What A has said to B'; and they are concluded by the notary's name. Clauses in this type of text are more or less fixed and witnesses are essential for the contract's validity. Their presence is reflected in autograph signatures on the verso or on the recto of the document, occasionally even in full copies of the contract on the same papyrus. The number of witnesses is determined by the period in which the document was written and the importance of the agreement.

Although one spontaneously thinks of the very large papyri, occasionally even more than four metres long,[5] there are in this category also less luxurious manu-scripts. A distinction has been made between a broad type, with long lines, broad margins, and the witness-list on the verso (e.g. P.Teos 2) and a more economic nar-

3 Depauw 2006: 72–6.
4 Depauw 2006: 113–237.
5 For the probably longest example so far (463.5 cm), see Depauw 2009.

row type with shorter lines, smaller margins and witnesses either on the recto or the verso (e.g. P.Tsenhor 15).[6]

2.2.2 Contracts in Epistolary Style

The notary contracts are traditionally distinguished from the so-called *šʿ.t* or 'contracts in epistolary style', which are far less formal (e.g. P.Teos 12). The scribe can be a notary, but this is often not the case. The parties are generally identified by *A pꜣ nty ḏd n B* 'A is the one who says to B', and the date usually follows at the end without mentioning the name of the ruling pharaoh. Some of the so-called contracts in epistolary style, however, do have a date at the beginning, while others do not identify a scribe at all. In many cases the document was probably written by the first party himself. Witnesses can be present but are apparently not compulsory. Some of these contracts are 'double documents', thus called because the text is provided twice: the *scriptura exterior*, which is freely accessible and usually more elaborate; and the *scriptura interior*, which is sealed and normally shorter.

Because of the *šʿ.t*'s informal character and flexibility, Demotists have not always found it easy to distinguish them from *sẖ*'s or notary contracts, at least in the Ptolemaic and – to a lesser extent – the Roman period. This can be illustrated by the confusion when categorising sureties, papyri in which someone guarantees an obligation of someone else before the local authorities. Felber refers to them as notary contracts, while I myself have called them double documents in epistolary style.[7] Seidl identifies some examples as *šʿ.t*'s, but adds that others seem to be notary contracts with an additional *scriptura interior*, combining features of Greek and Demotic legal documents. His conclusion can be paraphrased as: 'every legal document which is not a *sẖ*, for whatever reason, is a *šʿ.t*'.[8] The nature of these reasons is not specified, but the presence of witnesses seems to be a central criterion to suggest that the document is a *sẖ* rather than a *šʿ.t*. Yet in some cases the document itself contradicts this, as Seidl himself admits:[9]

> "Würde sich jedoch P. [Michigan] 4526 nicht selbst als šʿ.t bezeichnen, müßten wir eine Schreiber- und Zeugenurkunde annehmen; denn auf dem Verso stehen 5 Zeugennamen".

6 For the distinction between broad and narrow format see Pestman & Vleeming 1994: 26–32.

7 Felber 1997: 87 n. 77; Depauw 1997: 138.

8 Seidl 1962: 57–8. For further literature on the distinction between sẖ and šʿ.t, see Depauw 1997: 123–5; Felber 1997: 86–8.

9 Seidl 1962: 57.

3. Informality versus Epistolary Style in Early Demotic (644 – 332 BC)

3.1 Defining Epistolary Style in Early Demotic

There thus seems to be considerable terminological confusion, which I will try to elucidate by first going back to the early Demotic period. If a few criteria of those mentioned above are selected, the formal differences between contracts and letters in the early Demotic period seem to be quite strict.

Place of the Date Clause
The date is given at the very beginning of early Demotic contracts, both of the broad and of the narrow type, while in letters it always comes at the end.

The Name of the Pharaoh and the Day in the Date Clause
In early Demotic (unlike in abnormal hieratic), contracts of both the broad and the narrow type always provide the name of the pharaoh, but never specify the day, whereas in letters invariably the opposite is true: no pharaoh, but a day.

The Introductory Formula
Whether broad or narrow format, the introductory formula identifying the parties is in early Demotic always *ḏd A n B* 'What A has said to B', whereas letters normally use *ḫrw A m-bꜣḥ B* 'the voice of A before B' or *A smꜣʿ r B (m-bꜣḥ G)* 'A greets B (before the god G)'.

Witnesses
Witnesses never appear in letters, but are essential in Demotic contracts. Their exceptional absence in the latter may in most cases be apparent only and due to the state of conservation (e.g. when the verso is not accessible). I have opted not to reduce the number of possible cases of contracts in epistolary format further by adding this criterion, but will always draw attention to the presence or absence of witnesses.

The definition of a contract in epistolary style for the early Demotic period is thus a text with formulaic, legally binding contents in which a typical epistolary formula such as *ḫrw A m-bꜣḥ B* 'the voice of A before B' or *A smꜣʿ r B (m-bꜣḥ G)* 'A greets B (before the god G)' is used at the very beginning of the text and in which the date is only given at the end, without giving the name of the ruling pharaoh but specifying the precise day of writing.

3.2 Contracts (Receipts) in Epistolary Style in Early Demotic

There are only a handful of texts answering to (most of) this definition in the early Demotic period. Of the 78 early Demotic papyrus contracts in my corpus, none qualifies, but there are a few receipts rather than contracts. A first example is

P.Louvre 7854 (6th or 5th century BC),[10] a document with all the typical epistolary formulae including even an exterior address, which contains a very polite request to a superior to draw up a receipt for payment of grain. Despite the epistolary fiction, it seems likely that the letter replaced the receipt as sufficient proof for payment and was never meant to be sent to the addressee. A second example is P.Louvre 7850 (between 29 November and 28 December 533 BC), a letter from the chief of the necropolis to his superior, confirming to have received a bull as payment for the fee owed. In this case there is clearly no exterior address and the date clause at the end does not specify the day. The scribe is furthermore not identical to the sender, which is not unattested for letters but still rather suggests that the epistolary form is only fiction. The last and perhaps clearest example is P.Berl.Dem. 1 13572 (6 June 492 BC), a receipt of money in the form of a letter starting with *A smꜣ' r B (m-bꜣḥ G)* 'A greets B (before the god G)' followed by a pious wish, and ending in a date clause without the pharaoh's name but with a day. Here the presence of three witnesses confirms the legal character of this letter.

Other informal early Demotic texts are not contracts in epistolary style, but informal, narrow type 'notary' contracts. This is a very heterogeneous group, including many sheets with a non-calligraphic *ḥꜣ.t-sp* 'year' sign at the beginning, but also some texts which except for the absence of large decorative margins have all the characteristics of a broad format contract.[11] With 13 examples these informal contracts clearly form a minority (17%).

4. Informality versus Epistolary Style in Ptolemaic Demotic (332 – 30 BC)

4.1 Defining Epistolary Style in Ptolemaic Demotic

In the Ptolemaic period matters suddenly seem less clear-cut, mainly because of formal evolutions. Concentrating on the basic criteria identified for early Demotic, the following changes can be observed for all texts containing formal, legally binding contents.

Date Clauses with the Day

Although there are 3rd century BC attestations of broad format deeds specifying the day on which they were written,[12] this was exceptional before the end of the Theban revolt in 186 BC. From then onwards, however, the day is almost always specified,

10 P.Louvre 7854 and 7850 have been published as P.Louvre Eisenlohr (Diss.) 10 (TM 46774) and 22 (TM 46143).

11 For the latter type, see P.Tsenhor 1.

12 With the exception of some early Demotic contracts with influence from abnormal hieratic, to my knowledge the earliest example of a day indication seems to be P.Cair. III 50066, probably even pre-Ptolemaic.

even in the most formal contracts and its presence can no longer be used as a distinctive feature.

The Introductory Formula

Here the situation is more complicated than in early Demotic, as a result of the emergence of *A pꜣ nty ḏd (n B)* 'A is the one who says to B' as an introductory formula both in informal contracts and in letters. It appears around the same time in both contracts and letters, at the end of the 4th century BC. In texts with legal contents the earliest dated examples are P.Teos 12 from 306 BC and P.Brit.Mus. Reich 10077 A – B from 269 BC (there *A nty ḏd n B* without article). In letters it is first attested in the Loeb archive, e.g. in P.Loeb 6 (8 November 308 BC). It may be earlier in origin, but this is hard to ascertain because of the rather patchy preservation of Demotic texts in the period between 450 BC and the beginning of the Ptolemaic rule.

As a formula, *A pꜣ nty ḏd (n B)* at first sight looks like a grammatical reinterpretation of the *ḏd A n B* typical for contracts. The latter was in all likelihood an archaic relative form 'what A has said to B' which was no longer readily understood using contemporaneous grammatical rules,[13] and this may well have led to the invention of a new, 'modern' form in less formal contracts. On the other hand a reference to the oral character of the letter – one party speaking to another – is typical for early epistolography. There are New Kingdom antecedents for the use of *ḏd* 'say, speak' in the introductory formula and early Demotic *ḫrw* 'voice' also stresses the oral character.[14] Furthermore it is striking that in some of the earliest examples (all in the late 4th century Loeb archive) *A pꜣ nty ḏd (n B)* is used in letters which may be formal or official, but in no way contain legal obligations and are not formulaic in the legal sense at all. And P.Teos 12 (306 BC), the earliest text with contractual obligations using this formula, otherwise follows the epistolary pattern, since the date clause, providing no pharaoh but specifying the day, is given at the end rather than at the beginning. It does, however, have four witness signatures at the bottom of the recto. On balance the evidence rather seems to suggest that the epistolary formula was not 'borrowed' from contracts but arose independently, perhaps even influencing informal contracts.

The definition of contracts in epistolary style for the Ptolemaic period is thus a text with formulaic, legally binding contents in which a typical epistolary formula such as – in this period – *A pꜣ nty ḏd (n B)* is used at the very beginning of the text and in which the date is only given at the end, without giving the name of the ruling pharaoh (and in the 3rd century BC specifying the precise day of writing).

13 Vleeming 1980: 14 n. 47.
14 Depauw 2006: 131,147,149,159.

4.2 Contracts in Epistolary Style in Early Ptolemaic Demotic (332 – 151 BC)

In the early Ptolemaic period, before 150 BC, there are again few texts answering (most of) this definition. Of the 339 Demotic contracts dated to this period in my corpus, strictly speaking only two qualify. One is the already mentioned P.Teos 12 from 306 BC, a cession after judgement introduced by *A pꜣ nty ḏd (n B)* 'A is the one who says to B' and ending with a date clause without pharaoh but with day. It is written by a third party scribe and has four witnesses. The other example is P.Brit.Mus. IV 11 (195 BC), a transfer of two tombs which completely follows the epistolary pattern and has no witnesses nor a named external scribe. Two possible further examples may be P.Berl.Dem. I 15609 and P.Berl.Dem. III 13578 (both 4th-3rd cent. BC), a loan without witnesses and a lease with four witnesses respectively. Although both have a date at the end, without pharaoh but with the day, the introductory formula and possibly another date at the beginning are lost.

Even if these examples are included, the proportion of contracts in epistolary form remains very small (1%). Like for early Demotic, all other informal texts are not contracts in epistolary style – as they have in this case often been called, e.g. by Depauw –, but informal, narrow type 'notary' contracts. With 77 examples or 23% they still form a minority compared with the 252 broad format contracts,[15] but are a sizeable group nonetheless. Most are documents issued for the authorities such as sureties, self-dedications or royal oaths, not in use before the Ptolemaic period,[16] but the format was also employed for other purposes.

Compared with the early Demotic period, these informal contracts seem to form a more homogeneous group. Few have a calligraphic *ḥꜣ.t-sp* 'year' sign at the beginning, but most stick to the 'archaic' introductory formula *ḏd A n B* 'What A has said to B': only 8 replace this with *A pꜣ nty ḏd n B* 'A is the one who says to B'.[17] There is one atypical contract with some epistolary features, which in the light of later evolutions deserves closer attention: the double document (!) P.Brit.Mus.Reich 10077 A – B (269 BC). Although both in *scriptura interior* and *exterior* it starts with a date clause identifying the pharaoh and omitting the day, the introductory formula is *A pꜣ nty ḏd n B* and at the end the date is repeated, now with the day. The third party scribe who signs at the end adds that he has written *r-ḫrw* 'at the behest of' the first party. There are no witnesses, but the declarant has added an autograph subscription.

4.3 Contracts in Epistolary Style in Later Ptolemaic Demotic (150 – 30 BC)

The larger group of informal contracts illustrates how rules seem to have been less strict in the early Ptolemaic period, and how certain 'epistolary elements' such as the

15 Of 6 contracts the format is unclear (copies, register, summary, …).

16 Fifty-one are sureties, self-dedications, or royal oaths.

17 Compare also P.Mil.Vogl. 3 Dem. 4 A-B where a hybrid ḏd A tꜣ nty ḏd m-bꜣḥ B is used. There is also a single broad format contract which uses A pꜣ nty ḏd n B: P.Hausw. 18b.

introductory formula *A nty ḏd n B* started to creep in. From 150 BC onwards this evolution seems to intensify, since of the 298 Demotic contracts dated to this period in my corpus, 41 or 14% can be considered contracts in epistolary form according to the criteria mentioned above (including 2 with a date in the body and 4 without date).[18] Together with the 120 informal contracts (40%), they even form a majority against the 136 broad format contracts.[19] This rise is all the more remarkable because documents issued for authorities which were such an important group in the early Ptolemaic period have become much rarer after 150 BC.

Some of the narrow, informal contracts of this period also show more 'epistolary elements' than their earlier counterparts. Four have a second date without the name of the pharaoh (but with the day) at the end, which makes them rather ambiguous examples, very similar to the contracts in epistolary style.[20] Another six have a date clause without mentioning the name of the pharaoh at the beginning, and in this case the only distinction with contracts in epistolary form is the place of the date clause.[21] And there are nine further informal contracts that employ the introductory formula *A pꜣ nty ḏd n B* 'A is the one who says to B' or the hybrid *ḏd A pꜣ nty ḏd n B* something like 'What A has said, the one who says to B'.[22]

Since the average dimensions of broad format contracts also decrease in the course of time, the contrast with the narrow format becomes less marked in other respects as well. Graph 1 provides a schematic survey of the number of epistolary, informal and formal contracts between 664 and 30 BC.

18 AcOr 25 (1960), pp. 296–7 (TM 302); Dem.Conf. VII (Copenhagen 1999) p. 46 no. P.Amiens 5 (TM 44912); Demotica 2 31 (TM 43540); Enchoria 7 (1977), pp. 52–3 second doc. (TM 97); Fs. 150 Berlin p. 289 no. A (TM 201); *JEA* 19 (1933), pp. 34–5 (TM 46029); P.Adl.Dem. 3,10,12V,17,24; P.Dryton 24,49; P.Erbstreit pp. 49–50 no. 18; P.Gebelen p. 30; P.Gebelen 15,31,32,33; P.Hawara 20, 24a,24b, 24c,24d,24e,24g; P.Loeb 52; P.Ryl.Dem. 34; P.Tor.Amen. 14; P.Tor.Botti 18,19,20,23,27, 29,34b,34c,40,42,43,44; P.Tor.Choach. 1.

19 Of one text the format is unclear (a copy).

20 Enchoria 7 (1977), pp. 52–3 first doc. (TM 97); P.Adl.Dem. 19; P.Tor.Botti 13,14. Two of these are anonymous, one adds r-ḫrw=f, and only one has a third party scribe.

21 P.Adl.Dem. 9; P.Berl.Spieg. 3108; P.Ryl.Dem. 33; P.Tor.Botti 15,28; ZÄS 91 (1964), p. 127 (TM 46322). All except a single draft have the introductory formula A pꜣ nty ḏd n B; none identify the scribe; two (P.Berl.Spieg. 3108 and P.Ryl.Dem. 33) have three witnesses.

22 A pꜣ nty ḏd n B: OMRO 44 (1963), p. 9–13 version I (TM 43705); P.Berl.Spieg. 3118; P.Cair. II 30611, 30614; P.Dryton 15; P.Oxf.Griffith 59,71,74. ḏd A pꜣ nty ḏd n B: P.Oxf.Griff. 73. The latter formula is also used in some formal deeds, e.g. P.Adl.Dem. 20 or P.Ryl.Dem. 29.

Graph 1. The Number of Contracts per Period and per formal Type:

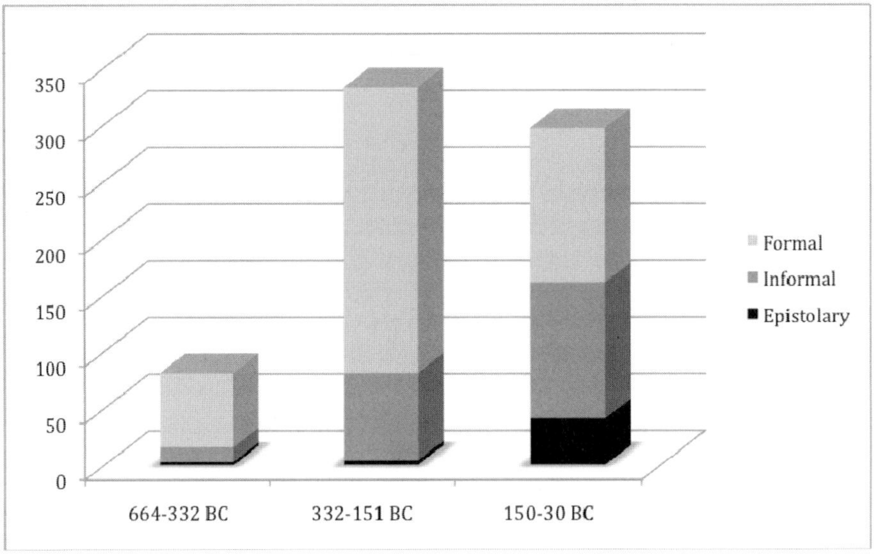

5. Informality versus Epistolary Style in Roman Demotic

The evolution of Demotic contracts in the Roman period falls outside the scope of this article. Suffice it to say that Demotic becomes very marginal for papyrus contracts after the middle of the 1st century AD, when the last notary contracts, always with elaborate Greek subscriptions, were written. From later periods some very informal contracts are known from a temple context, but these clearly take hybrid forms. Demotic letters practically disappear in the early 1st century AD as well, making the distinction increasingly less productive.

6. Autography and Epistolary Contracts in Later Ptolemaic Demotic

Epistolary contracts do not only become more numerous in the middle of the 2nd century BC, they also seem to take a specific form in two respects: autography and witnesses.

6.1 Autography on the Rise

The rise of autography is illustrated by Table 2. Although only in three cases the scribe mentioned at the end of the contract can with certainty be identified with the first party (A), it is very common that a third party scribe (P) complements his signature with the addition *r-ḫrw=f*, *r-ḫrw=w*, or *r-ḫrw=s* 'at his / their / her behest' and sometimes an expression such as *n p3 s 2* 'for the two people'.[23] It seems likely that in the 20 cases where the scribe is anonymous, the first party has also written the contract himself. Only a handful of (sometimes aberrant) examples remain where a third party scribe has not added that he has acted at the request of the declarant.[24]

Table 2. The Evidence for Scribes of Contracts in Epistolary Form (later Ptolemaic Period):

sẖ A	3
sẖ P r-ḫrw=f and variants	14
sẖ P	4
anonymous	20

At the very end of the 2nd century BC the addition *r-ḫrw=f* also appears in other contracts which are strictly speaking not in epistolary form because they have a date clause at the beginning with the name of the pharaoh (P.Berl.Spieg. 3118 and P.Tor.Botti 34a).

Although the earliest attestation of *r-ḫrw=f* is the already mentioned double document P.Brit.Mus.Reich 10077 A – B (269 BC), this stress on autography seems to be typical for the second half of the Ptolemaic period. Earlier it seems to have been considered relatively less important who actually wrote the contract. Thus although the Greek name μονόγραφος, literally something like 'sole scribe', has been interpreted as referring to the exclusive right of the temple notary to write contracts, the palaeography of these notary contracts casts some doubts on whether these officials always did the manual work themselves.[25] The earliest broad format contracts where scribes explicitly state that they are acting as representatives appear at the end of the 3rd century BC. In P.Ehevertr. 22 (220 BC) the scribe Psenchonis says that he is a representative (*rd*) of the royal scribe, and in P.Fam.Theb. 26 (217 BC) Horos son of Petechonsis labels himself the representative (*rd*) of Peteesis son of Paes *p3 sẖ qnb.t ḏmʿ* 'the scribe of official documents and contracts' and states that he has written *r-ḫrw=f* 'at his behest'.[26]

23 I have not included the strange addition P.Ehevertr. 28 (198 BC), where the scribe adds just before his signature sẖ=y r ḫrw Pa-t3-s.t-ʿ3.t ỉw=f ḏd [not p3y=y rt] ỉw=y ỉr r ẖ md nb nty ḥry.

24 P.Tebt.Botti 43 is an absolutely certain example, but the a sẖ P at the end of P.Gebelen p. 30 may be a witness. P.Adl.Dem. 17 and *JEA* 19 (1933), pp. 34–5 (TM 46029) are aberrant (royal oath and registration of priests respectively).

25 See e.g. Depauw 2000: 117–20 note m. Compare now also the observations of Arlt 2009: esp. p. 38, who shows that at least in larger cities there was not a single notary office, and even within one office family members apparently shared the work of a *monographos*.

26 Around the same time (earliest example in 220 BC) notaries start mentioning that they write in the name of institutions such as the notary office of the priests of Amon or Amonrasonther or the notary office of the prophet of Jeme: see Arlt, 2002: 30–2. For scribes who label themselves rd, compare also P.Dryton 12 (171 BC), P.Tor.Amen. 10 (118 BC) and 15 (126 BC); and P.Berl.Spieg. 3103 (114 BC).

The frequency of another autograph element, subscriptions by interested parties, also rises in the later Ptolemaic period.[27] Out of the 308 contracts from the period after the Theban revolt in my corpus, no less than 59 (19%) have autograph subscriptions, a substantially higher percentage than in the early Ptolemaic period (18 out of 345 = 5%).[28] Since most of these are not contracts in epistolary form, the proportion of Demotic contracts referring to autography rises to 27% (82 out of 308).

6.2 The Decline of Witnesses

This stress on autography is likely to be related to the absence of witnesses, since of all the contracts in epistolary form there is only a single certain example which adds these: AcOr 25 (1960), p. 296–297 (120 BC; TM 302), where 4 men have signed.[29] Without witnesses, the validity of the obligations contained in the document all rested on the fact that the first party had written it himself, or that a third party could vouch that he had written it at his request.

Quantifying the number of contracts without witnesses is problematic, however, because the back of Demotic documents is often inaccessible or the part where the witnesses were expected is lost. Nevertheless the increasing number of contracts without any trace of witnesses observed in Graph 2, culminating in their complete absence in the Roman period, suggests that this is more than just mere chance.

27 See Depauw 2003, but there without the percentages.

28 The percentage is, however, also quite high in the early Demotic period (19%).

29 In the fragmentary contract P.Gebelen 33 the two people who have signed at the end adding tw=y mtr.w n nȝ nty sẖ ḥry may be witnesses but could also be interested parties who add an autograph subscription.

Graph 2. The Proportion of Contracts without any Sign of Witnesses (early Demotic to Roman):

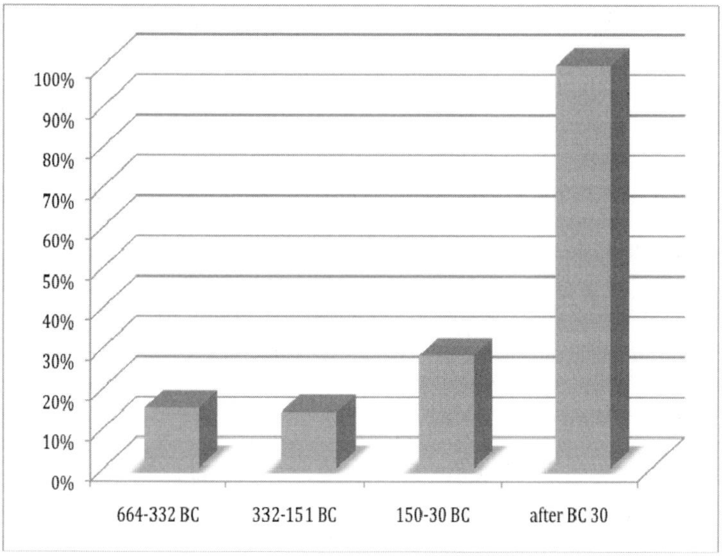

7. Conclusion

Contracts in epistolary style are very rare in early Demotic. The few examples of legal documents using formulae typical for letters are receipts rather than contracts. The emergence of the introductory formula *A pꜣ nty ḏd n B* 'A is the one who says to B' and its spread over both letters and contracts brought contracts in epistolary style and narrow type contracts closer together. After the Theban revolt the only formal difference was the place of the date clause and the identification of the reigning pharaoh. It is only logical that people writing a contract in the form of a letter would gradually start adapting those last two elements of epistolary convention, after which there would be no formal way to distinguish the two. The only distinctive element left may have been the identity of the scribe. As it seems, however, even notaries occasionally wrote contracts in epistolary style for clients: the notary Chestefnachtes son of Hariesis wrote several formal and informal deeds preserved in the archive of Totoes, but also P.Tor.Botti 27, a document in epistolary style.

Despite the increasing resemblance between the various categories of Demotic contracts, there is a clear quantitative shift towards the letter form. It is harder to determine an exact date for the start of this evolution. As Graph 3 illustrates, the middle of the 2nd century BC and especially the last quarter see a rise in the proportion of epistolary contracts.

Graph 3. The Proportion of Contracts in Epistolary Form 200 – 51 BC, per 25 Years:

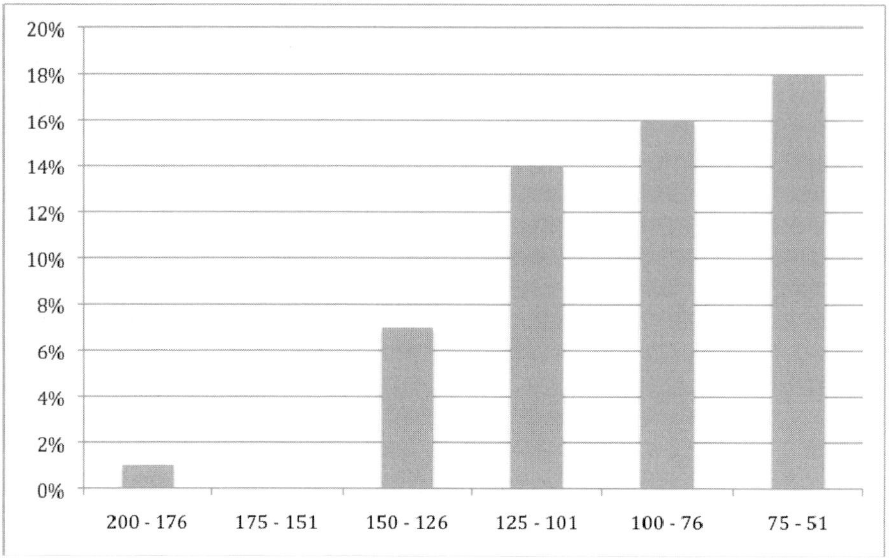

A more precise cut-off point when counting per decade as in Graph 4 is problematic in view of the likely influence of chance when working with low numbers.[30] Nonetheless, around 120 BC epistolary contracts seem to become more common. Since the shift is paralleled by a growing importance of the relation of the scribe to the first party and autograph confirmation, one wonders whether it was the result of an administrative reform. This is not unlikely in view of the compulsory registration decreed in 145 BC or the new rule that the language of the contract determined the competence of courts in 118 BC. That important changes took place in the format of Greek contracts around the same time only corroborates this hypothesis.

30 For 60 – 51 BC e.g. the 50% reflects the proportion in only 2 preserved contracts. All other decades count 11 or more preserved contracts, up to 68 for 110 – 101 BC.

Graph 4. The Proportion of Contracts in Epistolary Form 200 – 51 BC, per 10 Years:

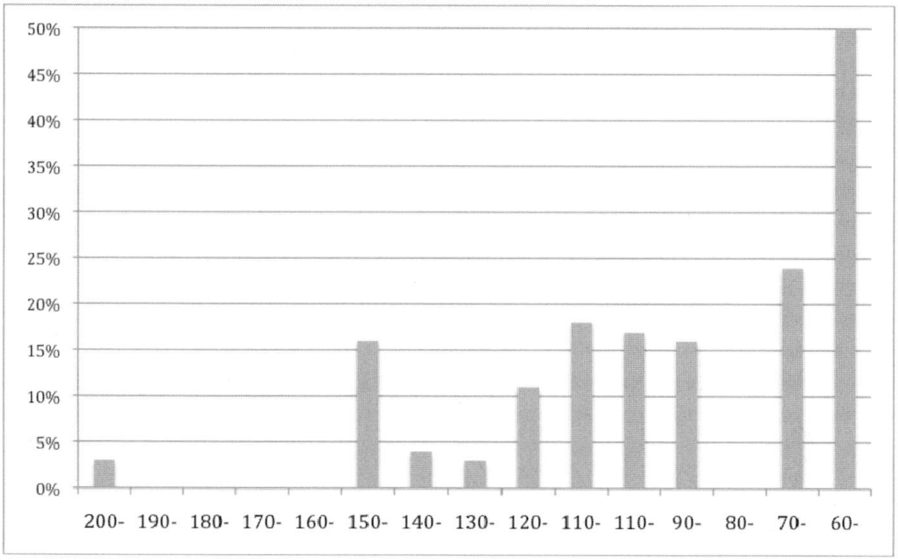

A final question is whether the distinctions between types of documents (formal, informal, epistolary) made above can be recognized in Demotic terminology (see Table 3). This is certainly not evident, and should be studied separately. That there seems to have been a difference in the eye of the law is suggested by the evidence of the so-called *Zivilprozessordnung*. This legal handbook seems to separate *sẖ* from *š*ʿ*.t*, whereby the latter can and often will be without witnesses.[31] Perhaps the large, broad format notary contracts were normally called *sẖ*, which could be extended to the narrow type contracts. The contracts in epistolary form were normally called *š*ʿ*.t*, but this could include the informal contracts as well. This does not imply that all these documents were letters, since *š*ʿ*.t* is just the general word for a (small) piece of papyrus cut from the roll. But it does suggest that the Egyptians may have looked at informal contracts and contracts in epistolary style in the same way, which further explains the gradual dissolution of their distinctive features.[32]

31 A further complication is the occurrence of the term qnb.t, but this seems a general term for any document admitted as evidence in court rather than a formal term for broad format contracts (the latter interpretation suggested by Mrsich): see Lippert 2003: 110.

32 The use of the term bꜣk 'letter' (see Depauw 2006: 257) for 'document, contract' in various contracts also points in this direction.

Table 3. A Typology of Demotic Documents:

	Dimensions	Layout	Scribe	Date	Formula	Identification	Registration	Witnesses	Meta-reference
Notary contract: broad type	broad sheet or roll	large margins	notary (always?)	beginning calligraphic with pharaoh without day (until early 2nd century)	*ḏd A n B*	with mothers (few exceptions)	after Greek conquest	yes, sometimes copies	*ḏmʿ*, *sẖ*
Notary contract: narrow type	narrow sheet	small or no margins	notary (always?)	beginning non calligraphic with pharaoh without day (until early 2nd century)	*ḏd A n B* *A pꜣ nty ḏd n B* (rare)	with mothers (mostly)	only in later periods	in most cases	*šʿ.t*, *sẖ* (?)
Contract in epis-tolary style	narrow rectangular sheet or strip	small or no margins	any scribe	(beginning or) end non calligraphic without pharaoh with day	*ẖrw A m-bꜣḥ B* *A smꜣʿ r B m-bꜣḥ G* *A pꜣ nty ḏd n B*	without mothers	no	very rare	*šʿ.t*, *bꜣk*
Letter	narrow rectangular sheet or strip	small or no margins	any scribe	end non calligraphic without pharaoh with day	*ẖrw A m-bꜣḥ B* *A smꜣʿ r B m-bꜣḥ G* *A pꜣ nty ḏd n B* others	without mothers	no	almost never	*šʿ.t*, *bꜣk*

Greek and Demotic Loan Agreements in Epistolary Style. Formalisation and Registration in the Later Ptolemaic Period[1]

Katelijn Vandorpe (Leuven)

Ptolemaic papyrus and ostraka archives contain Greek as well as Demotic private arrangements in epistolary style, bearing witness to economic activities. This paper compares the Greek documentation to similar Demotic 'letters'. A Greek private arrangement in epistolary style is known as a *cheirographon* (χειρόγραφον) or cheir (χείρ);[2] in Demotic it is simply referred to as *š῾.t*, 'letter',[3] or, more generally, *b3k*, 'document'. These agreements in epistolary style start with the greeting formula found in letters. Then, the writer of the document, party one, addresses himself to party two in the first person. Such arrangements are unilateral and, as a rule, party one writes the document himself, in his own hand and in his native language.[4] If he is illiterate, a third person writes for him by his request and the name of the writer is explicitly mentioned at the end of the agreement. The good-bye-formula typical of letters (ἔρρωσο) and/or a short date may be added at the end.

All kinds of agreements may be written in such autograph documents, but we focus here on acknowledgments of debt and compare this type to other types of contracts testifying to lending practices.[5] By doing so, we hope to find out how the Greek *cheirographon* and its Demotic counterpart developed in the course of the Ptolemaic period. In the overview of the different types of loans below, the validity of the contract is focused on: written arrangements, protecting the creditor,[6] were secured by the presence of witnesses or a notary, by seals or registration.

1 I would like to thank W. Clarysse and B. Feucht for several useful suggestions.
2 Seidl 1962: 61; Wolff 1978: 106–14; P.Dion., pp. 280–1; Yiftach-Firanko 2009.
3 See the contribution by M. Depauw in this volume.
4 P.Dryton §34; Von Reden 2007: 155.
5 Compare Rupprecht 1967.
6 Von Reden 2007: 155.

1. Types of Loans[7]

1.1. Greek Double Documents and Six-Witnesses Contracts[8]

Double documents are found throughout the Hellenistic world. In Egypt, Greek double documents are attested from the third century BC onwards.[9] In this kind of document the contract is written twice on one papyrus: the upper text (or *scriptura interior*) is folded and sealed and its contents cannot be altered, whereas the lower text (or *scriptura exterior*) is left unsealed and can be consulted whenever necessary. The double contracts are valid wherever they are presented and the stipulations of the transaction are protected not only by the duplicate form, but also by seals and sometimes by witnesses.

A specific type of double documents are the six-witnesses contracts. One of the witnesses present at the transaction is the *syngraphophylax*, a private person, who keeps the contract as long as it runs and has to produce it in a court of law when required. The upper text (*scriptura interior*) is sealed by both contracting parties and by the six witnesses, who impress their seal in clay. When public archives started to emerge at the end of the third century BC,[10] an abstract or copy of the double document could be kept or deposited there,[11] but as U. Yiftach-Firanko showed, these "registers were created in order to facilitate the working of the existent, private safe-keeping-mechanism, not as its substitute (…) There is no indication that the archives were meant to supplant the *syngraphophylax* as the organ which is in charge of producing the document in court (…)".[12]

In the later Ptolemaic period, the registration procedure was reformed somewhere between 130 and 113 BC: six-witnesses contracts could be registered in the record offices known as the *grapheia*[13] and their layout was drastically changed.[14] The new procedure was the cause of the degeneration (and thus the 'killing') of the six-witnesses contracts: the *scriptura interior* was shortened and the parties and wit-

7 Compare P.W. Pestman, in P.Dion., pp. 23–30, 176–93, 246–52, 280–2; P.Dryton §34–8.

8 Wolff 1978: 57–73; Vandorpe 1997; P.Dion., pp. 176–93 (Les actes à six témoins); Yiftach-Firanko 2008.

9 Double documents and/or six-witnesses contracts of the third century BC concerning loan, are, e.g.: BGU VI 1274, 218 BC, 6-witnesses; 1275, 215 BC, 6-witnesses; 1276, 215 BC, 6-witnesses (?); 1277, 215 BC, 6-witnesses; 1278, 215 BC, 6-witnesses; XIV 2393, 215 BC, duplicate; 2395, 221 BC, 6-witnesses; 2396, 213 BC, 6-witnesses; P.Cair.Zen. I 59001, 6-witnesses; P.Corn. 2, 250 BC, 6-witnesses (?); P.Hib. I 88, 263 BC, 6-witnesses (?); P.Iand.Zen. 2, 255 BC, 6-witnesses; P.Köln V 218, 215 BC, 6-witnesses; P.Lond. VII 1986, 252 BC, 6-witnesses; P.Sorb. I 17, 257 BC, duplicate; PSI IV 389, 243 BC, 6-witnesses; SB XVI 12812, 255 BC, 6-witnesses; XVIII 13255, 231 BC, 6-witnesses.

10 Yiftach-Firanko 2008: esp. 209, with bibliographical references.

11 Examples of six-witnesses contracts concerning loan that are deposited in such public archives are, e.g., CPR XVIII 14,16,24; P.Tebt. III 815 also contains several examples.

12 Yiftach-Firanko 2008: esp. 209.

13 P.Dion., pp. 25–8.

14 Yiftach-Firanko 2008.

nesses no longer impressed their seals in the clay; only one person (probably the *syngraphophylax*) put his imprint on the three clay seals.

Validity of Greek Double Documents, including Six-Witnesses Contracts:

- duplicate form, seals, witnesses (among them the *syngraphophylax*): these practices degenerate in the period 130 – 113 BC;
- from 130 – 113 BC onwards: (Greek) registration in a *grapheion* or a record office supervised by the state.

1.2. Greek Notarial or Agoranomic Contracts[15]

Greek notarial contracts are attested from ca. 240 BC onwards in the capitals of the Arsinoite, Herakleopolite and Oxyrhynchite nomes, whereas in Upper Egypt Greek notaries surface only after the great revolt, in 174 BC.[16] In such agoranomic contracts the transaction is secured by the notary or the *agoranomos* (or his deputy). The official enters the contract in a state register[17] and afterwards records the repayment. No witnesses are required. Whereas notarial *sale* contracts were usually of the long type, Greek notarial *loan* contracts, which were legally less important, could be of the short type.[18] In case of a contract of the short type, the size of the papyrus sheet is smaller and the text has shorter lines and small margins. The dating formula is more compact.

Validity of Greek Notarial or Agoranomic Contracts:

- guaranteed by a Greek notary or an *agoranomos*, who automatically registered the contract in the record office supervised by the state.

1.3. Demotic Temple Contracts[19]

As in pre-Ptolemaic times,[20] loans could be negotiated through temple notaries. The transaction was secured by the temple (and thus by Egyptian law) and by witnesses. In the Ptolemaic period, some Demotic temple contracts for loans were of the long (or broad) type,[21] but there was a tendency towards the use of the short (or narrow) type for loan transactions.[22] Whereas temple contracts of the long type (like sale

15 Messeri Savorelli 1980; Pestman 1985b: 9–27; for additions to the lists of *agoranomoi* of Krokodilopolis and Pathyris, see Vandorpe 2000: 195, n. 4 and 199, n. 32. See also P.Dion., pp. 246–52 and P.Dryton §34.

16 In 174 BC, the notarial office of the *agoranomos* of the Perithebas and of the Pathyrite nome is attested for the first time, see P.Dryton 11 + *AfP* 52 (2006), 198–9 no. 1.

17 For an example of such a register, see Vandorpe 2005.

18 See P.Dryton §34.

19 Zauzich 1968; Arlt 2009. See also P.Dryton §34 and the contribution by M. Depauw in this volume.

20 E.g., P.Hou 12 and 13, 487 BC.

21 E.g., *RdE* 24 (1972), p. 125, 217 BC; P.Tor.Botti 26, 107 BC.

22 P.Dryton §34.

contracts) are written on large papyrus sheets and have the names of sixteen witnesses on the verso, contracts of the short type are written on smaller sheets and bear the names of only four witnesses on the recto, below the contract.

Already from the Saite Period, most Demotic temple contracts were apparently not only written, but also registered and taxed by the temple notaries.[23] From about 145 BC onwards (UPZ I, pp. 596–614 = Sel.Pap. II 415), Demotic temple contracts could, in additon, be registered by state officials in the local record offices or *grapheia* in order that the state administration could keep track of these transactions; thus an additional layer of registration and taxation above the Demotic temple notaries was introduced. Some of these *grapheion*-registers were bilingual.[24]

Validity of Demotic Temple Contracts:

- guaranteed by witnesses and by temple notary, and entered in temple register;
- from about 145 BC onwards: also registration in a *grapheion* or a record office supervised by the state.

1.4. Demotic Contracts having a Hybrid Form (early Ptolemaic Period)

Some Demotic loan contracts combine characteristics of a notarial temple contract and of a Greek double document. They are written by a professional scribe, though not a Greek notary nor a temple notary. They have a date at the beginning of the contract, clauses found in notarial contracts and the name of the scribe and of (four) witnesses at the end. They take the form of a double document, like Greek documents (and unlike Demotic temple contracts). This type is attested for the early Ptolemaic period.[25]

Validity of Demotic Contracts having a Hybrid Form:

- duplicate form, witnesses;
- not found in the later Ptolemaic period.

23 Vleeming 1992: 343–50. Probably already before 150 BC, all kinds of Demotic contracts (and thus not only temple contracts) could be recorded in a Demotic register, but it is not clear who was in charge of such a register. See De Cenival 1987.

24 Pestman 1985a; P.Dion., pp. 25–8; Muhs 2005; Muhs 2009: 243–51. In the metropolis of the Fayum, registered Demotic contracts were stamped on the verso with red stamps in the late Ptolemaic period, see Vandorpe 1997: 254–5.

25 Few examples are attested, e.g., in chronological order: *WZKM* 25 (1911), pp. 312–4 no. 1 descr., 281/0 BC; P.Loeb 60, 243/3 BC (fragmentary, but probably a double document); P.David 12, 201 BC; P.Brit.Mus. IV 19, 199 BC. The fragmentary P.Berl.Dem. I 15609, of the early Ptolemaic period (year 18), may be a further example.

2. Greek Autograph Acknowledgments of Debt: Towards a Formal *Cheirographon* (End Second Century BC)

For the Greek documentation, I distinguish between formal and informal *cheirographa*. Informal *cheirographa* are only the expression of a private agreement between two parties who trust each other and are not tied by rules that make the document valid. They are already found in the early Ptolemaic period. P.Hib. II 259 (235 BC), for instance, concerns an *eranos*-loan, a type of loan between friends, known from Classical Greece. Informal *cheirographa* are not dealt with in this paper. Formal *cheirographa* are a valid alternative to above-mentioned types of documents such as notarial contracts. In his study of Greek loan documents in 1967, Rupprecht used the term 'novierende' and 'novatorische' *cheirographa*.[26]

2.1. Greek Cheirographa*: Transitional Stage*

In the third century BC hybrid forms combine the epistolary style and the duplicate form, popular at the time.[27] P. Hib. I 86 (248 BC) is an acknowledgment of debt in epistolary form (starting with the greeting formula and ending with 'good-bye' and date), but it is at the same time a double document which was partly sealed.[28] Such agreements were secured by the duplicate form.

Validity of early Greek *Cheirographa*:
- duplicate form, seal.

2.2. Formal Greek Cheirographa *versus Notarial Contracts: Similarities and Differences*

At the latest during the great Theban revolt (206 – 186 BC) a new type of document emerged which no longer needed a duplicate form, seals or witnesses to be valid. I call it a formal *cheirographon*,[29] as it takes over clauses of the above-mentioned notarial contracts. The earliest example is P.Köln V 220 of 191 BC, from the Arsinoite nome, but this document does not deal entirely with private matters: the loan of wine is negotiated between tax farmers of the wine-tax (*apomoira*) and a winegrower; as fiscal matters are involved, the loan has to be repaid to the royal bank and, according to the *praxis*-clause, the creditors can hold responsible the debtor and have a claim on his entire property as they act for the revenues of the

26 Rupprecht 1967: 37 and 104.

27 Many so-called *cheirographa* of the third century BC that do not take the duplicate form appear to be real letters and not acknowledgments of debt, e.g., P.Col.Zen. II 76, 247 BC.

28 A further example is undoubtedly the fragmentary P.Hib. I 129 = SB XII 10782, 247/6 BC.

29 Compare Wolff 1978: 108: „Kyriaklauseln treten erstmals in Handscheinen der späteren Ptolemäerzeit auf und gehörten seitdem zum regelmäßigen, aber nicht zum notwendigen Stil dieser Urkundsart".

crown (πρὸς βασιλικά). Formal loan-*cheirographa* of a true private nature surface only at the end of the second century and first century BC.[30]

A formal *Cheirographon* has some Characteristics of a Letter:
- it is formulated in the first person;
- it has sometimes 'good-bye' and a short dating formula at the end.

On the other hand, the clauses are clearly inspired by Greek notarial deeds.[31] Loan-*cheirographa* and agoranomic deeds contain similar clauses, except for the reciprocal surety-clause:

- the actual acknowledgment of debt mentions the loan object and the interest;
- the delivery clause records when and where the loan object has to be returned. In case of a loan of consumer goods the condition of the returned goods and the measure to be used are specified;
- a penalty clause is applied when the loan is not returned in time;
- (reciprocal surety clause appears only in case of multiple debtors, when the borrowers are surety for each other; this clause is not found in *cheirographa*);[32]
- according to the *praxis*-clause the creditor can hold the debtor responsible with a claim on the debtor's entire property; the creditor can act 'as if there was a legal decision' (καθάπερ ἐκ δίκης).[33]
- The *kyria*-clause stipulates that the deed is proof of the loan and that it is valid (κύριος) wherever presented; this clause is optional in *cheirographa* (see below).

Regional differences in the clauses in the *cheirographa* are linked to differences in the clauses of the notarial contracts. Documents from Pathyris and from the archive of Dionysios son of Kephalas illustrate this statement. A clear example is the *kyria*-clause, which is present in both notarial contracts and *cheirographa* from the archive of Dionysios (from Hermoupolis and Tenis-Akoris),[34] but is lacking in both notarial contracts and *cheirographa* from Pathyris.[35] Greek formal *cheirographa* do not – as

30 E.g., P.Tebt. I 110, 92 or 59 BC; 111, 116 BC (here, *sitologoi* are involved); for examples from Tenis-Akoris, see Table 1 (Date: 107 BC); for examples from Pathyris, see note 35. P.Fay. 240 descr. may be a further example of a loan-*cheirographon*, registered in the *grapheion* of Euhemeria, late second-first century BC. P.Amh. II 32^{v} is in my view an informal *cheirographon*.

31 Compare Rupprecht 1967; P.W. Pestman, in P.Dion., pp. 23–30; 176–93, 246–52, 280–2; P.Dryton §33–8 and pp. 118–9; Von Reden 2007: 156.

32 For loans based on pledge or on a mortgage, see Von Reden 2007: 162–74.

33 Wolff 1978.

34 E.g., the *cheirographon* P.Dion. 33 compared to the notarial contract P.Dion. 23.

35 Agoranomic loan contracts from Pathyris or neighbouring Krokodilopolis: *AfP* 52 (2006), pp. 201–3 no. 3; *AfP* 52 (2006), pp. 203–4 no. 4; P.Adl.Gr. 6;10;15; P.Amh. II 46;47;48;50; P.Bingen 39;40; P.Cair.Goodsp. 8 note; 8; P.Dryton 16;17;19;25;29;30; P.Grenf. I 28;31; II 18;21;24 + Pap.Flor. VII

one could expect – deal with small-scale transactions. The transactions in the archive of Dionysios son of Kephalas may illustrate this: similar amounts of grain are lent in *cheirographa* as in the notarial deeds and six-witnesses contracts.

Table 1. Loan Contracts from the Archive of Dionysios Son of Kephalas. All Contracts date from the Period 116 – 104 BC:

Six-Witnesses Contracts, *P.Dion.*:

13	55 artabas wheat + interest 50%
14	20 artabas wheat + interest 50%
15	26 artabas 2/3 wheat + interest 50%
16	166 artabas 2/3 wheat + interest 50%
17	33 artabas 1/3 wheat + interest 50%
18	66 artabas 2/3 wheat + interest 50%
19	16 artabas wheat + interest 50%
20	16 artabas wheat + interest 50%
21	20 artabas wheat
22	24 artabas wheat

Greek Notarial Contracts, *P.Dion.*:

23	150 artabas wheat + interest 50%
24	40 artabas wheat + interest 50%
25	54 artabas wheat + interest 50%
26 (novation)	150 artabas wheat
27 (novation)	142 artabas wheat

Demotic Temple Contracts, *P.Dion.*:

2	15 artabas wheat
3	50 artabas wheat

Greek *Cheirographa*, *P.Dion.*:

32	70 artabas wheat + interest 50%
33	33 1/3 artabas wheat

p. 223 no. 69;27;29; P.Lond. II 218, pp. 15–6; III 1205, p. 15; SB VI 9366; XVIII 13847; XXVI 16637; Greek *cheirographa*: P.Dryton 22 (after 140 BC) and P.Adl.Gr. 4 (109 BC). As only few people in Pathyris mastered the Greek language, few Greek *cheirographa* are found. Acknowledgements of debt are usually written in Demotic, see Table 2.

Why were *cheirographa* in Tenis-Akoris a good alternative to the six-witnesses contracts and notarial deeds? Unlike six-witnesses contracts, they do not need witnesses and they do not require traveling, whereas for notarial contracts, one had to travel to Hermoupolis. There are some further, minor differences: the loan negotiated through a *cheirographon* could be repaid under different conditions (for instance, in another month: Epeiph instead of Payni[36]), and the fine in case the loan was not returned was 2.000 drachmas per artaba instead of 3.000 drachmas recorded in the six-witnesses and notarial contracts.[37] The *cheirographa* therefore seem to be to the advantage of the debtor (Dionysios himself).

2.3. Validity and Registration of Greek Formal Cheirographa

Both notarial deeds and *cheirographa* become more popular in the later Ptolemaic period, probably because they do not require witnesses or seals; in addition, *cheirographa* do not require an *agoranomos*. People sometimes had to travel to appeal to an *agoranomos*, since not all towns had a Greek notarial office,[38] and a notarial contract involved costs.

How was the validity of the contract secured? *Cheirographa* might be registered in a registration office, as attested[39] for the archive of Dionysios son of Kephalas: apparently, several small villages that did not have a Greek notarial office had such a registration office like Tenis-Akoris and two neighbouring villages.[40] The registration procedure sufficiently protected these documents and to a considerable extent added to its success. From what date onwards could Greek formal *cheirographa* be registered? We will have a look at the registration of other documents, before answering this question.

- For Demotic temple contracts of the Peritheban nome (in Upper Egypt), registration by an official of a *grapheion* was possible from 145 BC onwards (see note 24).
- Demotic contracts registered in the Great Anubieion of Memphis were stamped on the verso already in 132 BC, whereas those registered in the *grapheion* of Ptolemais Euergetis, the capital of the Arsinoite nome, were stamped from 116/115 BC onwards at the latest.[41]

36 P.Dion. 32.
37 P.Dion., p. 280.
38 P.Dion., pp. 25–8.
39 See also P.Fay. 240 descr., probably a loan-*cheirographon*, registered in the *grapheion* of Euhemeria, late second-first century BC.
40 P.Dion. 32,33(?),34.
41 Memphis: P.Dem.Memphis 5 A-B; Fayum: P.Ashmol. 3; see Vandorpe 2002: 37–41.

- Six-witnesses contracts or double documents could also be registered in the *grapheia*[42]: U. Yiftach-Firanko showed that the reform imposing the registration of these documents is to be dated between 130 – 113 BC.[43]
- Formal *cheirographa* also surface at the end of the second century BC: the earliest example of a formal *cheirographon* for private matters is 109 BC.[44] Registration of such a *cheirographon* is attested for the first time in 107 BC.[45]

Whereas Demotic temple contracts were registered already in an earlier stage, reforms between 130 – 113/109 BC made it possible for double documents and *cheirographa* to be registered in the *grapheia*. The registration offices, found in numerous villages, were thus open to several types of documents, which were not automatically registered by the Greek notary.[46] Usually, a short registration note was added by an official on the original document.[47] Demotic contracts registered in the *grapheia* of Memphis and Ptolemais Euergetis, the capital of the Arsinoite nome, were, in addition, stamped on the verso: several of these red stamps have been preserved.[48] Thus, *grapheia* could have different habits. The question is whether all *grapheia* marked the registration on the original documents; in Pathyris, for instance, not a single registration note is found on the above-mentioned types of documents, although they are numerous and the major part of the evidence dates from the late second century BC. A Greek *cheirographon*-receipt from this town, recording the return of a loan, has no registration note, although the repayment was clearly registered by the local *archeion*, as shown by the Demotic summary on the back.[49] The absence of a registration note is, in my view, no proof that a document was not entered in a register.

As they had a *praxis*-formula and could be registered, Greek *cheirographa* were protected by the Greek laws of the chora. A case in the archive of Dionysios son of Kephalas shows at the same time the weaknesses of a *cheirographon*. According to P.Dion. 9, Dionysios received 300 *choes* wine from Lysikrates and promises in a *cheirogaphon* to return the price for the wine (24 talents) through a bank. He paid in two installments: 13 talents to the bank, for which he received a bank receipt, and the remaining 11 talents directly to Lysikrates. The latter, however, did not return the *cheirographon* nor did he issue a receipt, although Dionysios more than once insisted to

42 UPZ I, pp. 614–6.
43 Yiftach-Firanko 2008.
44 P.Adl.Gr. 4.
45 P.Dion. 32.
46 Compare Rupprecht 1967: 39 n. 97.
47 UPZ I, pp. 609–16.
48 See note 41.
49 P.Dryton 21: the Demotic summary has 'The Greek [document] which Onchasis has made in the *archeion* '.

get back the *cheirographon*: "As he had promised it, I was calm, because I did not suspect anything bad". Moreover, the creditor Lysikrates handed in an *enteuxis*, a petition to the king on the basis of the *cheirographon*, and the case was put in the hands of the *strategos*: "He tried to have me paid twice the same amount". Lysikrates entrusted the *cheirogaphon* to a third person, living in he same village, and forced family members of Dionysios to write an Egyptian surety contract, to guarantee the sum due by Dionysios, since a *cheirographon* does not have such a surety clause. In turn, Dionysios handed in a petition to the king, asking that the accused would not hold Dionysios responsible and that the *cheirographon* would be returned to Dionysios.

Formal Greek *Cheirographa* in the later Ptolemaic Period that took over Clauses from Deeds written by the Greek Notary are:

- Attested for private matters: from 109 BC at the latest.
- Valid: from 107 BC onwards at the latest, registration in a *grapheion* or a record office supervised by the state.
- Protected by Greek laws of the chora.
- Have a *praxis*-clause and deal with small and large-scale transactions.

3. Demotic Autograph Acknowledgments of Debt (the late Ptolemaic Period)

3.1. Demotic Autograph Acknowledgments of Debt versus Temple Contracts: Similarities and Differences

All kinds of Demotic contracts could be written in an epistolary style.[50] Self-written Demotic acknowledgments of debt, which are not of duplicate form, are attested mainly from the end of the second century BC onwards,[51] as are the formal Greek *cheirographa*. In Pathyris, for instance, they are better attested than their Greek counterparts, undoubtedly because most inhabitants mastered Egyptian better than Greek. Demotic acknowledgments of debt do not need witnesses. They are called, in a very general way, *b3k* in Pathyris, "document" (see below), and follow the clauses of Demotic temple contracts (compare the Greek *cheirographa,* which follow Greek notarial contracts). The same clauses as in the notarial temple documents are involved, but several clauses are optional and some are never included.

Overview of the Clauses Found in Demotic Acknowledgements of Debt from Pathyris:

- "You own" – loan object – "against me in the name of the grains you gave me".

50 For Demotic contracts in epistolary form in general, see the contribution by M. Depauw in this volume and see Depauw 1997: 124; Depauw 2006: 317–21.

51 Loan-*cheirographa* on papyrus: e.g., Theban examples: P.Tor.Botti 13,14,15, all of 114 BC; for examples from Pathyris, dating to the period 116 – 96 BC except for one fragmentary example from 139 BC, see Table 2. Theban loan-*cheirographa* on ostrakon from the Ptolemaic period: O.Leid.Dem. 413 (?) and 416 (not dated).

  - optional: an interest-clause (interest included or not included).
- "I shall return it to you up to year X, Pachon last day",
  - optional: a return "in seed clean without a second kind and without chaff".
  - optional: a transport-clause: "measured, conveyed and stored within (*p3 ḫn*) your house in Pathyris".
- Measure, e.g., "by the measure of Psenosiris": the measure is specified in a different way than in notarial temple contracts (which have 'in the measure with which you measured for me'):
  - optional: "without expenses of freightage".
  - optional: a penalty clause (50%).
  - never mentioned: the date in which the fine has to be paid.
  - never mentioned: a general security clause: notarial contracts have "All of everything that belongs to me with those things that I shall gain are in pledge of every word above until I do according to them, necessarily without delay ", compare the *praxis*-formula in the Greek notarial contracts.
  - sometimes: a specific surety in the form of an object (for instance, a veil and other woman's assets[52]).

Several clauses are similar to those used by the temple notaries of the town. One example from Pathyris may illustrate this regional diversity. According to the transport clause, the wheat to be returned has to be brought to the house of the creditor, normally denoted by *r p3y=k ᶜ.wy* ("to your house"). But the temple notaries Thotortaios and his grandson Nechthminis from Pathyris use the phrase *r p3 ḫn p3y=k ᶜ.wy* ("to the inside of your house").[53] Two acknowledgements of debt written by a private person in 116/5 and 101/99 BC, respectively,[54] take over the *p3-ḫn*-phrase and the acknowledgements of debt are indeed written in the period when Nechthminis was a temple notary.

There is one other conspicuous difference between autographs and temple contracts: whereas temple contracts have "Everything, all that belongs to me and all that I shall acquire, is security for every word above", Demotic acknowledgments of debt do not contain such a clause. There is therefore no equivalent to the Greek *praxis*-formula stipulating that all possessions of the debtor are taken as security. Only specific objects could be recorded as pledge (see note 52). The absence of such a clause may be the reason why Demotic autograph acknowledgments of debt, contrary to Greek *cheirographa*, usually deal with small-scale transactions.

52 Examples from Thebes (Memnoneia): P.Tor.Botti 13 and 14, 114 BC.
53 P.Adl.Dem. 5 and 6; P.Dryton 13,14,27.
54 P.Adl.Dem. 3 and 12.

Table 2. Amounts Lent in Demotic Self-Written Acknowledgements of Debt from Pathyris (period 116 – 96 BC, except for one fragmentary example from 139 BC):

Enchoria 7, pp. 51–4, 96 BC	300 deben (6000 dr.), worth 6 artabas wheat
P.Adl.Dem. 3, 116/5 BC	6 artabas wheat
P.Adl.Dem. 10, 102/1 BC	16 artabas wheat + interest 100%
P.Adl.Dem. 12, 99 BC	5 artabas wheat
P.BM 10494 ined.,[55] 104 BC	2 ½ artabas barley
P.Cair. II 30744 descr., 111 BC	8 keramia wine
P.Dryton 15, 139 BC	4 artabas wheat
P.Dryton 20, no date	1 1/3 artabas barley
P.Dryton 28, no date	3 ½ artabas barley

Table 3. Amounts Lent in Demotic Temple Contracts from Pathyris (period 164 – 89 BC):

P.Adl.Dem. 4, 110 BC	30 keramia wine
P.Adl.Dem. 5, 108/7 BC	21 artabas wheat
P.Adl.Dem. 6, 107 BC	7 artabas barley
P.Adl.Dem. 11, 101 – 99 BC	30 artabas barley
P.Adl.Dem. 25, 89 BC	5 3/4 artabas wheat
P.BM 10483 ined.,[56] 115 BC	6 ¼ artabas wheat
P. BM 10492 ined., 101 BC	15 keramia wine
P.Brux.Dem. E 8442,[57] 91/0 BC	3 3/4 artabas catror oil
P.Cair. II 30729, date unknown	22 ½ keramia wine
P.Dryton 10, 164 BC	15 artabas wheat, 14 artabas barley
P.Dryton 23, 124 – 16 BC	450 deben (9000 drachmas)
P.Dryton 26, 116 BC	15 7/12 artabas wheat
P.Dryton 27, 112 BC	15 artabas wheat
P.Gebelen 24, 139 BC	35 artabas wheat
P.Gebelen 27, 176 – 33 BC	13 ½ artabas wheat
P.Gebelen 29, date unknown	15 keramia wine
P.Ryl.Dem. 21, 111 BC	10 artabas wheat

55 See C.Dem.Conf. VII (= Ryholt 2002), pp. 243–4 no. 6 descr.
56 See C.Dem.Conf. VII (= Ryholt 2002), p. 243 no. 4 descr.
57 See C.Dem.Conf. VII (= Ryholt 2002), p. 246 no. 18 descr.

3.2. Validity of Demotic Autograph Acknowledgments of Debt

It is not clear whether Demotic autograph loans could be registered and thus were protected by the Greek laws of the *chora*, but they could be registered in some kind of Egyptian (Demotic) registers (see note 23) and were certainly protected by Egyptian law (after 118 BC).[58] The temple oaths contain some interesting information on this subject. When the Demotic autograph loan was still in the possession of the creditor and the debtor could not prove by a receipt that he had returned the loan in time, the creditor could turn to the village *epistates*, who tried to settle the dispute amicably. The *b3k*-documents, which are the Demotic autograph documents,[59] were considered valid documents. On the basis of such a *b3k*-document, the village *epistates* could decide to impose a temple oath.[60] This procedure was only needed in special cases, for instance, when the creditor or debtor died and it remained unclear whether the loan was returned and the *b3k*-document was still in the hands of the creditor. Several temple oaths mention such a *b3k*-document. O.Tempeleide 64 has: "Concerning this document (*p3y b3k*), which you made for my father about this amount of wheat I want to assert: he (my father) has not died while he owed you something according to this document, except for wheat [...]".

Demotic Autograph Acknowledgments of Debt in the later Ptolemaic Period, which took over Clauses from Deeds written by the Temple Notary:

- Are valid: not clear whether they were subject to registration in a *grapheion* or a record office supervised by the state; in any case, they could be registered in Egyptian (Demotic) registers.
- Are protected by Egyptian law.
- Have no *praxis*-clause regulating the responsibility of the debtor and deal with small-scale transactions.

4. Conclusions

In a multicultural society loan transactions could be secured by multiple types of contracts, which, in addition, influenced each other. Best secured were the contracts drawn up in the presence of witnesses or of a Greek notary or an Egyptian temple notary (section 1), but such contracts involved extra costs and not every village had

58 According to the *prostagmata* of 118 BC, agreements written in Greek had to be judged before the Greek judges-*chrematistai* and agreements written in Egyptian had to be judged before the native judges (the *laokritai*) in accordance with the national laws, see P.Tebt. I 5; C.Ord.Ptol. 53.

59 In *Enchoria* 7 (1977), p. 51–4, *b3k* is clearly distinguished from *sẖ*, a notarial temple deed. See also Depauw 2006: 320: "If a letter refers to itself, this most commonly happens by means of the word *b3k* (...)".

60 O.Tempeleide 64, 150 – 30 BC: *b3k*-document about a loan of wheat; O.Tempeleide 65, 108 – 43 BC: *b3k*-document about a loan of wheat; O.Tempeleide 66, 102/1 BC: *b3k*-document about a loan of wheat, which has only partly been repaid. If the oath is not sworn, the creditor has to return the *b3k*-document to the debtor; O.Tempeleide 149, 110 BC: *b3k*-document about money.

its own notaries. Therefore, autograph acknowledgements of debt were a good alternative (section 2–3). But how could this cheap and simple type of agreement be protected by law? A difference is to be made between the early and late Ptolemaic period and between Greek and Demotic autographs.

Early Ptolemaic Period

Greek self-written acknowledgements of debt are already attested in the early Ptolemaic period. In order to be valid in the eyes of the government, these documents needed in this early period an extra validation and the Greek examples usually took a duplicate form: the upper text (*scriptura interior*) of such a double document was folded and sealed by one or by both parties whereas the lower text (*scriptura exterior*) was left unsealed and could be consulted whenever necessary.

The non-notarial Demotic acknowledgements of debt in this early period were not written by the debtor himself and were thus no autograph documents: they were drawn up by a professional scribe and the document was secured by the presence of witnesses and by its duplicate form, a Greek practice, as described above.

<u>Autograph Acknowledgements of Debt in the early Ptolemaic Period</u>:
- Greek: secured by law if they took a <u>duplicate form</u>.
- Demotic:
  - no autograph acknowledgements of debt attested.
  - Demotic acknowledgements of debt were written by a professional scribe and
  - were secured by witnesses and by duplicate form.

The Late Ptolemaic Period

From the end of the second century BC, a more formal type of Greek *cheirographon* was established for loans of a private nature, using clauses similar to those of the Greek notarial contracts; this type needed neither witnesses nor seals. *Greek cheirographa* seemed to be a good alternative to the notarial contract. As they have a *praxis*-clause regulating the responsibility of the debtor, they deal with small-scale and large-scale economic activities. Demotic, self-written acknowledgements of debt, based on the clauses of the Demotic notarial temple contracts, surface in the same period, but as they have no *praxis*-clause regulating the responsibility of the debtor, they usually deal with smaller transactions than their Greek counterparts.

Both Greek and Demotic acknowledgements of debt of the late Ptolemaic period no longer needed a duplicate form nor witnesses in order to be valid. We assume that the registration of this type of documents by officials in the local record office, known as the *grapheion*, secured the validity of these self-written acknowledgements of debt. This is certainly the case with the Greek *cheirographa* from at the latest 107 BC onwards. It is not clear whether self-written Demotic acknowledgements of debt could be entered in the Greek register of the *grapheia* as well, but they could in any case be registered in some kind of Egyptian (Demotic) register.

Autograph Acknowledgements of Debt in the later Ptolemaic Period:

- Formal Greek *cheirographa*: no longer needed witnesses nor a duplicate form. They were secured by law, since
    - they took over the clauses of Greek notarial contracts (including the *praxis*-clause regulating the responsibility of the debtor, and as a consequence they dealt with small and large-scale transactions).
    - they could be registered by an official of the *grapheion* from 107 BC onwards at the latest.

- Demotic acknowledgements of debt: no longer needed witnesses nor a duplicate form nor a professional scribe. They were secured by (Egyptian) law, since
    - they took over the clauses of Demotic notarial temple contracts (but as they have no *praxis*-clause regulating the responsibility of the debtor, they deal with small-scale transactions);
    - arguably, they could be entered in the Greek register of the *grapheion*; in any case, they could be registered in Egyptian (Demotic) registers and were protected by Egyptian law.

U. Yiftach-Firanko[61] has shown that a new registration procedure, introduced between 130 – 113 BC in the local *grapheia*, 'killed' the Greek six-witnesses contracts and the double document-type in general (see section 1.1.). The above-mentioned evidence suggests that a similar registration procedure, introduced in the same period, was to the benefit of a new document type: autograph acknowledgements of debt, which we consider 'formalised' because they used clauses found in the local, notarial contracts. These formal autographs were less expensive than notarial contracts when loans had to be negotiated.

61 Yiftach-Firanko 2008.

Hybride Cheirographa

Andrea Jördens (Heidelberg)

Wer private Vereinbarungen schriftlich festhalten wollte, griff nicht ungern auf die Briefform zurück. Die in dieser Form abgegebene Erklärung händigte er sodann der anderen Partei aus, welche dadurch gegebenenfalls einen daraus resultierenden Anspruch geltend machen konnte. Zwar wurden die frühesten Verträge im griechischsprachigen Ägypten noch regelmäßig in Gestalt der Sechszeugenurkunde niedergelegt, die demnach bereits mit den Griechen in das Nilland gekommen sein sollte.[1] Schon bald erwuchs jedoch in dem an der Briefform orientierten sog. Cheirographon eine echte Konkurrenz. Als spezifischer Urkundstyp ist das Cheirographon Hans Julius Wolff zufolge, dem wir das maßgebliche Handbuch über das Urkundswesen im hellenistischen und römischen Ägypten verdanken, freilich erst seit dem späteren 2. Jh. v. Chr. anzusehen. Denn erst jetzt erlangte es seine endgültige Form, in der es dann wenigstens ein halbes Jahrtausend weiterleben sollte, um endlich in der spätantiken Tabellionenurkunde aufzugehen. Konkret bedeutete dies, daß die für den Eingang des Briefes typischen Höflichkeitsformeln[2] wie auch der anfangs noch häufiger gesetzte Schlußgruß[3] abgestoßen wurden, da sie zu dem Verwendungszweck als Vertrag als kaum mehr passend empfunden wurden; stattdessen wurde das nunmehr notwendige Datum hinzugefügt. In der Form des Präskriptes – ὁ δεῖνα τῷ δεῖνι χαίρειν, also ‚A dem B Grüße' – sowie der subjektiven Formulierung blieben sich Brief und Cheirographon jedoch gleich, während etwa das Hypomnema durch die Umkehrung der Adresse τῷ δεῖνι παρὰ τοῦ δεῖνος, also ‚dem B von A' – und das fehlende χαίρειν, das private Protokoll durch die objektive Stilisierung hiervon geschieden waren.[4]

Das Cheirographon war demnach einer der ältesten, zugleich aber, wie schon Wolff feststellte, der „allezeit wichtigste unter den festen Typen, die die Praxis auch für die ‚Privaturkunde' herausbildete".[5] Im folgenden soll nun eine kleinere Gruppe der Cheirographa näher betrachtet werden, in der die Grußformel abweichend von dem üblichen ‚A dem B Grüße' ὁ δεῖνα καὶ ὁ δεῖνα ἀλλήλοις χαίρειν, also ‚A und B

1 Mit Wolff 1978: 59ff.

2 Zu der sog. *forma valutudinis initialis* vgl. nur die Zusammenfassung bei Buzón 1984: 240f.

3 Wolff 1978: 109f.; vgl. auch Buzón 1984: 228 und 230, dessen Behandlung allerdings daran leidet, daß er Wolff überhaupt nicht und auch sonstige rechtshistorische Literatur allenfalls sehr selektiv herangezogen hat, obwohl der zweite Teil seiner Arbeit Urkunden gilt.

4 Hierzu Wolff 1978: 114ff. bzw. 122ff., zu letzterem auch unten Anm. 33 mit Text.

5 Wolff 1978: 106.

einander Grüße' lautet. Da eine solche gegenseitige Anrede dem Brief grundsätzlich fremd erscheint, möchte ich diese Untergruppe als ‚hybride Cheirographa' bezeichnen. Hinweise auf diese besondere Stilisierung finden sich zwar schon in Mitteis' Grundzügen und natürlich auch bei Wolff, doch sind diese Urkunden offenbar bisher noch nie im Zusammenhang betrachtet worden. Vor allem wird der Frage nachzugehen sein, ob es bestimmte Rechtsgeschäfte gab, bei welchen diese Form bevorzugt zur Anwendung kam. Dies könnte zugleich auch Rückschlüsse auf die Gründe erlauben, aus denen heraus man sich für diese eigenwillige Stilisierung entschied.

Ludwig Mitteis hatte dem jedenfalls keine allzu große Bedeutung beigemessen und lediglich notiert: „Bei gegenseitigen Verträgen nimmt das Cheirographon mitunter die Form an, daß beide Parteien sich mit χαίρειν anreden ... Doch ist das keineswegs unbedingt notwendig; es kann auch der eine Teil allein die beiderseitigen Erklärungen formulieren und der andere sie z. B. durch Unterschrift oder stillschweigend annehmen", wofür er jeweils zwei Beispiele benannte.[6] Ähnlich scheint dies auch noch Wolff eingeschätzt zu haben, demzufolge die „dem Briefstil zuwiderlaufende, doch bei beiderseitigen Zusagen ab und zu angewendete gegenseitige Anrede" nur zeige, „wie sehr auch sonst das Briefschema zur bloßen Form erstarrt" sei.[7] Immerhin machte er bereits auf regionale und zeitliche Unterschiede aufmerksam, wonach diese Stilisierung „namentlich im Hermupolites (sic), mindestens seit 135 n. Chr.", seit dem „späteren 3. Jh." dann auch im Arsinoites und Oxyrhynchites nachweisbar sei.[8] Konnte er sich dabei auf nur 15 Belege stützen,[9] hat sich die Beleglage in den vergangenen 30 Jahren noch einmal um zwei Drittel auf 26 erhöht, rechnet man allein, wie auch Wolff es tat, das bis zum 4. Jh. datierende Material. Nimmt man außerdem auch noch die späteren, in der Regel als Tabellionenurkunden ausgefertigten Verträge mit dieser Grußformel hinzu, wo sich die Frage nach den Gründen zweifellos ebenso stellt,[10] haben wir es sogar mit 34 oder gar 35 Belegen zu tun. Auch wenn wir damit gegenüber Wolff über mehr als die doppelte Menge an Texten verfügen, bleibt es insgesamt doch bei einer erstaunlich geringen Zahl.

Hinsichtlich der regionalen Verbreitung erweisen sich Wolffs Beobachtungen allerdings als weiterhin haltbar. Zuerst ist die fragliche Grußformel im Hermopolites anzutreffen, wo sie sich am häufigsten und auch am längsten, nämlich vom 2. bis zum 6. Jh., nachweisen läßt. Im Oxyrhynchites tritt sie dagegen nicht vor 274,[11] im Arsinoi-

6 Mitteis 1912: 57, mit Verweis auf P.Flor. I 47 = M.Chr. 146 und P.Lips. I 28 = M.Chr. 363 bzw. CPR I 10 = M.Chr. 145 (jetzt CPR XVII A 17) und BGU I 71.

7 Wolff 1978: 107.

8 Wolff 1978: 107f. Anm. 6.

9 Zu streichen ist das Naturaldarlehen P.Cair.Isid. 97 (Apr. 308).

10 Mit dem vom 31.12.381 datierenden P.Lips. I 28 = M.Chr. 363 hatte im übrigen auch schon Wolff eine Tabellionenurkunde in seine Aufzählung eingeschlossen.

11 Mit P.Köln II 101 = SB XII 11238 stammt der früheste sicher datierte oxyrhynchitische Vertrag vom 28.9.274 oder 280. Das von Wolff übersehene Vertragsfragment PSI IV 306 stammt nach der Einl. „dall'Epeiph dell'a. 3 di un imperatore (della prima metà del III sec., o anche della seconda metà del

tes sogar erst in der Tetrarchenzeit auf.[12] Im 4. Jh. begegnet sie schließlich in Kellis in der Großen Oase,[13] noch später auch in Antinoupolis und im Archiv des bekannten Notars Dioskoros.[14] Die nachdiokletianischen Urkunden bieten damit einen fast getreuen Spiegel der Überlieferungslage,[15] doch ist dies für die Verteilung der früheren Texte, namentlich das auffällige Übergewicht des Hermopolites, kaum zu behaupten. Nicht nur die im Verhältnis dazu geringe Zahl derartiger Urkunden aus Oxyrhynchites wie Arsinoites, die doch sonst dem Hermopolites an Funden weit voraus sind, sondern auch ihr spätes Auftreten verlangen vielmehr nach einer Erklärung. Sollte diese Stilisierung tatsächlich bei bestimmten Rechtsgeschäften bevorzugt worden sein, wäre demnach auch zu prüfen, wie man zur fraglichen Zeit außerhalb des Hermopolites mit solchen Vereinbarungen verfuhr.

Daß es sich dabei um eher seltene Vertragstypen handelte, deutet sich bereits in der geringen Zahl der Belege, aber auch in der gewaltsamen Konstruktion der gegenseitigen Anrede an. Dabei war nicht zufällig bei Mitteis der Hinweis auf ‚gegenseitige Verträge', bei Wolff auf ‚beiderseitige Zusagen' gefallen, wenngleich Mitteis' Nachsatz, daß „auch der eine Teil allein die beiderseitigen Erklärungen formulieren" könne, scheinbar Beliebigkeit suggeriert.[16] Nach den von ihm für letzteres angeführten Beispielen – beides Kaufverträgen – zu schließen, hatte er hierbei offenbar Verträge im Blick, die nur von einer Vertragspartei ausgestellt wurden, wiewohl eine vorherige Einigung zwischen den Parteien selbstredend vorauszusetzen ist. Eine solche einseitige Erklärung ist in den Papyri sogar der Normalfall, da Aussteller regelmäßig derjenige ist, der eine Verfügung trifft oder eine Verpflichtung eingeht – in Kaufverträgen also der Verkäufer, in Darlehen der Darlehensnehmer usw. Dem Empfänger der Erklärung blieb allenfalls die Anerkennung dieses Sachverhalts in der Subskription, wie zuletzt

II)", doch wird man letzteres demnach ausschließen dürfen. Was die Ortsangabe in Z. 5 betrifft, wird man entgegen dem Komm. in PSI V p. ix „non è possibile Νήσῳ Λαχανίας" (= BL I 395, wenngleich nicht ganz korrekt) vielleicht doch wieder auf diesen Gedanken Grenfells zurückkommen wollen, da die sonstigen Belege durchweg aus der Spätzeit datieren (vgl. nur Calderini – Daris, Diz. geogr. III 350; Suppl. II 134) und im Laufe der Jahrhunderte durchaus mit kleineren Lautveränderungen zu rechnen ist.

12 Frühester Beleg ist nunmehr P.Col. X 281 = SB XVI 12829 vom Juli/Aug. 287.

13 Aus den seit den späten 1980er Jahren durchgeführten Ausgrabungen in Ismant el-Kharab stammen P.Kell. I 13 (335) sowie 30 (22.5.363), während P.Sijp. 11a (390) bereits 1969 von der Duke University angekauft worden war.

14 In Antinoupolis wurden PSI XIII 1341 = SB V 8951 (425–50?, mit BL VIII 410) und der wohl ebenfalls hierher zu stellende P.Cair.Masp. II 67159 (16.12.568) ausgefertigt, wobei letzterer ebenso wie P.Lond. V 1705 (517/18 oder 532/33) zu dem in Kom Ishqaw, dem ehemaligen Aphrodites Kome, gefundenen Archiv des Dioskoros gehört.

15 Hierzu wie zum folgenden allgem. Habermann 1998, zum Dioskoros-Archiv bes. 151; zu Kellis bereits oben Anm. 13.

16 Vgl. oben Anm. 6f. mit Text.

noch einmal Dieter Hagedorn für die staatsnotariellen Urkunden des Arsinoites dargelegt hat.[17]

Hiervon wird man die hybriden Cheirographa *pace* Mitteis jedoch scharf zu scheiden haben, da demnach bereits die gegenseitige Anrede auf eine vom eben genannten Normalfall abweichende, da beiderseitige Verpflichtung verweist. Dies sei im folgenden an insgesamt drei Vertragsgruppen vorgeführt, nämlich an Tausch- und Gesellschaftsverträgen sowie den Liturgiestellvertretungen. Die zahlenmäßig größte Gruppe der Teilungsverträge, der hier neun Belege zuzuordnen sind, nehme ich dagegen aus, zumal sie in den Papyri in einer ganzen Reihe von Varianten begegnen – nicht zuletzt auch einseitigen Erklärungen, so etwa bei Erbschaftsteilungen seitens der Eltern.[18]

Tauschverträge oder, wie sie sich teilweise selbst bezeichnen, ἀντικαταλλαγαί gehören zu den seltensten in den Papyri belegten Vertragstypen überhaupt. Insgesamt liegen nur acht Zeugnisse vor, in denen zumeist Immobilien, zwei Mal auch Esel Tauschobjekte sind. In zwei Fällen ist ausdrücklich vermerkt, daß die Vertragspartner Brüder bzw. Halbbrüder sind,[19] doch auch dort, wo Hausanteile getauscht werden, wird man zuversichtlich mit einem familiären Hintergrund rechnen dürfen.[20] Bei Grundstücken mag vielleicht die relative Lage zum sonstigen Besitz eine Rolle spielen.[21] Weswegen es zu dem Tausch der Esel kam, ist dagegen allenfalls zu spekulieren; bemerkenswerterweise wird in beiden Fällen von der einen Partei noch eine Geldsumme als Ausgleich für den höheren Schätzwert des eingetauschten Esels gezahlt.[22] Die gegenseitige Anrede findet sich nun in der Hälfte der durchweg als Cheirographa gefaßten Belege; einmal treten beide Partner im Nominativ auf, während das erwartete ἀλλήλοις χαίρειν fehlt; in zwei weiteren Fällen ist der Anfang ganz verloren. Damit weist lediglich ein einziger Tauschvertrag die übliche Form des Präskriptes ὁ δεῖνα τῷ δεῖνι χαίρειν auf, auch wenn sich das Bild bei der geringen Zahl rasch ändern mag.

Etwas mehr Zeugnisse, nämlich zwölf, sind in den Papyri für Gesellschaftsverträge zu finden. Auch hier ist erneut die Hälfte als hybrides Cheirographon stilisiert.[23]

17 Hagedorn 1998. Anders als vielleicht erwartet wurden die Urkunden allerdings keineswegs ausschließlich von dem aus römischrechtlicher Sicht als ‚Schuldner' zu bezeichnenden Vertragspartner, sondern gelegentlich auch von dem ‚Gläubiger' ausgestellt. Welche Vertragspartei jeweils als ausstellende auftrat, war offenbar vor allem eine Sache lokaler Gewohnheiten, da anders als im römischen Recht eben keine Haftung begründet, sondern lediglich eine Erklärung über einen Sachverhalt abgegeben wurde, vgl. nur Wolff 1957: bes. 56ff. sowie 60.

18 Vgl. nur Jördens, Einl. zu P.Louvre I 8.

19 P.Flor. I 47 = M.Chr. 146 (14.1.217, + SB I 5671 = BL I 138f. 455; Herm.; Halbbrüder); P.Stras. VI 556 (nach 289; Herm.; Brüder, vgl. auch P.Stras. VI 555 und VII 627).

20 P.Kellis I 30 (22.5.363; Kellis); P.Thomas 28 = P.Michael. 51 (ca. 514–35, Aphr. K.).

21 So in PSI XIII 1341 = SB V 8951 (425–50?, mit BL V 127. VIII 410; Antin.).

22 P.Wisc. I 15 (24.6.236, mit BL VI 71. XI 126; Bubastos oder Oxy.); P.Sijp. 11a (390; Kellis).

23 P.Amh. II 100 (198–211); PSI IV 306 (2./3. Jh.); P.Köln II 101 = SB XII 11238 (28.9.274 oder 280); P.Lips. I 18 (308); P.Lond. V 1794 (21.6.488); in P.Lond. V 1705.5 wird man ἀλλήλοις ergänzen dürfen [so etwa auch Wolff, ZSSRA 93 (1976: 330) zu P.Oxy. XLIII 3139]; in P.Lond. V 1795 ist der An-

Diese Form scheint man aber nur dann gewählt zu haben, wenn die Parteien sich auf gleicher Basis trafen. Denn in den drei Verträgen, die mit dem für das Cheirographon üblichen ὁ δεῖνα τῷ δεῖνι χαίρειν beginnen, ist dies sichtlich nicht der Fall. Einmal geht es um die gemeinsame Nutzung eines Kamelstalles, der seinerseits vom Adressaten gepachtet worden war;[24] zwei andere Verträge betreffen ein gemeinsames Handelsunternehmen in die Oase, das der Transporteur gegenüber dem Finanzier, der ihm die nötigen Geldmittel vorgeschossen hatte, durchzuführen versprach.[25] Bei zwei weiteren Vereinbarungen handelt es sich um Tabellionenurkunden aus dem Jahr 568, die insoweit aber ebenfalls von der nunmehr üblichen Form abweichen, als auf die Datierung nicht sofort die Namen der Vertragspartner folgen, sondern eine feierliche Erklärung, daß eine gemeinsame Verständigung zustandekam; erst danach werden die beteiligten Parteien genannt, und zwar jede Seite betont für sich.[26] Hierauf ist noch zurückzukommen.

Eine deutlich größere Anzahl von Verträgen besitzen wir aus dem Bereich des Liturgiewesens.[27] Zumeist handelt es sich dabei um Liturgiestellvertretungen, in denen sich jemand gegenüber dem ernannten Liturgen bereit erklärt, gegen Entlohnung an seiner Stelle die ihm auferlegten Verpflichtungen zu erfüllen. Varianten hierzu stellen solche Verträge dar, in denen der Ernannte eine entsprechende Vereinbarung nicht mit dem Stellvertreter, sondern mit dem Ernennenden trifft, der dafür einen solchen Mann einzustellen verspricht,[28] wenn nicht gar ganz auf die Ernennung eines Liturgen verzichtet und gleich mit demjenigen kontrahiert wird, der die Arbeiten durchführen wird.[29] In weiterem Sinne sind schließlich auch die Verpflichtungen des ebenfalls

fang gänzlich verloren, doch firmieren beide Vertragspartner in der Subskription gemeinsam (Z. 13 Α[ὐρ(ήλιοι)] ... ạς Βίκτωρος καὶ Πέτρος Κούνθου οἱ προκ(είμενοι) ἐθέμεθα τ[ὴν] ọṃ[ολο]γίαν τῆς κοινωνείας καὶ πειθόμεθα κτλ.), zudem ist schon in der Ed. pr. die Nähe zu P.Lond. V 1794 vermerkt.

24 P.Oxy. X 1280 (Ende 4. Jh.), in dem schon Steinwenter (1936: 501) vielmehr eine „Untermiete nur ganz leicht als Gesellschaft verkleidet" erkannt hatte; vgl. auch Jördens 1990: 360f. Nur auf den ersten Blick vergleichbar erscheinen P.Amh. II 100 (198–211), wo jedoch der künftige κοινωνός schon aufgrund der sofortigen Zahlung seines Pachtzinsanteils eine ungleich stärkere Position besaß, und P.Lips. I 18 (308): Hier war der dritte Vertragspartner, ein Buleut, wohl sogar Eigentümer der künftig gemeinsam bearbeiteten $12^1/_4$ + 3 Aruren, doch wurde diese μισθομολογία (so nach Z. 20) bewußt als echter Gesellschaftsvertrag unter gleichen Partnern gestaltet, vgl. nur Jördens 1990: 361ff., bes. 363.

25 SB XVI 12530 = P.Genova I 20 (4.7.319); P.Genova I 21 (mit P.Genova II App. II; 25.7.320).

26 P.Cair.Masp. II 67158 = FIRA III 158.3ff. (28.4.568) bzw. der in 3 Ex. überlieferte P.Cair.Masp. II 67159, 67160 und III 67315^r.4ff. (16.12.568).

27 Vgl. zuletzt eingehend Jördens 1990: 185ff. Kap. III. Zu ergänzen sind inzwischen P.Oxy. LIX 3985 (9.5.473) und LXVII 4597 (19.11.294) sowie der damals übersehene P.Select 22 = Pap.Choix 14 (2. Jh.); P.Oxy.Elmagh. 11 (19.2.266?) ist nunmehr als P.Oxy. LVII 3912 wiederabgedruckt. Von den dort behandelten 34 Dokumenten zu entgeltlichen Leistungen im Liturgiewesen bleiben die Quittungen und eidlichen Verpflichtungen im folgenden allerdings unberücksichtigt.

28 P.Oxy. LI 3622 (29.8.356); P.Flor. I 39 = W.Chr. 405 (29.8.396); P.Oxy. LV 3796 (10.12.412).

29 P.Sakaon 58 = PSI VIII 873 (5.7.299); P.Michael. 28 (313/4); P.Oxy. XIV 1626 = Sel.Pap. II 361 = FIRA III 151 (16.5.325).

vom Liturgen zu finanzierenden Hilfspersonals,[30] aber auch eine Abrede über die Nachfolge im Amt des Dorfvorstehers hierher zu stellen.[31]

Von insgesamt 26 Verträgen dieser Art, die sich vom mittleren 2. bis zum 5. Jh. finden, sind anders als in den vorigen Fällen nur relativ wenige, nämlich vier, als hybride Cheirographa stilisiert.[32] Allerdings gibt es bislang kein einziges Zeugnis hierfür aus dem Hermopolites, wo diese Grußformel, wie wir gesehen hatten, besonders verbreitet war. Die vordiokletianischen Verträge stammen vielmehr überwiegend aus dem Oxyrhynchites und damit aus der Heimat des sog. privaten Protokolls.[33] Dieser vorzugsweise für Pachten und Mieten eingesetzte Urkundstyp begann stets mit der Feststellung eines Sachverhalts – beispielsweise ἐμίσθωσεν, ‚es hat verpachtet' – und war im Gegensatz zum Cheirographon immer objektiv stilisiert; wie dort waren die Verträge allerdings auch hier in der Regel als einseitige Erklärung formuliert. Dies galt jedoch nicht für Vereinbarungen im liturgischen Bereich, wo die Eingangsformel durchweg ὁμολογοῦσιν ἀλλήλοις ὁ δεῖνα καὶ ὁ δεῖνα, also ‚es anerkennen einander A und B', lautet.[34] Sowohl die Charakterisierung als Anerkenntnis wie vor allem die Nennung der beiden Vertragspartner im Nominativ weist ihnen insofern eine Sonderstellung zu, die derjenigen der hybriden Cheirographa, gerade auch in der betonten Wechselseitigkeit, durchaus vergleichbar ist. Im Arsinoites scheint es dagegen nie zu einer einheitlichen Vertragsgestaltung gekommen zu sein, doch sind neben zwei hybriden Cheirographa immerhin zwei private Protokolle mit der Einleitung συνέθεντο πρὸς ἀλλήλους, ‚es haben miteinander vereinbart', zu finden.[35]

30 P.Select. 22 = Pap.Choix 14 (2. Jh., mit BL V 64. VI 68. VII 99. VIII 200); P.Mich. XI 604 (31.5.223). Die meisten Belege hierfür sind allerdings Quittungen, vgl. die Übersicht bei Jördens 1990: 185.

31 P.Col. X 281 = SB XVI 12829 (7./8.287).

32 P.Col. X 281 = SB XVI 12829 (7./8.287, Ars.); P.Cair.Isid. 81 = SB V 7676 (9.4.297, Ars.); P.Oxy. XXXVIII 2859 (10.11.301, Oxy.); LXIII 4385 (22.5.386, Oxy.).

33 Vgl. nur Wolff 1978: 122ff., bes. auch 125 („In der frühen Kaiserzeit scheint das private Protokoll ein spezifisch zu *Oxyrhynchos* gehöriges Gebilde gewesen zu sein").

34 P.Select. 22 = Pap.Choix 14 (2. Jh.); P.Amst. I 49 (206 – 212); P.Oxy. XLIII 3095 = SB XII 10941 (217/18); P.Mich. XI 604 (31.5.223); P.Leit. 13 = SB VIII 10205 (222/3, 226/7 oder 242/3, mit BL V 48. VI 163); BGU IV 1062 = W.Chr. 276 (29.8.236, mit BL I 93. VII 18. VIII 40); P.Oxy. XXXVI 2769 (3.6.242); P.Harr. I 64 (269/70, mit BL III 77. VI 49. VII 66). So auch noch PSI IX 1037 (301, mit BL VIII 405. IX 319) sowie P.Oxy. XIV 1626 = Sel.Pap. II 361 = FIRA III 151 (16.5.325, mit BL V 79); verkürzt dagegen P.Osl. III 135 (286 – 93, mit BL III 127. VII 125. IX 176; ohne ἀλλήλοις) sowie P.Oxy. LXVII 4597 (19.11.294; ‹ὁμολογοῦσιν ἀλλήλοις› ergänzt, vgl. auch die Anm.).

35 So in P.Sakaon 58 = PSI VIII 873 (5.7.299) und wohl auch dem fragmentarischen P.Mich. IX 574 (frühes 4. Jh., mit BL IX 162), vgl. ebenso auch die Abrede zum Liturgietausch in P.Cair.Isid. 82 = SB VI 9268 (26.7.318); zu den beiden hybriden Cheirographa oben Anm. 32. Die beiden frühesten arsinoitischen Verträge – das Cheirographon BGU II 638 (18.6.143; Anfang verloren) und die staatsnotarielle Urkunde P.Lond. II 306 (p. 118) = W.Chr. 263 = Sel.Pap. II 358 (28.8.145) – folgen dagegen der üblichen Form, ebenso das private Protokoll BGU I 286 (συνέθετο ὁ δεῖνα τῷ δεῖνι). Angesichts der Variationsbreite war insofern auch Platz für gelegentliche Vertauschungen wie in P.Cair.Isid. 80 = SB VI 9267 (19.10.296), wo der Stellvertreter eher als Absender denn als Adressat des Cheirographons hätte erscheinen müssen; vgl. auch ebda. den Komm. zu Z. 2. Aufmerksamkeit mag zudem auch die hier verwendete gegenseitige Stipulation ἐπερωτήσαντες ἀλλήλους ὡμολογήσαμεν (Z. 21) verdie-

Man wird demnach kaum fehlgehen in der Annahme, daß hybride Cheirographa und mit dem wechselseitigen Anerkenntnis eingeleitete private Protokolle dieselbe Funktion erfüllten. Dennoch wurden Verbindungen zwischen beiden Phänomenen trotz der offenkundigen Gemeinsamkeiten bisher nicht gezogen – dies vielleicht auch deswegen, weil das Präskript des Cheirographons, sieht man einmal von den veränderten Kasus der Vertragsparteien und dem hinzugefügten ἀλλήλοις ab, weitgehend unverändert und damit relativ unauffällig blieb. Im Gegensatz dazu zog das bei den privaten Protokollen so prägnant an den Anfang gestellte ὁμολογεῖν schon bald die Aufmerksamkeit der Rechtshistoriker auf sich. Ihrem lebhaften Interesse am Charakter der Homologie ist daher hier auch eine erste Differenzierung nach Vertragstypen zu danken. Demnach wurde das private Protokoll nicht nur für Misthoseis oder Heiratsverträge eingesetzt, sondern auch, wie Wolff notiert, „für in der Form gegenseitiger Homologien gefaßte Lehrverträge (διδασκαλικαί) zwischen Eltern bzw. Herren der Lehrlinge und deren Meistern, wie auch für andere auf die – gewiß auch sonst, aber gerade hier typisch verwandte – Formel ὁμολογοῦσιν ἀλλήλοις gestellte Verträge (Teilungsabkommen, Vereinbarungen über Austausch oder Abnahme liturgischer Pflichten, Engagement von Vortragskünstlern)“.[36]

Wie nahe sich die beiden Urkundstypen stehen, wird zudem nicht nur an den soeben erörterten Verträgen aus dem Bereich des Liturgiewesens, sondern auch an den ebenfalls gern als hybride Cheirographa gefaßten, hier jedoch ausgeklammerten Tei-

nen, die in den hier in Rede stehenden Urkunden des häufigeren begegnet und der man daher vielleicht *pace* Simon (1964: 44ff.) noch einmal nachgehen sollte.

36 Wolff 1978: 124; zu den ebda. in Anm. 88 aufgeführten Ausbildungsverträgen sind inzwischen zu ergänzen P.Oxy.Hels. 29 (8. 8.54) und P.Oxy. LXVII 4596 (11./12.232 oder 264); SB XII 10946 (so) liegt verbessert in SB XXIV 16253 vor, bei dem am Ende aufgeführten Vertrag handelt es sich erneut um P.Oxy. XXXVIII 2875. Vgl. jetzt auch allgem. Bergamasco 1995: 98, demzufolge das Verhältnis zwischen der Fassung als „ὁμολογία oggettiva reciproca“ und einfachem Cheirographon in oxyrhynchitischen Ausbildungsverträgen 15 : 3 beträgt. Weitere Verträge mit Unterhaltungskünstlern (Wolff, a.o. Anm. 91) finden sich jetzt in P.Oxy. LXXIV 5014 und 5015 (beide 3. Jh.). Bei der überwiegenden Zahl der mehr als sechs Dutzend Dokumente, in denen nach einer Suche in der DDbDP die Formel ὁμολογοῦσιν ἀλλήλοις vorkommt, handelt es sich indessen um staatsnotarielle Urkunden. In jeder Hinsicht einen Ausnahmefall bildet das private Protokoll P.Sakaon 65 = P.Thead. 12 (11.9.328, mit BL VIII 302), das ein zinsloses Darlehen von 78 Talenten durch Sakaon und einen seiner Dorfgenossen aus dem arsinoitischen Theadelpheia betrifft und als „loan of money“ bzw. „fragment d'un prêt“ vorgestellt wurde. Das einleitende ὁμολογοῦσιν ἀλλήλοις ließ freilich schon den Erstherausgeber P. Jouguet aufhorchen, der im Komm. zu P.Thead. 12.1 notierte, „que les rapports entre les deux débiteurs étaient spécifiés dans notre contrat“, und eine Verbindung zur ἀλληλεγγύη erwog, während G. Parássoglou in seiner Neuedition kurzerhand ἀλλήλοις athetierte. Berücksichtigt man allerdings auch die weiteren Merkwürdigkeiten – daß zwar der Name des Gläubigers genannt wird, die Praxis jedoch unpersönlich formuliert und jedenfalls nicht ihm zugesprochen wird, dazu auf dem Verso Sakaon als Adressat erscheint –, handelt es sich vielleicht doch eher um eine interne Vereinbarung der beiden Schuldner über die Rückzahlungsmodalitäten. Vgl. etwa auch P.Köln XI 459 (436?) mit unten Anm. 41.

lungsverträgen offenbar.[37] Völlige Deckungsgleichheit, was ihren Einsatz für bestimmte Rechtsgeschäfte betrifft, ist freilich schon von der unterschiedlichen Herkunft und Zeitstellung unserer Quellen her kaum zu erwarten. Insofern sollte auch nicht erstaunen, wenn es bisher keine Lehrlings- und Künstlerverträge in der Form des hybriden Cheirographons und keine Tausch- und Gesellschaftsverträge in der des privaten Protokolles gibt. Immerhin ließ sich bei den Gesellschaftsverträgen der Spätantike eine besondere Stilisierung beobachten, worauf nunmehr zurückzukommen ist.

Diese Tabellionenurkunden zeichnen sich unter anderem dadurch aus, daß wie bei allen anderen hier in Rede stehenden Dokumenten beide Vertragsparteien im Nominativ stehen, aber zusätzlich noch durch ein präzisierendes ἐκ μὲν τοῦ ἑνὸς μέρους bzw. ἐκ δὲ θατέρου μέρους, also ‚von der einen Seite – von der anderen Seite', voneinander abgesetzt sind. Parallelen hierfür (im zweiten Teil mitunter auch mit einem prosaischeren ἐκ δὲ τοῦ ἑτέρου) lassen sich vom ausgehenden 5. Jh. bis in das frühe 8. Jh. benennen, und zwar nicht nur aus Ägypten allein, sondern auch aus Palästina und sogar Konstantinopel.[38] Auch die insgesamt 30 ägyptischen Urkunden bieten sonst eher selten belegte Provenienzen; so finden sich neben einzelnen Zeugnissen aus Lykopolis, dem Apollonopolites Heptakomias, aus Panopolis oder Syene sogar insgesamt zehn derartige Dokumente aus Antinoupolis.[39] In allen Fällen geht der Nennung der Vertragsparteien der ausdrückliche Hinweis auf die gemeinsame Errichtung der Urkunde voraus,[40] nicht selten folgt auch noch ein verstärkendes

37 Vgl. auch bereits Wolff 1957: 57f. Anm. 77.

38 Palästina: P.Petra I 1 (23.5.537, Petra); 2 (10.5.538, Gaza; beide mit BL XII 157); P.Ness. 22 (?.11.566, Nessana) – Konstantinopel: P.Cair.Masp. I 67032 = Sel.Pap. II 363 = FIRA III 179 = Jur.Pap. 52 (11.7.551, mit BL I 105f. 445. III 34). – Zu den ägyptischen Urkunden vgl. die folgende Anm. Die Eckdaten sind bislang die Jahre 481 und 719 (mit P.Princ. II 82 = SB III 7033 bzw. P.Rain.Cent. 121), die Hauptmasse stammt allerdings – nicht zuletzt wegen des gehäuften Auftretens im sog. Dioskoros-Archiv – aus dem 6. Jh. Eine Reihe dieser Verträge liegt sogar in mehreren Ausfertigungen vor, wovon im folgenden allerdings außer bei der ersten Nennung ebenso wie bei den – teilweise zahlreichen – Neuabdrucken stets nur ein Beleg als Referenz gegeben wird.

39 Lykopolis: P.Princ. II 82 = SB III 7033 (27.3.481, mit BL V 99. IX 246). – Apollonopolites Heptakomias: P.Lond. II 483 (p. 323) (5.8.615 oder 616). – Panopolis: P.Par. 20 (14.7.600; mit BL I 338. VI 113). – Syene: P.Münch. I 14 (15.2.594, mit BL I 311. VIII 227. XI 138). – Antinoupolis: P.Cair.Masp. II 67154[r] (527–65); P.Lond. V 1707 (5.10.566, mit BL XI 120); 1710 (566–73, mit BL X 107); P.Cair.Masp. II 67158 = FIRA III 158 (28.4.568); 67159 (16.12.568; 2./3. Ex. in 67160 sowie III 67315[r]); P.Lond. V 1712 (15.7.569); P.Flor. I 93 = M.Chr. 297 = FIRA III 22 (5.9.oder 5.10.569; 2. Ex. in P.Lond. V 1713); P.Cair.Masp. III 67311 (569/70?); II 67156 A (24.9.570; 2./3. Ex. in 67156 C sowie 67157); P.Münch. I 7 (23.6.583); vgl. auch P.Cair.Masp. I 67108 (Anf. 547, Aphr. K.). – Zu den arsinoitischen Belegen zuletzt Gagos (2008) 65 im Komm. zu Z. 6ff.; aus dem Herakleopolites stammen CPR VI 7 (6. Jh.), P.Rain.Cent. 121 (7.10.(?)719) und vermutlich SPP III 402 (6. Jh.) sowie 415 (7. Jh., beide äußerst fragmentarisch), aus dem Hermopolites P.Lond. III 992 (p. 253) = M.Chr. 365 = Sel.Pap. I 61 = FIRA III 182 (6./7.507, mit BL I 295), 1313[r] (p. 256) (1.12.507), P.Prag. I 42 (vor 533), BGU XII 2203 (7.7.571, mit BL IX 31. XII 24) und P.Herm. 29 = SB VI 9278 = CPJ III 513 (26.7.586).

40 In der Form ταύτην τίθενται καὶ ποιοῦνται πρὸς ἀλλήλους τὴν ὁμολογίαν o.ä., mit anschließender genauerer Kennzeichnung des Rechtsgeschäfts, vgl. außer den bereits von J.-L. Fournet und J. Gascou in der Ed. pr. von SB XXIV 16040 (6./7. Jh.) in BIFAO 98 (1998: 176) sowie zuletzt C. Rogl

ὁμολογοῦσιν (bzw. bei subjektiver Stilisierung ὁμολογοῦμεν) ἀλλήλοις;[41] gelegentlich ist sogar noch ein versprengtes χαίρειν angefügt.[42]

Fast schon erwartungsgemäß treffen wir unter den in dieser Form niedergelegten Rechtsgeschäften außer den bereits erwähnten Gesellschaftsverträgen auch wieder Teilungsvereinbarungen an, daneben aber auch auffällig viele Ehescheidungen.[43] Den Löwenanteil nehmen indessen die wenigstens 22 Streitbeendigungen ein, wobei es sich teils um die Unterwerfung der Parteien unter ein Schiedsgericht in der Form eines κομπρόμισσον, teils um διαλύσεις, also Vergleiche handelt, was übrigens auch die Scheidungen umgreift.[44] Nur nebenbei sei bemerkt, daß in drei Fällen auch die für die hybriden Cheirographa charakteristische wechselseitige Grußformel ihren Weg in solche Streitbeendigungen gefunden hat.[45]

in Einl. und Komm. zu Z. 4–5 von CPR XIX 50 (2. Hälfte 7. Jh.) genannten Belegen auch P.Cair.Masp. II 67159.4f. (16.12.568); 67156A.3 (24.9.570); P.München. I 7.6f. (23.6.583); 14.6 (15.2. 594); P.Par. 20.3 (14.600); P.Lond. II 483 (p. 323).4f. (5. 8. 615 oder 616).

41 ʽΟμολογοῦσιν ἀλλήλοις: P.Cair.Masp. II 67154^{r}.6 (527–656); 67156A.8 (24.9.570); P.Herm. 29.8 (26.7.586); vgl. auch P.Cair.Masp. III 67311.10 (569/70?); P.Lond. II 483 (p. 323) 11 (5.8.615 oder 616). – ʽΟμολογοῦμεν ἀλλήλοις: P.Princ. II 82.7 (27.3.481); P.Lond. III 1313 (p. 256).12 (1.12.507); V 1712.8 (15.7.569); vgl. auch als Partizip in BGU XII 2203.7 (7.7.571) sowie dem erst zu Ende des Präskriptes einsetzenden SB XIV 12043.3 (6. Jh.). Um so bemerkenswerter erscheint freilich die offenkundig einseitige Fortführung in der Abtretungsurkunde CPR XIX 50.9ff. (2. Hälfte 7. Jh.). Eine in dieser Weise formulierte Teilungsvereinbarung scheint auch in P.Köln XI 459.8 (436?) vorzuliegen, wobei die gegenseitige Erklärung hier allerdings gegenüber einem Dritten abgegeben wird.

42 So in P.Princ. II 82.8 (27.3.481); P.Lond. III 1313^{r} (p. 256).12 (1.12.507); P.Cair.Masp. I 67108.14 (Anf. 547); II 67158.10 (28.4.568); 67159.12 (16.12.568); P.Lond. II 483 (p. 323).12 (5.8.615 oder 616); BGU I 315.10 (22.7.627); in P.Lond. III 992 (p. 253).10 (6./7.507) endet das Präskript sogar wie in den hybriden Cheirographa mit ἀλλήλοις χαίρ(ειν).

43 Teilungsvereinbarungen: P.Lond. III 1313^{r} (p. 256) (1.12.507); P.Prag. I 42 (vor 533). – Ehescheidungen: P.Cair.Masp. II 67154^{r} (527–65); III 67311 (569/70?); P.Lond. V 1712 (15.7.569); P.Flor. I 93 (5.9. oder 5.10.569); BGU XII 2203 (7.7.571); P.Herm. 29 (26.7.586); SB XIV 12043 (6. Jh.); vgl. hierzu auch Steinwenter 1935: 80. Unklar bleiben die eherechtlichen Bezüge in dem fragmentarischen P.Lond. V 1710 (566–73). – Zu den Gesellschaftsverträgen vgl. oben Anm. 26, zu allen sonstigen Verträgen die folgende Anm. Aus dem Rahmen fallen insoweit nur die beiden Pachtverträge P.Cair.Masp. I 67108 (Anf. 547) und P.Lond. II 483 (p. 323) (5.8.615 oder 616), hier eine Emphyteuse auf Klosterland.

44 Kompromisse: P.Lond. III 992 (p. 253) = M.Chr. 365 = Sel.Pap. I 61 = FIRA III 182 (6./7.507, mit BL I 295); P.Lond. V 1707 (5.10.566); CPR VI 7 sowie SPP III 402 (beide 6. Jh.); SB XXIV 15899 = I 5266 (8.8.608); I 5271 (10.12.615); XIV 12194 = I 5258 + 5261 + 5263 (619 – 29 oder nach 641); BGU I 315 (22.7.627); SB I 5681 (8.6.654 oder 669); P.Rain.Cent. 121 (7.10.(?)719). – Dialyseis: Neben den in der vorigen Anm. genannten Scheidungen (in P.Flor. I 93.27 fällt immerhin das Verb διαλελύσθαι) auch P.Princ. II 82 (27.3.481); P.Lond. III 1008 (p. 265) (21.6.561); P.Cair.Masp. II 67156 A (24.9.570); P.Münch. I 7 (23.6.583); 14 (15.2.594); P.Par. 20 (14.7.600); vgl. auch die Abtretungsurkunde CPR XIX 50.9ff. (2. Hälfte 7. Jh.). Vergleiche konnten allerdings durchaus auch in anderer Form niedergelegt werden, vgl. nur A. Papathomas, P.Heid. VII 404, Einl. sowie Komm. zu Z. 8–14.

45 P.Haun. III 57.3 (412 – 5, mit BL XII 86: διάλυσις); P.Lond. III 992 (p. 253).10 (6./7.507); SB VIII 9775.9 (2. Hälfte VII. Jhdt., mit BL XII 201; beides κομπρόμισσα). In dem soeben von Gagos (2008) publizierten *compromissum* P.Corn. inv. II 48.6ff. (5.10.596) lautet die Grußformel zwar A καὶ B

Fragt man nun wiederum nach der Gestalt von Streitbeendigungen und Scheidungen in vordiokletianischer Zeit, fällt vor allem auf, daß es für ersteres kaum Zeugnisse gibt. Die früheste aus Ägypten bekannte Kompromißurkunde datiert nach wie vor vom Jahr 399,[46] und auch Dialyseis sind erst seit der zweiten Hälfte des 3. Jhs. nachweisbar.[47] Die Gründe hierfür sind erst kürzlich wieder mit neuen Argumenten erörtert worden, müssen im vorliegenden Zusammenhang jedoch nicht interessieren.[48] Von den drei vor dem Jahr 300 ausgestellten Vergleichen ist nun einer als hybrides Cheirographon stilisiert;[49] der zweite beginnt ungewöhnlicherweise mit einem bloßen μετοξὺ τοῦ δεῖνος καὶ τοῦ δεῖνος, also ‚zwischen A und B', wobei die Parteien wohlgemerkt wieder gleichgeordnet sind;[50] die dritte, äußerst fragmentarische Urkunde weist erneut ein wechselseitiges ὁμολογοῦμ[ε]ν ἀλλήλοις auf.[51]

Scheidungen sind demgegenüber im kaiserzeitlichen Quellenmaterial deutlich häufiger anzutreffen. Dabei sollte der Umstand, daß „der eigentliche Inhalt der Urkunde in der Bestätigung der Rückgewähr der Mitgift und der anderen Gütermassen

χ(αίρειν), doch fehlt sonst jeder weitere Hinweis – und sei es nur durch ein zusätzliches ἀλλήλοις – auf die sonst so betonte Zweiseitigkeit, was ohne Zweifel mit dem bereits von Gagos herausgearbeiteten großen sozialen Gefälle zwischen den beiden Vertragsparteien zu verbinden ist.

46 P.Giss. I 104 (30.6.399); vgl. bereits Ziegler 1971: 193f. sowie die Übersicht 289ff.; der ebda. versuchsweise in das „3. Jahrh.?" gesetzte, sehr fragmentarische P.Genova inv. Nr. 1126 = SB XII 10733 wird inzwischen deutlich später datiert, vgl. bereits die Neued. in P.Genova I 23 und bes. BL VII 275. Eine neuere Liste der Belege bietet H.A. Rupprecht, Tyche 12 (1997: 267f.) in der Besprechung von Gagos & van Minnen 1994; allgem. zuletzt Gagos 2008.

47 So jedenfalls nach der zuletzt erschienenen Übersicht bei Gagos & van Minnen 1994: 121ff., die entgegen der Überschrift sämtliche und keineswegs nur die ‚Late Antique Settlements in Greek' enthält, mit den Ergänzungen von J.F. Oates † & P. van Minnen, Einl. zu P.Sijp. 11b, bes. Anm. 9. Von den vier aus vordiokletianischer Zeit aufgeführten Belegen scheidet die Ekmartyresis P.Oxy. XII 1562 (279 – 82, mit BL VI 102. VII 140) für unsere Fragestellung aus; nachzutragen sind dafür SB XXIV 15957 (6. Jh.), 15958 (6./7. Jh.), 16039 (Anf. 7. Jh.), 16040 (Ende 6./Anf. 7. Jh.), 16126 (6./7. Jh., grch. Hypographe einer kopt. Urkunde), XXVI 16564 (5./6. Jh.) sowie möglicherweise die kürzlich von K. A. Worp bzw. A. V. Bakkers in BASP 44 (2007: 55f. # 5 bzw. 63ff. # 7) edierten, äußerst fragmentarischen Zusicherungen der ἀνεγκλησία P.Minnesota 13 (140/41, wenn nicht doch eher nach 212, vgl. nur die Stipulationsklausel in Z. 9ff.; der vermutete Bezug der offenbar singulären Titulatur in Z. 13ff. auf Antoninus Pius erscheint jedenfalls nicht zwingend) und 17 (5.5.191), die dann sogar als die frühesten Belege dieses Vertragstyps anzusehen wären. Vgl. zudem auch das – sichtlich eher als Teilung denn als Dialysis konzipierte – „agreement about a soldier's estate" zwischen der ‚Witwe' und den Gläubigern eines Soldaten P.Wisc. I 14 = Pap.Choix 6 (16.5.131), das als staatsnotarielle Urkunde im *praesidium* von Syene aufgesetzt wurde und ebenfalls mit einem wechselseitigen Anerkenntnis beginnt; hierzu auch bes. Wolff 2002: 160f., 169 Anm. 93f.

48 Vgl. nur Urbanik 2007 und Palme 2007.

49 P.Stras. IV 280 = I 20 = M.Chr. 94 (26.8.272, mit BL VIII 417. IX 326).

50 P.Oxy. XXXVI 2768 (vor 269, mit BL XI 164), laut Wolff (1978: 128) ein „anscheinend einem Gerichtsurteil nachgebildete(s) Vergleichsprotokoll", daher von ihm unter die „anspruchsvollere(n) Zeugnisse atypischer privater Beurkundung" gerechnet.

51 PSI XII 1256.11 (3. Jh., 14.7.).

an die Seite der Frau liegt“,[52] eher mit nüchternen Quittierungen rechnen lassen. Das Bedürfnis, zugleich auch die personenrechtlichen Implikationen dieses Rechtsaktes, insbesondere die Gestattung einer Wiederheirat festzuhalten, förderte jedoch auch hier die Tendenz zur Wechselseitigkeit. So sind nur vier der insgesamt 17 Scheidungsurkunden, die in Ägypten aus den ersten drei nachchristlichen Jahrhunderten erhalten blieben,[53] als einseitige Erklärungen der Frau über die Rückerstattung der Mitgift gefaßt.[54] Mehr als die Hälfte der Urkunden wird dagegen mit dem inzwischen schon vertrauten wechselseitigen Anerkenntnis ὁμολογοῦσιν ἀλλήλοις eingeleitet, und zwar nicht nur im Oxyrhynchites, wie immerhin ein privates Protokoll dieser Herkunft bezeugt, sondern auch in den Staatsnotariaten des Arsinoites.[55]

Demnach deutet alles darauf hin, daß bei bestimmten Rechtsgeschäften ein erhöhtes Bedürfnis an einer Betonung der Wechselseitigkeit bestand, das sich in einer spezifischen Ausgestaltung des Urkundenformulars niederschlug. Exemplarisch ließ sich dies an Tausch- und Gesellschaftsverträgen, an Verträgen aus dem liturgischen Bereich, an Streitbeendigungen und schließlich Scheidungen zeigen; für Lehrlings- und Künstlerverträge hatte es bereits Wolff vermerkt; es traf ebenso auf die hier nicht mehr systematisch geprüften Teilungsvereinbarungen zu. Nur wenige Änderungen an der Vertragseinleitung waren dazu vonnöten: Zum einen wurden die Vertragsparteien in denselben Kasus gesetzt und durch ein einfaches καί verbunden, zum anderen an passender Stelle eine Form von ἀλλήλων hinzugefügt; gegebenenfalls konnte noch das Verb in den Plural wechseln. Dies galt für private Instrumente

52 Rupprecht 1971: 43, vgl. auch 46.

53 Vgl. nur die Liste bei Merklein 1967: 109f., wobei die Quittung über die Rückerstattung der Mitgift P.Tebt. II 460 descr. (138–61) allenfalls formal hierher zu stellen ist, da sie dem Vater des verstorbenen Ehemannes ausgestellt ist; P.Flor. I 24 = M.Chr. 187 (3. Jh., mit BL III 55) enthält zudem lediglich eine Aufstellung banknotarieller Vertragsschlüsse. Hinzuzufügen sind nunmehr allerdings P.Mil.Vogl. III 184 (41–54?), der äußerst fragmentarische P.Kron. 51 (30.8.138; 2. Ex. von P.Kron. 52 = P.Mil.Vogl. II 85), P.Mil.Vogl. III 185 = SB VI 9381 (26.1.139), P.Oxy.Hels. 35 (2.,12. oder 22.8.151, mit BL VIII 274), der von K.A. Worp, BASP 44 (2007: 50f. # 2) edierte, erneut äußerst fragmentarische P.Minnesota 5^r (3. Jh.) und vielleicht noch P.Oxy. XLIII 3139 (3./4. Jh.); P.Brooklyn gr. 4 = SB VIII 9740 (2./3.177) ist inzwischen als P.Brook. 8 wiederabgedruckt.

54 So in den staatsnotariellen Urkunden P.Princ. II 31 (9./10.79 oder 80, Ars.), P.Oxy. II 266 = P.Lond. III 1187 descr. = M.Chr. 292 = Sel.Pap. I 7 (8./9.96) und P.Oxy. Hels. 35 (2.,12. oder 22.8.151, beide Oxy.) sowie dem Cheirographon unbekannter Herkunft P.Lond. II 178 (p. 207) (2 Ex., 5.4.145).

55 Oxyrhynchites: P.Oxy. XLIII 3139 (spätes 3./4. Jh.) mit Wolff 1978: 108 Anm. 6 a.E. – Arsinoites: P.Mil.Vogl. III 184 (41 – 54?); P.Fouad I 34 (70 – 9); P.Fam.Tebt. 13 (113/4); P.Lips. I 27 = M.Chr. 293 (17.3.123); P.Kron. 52 = P.Mil.Vogl. II 85 (30.8.138; 2. Ex. in P.Kron. 51); P.Mil.Vogl. III 185 = SB VI 9381 (26.1.139); P.Brook. 8 = SB VIII 9740 (2./3.177). Unklar ist die Konstruktion in dem durch syntaktische wie orthographische Mängel entstellten BGU III 975 (20.2.44, mit BL IX 24. XI 23), wo der in Z. 7ff. überlieferte Wortlaut ὁ[μ]ολουγια Πα[ο]ῦς ... γεγενεμένη αὐτοῦ γυνὴ Τεσενοῦφις ... συνῆρσθαι τὴν πρὸς ἀλλήρους συνβίοσιν bisher als einseitiges Anerkenntnis anstelle eines korrekteren ὁμολογεῖ Πα[ο]ῦς ... ‹τῇ› γεγενεμένῃ αὐτοῦ γυναικὶ Τεσενούφει gedeutet wurde. Nach Obigem wäre eine behutsamere Emendation zu ομολογία · Παοὺς ... ‹καὶ ἡ› κτλ. allerdings ebenso vorstellbar; vgl. zu einer solchen Form der Einleitung etwa auch A. Jördens, Einl. zu P.Louvre I 7 (4./5.41–54), bes. p. 53.

ebenso wie für δημόσιοι χρηματισμοί, so daß im Oxyrhynchites private Protokolle, im Arsinoites staatsnotarielle Urkunden in dieser Fassung auftraten. Im Hermopolites scheint es dagegen keinen solch bevorzugten Urkundstyp gegeben zu haben, was hier nun zur Abwandlung des Cheirographons führte, dessen Natur dem eigentlich entgegenstand. Wie erfolgreich dennoch dieser Kunstgriff war, zeigt die Ausbreitung der Hybridform in die anderen Gaue wie auch ihre Verwendung bis tief in die byzantinische Zeit hinein, wenngleich die Beleglage, wohl auch wegen des Siegeszugs der Tabellionenurkunde, insgesamt überschaubar blieb.

Ob man hierin mit Wolff ein Phänomen der Erstarrung erkennen oder eher eine aus dem Mangel an Alternativen geborene Flexibilität am Werke sehen will – deutlich wird daran doch so viel, daß das Bedürfnis nach Darstellung der Wechselseitigkeit größer war als alle von der Urkundsform her entgegenstehenden Hindernisse. Dies verweist freilich auf ein tieferes Interesse an einer solchen Gestaltung, das eben nicht auf andere Weise wie etwa durch den Austausch zweier jeweils von der anderen Vertragspartei ausgestellter Exemplare zu bewältigen war.[56] Daß es hierbei demnach um mehr gegangen sein muß als nur um die Entscheidung zwischen zwei gleichermaßen akzeptablen Möglichkeiten, legen auch die oben erörterten Tabellionenurkunden mit ihrer noch deutlicheren Markierung der beiden beteiligten Parteien nahe – um so bemerkenswerter, als diese auffällige Stilisierung in der Spätantike offenbar sogar reichsweit Verbreitung genoß.[57]

Als ich vor fast 25 Jahren im Rahmen meiner Untersuchungen von Arbeitsverträgen erstmals auf diese Erscheinung stieß, hatte ich in erster Linie ein soziales Moment dahinter vermutet: Die Wahl dieser Form in Liturgiestellvertretungen und Gesellschaftsvertragen habe vor allem die vom üblichen Gefälle zwischen Arbeitgeber und Arbeitnehmer unterschiedene Gleichrangigkeit der Kontrahenten zum Ausdruck gebracht.[58] Eine Bestätigung dessen hatte ich damals in den beiden Vereinbarungen über die Handelsgeschäfte in der Oase gesehen, die zwischen Finanzier und Transporteur und damit ungleichen Partnern geschlossen wurden, weswegen hier doch wieder die übliche Form des Cheirographons zum Tragen gekommen sei.[59] Selbst wenn mir diese Deutung nach wie vor Richtiges zu treffen scheint, wird man nun, nach erfolgter Durchmusterung der gesamten Dokumentation, doch auch zu fragen haben, ob dies allein als Erklärung ausreichen kann.

Läßt man noch einmal sämtliche hier behandelten Vertragsschlüsse Revue passieren, schälen sich zunehmend zwei große Bereiche heraus, denen diese Vereinbarun-

56 Zu dieser Praxis etwa auch Steinwenter 1935: 79ff.

57 Dies ergänzt insoweit die Beobachtungen Steinwenters (1935: 93), der einen „geradezu auffallenden Zusammenhang (…) zwischen dem Formular der byzantinisch-ägyptischen Dialysisurkunden und jene(m) Quellenmaterial, das wir als gemeinbyzantinisch bezeichnen könnten", konstatierte.

58 Jördens 1990: 196f., 357f., wobei anstelle von ‚hybriden' noch von ‚uneigentlichen Cheirographa' die Rede war.

59 Jördens 1990: 358f.

gen vornehmlich zuzuordnen sind: zum einen das Liturgiewesen, zum anderen die Familie. So gut wie nirgends ist das Geschäftsleben betroffen,[60] sieht man einmal von den besonderen Bedingungen unterworfenen Gesellschaftsverträgen ab; im übrigen ist einmal auch hier ein familiärer Kontext gegeben, da der in den Handwerksbetrieb aufgenommene Juniorpartner zugleich Schwiegersohn und künftiger Erbe ist.[61] Zumeist sind es allerdings Konflikte innerhalb der Familie, deren Ende auf diese Weise besiegelt wird: Vermögensauseinandersetzungen zwischen ehemaligen Ehepartnern bei der Scheidung, zwischen Verwandten bei Teilung oder Tausch oder auch bei den späten Dialyseis und Kompromissen.[62] Familiäre Bezüge liegen zudem bei zwei als hybride Cheirographa gefaßten Adoptionen vor,[63] desgleichen bei der ebenso stilisierten Abrede zweier Elternpaare über den den Kindern bei ihrer Eheschließung zugestandenen Erbanspruch, der nach deren Tod nunmehr auf die noch minderjährigen Enkel übergehen soll.[64] Selbst bei Ausbildungsverträgen war dies mitunter der Fall, abgesehen davon, daß schon die gelegentliche Aufnahme des Lehrlings in den Haushalt des Lehrherrn ein quasi-familiäres Nahverhältnis begründete.[65]

Ein zweiter Schwerpunkt dieser wechselseitigen Verträge liegt, wie erwähnt, im Liturgiewesen oder besser gesagt im öffentlichen Bereich. Zwar könnte man die Abrede der Geschwister, auch die Amtsübernahme des jüngsten Bruders wie die der beiden älteren aus dem Vermögen des inzwischen verstorbenen Vaters zu finanzieren,

60 Dies könnte auch gegen die bisherige Deutung des fragmentarischen P.Haun. III 56 (4./5. Jh.) als eines bloßen „Antichretic Loan?“ sprechen.

61 P.Cair.Masp. II 67158 = FIRA III 158 (28.4.568); vgl. hierzu schon Steinwenter 1936: 504, sowie bes. Jördens 1990: 368f.

62 Daß wechselseitige Anerkenntnisse grundsätzlich auch schon sozusagen vorbeugend eingesetzt werden konnten, bleibt davon unbenommen und bestätigt eher noch ihre konfliktentschärfende Funktion. Beispiele hierfür bieten etwa SB VIII 9824 (29.8.31, mit BL V 119), in dem vier Brüder nach der Aufteilung des geerbten Hauses in Oxyrhynchos der in der Fremde weilenden Schwester für den Fall ihrer Rückkunft noch Erbschaftsanteile zusichern; die „Testamentshomologie unter Eheleuten“ P.Münch. III 80 (103–14, mit BL XII 130); nicht zuletzt auch einige Eheverträge, so die staatsnotariellen Urkunden SB XXIV 16256 = P.Lond. II 294 descr.1–59 (24.7.109, mit BL XII 242; erg.) und SPP XX 5 = M.Chr. 288 = CPR I 24 (14.8.136, mit BL VIII 461. XII 275; 2. Ex. in CPR I 25, beide Ars.) wie auch die Tabellionenurkunde SB VI 8986 = III 6271 (1./2.641, mit BL VIII 337. X 194f.; erg.; Apoll. Magna). Vgl. zudem auch die unten in Anm. 64 genannten Texte; die entsprechende Ergänzung in P.Ness. 18.3 (5./6.537, mit BL IX 59. X 40) erscheint mit Blick auf die Fortführung dagegen wenig plausibel. Unklar bleiben die Details in dem nur bruchstückhaft überlieferten Vertragsregister SB I 5167 aus römischer Zeit, hier bes. Z. 3–5.

63 P.Oxy. IX 1206 = Sel.Pap. I 10 = Meyer, Jur.Pap.10 = FIRA III 16 (3./4.335) sowie P.Lips. I 28 = M.Chr. 363 = New Primer 76 (31.12.381, mit BL VII 79. VIII 170. IX 124).

64 SB XVIII 13176.56–138 (30.5.167); vgl. jetzt auch P.Petra I 1 (23.5.537).

65 Hierzu ausführlich schon Herrmann 1957–1958: 125f., knapp auch Hengstl 1972: 90; zur sozialen Lage allgem. Bergamasco 1995: 106ff. Bezeichnend erscheint überdies das die ‚Aushändigung‘ des Lehrlings an den Lehrherrn kennzeichnende Verb ἐκδιδόναι, das sonst namentlich aus Eheverträgen geläufig ist – vgl. nur Bergamasco 1995: 99f. resp. Yiftach-Firanko 2003: 41ff. und *passim* –, allerdings nicht zugleich, wie bes. von Herrmann (1957–1958: 136ff.) und jetzt auch Bergamasco (1995: 99f. Anm. 20) betont, eine Veränderung der Gewaltverhältnisse implizierte.

gut auch noch zu den innerfamiliären Vereinbarungen zählen.[66] In anderen Fällen ließen sich dagegen allenfalls bestimmte Rücksichtnahmen vermuten, so bei der Verständigung des amtierenden Dorfvorstehers mit seinem präsumptiven Nachfolger über die darauffolgende Ernennung seines Bruders,[67] bei den Bereitschaftserklärungen, den Anteil eines ebenfalls ernannten Kollegen mit zu erledigen,[68] oder auch bei den vielleicht nicht immer einfach zu gewinnenden Stellvertretern. Doch wurde auch mit Hilfspersonal in dieser Form kontrahiert, und womöglich zählt sogar ein – prodomatischer – Pachtvertrag mit den Vorstehern eines Dorfes hierzu.[69]

Fragt man nach den Gründen für diese vorderhand überraschende Parallelität, müssen sie in bestimmten Gemeinsamkeiten zwischen diesen beiden Bereichen bestanden haben, die in normalen Geschäftsbeziehungen, wie sie sonst das Vertragswesen prägten, nicht in vergleichbarer Weise gegeben sind. Dies verweist vor allem auf die soziale Kontrolle, der das Individuum in Familie und Öffentlichkeit in sehr viel höherem Maße als im geschäftlichen Leben unterworfen war. Denn anders als dort spielten sich die Vorgänge hier unter den Augen der für die soziale Existenz wesentlichen Bezugsgruppen ab, deren wertender Beobachtung man sich ununterbrochen ausgesetzt sah und die dadurch über genügend informelle Mittel verfügte, ihre Ansichten und Interessen bei Bedarf auch zur Geltung zu bringen. In diesem Umfeld stellten schriftliche Verträge noch mehr als sonst eine Ausnahme dar.[70] Sofern sie sich zur Streitbeendigung und vielleicht noch mehr zur Verhinderung von Konflikten einmal als unumgänglich erwiesen, war der Frieden in der Gemeinschaft nur durch eine sorgfältige Austarierung der Positionen zu sichern. Die für das Cheirographon typische Differenzierung in Adressat und Absender stellte hierfür allerdings keine guten Voraussetzungen bereit. Über die hier beschriebenen Änderungen im Eingangsformular war jedoch eine neue Parität zu erreichen, mit der die dieser Vertragsgestalt inhärente Ungleichheit sich wenigstens auf sprachlicher Ebene korrigieren ließ. Zwar hieß dies dem Briefschema erhebliche Gewalt antun, doch schienen die auf diese Weise zu erzielenden Vorteile ein solches Opfer offenbar wert.

66 P.Harr. II 227 (11./12.221).

67 P.Col. X 281 = SB XVI 12829 (7./8.287).

68 P.Lond. II 306 (p. 118f.) = W.Chr. 263 = Sel.Pap. II 358 (28.8.145, mit BL IX 129) und bes. P.Leit. 13 = SB VIII 10205 (222/3, 226/7 oder 242/3).

69 P.Gen. I^2 67 (19.1.382 oder 383).

70 Illustrativ erscheint hier der zuletzt noch einmal von Yiftach-Firanko (2003: 100ff.) eingehend erörterte P.Kron. 52 = P.Mil.Vogl. II 85 (30.8.138), der die Scheidung des inzwischen 54jährigen Kronion von seiner Schwester besiegelt, während bei der zweifellos schon mehrere Jahrzehnte zurückliegenden Eheschließung trotz der hohen Mitgift noch auf eine schriftliche Vereinbarung verzichtet worden war. Dieses Vertrauens muß sich Kronion in der Folge allerdings als unwürdig erwiesen haben. Zwar sind die genauen Hintergründe, die zu der Scheidung führten, nicht mehr im einzelnen zu rekonstruieren, doch wird aus den nunmehr festgehaltenen Bestimmungen immerhin so viel klar, daß der Druck, den die Familie daraufhin auf den unzuverlässigen Kronion zu entfalten wußte, erheblich war und seine Wirkung aller Wahrscheinlichkeit nach auch nicht verfehlte.

Der Brief in der Urkunde
Zur Briefform in spätantiken Verträgen

Sophie Kovarik (Köln)*

I. Die Tabellionenurkunde

Im 6. Jh. tritt uns in der ägyptischen Tabellionenurkunde eine Dokumentenform zur Niederschrift privatrechtlicher Geschäfte entgegen, die ihre endgültige Ausformung erreicht hat. Tatsächlich blickt sie aber auf eine längere Entwicklungsgeschichte zurück. Wie in so vielen Bereichen kommt es mit dem Beginn der Spätantike auch zu einem Wandel der Beurkundungspraxis von privaten Verträgen, dessen genauer Ursprung bisher nicht geklärt werden konnte. Das erste Auftreten dieser neuen Urkundsgattung in den frühen Jahren des 4. Jh. läßt an eine Reform unter Diokletian denken, die zum Verschwinden der herkömmlichen ägyptischen Urkundsformen römischer Ausprägung und dem Niedergang des Staatsnotariats, d. h. der amtlichen und öffentlichen Registrierung von Urkunden, geführt hat.[1] Stattdessen erscheint mit der Tabellionenurkunde eine Subjektivurkunde, die ihren Namen den *tabelliones*, also den Notaren, verdankt, die mittels ihrer Unterschrift (*completio*) diese Schriftstücke beglaubigen und dadurch Beweiskraft verleihen.

Diese Änderungen in der Rechtspraxis, die seit Jahrhunderten zu beobachten sind, finden erstmals in der ersten Hälfte des 6. Jahrhunderts mit der Konstitution CJ 4.21.17 aus dem Jahr 528 und den Novellen 44 und 47 aus dem Jahr 537 sowie der Novelle 73 von 538 unter Justinian Eingang in die Gesetzgebung. Zu diesem Zeitpunkt, an dem wir konkrete Vorschriften für diese neue Beurkundungsform endlich auch in der Legislation greifen können, hat sich in Ägypten, nach dem relativen

* Von 2008 bis 2010, zur Zeit der Tagung und Abfassung dieses Beitrages, war die Verfasserin DOC-Stipendiatin der Österreichischen Akademie der Wissenschaften, der an dieser Stelle ein herzlicher Dank ausgesprochen sei.
Papyruseditionen werden nach John F. Oates, Roger S. Bagnall, Sarah J. Clackson, Alexandra A. O'Brien, Joshua D. Sosin, Terry G. Wilfong, and Klaas A. Worp, *Checklist of Greek, Latin, Demotic and Coptic Papyri, Ostraca and Tablets*, http://scriptorium.lib.duke.edu/papyrus/texts/clist.html, June, 2011, gekürzt. Jahresangaben datieren immer nach Beginn unserer Zeitrechnung. Alle über die Urkunden getätigten allgemeinen Aussagen müssen aufgrund der Materialfülle als vorläufige Beobachtungen gelten.

1 „Am ehesten wird man vermuten dürfen, daß die unter Diokletian geschehene Einführung des amtlich konzessionierten Tabellionats in Ägypten die alten Beurkundungseinrichtungen verdrängt und allmählich, d. h. nicht in allen Gauen zur gleichen Zeit, hat absterben lassen" (Wolff 1978: 9).

Chaos im 4 Jh., mit einem Nebeneinander verschiedener Urkundsformen und der Konsolidierung der Tabellionenurkunde im späten 5. Jh., bereits ein Standardmodell durchgesetzt, nach dem regelmäßig bestimmte Elemente in einer Urkunde zu erwarten sind, obwohl, wie immer in Ägypten, mit großen regionalen Unterschieden zu rechnen ist.

Im 6. Jh. also, der „Blütezeit" der byzantinischen Tabellionenurkunde, stellt sich deren Ausgestaltung nun folgendermaßen dar: Zu Beginn der Urkunde erfolgt die Datierung, wie in Nov. 47 vorgeschrieben, ab dem späten 6. Jh. üblicherweise mit Voranstellung der Invokation. Dem schließt sich, vor dem eigentlichen Hauptteil der Urkunde, die Nennung der Vertragsparteien in Form einer Begrüßungsformel (ὁ δεῖνα τῷ δεῖνι χαίρειν) an. Danach geht die Urkunde im Corpus zur eigentlichen Beschreibung des erfolgten Geschäfts über, die aus Perspektive des Ausstellers, d. h. der Person, die etwa mietet, pachtet, ein Darlehen aufnimmt, eine Bürgschaft übernimmt oder etwas verkauft, in erster Person geschildert wird – nach dem Schema ὁμολογῶ + Verb, z. B. μεμισθῶσθαι (d. h. „Ich stimme überein", z. B. „gepachtet zu haben ..."). Dieses Urkundscorpus wird – zur Unanfechtbarkeit des Urkundsinhalts – mit der Kyria-Klausel beschlossen, etwa, um im Beispiel zu bleiben: ἡ μίσθωσις κυρία („der Pachtvertrag ist maßgeblich"). Damit wird auch der Vertragstyp angegeben. Es folgt die aus dem klassischen römischen Recht stammende Stipulation, die sich von einem Leistungsversprechen römischer Ausprägung zu einer persönlichen Zustimmungsklausel entwickelt hat und in der Form ἐπερωτηθεὶς ὡμολόγησα („auf Befragen habe ich zugestimmt") auftritt. Daran endlich schließt sich die *Hypographe* oder *Subscriptio* an, d. h. eine „Unterschrift" in Form einer subjektiv stilisierten Erklärung, die entweder eigenhändig oder unter Zurhilfenahme eines Schreibervertreters geschrieben wird, eventuell gefolgt von Zeugenunterschriften, die die Urkundserrichtung bestätigen. Beschlossen wird der ganze Vertrag durch die Unterschrift des Notars. Diese hat im allgemeinen die Form δι' ἐμοῦ + Name des Notars („durch mich N. N."), in Verbindung mit der Bezeichnung seines Berufes (z. B. *Symbolaiographos* oder *Nomikos*), oft ergänzt (vor oder nach der Notarsunterschrift) um Ausstellungsvermerke wie ἐπράχθη, ἐγράφη oder *esemioth* (von ἐσημειώθη), alles in allem also: „Durch mich N. N. Symbolaiographos (o.ä.) beglaubigt". Die Bestimmungen zur Notarsunterschrift enthält der vorgenannte Passus CJ 4.21.17. Die im Gesetzestext ebenfalls behandelte *absolutio* wurde im Osten offenbar als Ausgabe der Urkunde vom Aussteller an den Vertragspartner verstanden und findet sich, wenn vorhanden, am Ende von Stipulation oder Hypographe. Schließlich werden auf der Rückseite der Urkunde der Vertragstyp und der Name der beteiligten Parteien zumeist noch einmal angegeben.

Dieser *Cheirographon* genannte, zu Deutsch oft als Handschein bezeichnete Typus ersetzt nach landläufiger Meinung also alle davor gültigen Urkundsformen und wird zur alleinigen Dokumentationsform privater Rechtsurkunden, womit er zum

Standard der spätantiken Tabellionenurkunde wird.[2] Bezeichnend sind etwa Bemerkungen wie „Das Charakteristische des byzantinischen Urkundenwesens ist für Ägypten das, daß alle Objektivurkunden verschwunden sind und das Cheirographon die Alleinherrschaft gewonnen hat“ (Mitteis 1912: 87) oder „Trotzdem muß das Cheirographon der Bevölkerung geläufig geblieben sein; sonst hätte es nicht im 4. Jh. nach dem Verfall der öffentlichen Beurkundungseinrichtungen zur alleinherrschenden UForm der byzantinischen Zeit werden können“ (Steinacker 1927: 29) und wiederum ein wenig einschränkend „Der blosse, normalerweise subjektiv stilisierte Handschein, der schon im 3. Jh. in ständigem Vordringen gewesen war, gelangte für die meisten Geschäftsarten zur Alleinherrschaft und wurde zur Grundform der jetzt eindringenden Tabellionenurkunde“ (Wolff 1961: 115).

Aus der Struktur des *Cheirographons* ergibt sich aber auch der Briefcharakter der Tabellionenurkunde, einerseits aus der subjektiven Stilisierung und andererseits aus der Grußformel zur Einführung der Vertragsparteien.[3] Sogar die späteren koptischen Urkunden werden mit „der aus dem epistolaren Grundgedanken der Tabellionenurkunde stammenden, aber oft fehlenden (griechischen!) Grußformel“ (Steinwenter 1955: 12) ausgestattet.

Das zugrunde liegende römische *Cheirographon* hat im allgemeinen die Grußformel ὁ δεῖνα τῷ δεῖνι χαίρειν, also „Der A dem B, Grüße”, vor dem Vertragskörper, der mit ὁμολογῶ + Verb (ἐσχηκέναι) oder direktem Verb (z. B. ἔσχον) eingeleitet wird. Das Datum steht, anders als bei der späteren Tabellionenurkunde, am Ende des Dokumentes; Errichtungsort wird keiner gegeben.

Die Herkunft des *Cheirographons* in seiner spätantiken Ausprägung ist nicht gänzlich geklärt. Wolff (1961) erkennt zutreffend bestimmte Elemente der ägyptischen Tabellionenurkunde auch in Dokumenten aus Nessana (Palaestina), wohinter er als gemeinsame Vorlage das Notariat von Konstantinopel vermutet.[4] Der Grund

2 Zum *Cheirographon* s. allgemein Wolff 1978: 106–14 (§ 7. Private Urkunden I. Das Cheirographon), Wenger 1953: 736ff. und neuerdings eine Fallstudie zum Oxyrhynchites in Yiftach-Firanko: 2009.

3 In einer umfassenderen römischrechtlichen Definition ist jedes private Dokument, das ohne Mitwirkung eines Notars entstanden ist und eine Unterschrift, d. h. einer Erklärung in 1. Person, trägt, ein solcher Handschein und der Briefcharakter daher nicht entscheidend, vgl. etwa Wenger (1953: 736, Anm. 14): „Diese Erklärung kann in Briefform mit dem Briefgruß abgegeben werden, doch ist die Briefform fürs Chirographum nicht wesentlich. Auch eine unterschriftliche Erklärung in subjektiver Fassung unter einer objektiv gehaltenen Dispositivurkunde wäre ein Chirographum, so daß wohl jede Epistula ein Chirographum ist, nicht aber umgekehrt jedes Chirographum eine Epistula“. Im Griechischen aber ist im Unterschied zum römischen Recht der Terminus *Cheirographon* an die Briefform gebunden (Wolff 1978: 107, Anm. 4), allerdings ohne die Briefschlußformel (ἔρρωσο o.ä). Zum Unterschied zwischen Chirographum und Epistula im römischen Recht s. auch den Beitrag von Éva Jakab in diesem Band.

4 Die Datierung (nach Konsulat oder Postkonsulat und erst ab Justinian nach Regierungsjahren) zu Beginn der Urkunde, die (etwaige) Beiziehung von Urkundszeugen ab dem 5. Jh. und die die Tabellionenurkunde konstituierende Notarsunterschrift unterscheiden die notarielle Urkunde vom römischen *Cheirographon* in Ägypten und sind auf eine Einführung von außen zurückzuführen. Yiftach-Firanko (2009: 339, Anm. 66) führt zur Stützung von Wolffs Theorie einer ausländischen Herkunft

für eine solche Einführung eines neuen Dokumententypus und Notariats, die sich von dem in Ägypten bisher gebräuchlichen unterscheiden, ist allerdings nicht bekannt. Eine Einführung von außen würde vielleicht erklären, warum sich diese neue Dokumentationsform nicht sofort durchgesetzt hat. In Ägypten war das *Cheirographon* in der oben beschriebenen Form bereits seit ptolemäischer Zeit als privates Dokument in Gebrauch und besonders im römischen Oxyrhynchites verbreitet, weil es dort wohl als Standard-Format gedient hat.[5]

Generell herrschen in der Diplomatik der spätantiken Urkunden noch viele Unklarheiten. Eine systematische Analyse der Dokumententypen und der Frage wann und wo diese angewendet wurden, ist noch ausständig. Vor allem im 4. Jh. ist die Situation relativ chaotisch. Wie bereits erwähnt datieren die frühesten Tabellionenurkunden zu Beginn des 4. Jh., koexistierten aber lange Zeit an der Seite anderer Formate, die für die Dokumentation vertraglicher Aktivitäten herangezogen wurden. Diese verschiedenen Formate vermischten sich und verbanden alte Elemente mit neuen Bestimmungen. Es gibt etwa *Cheirographa* ohne Notarsunterschrift, die trotz allem, wie in der Tabellionenurkunde vorgesehen, daß Datum zu Beginn tragen (und manchmal auch am Ende),[6] auf der anderen Seite gibt es Tabellionenurkunden, in der es immer noch zur Personenbeschreibung der Vertragsparteien kommt, ein Charakteristikum des prä-tabellionischen Privatdokuments, das in der Tabellionenurkunde obsolet wird und dessen Funktion offensichtlich von der notariellen Beglaubigung übernommen wird.[7] Vor allem in der tabellionischen Frühzeit muß man sich vor Augen halten, daß diese Bestimmungen neu und daher nicht unbedingt bekannt sind.

Daß daher die von Mitteis (1912), Steinacker (1927) und Wolff (1961) postulierte „Alleinherrschaft" des *Cheirographons* (s. u. 205) nicht auf alle spätantiken Urkunden in absoluter Totalität zutrifft, soll eine Auswahl von Beispielen aus der ägyptischen Materialfülle veranschaulichen, die von dieser Norm in Form des oben skizzierten

die Ähnlichkeit der Tabellionenurkunde mit Dokumenten aus dem römerzeitlichen Judaea (z. B. P.Yadin 11) ins Feld.

5 S. dazu auch Yiftach-Firanko 2009: 327. Das *Cheirographon* ist ursprünglich, wie sein Name schon sagt, „bindend", weil es eigenhändig geschrieben wurde, denn es „bekannte im Cheirographon der Aussteller selbst mittels bindender Schrift, daß er die durch diese bezeugte Verfügung getroffen hatte oder die in ihr gekennzeichnete Verbindlichkeit eingegangen war". (Wolff 1978: 107).

6 In dieser Zerlegung spiegelt sich die Unsicherheit der Leute mit den neuen Regulationen wider, durch welche sie sich an diese zu halten glaubten: die Konsulatsangabe findet sich zu Beginn; während am Schluß zunächst noch einmal auf die Regierungsjahre rekurriert und Monat und Tag genannt werden, verschwinden im Laufe der Zeit jedoch die Regierungsjahre aus der Enddatierung; für Wolff (1961: 120ff.) zeigt sich darin die Schwierigkeit für die Urkundsbüros „aus der ihnen anbefohlenen Voransetzung der Konsulnamen eine neue Datierungsweise zu entwickeln" (p. 121), die Verschiebung der Datumsangabe vom Ende der Urkunde zu deren Beginn hält er für „eine direkte Folge der Einführung des Tabellionenwesens" (p. 120).

7 Eine genaue Untersuchung fehlt hier allerdings noch.

Schemas abweichen – denn wie schon Steinacker (1927: 74) schreibt: „Wie wenig es möglich ist, mit Hilfe der Rechtsbücher ein richtiges Bild des Uwesens zu gewinnen, haben die Papyri gezeigt“.

II. Abweichungen vom Briefformat

1. Die Umkehr der Briefformel (ὁ δεῖνα τῷ δεῖνι zu τῷ δεῖνι ὁ δεῖνα χαίρειν)

> „In der Grußformel steht jetzt der Adressat an erster Stelle; es lautet nicht mehr: ὁ δεῖνα τῷ δεῖνι, sondern τῷ δεῖνι ὁ δεῖνα χαίρειν“.
>
> (Mitteis 1912: 88)

Die *opinio communis*, die man vielerorts lesen kann, ist, daß die Standard-Grußformel in der Spätantike „Dem B (Name, Beruf, Herkunft) der A (Name, Beruf, Herkunft), Grüße“ lautet: τῷ δεῖνι ὁ δεῖνα χαίρειν und sich dadurch in der Form vom römischen *Cheirographon* unterscheidet. („Der A dem B, Grüße“: ὁ δεῖνα τῷ δεῖνι χαίρειν).[8] Das χαίρειν ist hier oft zu einer Sigle χ(αίρειν) – oder auf wenige Buchstaben χαί(ρειν) – reduziert. Der Aussteller des Dokumentes ist, da es sich um subjektiv stilisierte Urkunden handelt, die Person im Nominativ, die den stärkeren Vertragspartner im Dativ anspricht und damit auch diejenige Person, deren Hypographe am Ende des Vertrages erscheint, die also „unterschreibt“ und eine Verpflichtung eingeht, weil sie Land pachtet oder Geld leiht, und befindet sich daher üblicherweise in der sozial schwächeren Position. Diesbezüglich etabliert die Grußformel schon die soziale Hierarchie des Geschäftsvorganges.

Eine genauere Studie der Grußformeln der spätantiken Verträge aus dem Arsinoites – ohne Anspruch auf Vollständigkeit sind dies 183 Urkunden mit erhaltenem Präskript – zeigt aber, daß die Mehrheit (112 – beinahe 2/3 des untersuchten Urkundsmaterials) sich der Formel ὁ δεῖνα τῷ δεῖνι χαίρειν bedient, wie sie bereits als Standardformel für das römische *Cheirographon* bezeugt ist, und nicht der angeblichen neuen, für die spätantiken Verträge typischen Grußformel, die nun den Adressaten voranstellt. Dazu kommen 38 weitere, unedierte Stücke, die diese Tendenz bestätigen (22:16). Klar zeichnet sich hier ein chronologisches Gefälle ab: von den 71 edierten Urkunden mit neuer Grußformel stammen alleine 44–46 aus dem 7. Jh., aber nur 16–19 aus dem sonst so gut belegten 6. Jh. (aus dem 5. 6–7 und 2–3 aus dem 8. Jh.), wobei hier natürlich – wie immer bei paläographischen Datierungen –

8 Neben Mitteis (1912: 88), Zitat s. o. etwa Steinacker (1927: 30): „die Grußformel stellt den Namen des Empfängers voraus (τῷ δεῖνι ὁ δεῖνα χαίρειν)“. Gegen Mitteis schon einschränkend Herrmann (1958: 48) zu seinem Untersuchungsmaterial (den Pachtverträgen): „Die Anordnung ὁ δεῖνα τῷ δεῖνι endlich, die Mitteis in den byzantinischen Cheirographa als überlebt ansah, erscheint in dem bisher hinzugekommenen Material immerhin mindestens zehnmal“. Diese Vorrangstellung des Empfängers im Dativ wird auch der Mischung mit dem Formular des *Hypomnema* τῷ δεῖνι παρὰ τοῦ δεῖνος – s. unten unter **3**) zugeschrieben (vgl. Fn. 26). Vgl. die Entwicklungen im Privatbrief (Fn. 39).

Vorsicht geboten ist.[9] Darin zeigt sich, daß von einer grundlegenden Änderung nicht die Rede sein kann.[10] Die umgekehrte Anordnung (τῷ δεῖνι ὁ δεῖνα χαίρειν – „Dem B der A, Grüße“) scheint nur dann zur Anwendung gekommen zu sein, wenn es sich bei den Adressaten um Personen hohen Ranges handelte. Die Voranstellung wird als Ausdruck des Respekts diesen Leuten gegenüber gebraucht, hauptsächlich sind das Pagarchen, *stratelatai*, *duces*, *ekdikoi*, *comites*, die Kirche und Kirchenvertreter.[11] (Höhere) Militärs hingegen scheinen diese Ehre nicht zu verdienen, denn in den vielen Vertragsgeschäften zwischen Angehörigen der Armee oder Veteranen, die im Arsinoites zu greifen sind (die *numeri* der Leontoklibanarier und Transtigritani), kommt meistens die alte Formel zum Tragen, vgl. z. B. P.Würzb. 17 (454), P.Amh. II 148 (487), P.Worp 33 (501), P.Rain.Cent. 112 (509), P.Rain.Cent. 114 (526?), BGU II 369 (530), SPP XX 139 (531), CPR VIII 61 (543) oder CPR XXIV 14 (Ende 5., Anf. 6. Jh.) für Geschäfte mit Zivilisten und P.Prag. II 164 (493), SPP XX 131 (518), CPR XXIV 20 (Ende 5., Anf. 6. Jh.) für Geschäfte unter Soldaten; P.Prag. I 37 (466) und P.Paramone 13 (520?) sind unbestimmbar. Es handelt sich in allen Fällen um Kreditgeschäfte oder Miet-, Pachtverträge. Abweichungen im Formular, also der Gebrauch der „neuen“ Formel, ist in den untersuchten Beispielen, in welchen sich Armeeangehörige unter den Vertragspartnern befinden, im Dialysis-Vertrag SB XXII 15801 (419) zu bemerken, der sich an den Tribun der Transtigritani in der Funktion als Richter wendet. Dabei darf man aber nicht außer acht lassen, daß diese beiden *numeri* nur vom Ende des 5. bis Mitte des 6. Jh. belegt sind, eine Zeitspanne, in der die neue Anrede auch sonst noch nicht sehr verbreitet war. In P.Lond. I 113.5a (498) ist der angesprochene Veteran zugleich Grundbesitzer (*geuchos*),[12] eine Tatsache, die auch sonst eine Nennung an erster Stelle bewirkt, wie auch in SB XVIII 14001 (486 – *lamprotatos geuchos*), P.Ross.Georg. III 32 (504 – *megaloprepestatos* und *endoxotatos comes domesticorum* und *geuchôn* im Arsinoites) und BGU II 364 (553 – N. *Stratelates* und Strategios *illustris endoxotatoi geuchuntes*) zu beobachten ist. Nur in dem fragmentarischen Darlehen SB XVIII

9 Die „-“-Zahlen ergeben sich aus der Datierung in 2 Jahrhunderte.

10 In P.Dubl. 26 haben wir z. B. auch eine Musterurkunde bzw. einen Entwurf mit diesem Formular: Αὐρ(ήλιος) Κοσμᾶς υἱὸς τοῦ δ(εῖνος) – Αὐρηλίῳ τῷ δ(εῖνι) υἱῷ τοῦ δ(εῖνος), die zeigt, daß dies die Norm zu sein scheint.

11 BGU I 303, 305, 306, 320, 323; II 364, 366, 368, 396, 401; III 750, 752; CPR VIII 71, 82; X 127; XIV 1, 10, 11, 17, 32; XIX 11 (+ P.Vindob. G 25638), 32; XXIV 24, 26, 27, 28, 32; P.Berl.Zill. 8; P.Bodl. I 53; P.Eirene II 5, 29; P.Flor. III 336; P.Grenf. II 100; P.Harrauer 54; P.Koeln. III 152; P.Lond. I 113, 5a, 5c, 6b, 6c, 10; P.Paramone 13; P.Prag. I 64; P.Ross.Georg. III 32, 50, 52, 53; SB I 4488, 4490, 4658, 4659, 4666, 4694, 4819; VI 9461, 9592; XVI 12481, 13016; XVIII 13860, 13951, 13952, 14001; XXIV 16107, 16288, 16362; SPP XX 209; P.Vindob. G 21285 + 25908, ed. Kruit/Worp, Tyche 18 (2003), S. 47.

12 Eventuell fällt auch BGU I 303 (586) in diese Kategorie, ein Pachtvertrag mit einem *megaloprepestatos tribunos* und *antigeuchos*.

13860 (511) gibt es keine vordergründige Erklärung dafür, daß der Darlehensgeber, ein *draconarius* der Leontoklibanarier, an erster Stelle genannt wird.

Es finden sich aber auch ganze Vertragstypen, die sich immer dieser neuen Formel bedienen, wie etwa die Gestellungsbürgschaften. Das zugrundeliegende „Geschäft" kennt keine Gleichheit, bei den Bürgschaftsempfängern handelt es sich immer auch um die obersten Beamten der Lokalverwaltung oder lokale Würdenträger. Im Arsinoites sind das in byzantinischer Zeit eigentlich zumeist die Pagarchen, ab dem Ende der byzantinischen Herrschaft auch der vorher nicht vorhandene *dux*, an welche die folgenden Bürgschaften gerichtet sind: SPP XX 128 (487), SB XVIII 13951 (ca. 487), CPR X 127 (584), CPR XIX 11 + P.Vindob. G 25638 (590),[13] SB XVIII 13952 (591–592), CPR XXIV 24 (591–602), P.Lond. I 113, 5c (600), CPR XXIV 27 (610), BGU II 401 (618), BGU I 323 (vor 651), CPR XXIV 32 (651), CPR XIV 17 (652?), SB I 4659 (653/668), BGU III 750 (655), CPR VIII 83 (ca. 700). Auch wenn der Bürgschaftsempfänger nicht der lokalen Oberschicht zugehörig ist, wird die „neue" Formel verwendet, etwa in SB I 4658 (2. Hälfte 7. Jh.) ein Priester, Schreiber und *epistates* oder in BGU III 752 (655 ?)[14] ein Dioiket (beide außerhalb byzantinischer Herrschaft).

Es ist also wohl vielmehr als ein Zeichen der Hierarchisierung der Gesellschaft zu werten als eine Änderung der Urkundsformulars, daß ein hoher Funktionär oder Flavius in den Urkunden aus der fortgeschrittenen Spätantike nicht mehr dem Namen des Ausstellers folgen kann. Außerdem ist es im Laufe der Jahrhunderte zur Entwicklung von Urkundsformen gekommen, die eine solche Respektsanrede erst notwendig machen, wie etwa die Gestellungsbürgschaften vor Augen führen, die in dieser Form erst seit dem 5. Jh. entstanden sind und im Laufe der Zeit immer mehr zunehmen.[15]

2. Briefadresse ohne χαίρειν

> „Das Fehlen von χαίρειν spricht … natürlich nicht gegen die Auffassung, daß hier Briefform vorliegt".
>
> (Wilcken 1913: 294)

13 Dieser Papyrus wurde im Zuge meiner Diplomarbeit ediert und konnte im Nachhinein mit CPR XIX 11 vereinigt werden (vgl. Fn. 11).

14 Die Datierung im HGV 7.-8. Jh. ist aus mehreren Gründen zu hinterfragen, die an anderem Ort näher ausgeführt werden sollen.

15 Diese Form der Anrede findet sich auch bei dem Großteil der Bürgschaften aus Rest-Ägypten. Eine Ausnahme stellt hier nur der Antaiopolites dar, wie sich in dem Vertragsregister P.Cair.Masp. III 67328 (521), das ausschließlich aus Gestellungsbürgschaften besteht, gut verfolgen läßt (vgl. auch Fn. 28). Das Formular entspricht dem unter **3a.** behandelten *Hypomnema*-Misch-Gruß „Dem B, von A, Grüße" (τῷ δεῖνι παρὰ τοῦ δεῖνος χαίρειν), das typisch für die Urkunden des Dioskorosarchivs ist, aus dem alle Gestellungsbürgschaften des Antaiopolites stammen – siehe dazu weiter unten. Interessanterweise kommt die einzige Ausnahme aber – soweit ich das überblicke – auch aus Oberägypten: P.Lond. V 1732 (580) aus Syene bedient sich der herkömmlichen Formel „Der A dem B, Grüße" (ὁ δεῖνα τῷ δεῖνι χαίρειν).

Das Briefformular wird in der Literatur zwar als wesentlich für die Tabellionenurkunde angesehen, dem Fehlen des χαίρειν darin jedoch kaum Bedeutung beigemessen (vgl. auch unten Fn. 16). Nach Herrmann (1958: 44) etwa sei die Grußformel „kein integrierender Bestandteil dieser Urkundenform, und so finden sich nicht wenige Fälle, bei denen das χαίρειν fehlt." – daß solche Abweichungen eher funktionellen und geographischen Sonderformen zuzuschreiben sein könnten als dem reinen Zufall, sollte dabei aber nicht von vornherein abgetan werden.

Die Idee, die wir vom Standard-Formular der Tabellionenurkunde haben, geht hauptsächlich auf den Gebrauch in Mittelägypten zurück, weil von da der Großteil der erhaltenen Urkunden stammt. Über Oberägypten wissen wir, abseits von Archivfunden (wie das Dioskoros-Archiv aus Aphrodito), weniger Bescheid, weswegen es dort also schwieriger ist, von geographischen Eigenheiten im Urkundsformular auszugehen. So kann man also beim Fehlen von χαίρειν in der Grußformel einer gut dokumentierten Region, etwa dem Arsinoites, von einem Fehler des Schreibers ausgehen (abgesehen davon, daß dieses manchmal nur in den Ergänzungen der Editoren nicht berücksichtigt wurde). In schlecht dokumentierten Gegenden mag es sich dabei aber vielleicht um eine zugrunde liegende Gesetzmäßigkeit handeln, die auf den ersten Blick nicht erkennbar ist. Als Beispiel wäre hier der Panopolites anzuführen. In späterer Zeit findet sich aus diesem oberägyptischen Gau nur wenige Belege, die für diese Fragestellung herangezogen werden können: P.Stras. IV 229 (502) sowie SB I 5285 und SB I 5286 (beide 607) nennen die Vertragsparteien zu Beginn des eigentlichen Vertragstextes in folgender Weise: „Der A dem B",[16] direkt gefolgt von dem Corpus, das mit ὁμολογῶ / ὁμολογοῦμεν eingeleitet wird – χαίρειν wird also ausgelassen. Vor-tabellionische *Cheirographa* aus dem 4. Jh und frühen 5. Jh. – P.Panop. 21 (315), P.Lips. I 59 (371), P.Lond. III 870 (4. Jh.) sowie P.Grenf. II 80 (402) und P.Grenf. II 81 (403) – zeigen allerdings, daß dort vor der Einführung der Tabellionenurkunde χαίρειν durchaus in Gebrauch war.[17] P.Par. 20 (600) zählt zu den *dialyseis*, die als eigene Gruppe betrachtet unter **3b.** behandelt werden.

16 Ein Gruß, der mitunter natürlich auch anderswo begegnet, vgl. auch **2.** weiter unten mit Fn. 20. Man muß hier auch im Auge behalten, daß diese Formulierung zu Erfüllung des Briefformats ausreichend und χαίρειν daher eigentlich entbehrlich ist, und nicht zwingend anzuwenden, wie U. Wilcken bereits in O.Wilck, S. 104 und später in Wilcken 1913: 294 in Anmerkung dazu darlegt: „Das Fehlen von χαίρειν spricht nach den Proben aus älterer Zeit auf S. 103 natürlich nicht gegen die Auffassung, daß hier Briefform vorliegt: ὁ δεῖνα τῷ δεῖνι" (s. Zitat oben) zu SPP VIII 268 über Wesselys „Leugnen des briefartigen Formulares" (Wilcken 1913: 294).

17 Im 3. Jh. zeigen die in CPR XVIIB innerhalb des Vertragsregisters vermerkten unter Mitwirkung des Bankiers Aurelios Zoilos enstandenen Verträge (erhalten in 8, 11, 13, 16, 17, 20, 21, 24, 27–29) diesen Brauch, der offenbar nur bei Darlehensgeschäften Anwendung fand. Auch die oben erwähnten Beispiele betreffen Kreditgeschäfte (P.Lips. I 59 und P.Grenf. II 80, 81 sind Quittungen, die beiden letzteren eigentlich keine Homologien). Ein geraumer Teil der panopolitischen Vertragsurkunden bedient sich hingegen, wenn der entsprechende Passus erhalten ist, der Grußformel, die für *Hypomnemata* typisch ist – also „Dem B, von A" (τῷ δεῖνι παρὰ τοῦ δεῖνος) – auch wenn es sich dem Vertragstypus nach um ein *Cheirographon* handelt. Diese Grußformel scheint also Norm in

Es ist nicht auszuschließen, daß in der von geographisch bedingten Unterschieden geprägten ägyptischen Urkundslandschaft nicht auch andernorts mit solchen regionalen Abweichungen zu rechnen ist, deren Muster noch nicht offensichtlich geworden ist.[18]

Daß also P.Cair.Masp. 67170 (562/3/4), in welchem die Vertragsparteien aus dem Panopolites stammen, dem Dioskoros-Archiv zuzurechnen ist, bestätigt auch die hypomnematische Grußformel – „Dem B, von A, Grüße“ (mit χαίρειν) – im Präskript, die im Panopolites nicht zu erwarten wäre, vgl. dazu unten **3a.** und Fn. 28.

Es gibt allerdings keinen Grund für ein Fehlen des χαίρειν an Orten, wo es normalerweise so gut wie immer angewandt wird, wie etwa in Arsinoites und Herakleopolites. Nach Wolff (1961) war ein etwaiges Fehlen ein Zeichen von Respekt,[19] was sich allerdings durch die Belege nicht wirklich bestätigen läßt. Unter den arsinoitischen Dokumenten, in denen das χαίρειν ausfällt[20] – verschiedene Urkundengattungen – gibt es einige Vertragsadressaten höheren Ranges (Pagarchen, *comites* etc.), aber nicht immer ist ein sozialer Unterschied zwischen den Vertragsparteien gegeben (s. etwa SPP XX 217, einem Arbeitsvertrag zwischen Flaviern und *buleutai*).

3. χαίρειν wo es nicht zu erwarten ist

a) „Dem B, von A, Grüße“ (τῷ δεῖνι παρὰ τοῦ δεῖνος χαίρειν)

„Die Verknüpfung von παρά und χαίρειν düfte hingegen purer Gedankenlosigkeit entspringen: die spätzeitliche Gewohnheit, das letztere

Pacht- und Mietverträgen gewesen zu sein. Das zeigen die panopolitischen Urkunden aus Ann Arbor, die auch ins späte 3., frühe 4. Jh. datieren (P.Panop. 1–13). Es ist also richtig, hier mit den Herausgebern von „modifizierten Cheirographa“ zu sprechen (Youtie, Hagedorn & Youtie 1971: 2). Weitere Beispiele sind PSI XII 1233 (323/4?), SB V 7666 (330) und P.Dubl. 31 (355). Diese Formulare verlangen natürlich kein χαίρειν. Vielleicht ist in der überwiegenden Verwendung der *Hypomnemata*-Grußformel der Grund für das spätere Fehlen des Grußes in den *cheirographischen* Tabellionenurkunden zu vermuten. Vgl. zu dieser Hybridform die unter **3a.** behandelten Beispiele für Hermopolites und Antaiopolites, mit Fn. 26.

18 In den wenigen Urkunden des benachbarten This etwa wird regelmäßig die „reguläre“ Grußform ὁ δεῖνα τῷ δεῖνι χαίρειν verwendet: P.Par. 21 (616), P.Par. 21bis (592), SB I 4503 (605/7), SB I 4504 (613), SB I 4505 (606/8).

19 „In den neuen Formen des Präskripts dürfte sich byzantinische Unterwürfigkeit gegenüber dem nach Autorität oder Stand Höheren ausdrücken. Viele werden es als unangebracht empfunden haben, ihn an zweiter Stelle zu nennen oder mit dem vertraulichen Wort χαίρειν zu begrüssen“ (Wolff 1961: 118). Das scheint sich tatsächlich für die Umkehr der Briefformel zu bestätigen, s. o. unter **1.**, wie auch schon von Wolff (1961: 118, Anm. 10) bemerkt.

20 SPP XX 128 (487); CPR X 120 (523); CPR XIV 5 (531/2); SB VI 9596 (579); SPP XX 217 (581); SB I 5139 (6. Jh.); SB XVIII 13963 (6.-7. Jh.); CPR VII 51 (629/44); SB VIII 9754 (647); BGU II 404 (arab.)

Wort abgekürzt zu schreiben, muss es in den Augen vieler zur sinnlosen Floskel degradiert haben".

(Wolff 1961: 118–119, Anm. 10)

In einigen Urkunden aus dem Hermopolites und dem Antaiopolites kommt zur Einführung der Parteien eine andere Grußformel zum Einsatz, und zwar „Dem B, von A, Grüße" (τῷ δεῖνι παρὰ τοῦ δεῖνος χαίρειν).

„Dem B, von A" ist typisch für das Formular des sogenannten *Hypomnema*,[21] dessen Corpus mit einem Wunsch eingeleitet (τῷ δεῖνι παρὰ τοῦ δεῖνος. βούλομαι + Verb) und das in Form eines „Angebots" für die Beurkundung von Pachtverträgen verwendet wird. Es stellte im römischen Arsinoites den bedeutendsten Urkundstyp für diesen Zweck dar und war hauptsächlich dort, aber auch in Hermopolites und Oxyrhynchites verbreitet. Diese hypomnematische Grußformel also, die große soziale Unterschiede zwischen den Parteien[22] suggeriert und in welcher das χαίρειν korrekterweise unterbleibt, verschwindet auch in den spätantiken hermopolitanischen Rechtsurkunden nicht – jedoch kommt es zu einer Vermischung mit dem *Cheirographon*: Vom *Hypomnema* überlebt nur das Präskript, wie in der Tabellionenurkunde üblich, wird der Vertragsgegenstand aber mit ὁμολογῶ + Verb eingeleitet – ein Formulartyp, der sich andernorts, soweit die Überlieferungslage eine Aussage zuläßt, in keiner regelmäßigen Verwendung nachweisen läßt (zu Aphrodito vgl. S. 212 mit Fn. 28). Im Hermopolites hingegen dürfte in den spätantiken Urkunden der *Cheirographon*-Stil mit hypomnematischen Präskript sogar überwiegen.[23] Ihnen

21 Zum *Hypomnema* s. Wolff 1978: 114–22, Herrmann 1958: 25–43 und zuletzt Yiftach-Firanko 2007: 1051–2 mit Anm. 3, besonders zu dessen Verbreitung.

22 S. Wenger 1953: 739 und Wolff 1978: 119–20. Yiftach-Firanko (2007) erklärt die Popularität des Hypomnema im Arsinoites mit der im Vergleich zu der staatsnotariellen Snygraphê unkomplizierteren und schnelleren Beurkundung. Gerade in den arsinoitischen Urkunden aber ist später interessanterweise die für das *Hypomnema* charakteristische Grußformel mit der Tabellionenurkunde völlig verschwunden (zu den „Ausnahmen" P.Dubl. I 34, und SB XVIII 14001 vgl. Fn. 29).

23 Beispiele sind P.Herm. 69 (412); P.Alex. 32 (447/62); SB XVI 12948 (448); P.Lond. V 1793 (472); BGU XVII 2682 (481); CPR X 118 (482); SB VIII 9776 (496); P.Stras. V 470 (497); SB XIV 12050 (498); P.Stras. V 471 (500); P.Stras. V 471bis (505); P.Stras. VII 656 (506); P.Vind.Sal. 9 (509); P.Berl.Frisk 5 (510); P.Stras. V 483 (512); SB IV 7369 (512); BGU XVII 2683 (513); P.Lond. III 994 (517); BGU XII 2187 (520); P.Strasb. VI 579 (521); P.Flor. III 283 (536); P.Stras. V 481 (538); P.Stras. V 482 (538); P.Berl.Möller 3 (540); SB XVIII 13583 (547); P.Lond. V 1872 (548); P.Stras. IV 338 (550); P.Stras. I 4 (551); P.Stras. VI 574 (553); P.Stras.V 398 (553); SB XIV 12131 (553); SB XVIII 13584 (6. Jh.); BGU XVII 2684 (555); P.Stras. IV 248 (560); P.Lond. V 1767 (561); BGU XII 2202 (565); CPR IX 33 (566); P.Lond. V 1872 (568); BGU XII 2204 (574); SB XVI 12865 (576); P.Vind.Tand. 28 (576/577); P.Heid. VII 405 (577); P.Bad. II 30 (ca. 577); SB XVI 12866 (583); BGU XVII 2685 (585); SB VI 9085 (585); P.Ross.Georg. III 40 (589); P.Stras. IV 190 (592); P.Stras. VI 580 (6. Jh.); SB XIV 12052 (6. Jh.); SB XVIII 13889 (6. Jh.); P.Hamb. III 222 (6.-7. Jh.); P.Stras. VI 600 (600); P.Stras. VIII 758 (600); P.Thomas 30 (603); SPP XX 218 (624); P.Lond. III 1012 (633); P.Paramone 18 (641?); P.Stras. VI 600 (7. Jh.); P.Flor. I 38 (7. Jh.) und besonders beliebt im Taurinos-Archiv: BGU XII 2141 (446), 2146 (457), 2147 (464), 2149 (470), 2151 (476), 2155 (481),

gegenüber stehen die Verträge, die sich regulär der Adresse „Der A dem B, Grüße“ (ὁ δεῖνα τῷ δεῖνι χαίρειν), die oben exemplarisch für den Arsinoites vorgestellt wurde, bedienen.[24] Bei der Menge von Belegen für beide Varianten ist es unwahrscheinlich, die Wahl des Grußes reiner Willkür zuzuschreiben. Vielmehr scheinen sich hier funktionelle Unterschiede zu manifestieren, in denen Erinnerungen an frühere Konventionen nachhallen. Bei einer unsystematischen Analyse hat es den Anschein, als ob die erste Gruppe, wie es der Ursprung des Formates nahe legt, Pacht- und Mietverträge enthält, während der *Cheirographon*-Gruß auch in seinem Element bleibt und vor allem für Kreditgeschäfte (Darlehen, Lieferungskäufe, Arbeitsverträge mit Vorauszahlung) Anwendung findet, für deren Beurkundung das *Cheirographon* ab dem 3. Jh. als bevorzugter Dokumententyp gelten kann.[25] Besonders im Taurinos-Archiv und den anderen in BGU XII edierten Urkunden läßt sich das gut beobachten (s. Fn. 23 und 24).

In der eingangs zitierten Grußformel dringt aber mit der fälschlichen Erweiterung um χαίρειν noch ein weiterer Bestandteil des *Cheirographons* in die Mischform ein: „Dem B, von A, Grüße“.[26] Besonderer Beliebtheit erfreute sich diese For-

2156 (483), 2157 (485), 2159 (485), 2160 (488), 2162 (491), 2164 (494), 2174 (501), 2182 (510), 2186 (514?). Viele der oben angeführten Urkunden sind oft nur fragmentarisch erhalten – obwohl der Kontext für Notarsurkunden spricht, ist nicht auszuschließen, daß manche von ihnen, besonders im 5. Jh., noch ohne Beteiligung eines Notars ausgefertigt wurden. „Echte“, notariell beglaubigte *Hypomnemata* datieren naturgemäß früh und finden sich in SB VIII 9931 (405); BGU XII 2139 (432), vielleicht P.Berl.Zill 5 (417) – wahrscheinlich handelt es sich auch bei BGU XII 2148 (466) und P.Stras. VI 597 (541) um solche, jedoch ist die Notarsunterschrift nicht erhalten. Interessant ist auf jeden Fall, daß sich mitten unter den Tabellionenurkunden mit Mischstil im Taurinos-Archiv neben dem eben erwähnten notariellen *Hypomnema* BGU XII 2139 (432) auch private *Hypomnemata* – BGU XII 2148 (466) und BGU XVII 2675 (481) – finden.

24 P.Herm. 37 (4. Jh.); SB XVI 12486 (470); PSI VI 703 (480); P.Amst. I 45 (501); SB XVI 12864 (506); SB XVI 13037 (523); BGU XII 2188 (526); SB XXIV 16284 (533); SB XXII 15597 (537); SB XVI 12488 (538); P.Lond. III 1001 (539); P.Athen.Xyla 4 (541); P.Athen.Xyla 10 (543); P.Lond. III 1319 (544/545); CPR IX 25 (Mitte 5. Jh.); SB XVI 12489 (Mitte 5. Jh.); P.Lond. III 1006 (555); BGU XII 2201 (565?); P.Lond. V 1774 (570); SPP XX 261 (570); CPR IX 31 (581); SB XVI 12867 (584); BGU XII 2205 (590); SB XVI 12868 (593); BGU XII 2206 (591–602); SB XXII 15322 (595); P.Flor. III 300 (597); P.Lond. V 1772 (6. Jh.); SB VI 9586 (600); P.Grenf. II 87 (602); SB XVI 12604 (602); P.Bodl. I 41 (604); BGU XII 2207 (606); b (608); BGU XVII 2695 (608); BGU XII 2208 (614); BGU XII 2209 (614); BGU XVII 2696 (616); BGU XII 2210 (617); P.Flor. I 70 (627); SB XVI 12492 (638); SB XVIII 13170 (7. Jh.) und Taurinos-Archiv: BGU XII 2140 (432), BGU XII 2180 (504), BGU XII 2185 (512), BGU XII 2198 (6. Jh). Die umgekehrte Briefformel mit Voranstellung des Adressaten („Dem B der A, Grüße“), scheint wenig vertreten, s. P.Vind.Sijp. 11 (453); CPR XXIII 33 (550); BGU XII 2200 (561), 2199 (6. Jh.), 2209 (614); in P.Stras. V 310 (7. Jh.) fehlt χαίρειν.

25 Einige Überlegungen dazu werde ich in Kürze an anderer Stelle vorlegen.

26 Zur Vermengung der beiden Urkundstypen s. Wolff 1961: 116–7: „Die Unterschiede zwischen Hypomnema (τῷ δεῖνι παρὰ τοῦ δεῖνος) und briefartigem Cheirographon (ὁ δεῖνα τῷ δεῖνι χαίρειν) verwischen sich, indem in der Grussformel des letzteren nicht selten der Name des Adressaten vor den des Ausstellers tritt, ferner das Grusswort χαίρειν häufig fortgelassen oder auch umgekehrt, mit

mel in späterer Zeit in den Tabellionenurkunden des Hermopolites[27] und im Archiv des Dioskoros von Aphrodito im 6. Jh.[28] Außerhalb dieser beiden Gaue tritt die Formel τῷ δεῖνι παρὰ τοῦ δεῖνος (χαίρειν) nur selten und ausnahmsweise in Erscheinung.[29]

Anders als bei Dioskoros ist dieses Präskript (mit oder ohne χαίρειν) jedoch im restlichen Antaiopolites und bei Texten, die zumindest nicht im engeren Sinne zum Archiv des Dioskoros gehören (wie z. B. das Archiv des Phoibammon, Sohn des Triadelphos),[30] soweit ich sehe, gar nicht in Verwendung, sondern es wird die

der παρά-Formel verbunden wird". Ferner auch Wolff (1978: 122) und Herrmann (1958: 42). Ein solches Eindringen des χαίρειν ist bereits in den „echten" *Hypomnemata* römischen Stils, also ohne Notarsunterschrift, zu bemerken. Beispiele sind etwa BGU II 519 (Ars., 388), P.Lips. I 22 (Herm., 388) und wahrscheinlich SB XX 15035 (Herm., 369). Zahlreicher sind hingegen, als direkte Vorläufer, die prä-tabellionischen „modifizierten" *Cheirographa*, in deren Grußformel sich ein παρά eingeschlichen hat (vgl. Fn. 17).

27 In diese Kategorie fallen CPR XXIV 10 (475 – Taurinos-Archiv); SB III 7167 (477); SB XVI 12378 (504); P.Strasb. V 472 (533/4); P.Horak 10 (555) und P.Lond. III 1003 (562/3) – SPP XX 121 (439) hat, obwohl aus dem 5. Jh., noch keine Notarsunterschrift und ist ein Kaufvertrag, während alle anderen Beispiele Pacht- oder Mietverträge sind.

28 P.Cair.Masp. I 67094, 67095, 67100, 67101, 67106, 67113, 67123, 67125, 67127, 67130; II 67170, 67235; III 67296, 67297, 67300, 67328, 67332; P.Flor. III 342; P.Lond. V 1661, 1687, 1690, 1692; P.Ross.Georg. III 36, 37; PSI VIII 931 (wie immer ohne Anspruch auf Vollständigkeit – παρά, aber kein χαίρειν haben etwa P.Flor. III 281, 283, 284). Eine Besonderheit ist P.Lond. V 1692, bestehend aus 2 Urkunden (a, b), die beide vom selben Notar beglaubigt wurden und dieselben Vertragspartner haben. In a findet sich die für Dioskoros weniger gebräuchliche Formel „Dem B der A, Grüße" (τῷ δεῖνι ὁ δεῖνα χαίρειν); in b hingegen „Dem B, von A, Grüße" (τῷ δεῖνι παρὰ τοῦ δεῖνος χαίρειν). Es fällt in diesen Beispielen auf, daß, vielleicht anders als im Hermopolites, unterschiedliche Geschäfte beurkundet werden; signifikant ist hier, daß, soweit ich sehe, unter den Bürgschaften das Präskript τῷ δεῖνι παρὰ τοῦ δεῖνος χαίρειν nur einmal ohne χαίρειν geschrieben wird (P.Flor. III 284), und dessen Funktion damit tatsächlich derjenigen der „neuen" Grußformel des Arsinoites entspricht (vgl. etwa P.Cair.Masp. III 67328, ein Register von 10 Bürgschaften, vgl. Fn. 15).

29 In Mitteläg ypten sind das für den Arsinoites SB XVIII 14001 und P.Dubl. I 34 (511), für den Herakleopolites P.Dubl. I 24 (7. Jh.) – den beiden letzteren Urkunden fehlen wesentliche Charakteristika der Tabellionenurkunde. Nach der Grußformel folgt in P.Dubl. I 34 34 ὁμολογῶ (l. ἐπειδὴ) γεγράφηκα ... den Satz mit τῶ (l. τὸ) ἐμὸν χαρτίον ἄγυρόν (l. ἄκυρόν) ἐστιν beendend. Die für diese Zeit im Arsinoites vollkommen aus dem Rahmen fallende griechisch geleistete „Notarsunterschrift" und das Fehlen einer für die Tabellionenurkunde erforderlichen Datierung und Errichtungsort spricht für die Imitation einer Notarsurkunde. Ähnlich verhält es sich in P.Dubl. I 24; die lateinisch-griechische Notarunterschrift wirkt zwar professionell, aber der Rest der Urkunde läßt einiges vermissen. In SB XVIII 14001 (486) scheint mir mit dem Genitiv vielleicht doch eher ein Fehler des Schreibers vorzuliegen παρά ist keines erhalten. Im Oxyrhynchites ist der sehr früh datierende Papyrus P.Oxy. VIII 1122 (407) fragmentarisch, also vielleicht ebenfalls noch nicht als Tabellionenurkunde zu werten. Die Zuordnung von P.Grenf. II 90 (525) zum Apollonopolites erscheint aufgrund des Formulars fragwürdig, allerdings handelt es sich auch hier nicht um eine Tabellionenurkunde, da Datierung und Notarsunterschrift fehlen.

30 Vgl. Fournet 2008: 18 mit Anm. 3.

Standard-Grußformel „Der A dem B, (Grüße)“ – ὁ δεῖνα τῷ δεῖνι (χαίρειν) gebraucht,[31] die allerdings auch im Archiv des Dioskoros vorhanden ist.

Das Eindringen oder Beibehalten eines rudimentären *Hypomnema*-Bestandteiles, nämlich des Präskripts, innerhalb der cheirographischen Tabellionenurkunde könnte also – da die Formel τῷ δεῖνι παρὰ τοῦ δεῖνος (χαίρειν) genau wie die umgekehrte Grußformel des Arsinoites den Adressaten im Dativ voranstellt – darin begründet sein, durch diese vom Formular vorgegebene Nennung an erster Stelle besonderen Respekt zu bezeugen.

Es zeigt sich auf jeden Fall auch hier, daß die Grußformel mit χαίρειν ein solches Charakteristikum der Vertragsurkunde gewesen sein muß, daß sie auch in Kontexten angewendet wurde, wo sie fremd und fehl am Platz war bzw. gerade bei Verwendung des importierten Präskripts mit einem essentiellen Bestandteil bekräftigt werden sollte, daß es sich trotzdem tatsächlich um eine Tabellionenurkunde handelte.[32]

b) Sonderformen und Objektivurkunden

> „Das Charakteristische des byzantinischen Urkundenwesens ist für Ägypten das, daß alle Objektivurkunden verschwunden sind und das Cheirographon die Alleinherrschaft gewonnen hat“.
>
> (Mitteis 1912: 87)

Abschließend sollen noch zwei Varianten von Grußformeln besprochen werden, die hauptsächlich in zwei Urkundstypen erscheinen, dem *compromissum* (Übereinkunft zur Bestimmung eines Schiedsrichters) und der *dialysis* (Vergleich, Eheschließung oder Scheidung), die in einer Art Erklärung, manchmal auch objektiv stilisiert, formuliert sind.[33] Man verwendet sie, um einen Vorgang zu dokumentieren, in dem zwei zumindest theoretisch auf formaler Ebene gleichberechtigte Parteien über eine Sache übereinkommen, eine einseitige Obligation also außer Frage steht. Da aber auch diese Art Urkunde von einem Notar aufgesetzt wurde und das χαίρειν als

31 Mit χαίρειν P.Bingen 132; P.Mich. XIII 662, 664, 666, 669, 671; P.Michael. 44, 45, 46, 47; P.PalauRib. 24; P.Vat.Aphr. 1; PSI IV 283; P.Genova I 30; SB III 7201; SB XVIII 13320, SB XXII 15477 – aber auch Beispiele ohne χαίρειν, wie etwa P.Michael. 48.

32 Worin aber besteht nun der Unterschied zwischen *Hypomnema*-Präskript mit oder ohne χαίρειν? Es lassen sich keine auf den ersten Blick evidenten Gründe beibringen – in dem Dossier von *misthoseis* mit der Bischofskirche von Hermupolis (P.Stras. V 470–474) wird z. B. im Gruß einmal (P.Stras. V 472) χαίρειν verwendet und die anderen Male nicht. Generell sind diese Beobachtungen nur unsystematische Streiflichter auf eine bemerkenswerte Vielfalt in der Urkundsgestaltung, welche z. B. im Arsinoites in der Form nicht besteht. Die gesamte Problematik bedarf noch einer umfassenderen Analyse; die hier vorgelegten gesammelten Eindrücke erheben keinesfalls Anspruch auf Vollständigkeit, sondern sollen nur interessante Aspekte aufzeigen.

33 So auch schon Wolff 1961: 115: „für manche Typen von Geschäften, wie z. B. διαλύσεις, traten allerdings auch neuartige Formen der objektiv stilisierten Erklärung in Erscheinung“. Bei dieser Art Verträge handelt es sich allerdings nicht unbedingt, aber auch, um Homologien.

essentieller Bestandteil einer solchen Tabellionenurkunde verstanden wurde (s.o.), kann es in diesen bilateralen Erklärungen zu zwei merkwürdigen Konstruktionen kommen, um dieser signifikanten Rolle des χαίρειν Rechnung zu tragen.

a. „A und B [einander], Grüße" (ὁ δεῖνα καὶ ὁ δεῖνα [ἀλλήλοις] χαίρειν)[34]

b. „auf der einen Seite A – auf der anderen Seite B – Grüße" (ἐκ μὲν ἑνὸς μέρους *N. (Nom.)* – ἐκ δὲ ἑτέρου / θατέρου μέρους *N. (Nom.)* – χαίρειν)

Diese Urkunden zeigen oft noch eine andere anachronistische Eigenheit: den Gebrauch der dritten Person. Da auch dieses Phänomen, wie die abweichende Grußformel, großteils im selben Kontext, nämlich im *compromissum* und der *dialysis*, auftritt, kann hier vielleicht mit derselben zugrundeliegenden Ursache gerechnet werden: Das Hauptmerkmal der notariellen Urkunde, nämlich die subjektive Stilisierung im gesamten Dokument, ist darin begründet, daß es sich bei der Tabellionenurkunde um eine unilaterale Erklärung der Person handelt, die eine Verpflichtung eingeht und damit zumeist die schwächere Position innehat. Die objektive Stilisierung bezweckt also die formelle Gleichstellung der involvierten Parteien.

Auch ein Partnerschaftsvertrag zweier Obsthändler wie P.Lond. V 1794 (Herm., 488) mag nach einer Möglichkeit verlangen, Gleichheit zwischen den Vertragspartnern auszudrücken und bedient sich daher des reziproken Grußes: Αὐρήλιοι *N. und N.* ἀλλήλοις χαίρειν.

Typischerweise beginnt ein Kompromiß, wie BGU I 315 (Ars., 627), mit:

> Τόδε τὸ κομπρόμισσον ποιοῦνται πρὸς ἀλλήλ(ους) ἑκουσίᾳ γνώμῃ ἐκ μὲν τοῦ ἑνὸς μέρους Αὐρήλ(ιος) Ἄπα Ἰούλιος κναφεὺς υἱὸς τοῦ μακαρίου Ἰωσήφ, ἐκ δὲ τοῦ ἑτέρου μέρους Αὐρήλιος Ἰωσὴφ κάπηλος υἱὸς Αἰουλίου ὁρμώμ(ενοι) ἀπὸ τῆς Ἀρσινοιτῶν πόλεως χ(αίρειν).
>
> „Diesem Kompromiß stimmen einander gegenseitig und freiwillig zu auf der einen Seite Aurelios Apa Iulios, Walker, Sohn des seligen Ioseph, und auf der anderen Seite Aurelios Ioseph, Sohn des Aiulios, Kaufmann, beide stammend aus Arsinoiton Polis, Grüße".

Das hinzugefügte χαίρειν am Ende hat keine syntaktische Bestimmung in dieser Konstruktion. Oftmals erfolgt nach dieser objektiven Einleitungsformel ein Wechsel in die erste Person ὁμολογοῦμεν, manchmal erst später, in den Unterschriften. Die Rückkehr zum vertrauten Gebrauch der ersten Person scheint legitim, sobald mit der

34 Vereinzelt finden sich bereits in den prä-tabellionischen *cheirographa* des 3.-4. Jh. Beispiele für diese Praxis in ähnlichem Kontext (Erbschafts-, Kooperationsverträge, generell Übereinkommen). Vgl. zum Folgenden die Ausführungen von Andrea Jördens zu den hybriden Cheirographa im selben Band.

objektiven Stilisierung des Präskripts Klarheit über die Art der Vereinbarung geschaffen wurde.

Kompromisse und Dialyseis mit den besagten Grußformeln zeigt die folgende Aufstellung:

Publikationsnr.	Datierung	Herkunft	Gattung	Zitat
P.Haun. III 57	412–415?	Arkadia (?)	Dialysis	*N. (Nom.) und N. (Nom.)* ἀλλήλοις χαίρειν. ἐπειδὴ ἐγώ...
P.Princ. II 82	481	Lykopolis	Dialysis	[ταύτ]ην π[οιοῦνται πρὸς ἑαυτο]ὺς τὴν κοινὴν ὁ[μο]λ[ογ]ία[ν τ]ῆς διαλύσεως ἐκ μὲν τοῦ ἑνὸς [μέρους] *drei Brüder (Nom.)* --- [ἐκ δὲ θατέρου *N. (Nom.)*] --- [ὁμολογοῦμεν ἀλλήλοις τ]ὰ ὑποτεταγμένα. χ]αίρειν. μικρῷ πρότερον...
P.Lond. III 992	507	Hermupolis	Kompromiß	[οἱ ὑπογρ(άφοντες)] ποιοῦντ[ες] πρὸς ἑαυτοὺς τὴν ὁμολογίαν τοῦ κομπρομίσσου [ἐκ μὲν τοῦ] ἑνὸς μ[έ]ρους *drei Brüder und Erben eines verstorbenen Bruders (Nom.)* --- ἐκ δὲ [τοῦ] ἑτέρου μέρους *N. und Gattin, Schwester der Vorgenannten (Nom.)* ἀλλήλοις χαίρ(ειν). ἐπειδὴ ἠμφιβητήσαμεν πρὸς ἑαυτούς...
P.Corn. inv. II 48, ed. T. Gagos, *BASP* 45 (2008), S. 62–63	596	Arsinoites	Kompromiß	*N. (Nom.) und N. (Nom.)* χ(αίρειν). ὁμολογοῦμεν ἑκουσίᾳ γνώμῃ [αἱρ]ῆσα[σ]θαι...
BGU I 315	602	Arsinoites	Kompromiß	τόδε τὸ κομπρόμισσον ποιοῦνται πρὸς ἀλλήλ(ους) ἑκουσίᾳ γνώμῃ ἐκ μὲν τοῦ ἑνὸς μέρους *N. (Nom.)* ἐκ δὲ τοῦ ἑτέρου μέρους *N. (Nom.)* χ(αίρειν). δίκην ἔχοντες πρὸς ἀλλήλους...
P.Prag. I 48	615	Arsinoites	Kompromiß	*N. (Nom.) und N. (Nom.) und N. (Nom.) und N. (Nom.) und N. (Nom.)* χ(αίρειν). ὁμολογοῦμ[εν
P.Prag. I 49	628	Arsinoites	Kompromiß	*N. (Nom.) und N. (Nom.) und N. (Nom.)* χ(αίρειν). ὁμολογοῦμεν δικάσασθαι πρὸς ἀλλήλους...

SB VIII 9775	2. H. 7. Jh.	Arsinoites	Kompromiß	*N. (Nom.) und N. (Nom.)* [ἀλλ]ή[λοις] χ[αίρειν]. ὁμολογοῦμε[ν
SB XIV 12194	7. Jh.	Arsinoites	Kompromiß	[τόδε τὸ κομπρόμισσον π]οιοῦνται πρ[ὸ]ς [ἀλλήλους ἑκουσίᾳ γνώμῃ ἐ]κ μὲν τοῦ [ἑνός μέρους *N. (Nom.)*] ἐκ δὲ τοῦ ἑτ[έ]ρ[ου μέρους *N. (Nom.)*] *für seinen Bruder* χ(αίρειν)]*. ὁμολογοῦμεν δικάσασθαι [

* χαίρειν wird an dieser Stelle vom Herausgeber nicht ergänzt, ist aber doch sehr wahrscheinlich.

Korrekterweise kein χαίρειν verwenden folgende, z. T. objektive Urkunden: CPR VI 7 (Hera., 6. Jh.), P.Lond. V 1707 (Ant., 566), P.Münch. I 14 (594), P.Par. 20 (Pan., 600),[35] SB I 5681 (Ars., 654?), P.Rain.Cent. 121 (Hera., 719), SPP III 402 (Hera., 6. Jh.). Es fällt auf, daß es sich bei dem Gebrauch des χαίρειν innerhalb dieser Urkundsform also besonders um ein arsinoitisches Phänomen handelt.

In den Fällen, in denen man sich innerhalb dieses Urkundstyp an die gewöhnliche Grußformel, „Der A dem B", Grüße hält – wie etwa SB XXII 15477 (Ant., 537), P.Herm. 31 (Theben, 6. Jh.), P.Münch. I 1 (574),[36] SB VI 9456 (Ars., 594) oder SPP XX 243 (Ars., 633/648) – zeigt sich ein hierarchisches Ungleichgewicht, da weder eine objektive Stilisierung noch eine „Unterschrift" von allen beteiligten Personen vorliegt, sondern nur vom Aussteller.[37] All diese Elemente also – die konventionelle Grußformel in der gängigen unilateralen subjektiv stilisierten Tabellionenurkunde – zeugen von einem Ranggefälle.

Es gibt allerdings auch Objektivurkunden außerhalb der beiden erwähnten Gattungen: In P.Dubl. I 32 (512) und 33 (513), dem Verkauf eines Klosters, folgt auf das Datum direkt die Einführung des Vertragsgegenstandes, ohne Grußformel, aber objektiv stilisiert. P.Dubl. I 32: ὁμολογεῖ Εὐλόγιος μονάζων ... πεπρακέναι καὶ καταγεγραφηκέναι πρὸς πᾶσαν δεσποτίαν ... Πούσι πρεσβυτέρῳ Μελιτιανῷ „Der Mönch Eulogios stimmt zu ..., daß er verkauft und vollständig als Eigentum übertragen hat ... dem Pusis, Melitanischer Priester ...". Beide Dokumente sind vollständig in dritter Person verfaßt (mit Ausnahme der Zeugenunterschriften) und haben eine Notarsunterschrift am Ende der Urkunde – meines Wissens handelt es sich

35 Nach den Ausführungen oben, unter **2.** auch nicht anders zu erwarten.

36 Zwischen der Nennung der einen Partei und dem Gruß an die andere Partei finden sich bereits 10 Zeilen Information zur Beschreibung der familiären Situation.

37 Auch von den oben in der Tabelle angeführten Belege unterschreibt allerdings in BASP 45 (2009) nur die eindeutig schwächere Partei und in BGU I 315 überhaupt niemand.

(abgesehen von den oben behandelten Kompromissen) um die einzigen notariellen Objektivurkunden im Arsinoites (nach dem 4. Jh.). Auch das Format – die beiden Verträge sind Papyrusrollen, die in der Breite 77 bzw. 84 cm messen – und das dahinterliegende Geschäft sind ungewöhnlich (Garantie für ein Darlehen in Form eines fiktiven Verkaufes).

Schlußbemerkung

Eindeutig scheint also, daß χαίρειν und damit das Briefformat als wesentlicher Bestandteil der Tabellionenurkunde betrachtet wurde, wodurch es auch in solchen Fällen zur Anwendung kommt, in welchen dieser Gruß nicht zu erwarten oder sogar grammatikalisch falsch ist. Bedingt wird das dadurch, daß in manchen Teilen Ägyptens und in manchen Urkundengattungen auch nach der Einführung der Tabellionenurkunde ältere Traditionen überlebt haben, wie z. B. die Grußformel des *Hypomena* oder die objektive Stilisierung, der Siegeszug des *Cheirographon* also nicht allumfassend war.

An dieser Stelle sei auch darauf hingewiesen, daß zeitgleich mit der endgültigen Ausformung der privaten Rechtsurkunden Ende des 5. Jh. auch beim Brief ein Wandel zu bemerken ist, diesbezüglich nämlich, daß zunächst χαίρειν aus den Grußformeln und überhaupt diese selbst verschwindet, einhergehend mit einer Änderung im Format.[38]

Man könnte also von der Verbrieflichung der Urkunde sprechen, da es zu einer Übertragung der Briefcharakteristika vom Brief auf die Urkunde kommt, die in Folge als Eigenheit der Urkunde empfunden werden, während gleichzeitig der Brief sich ab dieser Zeit dadurch auszeichnet, daß er ohne Gruß *in medias res* geht.[39] Der Umbruch im Format zieht außerdem nach sich, daß die Urkunde im Längsformat sich dann auch äußerlich vom Brief neueren Typs im Querformat abhebt.

38 Vorbildlich herausgearbeitet hat das Fournet (2009) in seiner Studie zur „Anatomie des Briefes".

39 Fournet (2007: 356) spricht bereits in einer früheren Arbeit von dem „changement de diplomatique que connaît la lettre au Ve s. (*Fig. 3*) : la disparition de la formule d'introduction (*praescriptum*: ὁ δεινα τῳ δεινι χαιρειν) et de la salutation finale". Die Grußformel in den Briefen durchläuft vor ihrem Verschwinden auch ähnliche Stadien wie die der Urkunde (Weglassen des χαίρειν, Inversion der Grußformel), vgl. Fournet 2009: 43, mit Anm. 61.

Urkunden in Briefform: Chirographum und Epistula im römischen Privatrecht

Éva Jakab (Szeged)

Der Briefverkehr war bereits in der Antike ein wichtiger Bestandteil der alltäglichen Kommunikation. Ein Brief wurde meistens vom Verfasser eigenhändig geschrieben und an den Adressaten vertraulich gerichtet; der Anfang folgte typischerweise dem Schema „A grüßt B". Briefe können Nachrichten, Bestätigungen, Glückwünsche oder Bitten mitteilen. Im rechtshistorischen Kontext sind diejenigen Schriftstücke von Interesse, die unter den Parteien (oder auch Dritten) Rechtswirkungen erzeugen oder tilgen; auf diese „privatrechtlichen Urkunden in Briefform" werde ich den vorliegenden Beitrag beschränken.[1]

Briefe werden üblicherweise unter Personen gewechselt, die einander privat oder geschäftlich bekannt sind. Die Korrespondenz trägt immer einen persönlichen Charakter, unabhängig davon, ob sie unter sozial Gleichgestellten oder Abhängigen entsteht. Der Brief spricht den Adressaten oft in einem vertrauten Ton an. Bereits dieses Merkmal macht wahrscheinlich, dass Briefe im Rechtsverkehr in einem speziellen Kontext eingesetzt worden sein dürften. Es gibt Rechtsverhältnisse, die auf dem Vertrauen unter den Parteien basieren oder die Öffentlichkeit diskret meiden wollen. Hierher zählen vor allem die Kreditgeschäfte: Gläubiger und Schuldner sind daran interessiert, ihren Vermögensstand nicht restlos öffentlich zu bekennen.

In den lateinischen Quellen wird der Brief *epistula* genannt. Im juristischen Kontext werden zwei technischen Wörter verwendet, die Schriftstücke in Briefform, mit persönlicher Formulierung, bezeichnen: *chirographum* und *epistula.* Im Folgenden werde ich die Schriften der klassischen römischen Juristen (die Jurisprudenz) und die Dokumente des Rechtslebens (Urkunden) unter diesem Aspekt untersuchen.[2]

Leopold Wenger hat 1953 sein umfassendes Werk über *Die Quellen des römischen Rechts* veröffentlicht; seine Thesen bestimmen bis heute die wichtigsten Grundsätze der römischrechtlichen Quellenlehre.[3] Wenger versucht seine Quellen-

1 Ausgeklammert bleiben dabei etwa die *epistulae* der römischen Kaiser, die eher zur Gesetzgebung einzuordnen sind; vgl. Wenger 1953: 466ff.

2 Gegen die Ignoranz gegenüber der Praxis in rechtshistorischen Arbeiten s. bereits Friedman 1977: 47f. Zum Spannungsfeld zwischen Rechtsleben und Rechtswissenschaft s. Jakab 2009: 1ff.

3 Der Band bietet auf 973 Seiten einen Einblick in die römische Rechtsgeschichte und eine detaillierte Beschreibung der Rechtsquellen aller Form.

masse nach Logik und Systematik zu ordnen, aber bereits er gibt zu, dass die Terminologie und die Arten der privatrechtlichen Urkunden „in der lateinischen Rechtssprache von einer auffallenden Unbestimmtheit und mehrfach durch äußere Umstände eher als durch juristische Momente veranlasst“ gewesen seien.[4] Bei den Dokumenten unter Privatleuten bemüht er sich die Texte in folgende Gruppen einzugliedern: Dispositiv- und Beweisurkunde; öffentliche und Privaturkunde; subjektiv und objektiv gefasste Urkunde.

Für das vorliegende Thema ist die letztgenannte Gruppierung von Interesse. Wenger sieht dabei den wesentlichen Unterschied in der Art der Formulierung: „In jenen gibt der erklärende seine rechtsgeschäftliche Erklärung selbst in der Ich-Form eines Bekenntnisses ab, in diesen berichtet ein außenstehender Beobachter, z.B. ein Notar, oder auch die Gegenpartei über eine rechtsgeschäftliche Erklärung“.[5] Die Urkunden in Briefform (*epistulae* und *chirographa*) gehören jedenfalls der Gruppe der subjektiv stilisierten Urkunden an.

Die herrschende Lehre betrachtet die beiden (mit Wenger) als Synonyme und betont, dass die *epistula* bloß ein Unterbegriff des Chirographum sei: „Epistula besagt nichts über den dispositiven oder bloß beweisenden Charakter der Urkunde, sondern geht auf die Briefform mit beginnendem Gruß. Die Epistula fällt unter den weiteren Begriff des Chirographums, wie denn die urkundlichen und literarischen juristischen Quellen Epistula mit Chirographum im angegebenen Rahmen synonym gebrauchen“.[6]

Seit dem Erscheinen Wengers grundlegenden Werkes, seit 1953 wurden zahlreiche neue Quellen veröffentlicht, die Indizien zur Neuuntersuchung des Themas Chirographum und Epistula liefern könnten. Es reicht hier etwa auf das „Archiv der Sulpizier“ zu verweisen, das G. Camodeca 1999 musterhaft edierte.[7] Auch die Auffassung der Forschung bezüglich der Bedeutung des Urkundenmaterials nahm langsam eine gewisse Wende. Es wurde das Spannungsfeld zwischen „gelebtem und gesetztem Recht“, zwischen der Alltagspraxis und der Rechtswissenschaft erkannt.[8] Die Berücksichtigung der Praxis wurde in den Vordergrund gerückt, die Funktion der rechtshistorischen Forschung wurde neu überlegt. Es gibt immer wieder Versuche, aus den Entscheidungen der klassischen römischen Juristen die typischen Formulare der Geschäftspraxis zu rekonstruieren und dadurch die lückenhafte epigraphische Überlieferung zu ergänzen.[9] Neue Fragestellungen können zu überraschenden Ergebnissen führen, wenn man an die Texte ohne große dogmatische Erwartungen herangeht.

Mein vorliegender Beitrag versucht, die Aussagen der neuen Quellen und die Ergebnisse der neuen Methodik zu verwerten, um Wengers Thesen und deren Einfluss

4 Wenger 1953: 737.
5 Wenger 1953: 736.
6 Wenger 1953: 737–8.
7 Camodeca 1999.
8 Siehe dazu etwa Zweigert & Kötz 1996: 10ff.; Friedman 1990: 53.
9 Siehe etwa Jakab 2009: 117ff., 157ff.

auf die römischrechtliche Forschung kritisch zu überprüfen. Die Untersuchung konzentriert sich auf folgende Fragen: Kann die Differenzierung zwischen subjektiv und objektiv gefassten Urkunden konsequent beibehalten werden? Stimmt die traditionelle Definition des Chirographum mit den neuen Quellen überein? Sind die Begriffe Chirographum und Epistula in den literarischen und juristischen Quellen wirklich immer synonym verwendet? Oder könnten doch wesentliche Unterschiede zwischen den beiden festgestellt werden?

1. Chirographum

Das rechtshistorische Schrifttum nimmt von der Funktion und der Bedeutung der Epistula in der Rechtspraxis beinahe keine Kenntnis; allein das Chirographum wird in den Handbüchern zum römischen Recht kurz erwähnt.[10] Zum Chirographum liegen jedenfalls Definitionen vor, deshalb empfiehlt es sich, die Abhandlung mit diesem Urkundentyp zu beginnen. Leopold Wenger definiert das Chirographum als „subjektiv stilisierte Erklärung";[11] damit stellt er auf ein sehr breites Bedeutungsfeld ab. Bereits er sah, dass die Terminologie der hellenistischen Rechtssprache entstamme. Unten werden wir sehen, das auch das in Italia verbreitete Formular enge Verwandtschaft mit dem Formular in den Papyri zeigt.

Hans Julius Wolff bemüht sich um eine exaktere Definition des Chirographum, wobei er die juristisch relevanten Charakteristika hervorhebt: Im *cheirographon* bekannte „der Aussteller selbst mittels bindender Schrift, dass er die durch dieses bezeugte Verfügung getroffen hatte oder die in ihr gekennzeichnete Verbindlichkeit eingegangen war ... Der Deklarant stellte entweder mit direkten Worten ... oder indirekt mittels Anerkenntnisses das Vorliegen eines bestimmten Sachverhaltes fest; hieran schloss sich, wenn der Charakter des Geschäfts es erforderte, ein in der 1. Person des Futurs gehaltenes Leistungs- oder Garantieversprechen ...".[12]

Dem römischrechtlichen Schrifttum ist bekannt, dass das Chirographum als Beweisurkunde nach griechischem Muster entstanden sei. Die Urkunde wird als „zeugenlose, eigenhändig geschriebene und durch die Handschrift beweiskräftige, subjektiv (in der 1. Person) gefasste Erklärung" definiert.[13] Der Urkundentyp soll insbesondere in Kreditgeschäften (Darlehen, Bürgschaften, Verpfändungen, Schuldanerkenntnisse, Quittungen usw.) verwendet worden sein.[14]

10 Diese Beobachtung ist sogar für das sonst ausgezeichnete Werk von Wenger treffend, s. Wenger 1953: 734ff. Epistulae analysiert er vor allem im öffentlichrechtlichen Bereich, s. Wenger 1953: 148, 381ff., 407, 425ff., 440ff., 464.

11 Wenger 1953: 736.

12 Wolff 1978: 107, 203.

13 Kaser 1971: 234; ebenso Kaser & Knütel 2005: 51.

14 Siehe in den literarischen Quellen etwa Cic. *Fam.* 7.18.1; Gell. *NA* 14.2.7; weiter unten werden noch zahlreiche juristische Quellen genannt.

Die herrschende Lehre zählt also zu den begriffswesentlichen Elementen eines jeden Chirographums die subjektive Formulierung, die Eigenhändigkeit und den Verzicht auf die Mitwirkung von Zeugen. Im Folgenden soll geprüft werden, ob das Quellenmaterial diese Definition bestätigt.

Blättert man in den Quellen, findet man auch Chirographa, in welchen Verpflichtungen übernommen werden, die nach *ius civile* nicht klagbar sind.[15] Solche Belege würde ich hier als Chirographa im „weiteren Sinne" ausklammern; im Rahmen des vorliegenden Beitrags kann ich auf sie nicht näher eingehen.

In anderen Texten bedeutet das Wort Chirographum bloß ein eigenhändig geschriebenes Schriftstück; es wird als Synonym für *manu sua scribere* verwendet.[16] Dokumente dieser Art können allerlei Vertrags- oder Urkundentypen vertreten. Wegen des untechnischen Sprachgebrauchs scheiden sie in der vorliegenden Untersuchung ebenfalls aus. Für unser Thema haben nur die Chirographa Relevanz, die ein gefestigtes Formular zeigen und dadurch klagbare Verpflichtungen erzeugen.[17]

Das Formular des Chirographums war im klassischen römischen Recht bereits so verbreitet, dass Gaius, Verfasser einer elementaren juristischen Einführungsschrift im 2. Jh., es einigermaßen definieren bzw. in das geschlossene System der römischen Verträge eingliedern wollte (Gai. 3.134):[18]

> „Praeterea litterarum obligatio fieri videtur chirographis et syngraphis, id est, si quis debere se aut daturum se scribat, ita scilicet, ut, si eo nomine stipulatio non fiat. Quod genus obligationis proprium peregrinorum est".

In seinen Institutionen[19] untersucht Gaius ab dem Abschnitt 3.89 (Obligationen *ex contractu*, Vertragsrecht) den Aspekt, wann eine Obligation wirksam entsteht, also mit welchem Akt jeweils die Klagen auf Erfüllung erzeugt werden. Bekanntlich gliedert er die Kontraktobligationen in vier Gruppen ein: *re, verbis, litteris, consensu*. Beim Litteralkontrakt (Entstehung einer Obligation, einer Verpflichtung aus Schriftakt) kommt er auf das Chirographum zu sprechen.

Der praxisorientierte Jurist ist vor allem an den römischen *nomina transscriptitia* interessiert; er betont, dass diese nur unter römischen Bürgern eine strengrechtliche Klage begründen können. Bei Nichtbürgern kann jedoch die mangelnde Rechtswirkung der Eintragungen im „Kassenbuch" durch Chirographa und Syngrapha (ebenfalls durch Schrift) ersetzt werden. Die Wendung *ius proprium peregrinorum* dürfte

15 Siehe etwa D. 30.103 Julian oder D. 2.14.47.1 Scaevola.

16 So etwa D. 2.14.47.1 Scaevola.

17 Siehe etwa D. 30.44.5 Ulpian; D. 38.4.7 Scaevola; *Paul.Sent.* 5.25.5.

18 Gai. 3.134: „Ferner ist es herrschende Meinung, dass eine Verpflichtung aus Schriftakt durch Chirographa und Syngrapha entsteht; das heißt, wenn jemand schreibt, dass er schulde, oder schreibt, dass er zahlen werde – selbstverständlich nur dann, wenn in jener Angelegenheit keine Stipulation stattfindet. Diese Art der Obligation gehört dem Sonderrecht der Peregrinen an". Übersetzung nach Manthe 2004: 275.

19 Zum Werk s. Nelson & Manthe 1999: 26ff.

den Gegensatz zu den *nomina transscriptitia* als *ius proprium Romanorum* hervorheben wollen. Mit dieser Eingliederung in das römische Vertragssystem kommt Gaius eigentlich bei der hellenistischen Rechtsauffassung an, die der Urkunde konstitutive Wirkung bzw. unwiderlegbare Beweiskraft verleiht. Gaius zeigt damit die Durchlässigkeit der Grenzen zwischen römischer und hellenistischer Alltagspraxis. Er gliedert die konstitutive Wirkung der hellenistischen Urkunde in das römische Vertragssystem als „Litteralobligation“ (Verpflichtung aus Schriftakt) ein.[20] Offenbar hat Gaius ein Chirographum vor Augen, wodurch ein *nomen*, eine Schuldforderung mit einer Klage auf *certa pecunia* begründet wird. Solche Chirographa folgen einem gefestigten Formular und werden vor einem römischen Gericht als klagbare Schuldscheine anerkannt. Gaius beschränkt seine kurz gehaltene Bewertung auf die Entstehung der Obligation; das Formular und die nähere Definition der Begriffsmerkmale bleiben in seinen Institutionen unbehandelt.

Über das Formular und den Wortlaut der Chirographa wurden Belege direkter und indirekter Art überliefert: einerseits epigraphische und papyrologische Zeugnisse und andererseits wörtliche Zitate von Urkunden als Entscheidungsgrundlagen in den Schriften der römischen Juristen.

Im lateinischen Formular fehlt am Anfang oft die Grußform; der Text setzt mit dem Namen des Schuldners ein und mit dem Verbum in der 1. Person *scripsi*. Dem folgt die juristisch relevante Handlung mit einem Infinitiv ausgedrückt, etwa *scripsi me debere, scripsi me accepisse, scripsi me repromisisse.*[21] Zitieren wir z. B. den Wortlaut eines typischen Darlehensgeschäfts bei Modestin (D. 22.1.41.2):[22]

> „Ab Aulo Agerio Gaius Seius mutuam quandam quantitatem accepit hoc chirographo: ‚ille scripsi me accepisse et accepi ab illo mutuos et numeratos decem, quos ei reddam kalendis illis proximis cum suis usuris placitis inter nos‘ ...“

Die Entscheidung stammt aus den *Responsa* (Rechtsgutachten) des Herennius Modestinus. Er war der Schüler Ulpians und damit der letzte Vertreter der klassischen Jurisprudenz.[23] Er entschied hier ein juristisches Problem auf Anfrage einer der Parteien. Gaius Seius und Aulus Agerius sind typische Blankettnamen. Es ist denkbar, dass Modestin die Parteien nicht öffentlich nennen wollte oder er behandelte bloß einen Entwurf als Schulfall. Im Sachverhalt geht es um ein Darlehensgeschäft mit unbestimmter Zinsabrede. Der Jurist wurde darüber gefragt, ob auf-

20 Ähnlich fasst den Text auf Nelson & Manthe 1999: 216.

21 FIRA III Nr. 130; TH Nr. 4, Nr. 8; vgl. Arangio-Ruiz 1948.

22 D. 22.1.41.2: „Gaius Seius hat von Aulus Agerius einen bestimmten Geldbetrag als Darlehen mit dem folgenden Chirographum erhalten: ‚Ich, der und der, habe geschrieben, dass ich erhalten habe und erhielt von dem und dem zehn (Goldstücke) als Darlehen zugezählt, die ich ihm zurückgeben werde am kommenden Ersten des und des Monats mit den zwischen uns vereinbarten Zinsen‘...“ Die Übersetzungen aus den Digesten folgen überwiegend der Ausgabe Behrends, Knütel, Kupisch & Seiler 1995–2005.

23 Er war der juristische Lehrer des Sohnes des Kaisers Maximinus Thrax; seine Ämterlaufbahn entfaltete sich in den ersten Jahrzehnten des 3. Jhs. n.Chr., vgl. Kunkel 2001: 259.

grund der wörtlich zitierten Beweisurkunde (eines Chirographums) vom Schuldner überhaupt Zinsen verlangt werden können.[24]

Uns interessiert vor allem das korrekt zitierte Formular, das außer dem Zinsfuß alle juristisch relevanten Elemente enthält: Die Bestätigung des Empfangs eines gewissen Geldbetrags, die Bezeichnung der *causa numerationis* (*mutuum*) und die deklarierte Rückzahlungspflicht, die hier mit einem genauem Rückzahlungstermin festgehalten wurde. Bemerkenswert ist noch, dass die Verpflichtung zur Rückzahlung aus dem Darlehen nach *ius civile* automatisch folgt, die Parteien wollten sie trotzdem (zusätzlich) auch als *lex contractus* festhalten. Die Wendung *mutua accipere* ermöglicht die Klage aus dem Realkontrakt *mutuum,* aber das Chirographum als Litteralkontrakt begründet ebenfalls eine strengrechtliche Klage.[25] Der Gläubiger kann also nach Belieben auswählen, welche Klageformel bzw. welches Beweisprogramm ihm am günstigsten erscheint.[26]

Zur Grundlage der Entscheidung Modestins lag wahrscheinlich eine Beweisurkunde aus der Alltagspraxis vor. Die Juristen Roms reagierten oft auf die Herausforderung der Interpretation der im Geschäftsverkehr üblichen Vertragsklauseln, die ebenfalls als Quelle des römischen Rechts anzusehen sind.[27] Ein ähnliches Formular ist in griechischer Sprache im Archiv der Sulpizier überliefert (T.Sulp. 78):[28]

> „Ich, Menelaos ... habe geschrieben, dass ich erhalten habe von Primus, Sklaven des Publius Attius Severus, tausend Denare aus einer besiegelten *naulotike*, und ich werde sie zurückgeben (zahlen) gemäß der *naulotike*, die ich mit ihm errichtet habe ...“

Das Schriftstück wurde am 11. April 38 n.Chr. in der bedeutenden Hafenstadt Puteoli (im Golf von Neapel) angefertigt.[29] Der griechische *naukleros* Menelaos stellte seinen Schuldschein für seinen Latein sprechenden Geschäftspartner in griechischer Sprache aus. Menelaos stammt aus der kleinasiatischen Hafenstadt Keramos.[30] Wenn er Anfang April in Puteoli Geschäften nachgeht, dürfte er an der italischen Küste überwintert haben.[31] Die Bank der Sulpizier ist am Geschäft als Zahlungs-

24 Modestin verneint es: Der Schuldner könne nicht dazu gehalten werden, weil die Höhe der vereinbarten Zinsen aus dem Schriftstück nicht hervorgehe. Zu dem Problem der unbestimmten Zinsabreden s. Gröschler 1997: 156ff.

25 Siehe dazu oben Gai. 3.134.

26 Jakab 2008: 328ff.

27 Siehe Coing 1951: 98f.

28 T.Sulp. 78.5-12: Μενέλαος Εἰρηναίου Κερα|μιήτης ἔγραψα ἀπέχιν μαι | παρὰ Πρίμου Ποπλίου Ἀττίου Σεβή|ρου δούλου{λου} δηνάρια χίλια | ἐκ ναυλωτικῆς ἐκσφραγισμένης | ἃ καὶ ἀποδώσω ἀκουλούθως | τῇ ναυλωτικῇ ἥ‹ν› πεποίημαι πρὸς | αὐτόν.

29 Siehe dazu Jakab 2000: 259–63.

30 Ankum 1978: 159; Camodeca 1999: 178.

31 Zur Seefahrt in der Antike s. Casson 1971: 270ff.

stelle beteiligt:[32] Ein gewisser Primus lässt die tausend Denare durch die Bankkasse an Menelaos auszahlen. Der eigenhändig geschriebene Schuldschein des Menelaos über den Empfang des Geldbetrages ist im Bankarchiv erhalten geblieben. Der Sklavenname Primus verrät nichts über seinen Träger; wir wissen nicht einmal, ob er im Rahmen seines Sondervermögens (*peculium*) oder für seinen Herrn, Publius Attius Severus,[33] handelte.

Menelaos verspricht, dass er die erhaltenen tausend Denare zurückzahlen werde; die Festsetzung einer Frist oder von Zinsen fehlt aber im Dokument. Es fehlt auch der ausdrückliche Hinweis auf ein Darlehen; allein die bestätigte Rückzahlungspflicht zeigt das Recht des Primus zur Rückforderung. Als *causa* der empfangenen Zahlung wird eine „besiegelte *naulotike*", ein Frachtvertrag, genannt. Menelaos dürfte die tausend Denare als Frachtlohn erhalten haben.[34] Die Beurkundung als Darlehen erleichtert jedoch die Rückforderung, wenn der Transport nicht erfolgreich durchgeführt wird.[35] Die Bestellung eines Bürgen ab Z. 12[36] und die Bedeutung der Zeugen sollen hier ausgeklammert bleiben.

Die beiden bis jetzt zitierten Texte überliefern das Formular eines nach dem üblichen Schema angefertigten, eigenhändig geschriebenen Chirographums. Wie oben bereits erwähnt, ist dieses Formular durch die subjektive Stilisierung, die eigenhändige Anfertigung und das Fehlen von Zeugen gekennzeichnet. Urkunden nach diesem Muster werden gerne im Schrifttum den feierlichen altrömischen Zeugenurkunden (*testationes*) gegenübergestellt.[37] Im gut dokumentierten Rechtsleben des antiken Puteoli findet man jedoch zahlreiche Dokumente, die das Formular mit einer Stipulation kombinieren. Ein schönes Beispiel liefert T.Sulp. 50 (35 n.Chr.):[38]

> „M(arcus) An[tonius M(arci) f(ilius)] M[a]ximus [scripsi] me acce|pi[sse et deber]e C(aio) Sul[pi]cio Fau[sto HS] ∞ ∞ n(ummum), | [quae ab eo mutua] et n[umerata a]cc[epi] | [e]aq[ue HS ∞ ∞] nummu[m, q(uae) s(upra) s(cripta) s(unt), p(roba) r(ecte) d(ari)] | stip[ulat]us est C(aius) Su[lpicius Faustus spopo]ndi | eg[o] M(arcus) Anton[ius Maximus …]"

32 Verboven 2000: 161ff.; Verboven 2003: 10.

33 Der Name seines *dominus* ist als Händler auf Transportamphoren überliefert, vgl. Camodeca 1999: 178.

34 Zum umstrittenen Inhalt der Urkunde vgl. auch Wolf 2003: 440ff.

35 So etwa Ulpian D. 19.2.15.6; s. dazu Jakab 2000: 263ff.

36 Es ist bemerkenswert, dass die Bürgschaft bereits in lateinischer Sprache formuliert ist.

37 So etwa Kaser & Knütel 2005: 50f.; ähnlich auch Jörs, Kunkel & Wenger 1949: 99f.

38 T.Sulp. 50: „Ich, Marcus Antonius … habe geschrieben, dass ich erhalten habe und schulde dem C. Sulpicius Faustus Sesterzen 2.000, die ich von ihm, als Darlehen zugezählt, empfangen habe; und diese 2.000 Sesterzen, die oben geschrieben sind, in geprüfter Münze und richtig zu geben hat sich C. Sulpicius Faustus versprechen lassen und habe ich, Marcus Antonius, versprochen …". Übersetzung nach Gröschler 2006: 261–87.

Der erste Teil des Textes enthält den eigenhändigen Schuldschein des Marcus Antonius darüber, dass er von Caius Sulpicius Faustus (ein Mitglied der Bank der Sulpizier) zweitausend Sesterzen als Darlehen empfangen hat. Die Wendung *accipere et debere* ist eine neue Variante.[39] Das Chirographum bestätigt die *numeratio*, die Zuzählung in baren Münzen, in die Hände des Schuldners. Der terminus technicus Darlehen (*mutuum*) ist im römischen Recht eng aufzufassen: Es bezeichnet nur die unmittelbare Zuzählung von vertretbaren Sachen, wodurch der Schuldner verpflichtet wird, die gleiche Menge in gleicher Art und Güte zurückzuzahlen (Gattungsschuld). Beide Rechtsgründe – Chirographum und *numeratio* – erzeugen je eine Klage. Dem subjektiv gefassten Schuldschein folgt noch eine Stipulation (*testatio* mit Zeugen), woraus eine weitere strengrechtliche Klage auf die Rückforderung entsteht. Das Beweisprogramm in einem künftigen Prozess muß – je nach der gewählten Klage – unterschiedlich aufgebaut werden: Wird aus dem *mutuum* geklagt, muß die Zuzählung der Darlehensvaluta (*numeratio* = Traditio = Eigentumsübertragung) bewiesen werden; wird aus dem Chirographum geklagt, muß der geschriebene Schuldschein vorgelegt werden; wird aus der Stipulation geklagt, muß die mündlich ausgeführte Frage und die übereinstimmende Antwort bezeugt werden.[40]

Auch in diesem Text wurden weder eine Rückzahlungsfrist noch Zinsen erwähnt. Eine mögliche Erklärung dafür dürfte darin liegen, dass die jeweils fälligen Zinsen in der Alltagspraxis am Monatsanfang gezahlt werden mußten: Der Schuldner wurde dadurch mittelbar zur pünktlichen Leistung gezwungen, weil der Gläubiger bei Verzug sofort das ganze Kapital samt Zinsen einklagen konnte.[41]

Die Kombination von Chirographum und Stipulation ist auch in den Entscheidungen der Juristen überliefert (Paulus D. 12.1.40):[42]

> „Lucius Titius scripsi me accepisse a Publio Maevio quindecim mutua numerata mihi de domo et haec quindecim proba recte dari kalendis futuris stipulatus est Publius Maevius, spopondi ego Lucius Titius".

Auch dieses Formular zeigt die gemischte Form, die wir oben beobachtet haben. Der erste Teil enthält ein typisches Chirographum; die Wendung *ex domo* kommt in Darlehensurkunden öfter vor und soll die Zuzählung in barem Geld, ohne Mitwirkung einer Bank bezeichnet haben.[43] Bemerkenswert ist, dass die anschließende Stipulation hier ebenfalls subjektiv stilisiert ist. Solch kleine Abweichungen zeigen, dass

39 Die Wendung kommt übrigens auch in griechischen Urkunden vor, s. etwa P.Yadin 11.2–3; die Urkunde wurde in En Gedi, Judea, im Jahre 124 n. Chr. angefertigt.

40 Der Gäubiger konnte die alternativen Klagen wahlweise geltend machen, s. dazu Jakab 2008: 328f.

41 So bereits Gröschler 1997: 152ff.

42 D. 12.1.40: „Ich, Lucius Titius, habe geschrieben, dass ich erhalten habe von Publius Maevius fünfzehn Goldstücke als Darlehen, von zu Hause mir zugezählt; und Publius Maevius hat (in Stipulationsform) gefragt, ob diese fünfzehn in guter Münze und rechtmäßig an einem künftigen (bestimmten) Monatsersten zurückgezahlt werden und ich habe zugestimmt …".

43 Camodeca 1999: 154.

das Formular von den Parteien (vom Schreiber?) an das konkrete Rechtsgeschäft angepasst wurde.

Das soeben dargestellte Formular des Chirographums wird im Archiv der Sulpizier mit großer Vorliebe angewendet. Wir begegnen ihm bei Darlehensgeschäften,[44] bei Quittungen,[45] bei einer Empfangsbestätigung aus einem Frachtvertrag,[46] bei Versteigerungen,[47] bei Schiedsverfahren[48] und auch bei Verpachtungen von Lagerhäusern.[49] Aus den 95 gut erhaltenen Urkunden des Bankhauses zeigen 31, also beinahe ein Drittel, diese Beurkundungsform.

Die Beurkundung in Form eines Chirographums mit anschließender Stipulation (mit einer subjektiv oder objektiv gefassten *testatio*) war bei den Sulpiziern ebenfalls sehr häufig. Wir finden diese Praxis in allen Darlehensurkunden,[50] in den Quittungen[51] und in diversen weiteren Geschäften.[52] Das Formular bietet einen klaren, übersichtlichen Aufbau. Am Anfang wird der sich Verpflichtende (Schuldner) genannt, gleich darauf der Gläubiger und das Objekt der Obligation. Die anschließende Stipulation nennt hingegen zunächst das Objekt, dann die Verpflichtung und erst am Schluss die Parteien. Das gemischte Formular zeigt eine bemerkenswerte Symmetrie: Das Chirographum setzt mit den Parteien ein, während die Stipulation mit ihren Namen endet; in der Mitte wird das Objekt und die Haftungsgrundlage in beiden Formularen korrespondierend wiederholt.

Die Häufigkeit solcher gemischten Formulare bereits am Anfang des 1. Jhs. spricht gegen die herrschende Lehre, die für die Unvereinbarkeit von Chirographum und Stipulation argumentiert: „Der nichtrömische Litteralkontrakt durch Errichtung eines Schuldscheins (*chirographum*, genauer: eigenhändige Schuldurkunde …), also ohne *stipulatio*, gilt nach römischer Auffassung als den Peregrinen vorbehalten (Gai. 3.134). Seit der späten Klassik verschmilzt er mit der regelmäßig beurkundeten *stipulatio*“.[53] Die Täfelchen aus dem Archiv der Sulpizier zeigen hingegen, dass Chirographum und Stipulation im Rechtsleben bereits Anfang des 1. Jhs. n. Chr. kühn kombiniert wurden.

44 T.Sulp. 50–7, 66–9.
45 T.Sulp. 70–7.
46 T.Sulp. 78.
47 T.Sulp. 78, 81, 100–3.
48 T.Sulp. 22, 27.
49 T.Sulp. 45–6.
50 T.Sulp. 50–7, *mutua cum stipulatione*; 66–9 *pecunia debita in stipulatione deducta.* Verboven (2003 10–1) stuft sie als *stipulationes purae* ein, weil sie weder die Zinsen noch die Rückgabefrist geregelt haben.
51 T.Sulp. 70–7 alle *apochae.*
52 T.Sulp. 22, 27, 45, 46.
53 Kaser & Knütel 2005: 203.

Das Chirographum wird im Schrifttum, wie oben bereits erwähnt, als eigenhändig geschriebener Schuldschein definiert.[54] Es sind jedoch Dokumente auch von Puteoli überliefert, die von fremder Hand ausgestellt wurden.[55] Blättert man das Archiv der Sulpizier durch, stößt man etwa auf T.Sulp. 98 (Tab. I pag. 2, Z. 4–7):

> „*Q. Poblicius C. scripsi rogatu et mandatu Philocomi coram ipso, quod is negaret se litteras scire, eum accepisse* ...“

Anstatt der eigenhändigen Schrift wurde hier die Beurkundung durch dritte Hand, durch einen Vertreter, ausgeführt, weil der Schuldner nicht schreiben konnte. Es ist bemerkenswert, dass der rechtsgeschäftliche Inhalt dem entsprechend korrekt in dritter Person formuliert wurde.

Einen ähnlichen Fall zeigt T.Sulp. 82 (Tab. I pag. 2, Z. 4–7):

> *„scripsi rogatu et mandatu Patulciae ... libertae meae, coram ipsa eam accepisse ab ... “*

Es handelt sich um eine Empfangsbestätigung in Form eines Chirographums, die der Patron an Stelle seiner Freigelassenen, Patulcia, schreibt. Ob Patulcia nicht schreiben konnte oder ihr Patron sie aufgrund seines *ius patronatus* vertritt, lässt sich nicht sagen.

Chirographa von fremder Hand werden auch in den Schriften der römischen Juristen mehrmals erwähnt. Ich möchte hier bloß auf eine Entscheidung des Herennius Modestinus verweisen (Modestin D. 20.1.26.1):[56]

> „*Pater Seio emancipato filio facile persuasit, ut, quia mutuam quantitatem acciperet a Septicio creditore, chirographum perscriberet sua manu filius eius, quod ipse impeditus esset scribere* ...“

Der berühmte Jurist bespricht den wahrscheinlich nicht seltenen Fall, dass ein *pater familias* anlässlich seiner Kreditgeschäfte die Hilfe seines erwachsenen, aus der väterlichen Gewalt bereits entlassenen (emanzipierten) Sohnes in Anspruch nimmt. Der Vater hat mit dem Gläubiger Septicius (vielleicht handelt es sich um einen Bankier) vereinbart, dass er bei ihm eine bestimmte Summe Geldes als Darlehen aufneh-

54 So besonders das römischrechtliche Schrifttum, s. dazu zusammenfassend etwa Kaser & Knütel 2005: 51. Anders jedoch bereits Kunkel, s. Jörs, Kunkel & Wenger 1949: 100: „Ihr Schreiber kann der Erklärende selbst, aber auch ein Dritter sein“. Also bereits Kunkel sah, dass die Eigenhändigkeit kein zwingendes Element der Definition sei.

55 Etwas vorsichtiger Kaser 1971: 234: „In Ägypten wurden auch Chirographa unter griechischem Einfluss zuweilen von dritter Hand geschrieben und von den Parteien oder von Zeugen oder beiden unterschrieben“. Er bezieht sich auf FIRA III Nr. 121 und Nr. 131, Darlehen- bzw. Kaufurkunden von römischen Soldaten. Mit neuen Ergebnissen zum Thema s. Yiftach-Firanko 2009: 325ff.

56 D. 20.1.26.1: „Ein Vater, der ein Darlehen vom Gläubiger Septicius aufnehmen wollte, überredete ohne Schwierigkeiten seinen aus der Hausgewalt entlassenen Sohn Seius dazu, dass der Sohn einen Schuldschein (Chirographum) eigenhändig ausstellte, weil er selbst am Schreiben gehindert war ...“.

men werde. Septicius bestand offenbar darauf, dass als Beweisurkunde ein eigenhändig geschriebener Schuldschein ausgestellt werden soll. Der Jurist teilt komprimiert mit, dass der Vater am Schreiben gehindert gewesen sei. Als Ursache dafür käme Krankheit oder Abwesenheit in Frage – oben haben wir gesehen, dass die Ausstellung eines Chirographums die Anwesenheit der Vertragsparteien (zumindest des Schuldners) voraussetzt. Die Fortführung des Textes macht eindeutig, dass der Sohn *mandante patre manu sua perscripsit*, er hat also das Chirographum zwar eigenhändig, aber bloß im Auftrag des Vaters (nicht im eigenen Namen) ausgestellt. Modestin wurde darüber gefragt, ob ein dem Sohn gehörendes Haus, das auf Bitte des Vaters im Schriftstück als Pfand erwähnt wurde, aufgrund des eigenhändig geschriebenen Schriftstücks (als konstitutiv verpflichtender Urkunde) heraus verlangt werden könne. Das pfandrechtliche Problem kann hier ausgeklammert bleiben. Uns interessiert allein die Tatsache, dass Seius das Chirographum für seinen Vater (quasi stellvertretend) ausgestellt hat. Modestins Fall zeigt, dass die allgemein anerkannte und sehr verbreitete Definition des Chirographums als „eigenhändig geschriebener Schuldschein" präzisiert werden muss. Es ist auch denkbar, dass das Chirographum im Auftrag des Schuldners von fremder Hand geschrieben wird. Das Schriftstück erzeugt auch in diesem Fall die Obligation zwischen den in der Urkunde schriftlich festgelegten Parteien, zwischen Schuldner und Gläubiger.

Schließlich möchte ich kurz darauf aufmerksam machen, dass Schuldscheine vom Gläubiger weitergegeben werden konnten – die Obligation konnte übertragen werden. Die Chirographa dienten in gewisser Hinsicht als Wertpapiere. Dem Gläubiger stand es frei, die Chirographa seiner Schuldner zu verschenken,[57] im Legat zu vermachen[58] oder zu verkaufen.[59]

Typischerweise wurden die in Chirographa beurkundeten Forderungen konsequent in die *rationes* eingetragen.[60] Hat der Gläubiger das Chirographum jemandem überreicht, wurde damit auch die Forderung übereignet – der Schuldschein verkörperte also das *nomen*, die Schuldforderung, die Klage aus dem Chirographum stand sodann dem Empfänger zu. Weil der Besitz eines Schuldscheins jeden automatisch in die Lage des Berechtigten versetzt, konnten Chirographa sogar Gegenstände von Diebstahl werden.[61] Diese Sachverhalte aus den Schriften der römischen Juristen zeigen, dass der eigenhändig geschriebene Schuldschein als Urkunde über ihre Beweiskraft hinaus konstitutive Wirkung hatte.[62]

57 In den Digesten findet man Entscheidungen, in denen Chirographa unter Lebenden oder von Todes wegen verschenkt wurden, s. etwa Julian D. 39.6.18.2.

58 Siehe etwa D. 30.43.5 Ulpian.

59 Einen Kauffall schildert Julian in D. 32.59.

60 Siehe etwa D. 48.10.23 Paulus.

61 Siehe etwa D. 47.2.27.1 Ulpian.

62 Urkunden mit konstitutiver Wirkung kennen wir aus der hellenistischen Rechtskultur, vgl. Wolff 1978: 143.

Zusammenfassend kann Folgendes über die Chirographa als subjektiv stilisierten Urkunden in Briefform festgestellt werden: Das Chirographum als eigenständiger Urkundentyp erschien in den römischen Quellen bereits in der republikanischen Zeit.[63] Im juristischen Kontext wird das Chirographum als unwiderlegbare Beweisurkunde angesehen, die insbesondere im Kreditwesen mit großer Vorliebe verwendet wurde.

Gellius erwähnt das Chirographum als verbreitete Alternative der denkbaren Beweismittel über geschuldetes Geld (Gell. *NA* 14.2.7):

> „*probari apud me debere pecuniam datam consuetis modis, expensi latione, mensae rationibus, chirographi exhibitione, tabularum obsignatione, testium intercessione*".

Der Gläubiger kann nach Gellius in einem eventuellen Prozess folgende Beweismittel über das Bestehen seiner Forderung vorlegen: Eintragung im Kassenbuch, Banküberweisung, Chirographa, versiegelte Täfelchen oder Zeugenaussagen. Um die Sicherheit des Gläubigers zu erhöhen, konnten über dasselbe Rechtsgeschäft mehrere Beweismittel sichergestellt bzw. die oben erwähnten Urkundentypen kombiniert werden.

Die rasche Prüfung der Juristenschriften und des Urkundenmaterials hat zu dem Ergebnis geführt, dass die lateinischen Chirographa ein festes Formular zeigen („scripsi me accepisse"). Sie wurden überwiegend subjektiv formuliert, vom Schuldner in Ich-Form eigenhändig geschrieben. Es sind jedoch auch Belege für Chirographa erhalten, die stellvertretend von einem Dritten und dementsprechend in der 3. Person ausgestellt wurden. Die im Schrifttum verbreitete Definition erfasst zweifelsohne die überwiegende Tendenz der Merkmale des Chirographums, kann aber durch ihre systematisierende Bemühung zu Verzerrungen und Missverständnisse führen. In Irre führend ist jedenfalls die strikte Trennung zwischen Chirographa und *testationes*. Oben wurde gezeigt, dass die beiden Urkundentypen in der Rechtspraxis des Alltags oft kombiniert wurden. Die oben zitierten Entscheidungen der römischen Juristen verweisen darauf, dass die Chirographa immer Verpflichtungen zwischen zwei Parteien (Schuldner und Gläubiger) erzeugten, wobei die Anwesenheit der Kontrahierenden meistens vorausgesetzt werden kann. In Ausnahmefällen war jedoch eine Stellvertretung bei der Beurkundung denkbar.

2. Epistula

Nach dem kurzen Überblick über die römische Praxis der Chirographa ist die Verwendung von *epistulae* im juristischen Kontext zu behandeln. Eine summarische Prüfung der Quellenlage zeigt, dass diese Form der Willenserklärung von den Juristen – nach der Überlieferung der justinianischen Gesetzessammlung, der Digesten, – in mehr als hundert Texten besprochen wurde. Der Menge nach dürften

63 Jörs, Kunkel & Wenger 1949: 100.

die *epistulae* im Rechtsleben sogar bedeutender gewesen sein als die soeben dargestellten Chirographa. Bereits dieser Befund spricht dagegen, in der *epistula* bloß einen Unterbegriff des Chirographum zu sehen, wie es die herrschende Lehre mit Wenger immer noch konsequent vertritt.[64]

Zweifelsohne gibt es einerseits Quellen, in denen uns die Wörter Chirographum und Epistula als Synonyme begegnen.[65] In diesen Texten wird das Wort Chirographum untechnisch, als handgeschriebenes Schriftstück im weiteren Sinne, verwendet. Der Gebrauch eines für das Chirographum typischen Formulars (*scripsi me accepisse*) kann in diesen Texten nie nachgewiesen werden. Diese Quellen bleiben in der vorliegenden Untersuchung ausgeklammert.

Von Interesse sind vielmehr die Texte, die eine starke Tendenz andeuten, dass *epistulae* im Rechtsleben von den Chirographa abweichend eingesetzt wurden. Eine Epistula wurde überwiegend in solchen Rechtsverhältnissen geschrieben und an den Adressaten weggeschickt, in denen ein *chirographum* oder eine *testatio* nicht ausgestellt hätte werden können. Meine Arbeitshypothese lautet also, dass die *epistulae* in der Urkundenpraxis eine typische, eigenständige Funktion hatten, weshalb sie nicht bloß als Synonym von Chirographa angesehen werden dürfen. Der unterschiedliche Wirkungsbereich hatte auch Konsequenzen auf die Durchsetzbarkeit der durch sie begründeten Forderung auf dem Prozesswege.

Über die Formulierung einer *epistula* lässt sich feststellen, dass sie sich immer getreu an die Briefform hält. Sie wurde zwar subjektiv stilisiert, wie das Chirographum, aber sie folgt keinem festen Schema. Die Epistula bewahrt auch als Geschäftsurkunde den formlosen, oft vertraulichen Ton der Privatkorrespondenz. Ein gutes Beispiel zeigt dafür Paulus (D. 17.1.59.5):[66]

> „*Ille illi salutem. Mando tibi, ut Blaesio Severo adfini meo octoginta credas sub pignore illo et illo: in quam pecuniam et quidquid usurarum nomine accesserit indemnem rationem tuam me esse ex causa mandati in eum diem, quoad vixerit Blaesius Severus, praestaturum*“.

Paulus begutachtet einen Rechtsstreit, der aus einem typischen Geschäftsbrief (*epistula*) hervorgegangen ist. Der Jurist zitiert den Wortlaut des Briefes, weil er in seiner Entscheidung diesen Wortlaut auslegen muß. Er tilgt dabei die ursprünglichen Namen der Betroffenen (des Schreibers und des Adressaten), behält jedoch den Namen des Dritten, des begünstigten Blaesius Severus bei.

64 Wenger 1953: 737f.; siehe dazu bereits oben bei Anm. 6.

65 Siehe dazu bereits oben bei Anm. 15.

66 D. 17.1.59.5: „A grüßt B. Ich beauftrage dich, meinem Schwager Blaesius Severus gegen dieses und jenes Pfand achtzig zu leihen. Dafür, dass wegen dieses Geldes und all dessen, was an Zinsen hinzukommt, für dein Vermögen kein Nachteil entsteht, werde ich aufgrund des Auftrages einstehen, solange Blaesius Severus lebt“.

Der Geschäftsbrief setzt mit der üblichen Grußform ein; ihr folgt der juristisch relevante Inhalt, der bereits vom antiken Juristen als Auftragsvertrag (*mandatum*) eingestuft wird. Die Briefform ist die vertraute, persönliche Umgangsform, die zum freundschaftlichen Charakter des *mandatum* besonders gut passt.[67] Trotz vertrauter Beziehungen achtet der Mandant pedantisch auf die juristisch korrekte Formulierung. Er beauftragt B, den Adressaten, einem Dritten (hier seinem Schwager) eine bestimmte Summe Geldes darzuleihen. Der Geschäftswille wird mit dem technisch gebrauchten Verbum *mandare* ausgedrückt. Anschließend nennt der Auftraggeber den künftigen Schuldner, die Höhe des Betrags, wofür er sich einzustehen bereit erklärt und die zusätzlichen Sicherheiten (Pfand), die er zu verlangen wünscht. Am Schluss erklärt er ausdrücklich seine Obligation zum Einstehen (*praestare*) für Kapital und Zinsen, befristet mit dem Ableben des Schuldners.[68] Von Interesse ist noch die präzise Wendung

> „*me esse ex causa mandati … praestaturum*“:

Der Auftragsvertrag wird ausdrücklich als Haftungsgrundlage des Bürgen genannt.

Auf den ersten Blick fällt auf, dass an diesem Rechtsverhältnis nicht zwei, sondern drei Personen beteiligt sind. Der Schreiber des Briefes, der Adressat und der Begünstigte, Blaesius Severus. Der Brief wurde im Interesse eines Dritten geschrieben, um ihm bei seinen Kreditgeschäften zu Hilfe zu kommen. Das Hauptschuldverhältnis, der Darlehensvertrag entsteht zwischen dem Adressaten und dem hier nur erwähnten Schwager, Blaesius Severus. Der Schreiber der *epistula* übernimmt dabei das *praestare* für fremde Schuld, die bereits von Gaius als eine zulässige Form der Bürgschaft angesehen wird.[69] Der Brief dient also als Geschäftsurkunde, womit der Schreiber die Rolle eines Bürgen auf sich nimmt.

Weitere Quellen zeigen, dass *epistulae* oft in Rechtsverhältnissen eingesetzt wurden, in denen drei oder mehr Personen involviert waren. Eine besonders schöne Entscheidung bietet Scaevola (D. 17.1.62.1):[70]

> „*Lucius Titius Gaio suo salutem. Peto et mando tibi, ut fidem dicas pro Publio Maevio apud Sempronium: quaeque a Publio soluta tibi non fuerint, me repraesentaturum hac epistula manu mea scripta notum tibi facio*“.

67 Vgl. dazu Nörr 1993: 17: „Mandatsverhältnisse beruhen zumeist auf freundschaftlichen Beziehungen.“

68 Zur Haftung des Auftraggebers und zu seinem Anspruch auf Regress s. Giménez-Candela 1993: 169ff.

69 Gai. 3.156; vgl. dazu Nelson & Manthe 1999: 342ff.

70 D. 17.1.62.1: „Lucius Titius grüßt seinen Gaius. Ich bitte und beauftrage dich, dass du für Publius Maevius bei Sempronius gutstehst. Alles, was dir von Publius nicht gezahlt werden wird, werde ich dir bar auszahlen, wie ich dir durch diese eigenhändig geschriebene *epistula* zur Kenntnis gebe“.

Cervidius Scaevola bedient sich typischer Blankettnamen: Lucius Titius oder Gaius werden die Parteien in Fällen genannt, die aus dem Schulunterricht stammen oder worin die konkreten Parteien aus welchem Grund immer nicht öffentlich gekannt werden sollten. Lucius Titius schreibt einen gewöhnlichen Brief an einen gewissen Gaius, in dem die Begründung eines komplizierten Rechtsverhältnisses angeregt wird. Die knapp, aber juristisch-technisch präzis formulierte *epistula* bittet bzw. beauftragt den Gaius, für einen Dritten, den genannten Publius Maevius, die Bürgschaft in Form einer *fideiussio* bei dessen Gläubiger, Sempronius, zu übernehmen. Am Rechtsverhältnis sind also insgesamt vier Personen beteiligt: Der Schreiber des Briefes (hier Lucius Titius genannt), der Adressat (hier Gaius genannt), der Begünstigte Dritte (hier Publus Maevius genannt), der Hauptschuldner, der hofft ein Darlehen bei Sempronius aufnehmen zu können und dafür eine Bürgschaft benötigt. Der Schreiber unserer Epistula wollte ihm dabei helfen, aber er wünschte nicht – aus welchem Grund immer – persönlich als Bürge bei Sempronius aufzutreten. Er wollte sich offenbar nicht ins Rampenlicht stellen, versprach jedoch im Hintergrund das Einstehen für die Schulden des Publius Maevius. Vielleicht war er auch abwesend und konnte deshalb keine formal gültige Bürgschaft übernehmen. Cervidius Scaevola zeigt uns, dass *epistulae* einen Zweck erfüllen können, wenn man mit Urkunden im Zweipersonenverhältnis überhaupt nicht weiterkommen würde. Der soziale Aspekt, der Charakter der Kreditverhältnisse auf Vertrauensbasis spielte dabei eine nicht unwesentliche Rolle.[71]

Für den formlosen Wortlaut und freundschaftlichen bzw. familiären Charakter solcher Geschäftsbriefe führt Marcellus ein gutes Beispiel an (D. 46.1.24):[72]

> „*Lucius Titius cum pro Seio fratre suo apud Septicium intervenire vellet, epistulam ita emisit: ‚Si petierit a te frater meus, peto des ei nummos fide et periculo meo …*“

Der Jurist verwendet wieder Blankettnamen, trotzdem können wir annehmen, dass der Geschäftsbrief die alltägliche, in Rom übliche und juristisch anerkannte Praxis widergibt. Ein ehrenhafter Römer (hier Lucius Titius genannt) erfährt, dass sein Bruder in Geldnot steckt und er will ihm zu Hilfe kommen. Er hätte seinen Bruder aufsuchen und ihm seine Bürgschaft in Form der üblichen Stipulation (*sponsio, fidepromissio* oder *fideiussio*) anbieten können. Es ist denkbar, dass er sich vom Ort der Kreditgewährung weit entfernt aufhielt und deshalb die Briefform wählte. Es scheint mir jedoch wahrscheinlicher, dass er jedes Aufsehen vermeiden wollte, deshalb eher diesen diskreten Geschäftsbrief verfasste. Er schrieb an den künftigen Gläubiger (vielleicht einen Bankier, der mit der Familie schon länger in Kontakt stand) und

71 S. dazu auch Choe 1993: 138.

72 D. 46.1.24: „Als Lucius Titius für seinen Bruder Seius bei Septicius (als Bürge) eintreten wollte, schickte er einen Brief folgender Art: ‚Wenn mein Bruder von dir (Geld) erbittet, gib es ihm bitte auf meine Treue und Gefahr …“

übernahm formlos das Einstehen für die künftigen Schulden seines Bruders. Sein Einstehen wird technisch mit der Wendung *fide et periculo meo* ausgedrückt: Er verspricht auf seine Treue, dass er das Risiko der Kreditgewährung (die Insolvenz des Schuldners) auf sich nehme, d. h. für die Schulden seines Bruders wie ein Bürge einstehen werde.[73]

In Rechtsverhältnissen solcher Art konnte die gewünschte Rechtsfolge allein *per epistulam* erreicht werden; ein Chirographum im engeren Sinne (mit dem gefestigten Formular *scripsi me debere* …) hätte diese Funktion nie erfüllen können.

Blättert man in den Schriften der römischen Juristen, findet man zahlreiche Anwendungen der *epistula*, in denen der persönliche Brief ebenfalls nicht durch ein Chirographum hätte ersetzt werden können. Hierher zählen etwa die Freilassung von Sklaven; die Gewährung der Testierfreiheit einem *libertus*; die spätere Ergänzungen zum eigenen Testament; die einvernehmliche Bestellung eines Richters in der Phase der Prozessvorbereitung; die Schenkung eines *fundus* mit Besitzübergabe durch den *colonus* … Die Liste könnte man noch lange weiter führen.

Kehren wir jedoch zu den Kreditgeschäften zurück. Man hat den Eindruck, dass beide Urkundentypen (Chirographum und Epistula) in erster Linie bei Geldtransaktionen verwendet wurden. Das typische Formular des Chirographum haben wir bereits oben kennen gelernt; es setzt überwiegend voraus, dass der Schuldner bei der Kreditgewährung persönlich anwesend ist und den handgeschriebenen Schuldschein niederschreibt. Es besteht meistens ein persönlicher Kontakt zwischen den Parteien. Die persönliche Beziehung, ein gewisses Naheverhältnis ist noch mehr typisch für die *epistula*. Die oben zitierten Quellen zeigten, dass im alltäglichen Geschäftsverkehr zwischen den korrespondierenden Parteien ein geschäftliches Vertrauensverhältnis herrschte, was die formlose Formulierung und den vertraulichen Ton ermöglichte.

Ein weiteres Beispiel für die Verwendung von Briefen in geschäftlichen und rechtlichen Beziehungen stammt von Papinian (D. 16.3.24):[74]

> „*Lucius Titius Sempronio salutem. Centum nummos, quos hac die commendasti mihi adnumerante servo Sticho actore, esse apud me ut notum haberes, hac epistula manu mea scripta tibi notum facio: quae quando voles et ubi voles confestim tibi numerabo*“.

Die Blankettnamen Lucius Titius, Sempronius und Stichus vertreten wieder die ursprünglichen Parteien, die der Jurist in der schriftlichen Fassung seiner Entscheidung nicht öffentlich bekannt machen wollte. Der Geschäftsbrief zwischen Lucius Titius und dem Adressaten, Sempronius, bestätigt einen vollzogenen Zahlungsvorgang, der

73 Zum Kreditmandat s. Krampe 2003: 125ff.

74 D. 16.3.24: „Lucius Titius grüßt Sempronius. Damit du weißt, dass die hundert Geldstücke, die du mir anvertraut hast und die mir der Sklave Stichus, dein Vermögensverwalter, ausgezahlt hat, sich in meinen Händen befinden, gebe ich dir davon durch diesen von mir eigenhändig geschriebenen Brief Kenntnis. Diese Geldstücke werde ich, sobald du willst und wo du willst, unverzüglich zurückzahlen“.

durch Stichus, den Sklaven des Adressaten, ausgeführt wurde. Der erste Teil des Textes ist also eine Quittung über den Empfang des genannten Geldbetrages im Dreipersonenverhältnis: Sempronius hat seinen Sklaven angewiesen, seinem Agenten (*argentarius*?), der hier Lucius Titius genannt wird, hundert zu übergeben. Das Geld wurde zwischen den Parteien, die in eine Obligation getreten sind, nicht von Hand zu Hand zugezählt; deshalb dürfte Lucius Titius kein Chirographum, sondern eine *epistula,* verfasst haben. Wie wir oben gesehen haben, waren die Chirographa überwiegend auf Zweipersonenverhältnisse beschränkt.

Der letzte Satz, den Papinian aus dem Formular zitiert, legt die Rückzahlungspflicht des Empfängers (des Lucius Titius) fest. Die Rückgabe auf jederzeitiges Verlangen spricht für eine Verwahrung (*depositum*). Die Wendung *ubi voles* ist ein starkes Argument dafür, dass es hier um eine uneigentliche Verwahrung (*depositum irregulare*) geht. Der Empfänger verspricht, den geschuldeten Betrag auf Wunsch auch an einem anderen Ort (etwa in Alexandria, Berytos) zu leisten; es handelt sich also um eine Rückgabe nach Gattung.[75] Papinians lange Ausführungen zeigen, dass der rechtsgeschäftliche Inhalt (der für den Bankier und seinen Kunden zur Alltagspraxis gehörte) schwer in ein systematisch geordnetes Vertragsrecht eingegliedert werden konnte. Der Jurist kann kaum einen festen Klagegrund nennen. In geschäftlichen Beziehungen solcher Art kam es gewiss selten dazu, dass die Parteien ihren Anspruch auf dem Gerichtswege hätten durchsetzen wollen.

Der Bankier teilt hier seinem Kunden mit, dass der durch einen Sklaven geschickter Betrag bei ihm restlos angekommen ist. Ferner sichert er verbindlich zu, dass der Deponent es zu jedem beliebigen Zeitpunkt und an jedem beliebigen Ort abrufen kann.

Scaevola, der an praxisnahen Sachverhalten immer interessiert war, legt einen ähnlichen Brief zur Auslegung vor (Cervidius Scaevola D. 16.3.28):[76]

> „*Caecilius Candidus Paccio Rogatiano suo salutem. Viginti quinque nummorum quos apud me esse voluisti, notum tibi ista hac epistula facio ad ratiunculam meam ea pervenisse: quibus ut primum prospiciam, ne vacua tibi sint: id est ut usuras eorum accipias, curae habebo*".

Der Geschäftsbrief, der mit der üblichen Grußform einsetzt, berichtet über ein Rechtsverhältnis, das mit Hilfe eines Dritten zustande kam. Das Fragment steht in den Digesten unter dem Titel *Depositi vel contra*, über die Klagen aus dem Verwahrungsvertrag. Der Schreiber des Briefes, Caecilius Candidus (wahrscheinlich ein *nummularius*) versichert seinem Kunden, dass er die durch Boten (Sklaven) geschickte Summe erhalten

75 Vgl. dazu Jakab 2006: 86ff.; Backhaus 2004: 253f.

76 D. 16.3.28: „Caecilius Candidus grüßt seinen Paccius Rogatianus. Die 25 Geldstücke befinden sich nach deinem Willen in meinen Händen und sind, wie ich dir durch diesen Brief bekannt mache, in meiner Kasse verbucht. Für diese sehe ich sobald wie möglich zu, dass sie nicht brachliegen, das heißt, ich werde Sorge tragen, dass du Zinsen auf sie erhältst".

habe. Ursprünglich ging es wohl um 25 000 Sesterzen, also um eine hübsche Summe. Wertvoll ist die Information, dass der Betrag im Geschäftsbuch des Empfängers eingetragen wurde. Der letzte Satz deutet das Agentengeschäft an, worüber uns Ulpian anderswo belehrt:[77] Der Kleinbankier verwaltet das Kapital und legt es für den Hinterleger gewinnbringend an, wobei das Risiko nicht der Bankier, sondern der Geldanleger trägt.

Zusammenfassend ist festzuhalten, dass zwischen den beiden Urkundentypen (Chirographum und Epistula) mehrere Unterschiede nachgewiesen werden können. Äußerlich, ihrem Schema nach, ist eine *epistula* immer formlos abgefasst. Sie hat kein gefestigtes Formular, wie wir es bei den Chirographa beobachtet haben. Die formlose Ausfertigung ist bestens geeignet, auch atypische Vertragsverhältnisse festzuhalten. Eine Epistula wird gerne in Rechtsverhältnissen eingesetzt, in denen mehr als zwei Personen involviert sind (Dreipersonenverhältnis). Solche Obligationen konnten in dem typischen und bereits in der Republik gefestigten Chirographum-Formular nicht beurkundet werden.

Schließlich möchte ich noch auf einen weiteren, juristisch wesentlichen Unterschied verweisen, der mit einem interessanten Fall des Paulus anschaulich dargestellt werden kann (D. 16.3.26.2):[78]

> „*Titius Semproniis salutem. Habere me a vobis auri pondo plus minus decem et discos duos saccum signatum: ex quibus debetis mihi decem, quos apud Titium deposuistis: item quos trophimati decem: item ex ratione patris vestri decem et quod excurrit*“. *Quaero, an ex huiuscemodi scriptura aliqua obligatio nata sit, scilicet quod ad solam pecuniae causam attinet. Respondit ex epistula, de qua quaeritur, obligationem quidem nullam natam videri, sed probationem depositarum rerum impleri posse: an autem is quoque, qui deberi sibi cavit in eadem epistula decem, probare possit hoc quod scripsit, iudicem aestimaturum*“.

Der Jurist zitiert wörtlich einen Geschäftsbrief, der eigentlich einen Saldo über den Stand der Geldgeschäfte zwischen den Parteien festhält. Es wurde gefragt, ob aus dieser *epistula* geklagt werden könne. Die Antwort des Juristen zeigt, dass das juristische Problem im Sinne von Gaius 3.134 zu verstehen ist:[79] Wird mit dem vor-

77 Siehe etwa D. 16.3.7.2. Vgl. dazu Andreau 1999: 229ff.; Jakab 2008: 324f.

78 D. 16.3.26.2: „‚Titius grüßt die Brüder Sempronius. Ich habe von euch Gold im Gewicht von mehr oder weniger zehn Pfund sowie zwei Teller und einen versiegelten Sack. Aus diesem Bestand schuldet ihr mir noch zehn, die ihr bei Titius hinterlegt habt, ferner die zehn, die ihr Trophius schuldet, ferner aus der Abrechnung eures Vaters zehn und den noch darüber hinausgehenden Betrag‘. Ich frage, ob aus diesem Schriftstück irgendeine Obligation entstanden ist, und zwar allein hinsichtlich des Rechtsverhältnisses des Geldes. Er hat das Gutachten erteilt, aufgrund der in Frage stehenden *epistula* sei zwar anzunehmen, dass keinerlei Obligation entstanden sei; durch sie könne aber der Beweis über die hinterlegten Sachen erbracht werden. Ob aber auch derjenige, der in demselben Brief bekundet hat, ihm würden zehn geschuldet, das, was er geschrieben hat, beweisen könne, werde der Richter beurteilen“.

79 S. dazu oben bei Anm. 18.

liegenden Schriftstück eine Obligation begründet? Oben haben wir gesehen, dass ein Geschäftsbrief, der dem festen Formular des Chirographum folgt, eine strengrechtliche Klage (*obligatio stricti iuris*) erzeugt (konstitutive Wirkung nach hellenistischem Muster). Diese Wirkung verneint Paulus entschieden im vorliegenden Fall. Die *epistula* hat keine konstitutive Wirkung. Sie dient bloß als Beweis dafür, dass die Verwahrung besteht. Geklagt werden kann also nur mit der *actio depositi directa*, nicht nach strengem Recht, *ius strictum*, sondern aufgrund der *bona fides*.

Pecunia constituta und *stipulatio* Grenzen des Rechtsschutzes für formlose Geschäfte im römischen Recht*

Johannes Platschek (Wien)

1. Pecuniam constituere

„Von Briefen und *Chirographa*" bei den römischen Juristen hat uns Éva Jakab berichtet. Ich darf unmittelbar anknüpfen und einen weiteren Schritt in das scheinbare Dickicht der römischen Rechtswissenschaft wagen. *Chirografa* und *syngrafae*, schriftliche Erklärungen, dass jemand „schulde oder geben werde" („si quis debere se aut daturum se esse scribat"), können – so berichtet uns der Jurist Gajus in seinem Elementarlehrbuch – unter Nichtrömern (Peregrinen), nicht aber unter Römern eine Verbindlichkeit (*obligatio*) nach *ius civile* begründen.[1] Inwieweit dies für die Peregrinen tatsächlich zutrifft, sei dahingestellt.[2] Für die Römer jedenfalls bedarf es zur *Schuldbegründung* insbesondere einer tatsächlichen Auszahlung eines Darlehens (Realvertrag) oder eines förmlichen mündlichen Versprechens in Frage und Antwort (*stipulatio*; Verbalvertrag). Ein schriftliches Zahlungssprechen begründet keine zivilrechtliche Klage.

In seinem Edikt verheißt der römische Prätor jedoch eine Klage gegen denjenigen, „qui pecuniam debitam constituit" – „der geschuldetes Geld festgesetzt hat" (D. 13.5.1.1 Ulp. 27 ed.), die *actio de pecunia constituta*.[3] Sie setzt folgendes voraus:

* Die Vortragsform wird beibehalten. Die Anmerkungen bringen Quellentexte, Hinweise auf flankierende Probleme und sporadische Literaturangaben.

1 Gai. 3.134: „Praeterea litterarum obligatio fieri videtur chirografis et syngrafis, id est si quis debere se aut daturum s<e> es<se> scribat, ita scilicet, si eo nomine stipulatio non fiat. Quod genus obligationis proprium peregrinorum est".

2 Nach griechischer Vorstellung macht eher die Auszahlung eines Darlehens (Realverfügung) die fehlende Rückzahlung zu einem Akt der Vorenthaltung und damit die Rückzahlung zur Pflicht; die Urkunde macht durch ihren Beweiswert diese Schuldbegründung unwiderlegbar (Rupprecht 1967: 137–41). Im übrigen ist die Beschreibung (auch) der *syngrafa* durch Gaius mit *si quis debere* ***se*** *aut daturum* ***se*** *esse scribat* nicht unproblematisch: Die συγγραφή ist im Gegensatz zum χειρόγραφον objektiv stilisiert. Der Verfasser der Urkunde schreibt: „*N.N. hat* zum Darlehen gegeben/erhalten", „*er* soll zurückzahlen" usw., nicht: „*ich* schulde" oder „*ich* werde geben"; gerade das aber vermittelt das reflexive *se*.

3 Zur Klage siehe Lenel 1927: 249ff. Zum *constitutum debiti* grundlegend Bruns 1861; Standardwerk von Astuti 1938 und 1941; seitdem Magdelain 1958; Roussier 1958; Ricart Martí 1994 und passim; zuletzt La Rosa 1997 und 2008; Waelkens 2008 (beide mit bedenklichen Quellenexegesen und

Es muss bereits eine Geldschuld bestehen (*pecunia debita*). In der fragmentarisch überlieferten Klageformel erscheint als eine Verurteilungsvoraussetzung: „eamque pecuniam cum constituebatur debitam fuisse" – „dass dieses Geld, als (es?) festgesetzt wurde, geschuldet war" (D. 13.5.18.1 Ulp. 27 ed.).

Die Erfüllung dieser Schuld wird sodann „festgesetzt" / „zugesagt". Das Vertrauen des Gläubigers in die Zusage ist schützenswert, wenn diese bestimmte Erfüllungsmodalitäten enthält, die sich noch nicht aus der Schuld selbst ergeben; wenn insbesondere Zeit, Ort oder Empfänger der Leistung bestimmt werden.

Tut der Erklärende nicht, was er zugesagt hat („neque fecisse reum quod constituit" – D. 13.5.16.4 Ulp. 27 ed.), muss er den Empfänger schadlos halten. Die Klage geht auf das *Interesse* des Empfängers der Zusage an ihrer Einhaltung.

Im Mittelpunkt steht die Erklärung des Schuldners oder eines Dritten über die Erfüllung der Schuld: *pecuniam constituere* bzw. *constituere se soluturum*. Geltungsgrund, genauer gesagt: Grund für den prätorischen Schutz des *constituere* ist nach dem Juristen Ulpian aber der *consensus*, die Willensübereinstimmung mit dem Empfänger der Erklärung. Dieser muss die Zusage entgegennehmen; weist er sie zurück, kann er keinen Schutz beanspruchen, was ihre Einhaltung betrifft. Wenn die Römer vom *consensus* als Geltungsgrund sprechen, so meinen sie damit regelmäßig den *bloßen consensus*. Was Geltung bereits aus dem *consensus* bezieht, bedarf keiner Form. Dazu Ulpian:

> „Festsetzen können wir aber sowohl unter Anwesenden als auch unter Abwesenden, ganz so wie bei einer Abrede (*pactum*); durch Boten oder höchstpersönlich; und mit jedem beliebigen Wortlaut".[4]

Darin unterscheidet sich das *constitutum* von der *stipulatio*, dem förmlichen Schuldversprechen in mündlicher Frage und Antwort, also unter Anwesenden. Der Gläubiger fragt dabei den Schuldner: „(Centum) dari spondesne?" – „Gelobst du, dass (Hundert) gegeben werde(n)?" Antwort: *Spondeo!* – „Ich gelobe es!" Eine *stipulatio* kann schriftlich dokumentiert werden, aber sie kann nicht schriftlich *abgeschlossen* werden. Aus der *stipulatio* ergibt sich eine Klage nicht erst durch das Edikt des Prätors, sondern bereits nach dem *ius civile*, das der Prätor vorfindet. Das *constitutum* ist prätorisch sanktioniertes, formloses Rechtsinstitut, die *stipulatio* ein förmliches Geschäft, sanktioniert durch das *ius civile*.

Ergebnissen); Varvaro 2007–2008. Siehe außerdem Kaser 1971: 583f.; Zimmermann 1990: 511ff. Eine Monographie des Verfassers des Folgenden ist in Vorbereitung.

4 D. 13.5.14.3 (Ulp. 27 ed.): „Constituere autem et praesentes et absentes possumus, sicut pacisci, et per nuntium et per nosmet ipsos, et quibuscumque verbis". Für La Rosa (1997: 202–4; 2008: 280) ist die *pecunia constituta* - unter Berufung auf eine alte Literaturmeinung und ohne Quellenbeleg - ein Formalgeschäft. Unsere Stelle, die explizit das Gegenteil besagt, wird als unecht eliminiert (La Rosa 1997: 209f.). Gegen entsprechende frühere Versuche schon Astuti 1938: 101f.; 138.

2. „My debtor just wrote me a letter …"

Um den Zusammenhang des *constitutum* mit unserem Generalthema deutlich zu machen, darf ich auf einige *Briefe* hinweisen, die uns in den Digesten unter dem Titel *De pecunia constituta* (D. 13.5) im Wortlaut überliefert sind und deren Relevanz für die Klage *de pecunia constituta* von den Juristen erörtert wird. Zum Teil stammen die Briefe vom Schuldner, bzw. dem vermeintlichen Schuldner selbst. Zwei andere haben Dritte an den Gläubiger geschrieben. Auf sie möchte ich kurz eingehen.

In D. 13.5.5.3 (Ulp. 27 ed.) findet sich eine „epistula ad me emissa", ein „an mich (den Gläubiger) gesendeter Brief" eines Dritten (Titius), der sich über mögliche Schulden des Sejus erklärt:

> „Scripsi me secundum mandatum Seii, si quid tibi debitum adprobatum erit me tibi cauturum et soluturum sine controversia".
>
> „Ich habe geschrieben, dass ich gemäß dem Auftrag des Sejus, wenn etwas als dir geschuldet bewiesen wird, dass ich dir dann Sicherheit leisten und zahlen werde ohne Widerrede".

Für den Fall, dass der Gläubiger dem Titius eine Schuld des Sejus nachweisen wird, kündigt Titius an, „ohne Widerrede Sicherheit zu leisten und zu zahlen". Bei *cauturum* – „Sicherheit zu leisten" könnte der Text gestört sein;[5] in jedem Fall verspricht Titius dem Gläubiger des Sejus schriftlich, Schulden des Sejus auf Vorlage eines Nachweises zu bezahlen. Titius „schreibt, dass er geben (bzw. zahlen) werde" – „scribit se soluturum". Wir erinnern uns an Gajus: Daraus entsteht keine zivile *obligatio*. Dennoch kann die Erklärung des Titius zu seiner Haftung führen. Denn schon der Jurist Julian sieht darin ein *pecuniam constituere*, das bei Nichteinhaltung haftbar macht. Die Festsetzung von Erfüllungsmodalitäten besteht hier in der Zusage von jederzeitiger sofortiger Leistung bei Nachweis der Schuld. Dass es sich dabei nicht um eine eigene Schuld des Titius handelt, ist für den Juristen irrelevant; denn das Edikt ist objektiv formuliert: „qui pecuniam debitam constituit". Durch seine formlose Erklärung kommt Titius in die Stellung eines Garanten. Wenn er sich nicht an die Zusage hält, also bei Vorlage von Dokumenten nicht unverzüglich leistet, haftet er mit der *actio de pecunia constituta* auf das Interesse. Allerdings muss der Gläubiger dazu auch den Richter vom Bestand der Schuld des Sejus zum Zeitpunkt des *constituere* überzeugen.

5 Verdächtigungen schon bei Roussier 1958: 24 Anm. 1 (*curaturum*). Statt *cauturum et* sind denkbar: *caute* - „sicher"? (identifiziert als *caut*(*urum*) *e*(*t*)); *actutum* - „sofort"/„unverzüglich"? (zunächst verdorben zu *acturum* - „klagen werde", verbessert zu *<c>auturum <et>*), vgl. Plaut. Mos. 603f.: … „faenus reddite. / Daturi n' estis faenus actutum mihi?"; ferner etwa P.Fouad I 45 (153 n. Chr.): „sine controversia et / ⌊spe futu⌋rae di⌊la⌋tionis"; gr. Papyri passim: „ἀποδώσω σοι … ἀνυπερθέτως" – „ich werde dir zurückzahlen … unverzüglich". Für unsere Fragestellung ist das Textproblem nicht entscheidend.

Eine andere *epistula emissa* begegnet in D. 13.5.24 (Marcell. sing. resp.). Ein Vormund (*tutor*) Titius schreibt an den Gläubiger Sejus seiner Mündel (*pupilli*):

> „Remanserunt apud me quinquaginta ex credito tuo ex contractu pupillorum meorum, quos tibi reddere debebo idibus Maiis probos: quod si ad diem supra scriptum non dedero, tunc dare debebo usuras tot".

> „Es sind bei mir verblieben fünfzig (tausend Sesterze) aus deinem Darlehen aus dem Vertrag meiner Mündel, die ich dir zurückgeben werden muss an den Iden des Mai in geprüfter Münze. In dem Fall, dass ich bis zu dem oben genannten Tag nicht geleistet haben werde, werde ich dann so und so viele Zinsen leisten müssen".

Bezuggenommen wird auf ein Darlehen der *pupilli* des Titius bei Sejus. Es geht um ein Kapital von 50.000 Sesterzen. Die zugesagten Erfüllungsmodalitäten bestehen in der Festlegung eines Zahlungstermins. Daneben verspricht Titius aber auch Strafzinsen für den Fall der Nichtleistung zum Termin.

Zunächst stellt der Jurist klar, dass Titius durch diese Erklärung nicht an die Stelle der *pupilli* getreten ist. Sie schulden weiterhin. Der Schuldner wurde nicht durch Erneuerung des Schuldverhältnisses (Novation) ausgetauscht. Dies ist nur durch Stipulation zu erreichen; eine Stipulation liegt aber nicht vor.

Die Schuld der *pupilli* besteht fort, Titius tritt durch formlose Erklärung als Garant hinzu. Er haftet aus der *actio de pecunia constituta*, nach der Entscheidung des Juristen aber nur „auf das Kapital" (*in sortem*).[6] Zahlt er an den Iden des Mai nicht, hat er Sejus dessen konkreten Schaden wegen Ausbleibens der pünktlichen Zahlung zu ersetzen. Er haftet *nicht* auf die versprochenen Strafzinsen. Eine Begründung dafür gibt der Jurist nicht. Liegt insofern kein *constituere* vor? Sind die Strafzinsen nicht *pecunia debita*? Schließt die Sanktionierung der pünktlichen Zahlung des Kapitals durch die *actio de pecunia constituta* einen weiteren Ver-

6 La Rosa 1997: 207f. bezeichnet den Text als „certamente manipolato", ohne sich über seine ursprüngliche Gestalt und Aussage zu erklären. Ihr stärkstes Argument ist die Formulierung im Pendant der Basiliken B. 26.7.24 (A IV 1300 Scheltema; III 137 f. Heimbach), der Erklärende hafte ὡς ἀπὸ τῆς ἀντιφωνήσεως - „quasi ex constituto" (so die Übersetzung von Heimbach III 138): „un accostamento al constitutum e non il riconoscimento di un vero rapporto di constitutum"; die byzantinische Tradition wäre insofern konservativer als die Kompilatoren. Sollten die Basiliken auf den Originaltext zurückgehen? Die Kompilatoren hätten in: „Marcellus respondit in sortem teneri quasi ex constituto" die letzten drei Worte gestrichen. „Ex constituto teneri" ist freilich nirgends belegt. Das ὡς der Basiliken muss – gleich dem lateinischen *quasi* – keineswegs eine Annäherung an etwas in Wahrheit nicht gegebenes kennzeichnen; es lässt sich auch mit „in der Eigenschaft als", „unter dem Gesichtspunkt" übersetzen, oder kann (in eben diesem Sinne) schlicht unübersetzt bleiben, vgl. nur etwa einerseits D. 16.1.17.2: „Mulier et Titius, cum in rem communem mutuarentur, eiusdem pecuniae rei facti sunt", andererseits B. 26.7(!).48.2 (A IV 1304 Scheltema; III 141 Heimbach): „Ἐὰν γυνὴ καὶ ἄλλος, ὡς δύο ἐναγόμενοι δανείσωνται ..." und schließlich die Übersetzung Heimbachs III 141: „Si mulier et alius quasi duo rei mutuam pecuniam acceperint ...".

trauensschutz hinsichtlich der Strafzinsen aus? Wie dem auch sei: Auf die Strafzinsen könnte sich Titius nur verpflichten, indem er sie in *Stipulationsform* verspricht; das ist in einem Brief nicht möglich.

3. Konkurrenz von constitutum und stipulatio

Die bisher betrachteten Stellen weisen bereits auf eine *Konkurrenz* zwischen formlosem *constitutum* und förmlicher *stipulatio* hin. Novation einer Schuld und Versprechen von Strafzinsen sind durch mündliche *stipulatio*, nicht aber in einem Brief bzw. durch *pecuniam constituere* möglich. Doch was die Haftung auf das Kapital (*in sortem*) betrifft, scheint es einen Überschneidungsbereich zu geben. Die Verfasser unserer Briefe wären jeweils auch durch Stipulation in die Haftung gekommen: als Bürge oder Schuldübernehmer.

Die Konkurrenz von *pecunia constituta* und *stipulatio* zeigt sich besonders deutlich bei der beabsichtigten, aber unwirksamen *stipulatio* (über eine bereits bestehende Schuld). Kann sie als wirksames und klagbares *constituere* aufrecht erhalten werden?

> D. 13.5.1.4 (Ulp. 27 ed.)
> „Eum, qui inutiliter stipulatus est, cum stipulari voluerit, non constitui sibi, dicendum est de constituta experiri non posse, quoniam non animo constituentis, sed promittentis factum sit".
>
> „Man muss sagen, dass derjenige, der sich *unwirksam* etwas förmlich versprechen ließ (‚stipulierte'), als er wollte, dass ihm förmlich versprochen, nicht dass ihm festgesetzt (‚konstituiert') werde, *nicht* mit der Klage wegen festgesetzten (Geldes) vorgehen kann, weil es nicht mit der Absicht eines Festsetzenden, sondern der eines Versprechenden geschehen ist".

Hier wird Schutz versagt, „quoniam non animo constituentis, sed promittentis factum est". Der Gläubiger des gescheiterten förmlichen zivilen Geschäfts erhält *keine* prätorische Klage. Das formlose *constituere* ist nicht im förmlichen Stipulationsversprechen enthalten. Die griechische Wiedergabe der Stelle in den Basiliken bringt dies auf den Punkt:

> B. 26.7.1.4 (A IV 1297 Scheltema; III 134 Heimbach)
> „Ἡ ἄχρηστος ἐπερώτησις οὐ ποιεῖ ἀντιφώνησιν". – „Die unwirksame ‚Frage' (=*stipulatio*) macht keine ‚Antwort' (= *constitutum*)".

Die beiden Geschäfte setzen unterschiedlichen Willen voraus. Eigenartigerweise ist in den Digesten zunächst vom *Gläubiger*: „stipulatus est, cum stipulari voluerit, non constitui", dann aber vom *Schuldner* die Rede: „non animo constituentis, sed promittentis" – ein unvermuteter Wechsel des Sinnsubjekts und der Perspektive.

Gegen die Echtheit der letzten Worte (*quoniam – sit*) in der überlieferten Form lassen sich Zweifel schwer unterdrücken.[7]

Schon aus der ersten Hälfte ergibt sich aber: Der Gläubiger kann nur *die* Klage erhalten, die sich aus der gewollten *Stipulation* ergibt. Ist diese unwirksam, kann er nicht auf die *actio de pecunia constituta* zurückgreifen. Dieselbe Schuldnererklärung kann offenbar einmal *constitutum* sein; ein anderes Mal nicht, dann nämlich, wenn in Wahrheit eine Stipulation gewollt war, das Zahlungsversprechen also eine verunglückte Stipulation ist.

4. Der Konträrfall: acceptilatio und pactum de non petendo

Bemerkenswert ist – und war es schon für die mittelalterlichen Glossatoren –, dass die römischen Juristen in einem Parallelfall zu einem anderen Ergebnis kommen.[8] Dort geht es um den Konträrakt zur *stipulatio*, den zivilen förmlichen Erlass (*acceptilatio*), einerseits und das prätorisch geschützte formlose *pactum de non petendo* andererseits. Eine *acceptilatio* besteht wie die *stipulatio* in Frage und Antwort, nur dass diesmal der Schuldner den Gläubiger fragt: „Acceptum habesne?" – „Hast du erhalten?" – „Acceptum habeo!" – „Ich habe erhalten!" Dieser Akt schafft eine Stipulationsverbindlichkeit endgültig aus der Welt. Sie erlischt nach *ius civile*. Das *pactum de non petendo* hingegen ist die formlose Vereinbarung der Parteien, dass der Gläubiger seine (fortbestehende) Forderung nicht gerichtlich geltend machen werde. Stammt die Forderung aus Stipulation und klagt der Gläubiger trotz *pactum de non petendo*, wird der Schuldner vom Prätor durch Auf-

7 Auf die ich aus Zeitgründen nicht genauer eingehen kann. Warum kann der Jurist in der Begründung der Entscheidung plötzlich unterstellen, dass der *Schuldner* kein *constitutum* wollte? Im Tatbestand ist nur vom *Gläubiger* die Rede. Ein ganz ähnliches Phänomen begegnet in D. 2.14.7.12 (*Ulp.* 4 ed.) über die Stipulationsklausel (zur Verwandtschaft der Problematik schon Astuti 1941: 262f.):

> „Quod fere novissima parte pactorum ita solet inseri ‚rogavit Titius, spopondit Maevius', haec verba non tantum pactionis loco accipiuntur, sed etiam stipulationis: ideoque ex stipulatu nascitur actio, nisi contrarium specialiter adprobetur, quod non animo stipulantium hoc factum est, sed tantum paciscentium".

Nicht nur stimmen die letzten Nebensätze der Stellen fast vollständig überein:

„quoniam	non animo constituentis,	sed	promittentis	factum sit"
„quod	non animo stipulantium,	sed tantum	paciscentium hoc	factum est"

„Contrarium ... adprobetur, quod ... factum est" ist grammatikalisch fragwürdig. Auch zeigt die Stelle inhaltlich ein mindestens ebenso handfestes Problem, um nicht zu sagen: einen eklatanten Fehler. Aus einer Stipulationsklausel, sie mag mit noch so viel *animus stipulantium* in die Urkunde aufgenommen worden sein, kann man nicht klagen. Geklagt wird vielmehr aus der tatsächlich vorgenommenen Stipulation. Sie wird aufgrund der Klausel *vermutet*; diese Vermutung kann aber im Einzelfall *widerlegt* werden: „nisi contrarium specialiter adprobetur". Würde die Stelle nach *adprobetur* enden, ergäbe sie besten Sinn. Die Worte *quod - est* aber schaffen etwas juristisch Unerhörtes: die Anerkennung der schriftlichen Stipulation!

8 Dazu zuletzt Krampe 1985: 20, 25.

nahme einer *exceptio pacti* in die Klageformel geschützt: Der Schuldner kann dann nicht verurteilt werden, wenn er das *pactum* nachweist.

Der Jurist Paulus, Ulpians Zeitgenosse und wissenschaftlicher Konkurrent, will jede, auch die unwirksame *acceptilatio* so behandelt sehen, als enthalte sie ein „stillschweigendes *pactum de non petendo*": „Wenn der förmliche Erlass unwirksam war, so scheint mittels einer stillschweigenden Vereinbarung verabredet worden zu sein, dass nicht geklagt werde", D. 2.14.27.9 (Paul. 3 ed.).

Auch Ulpian wirft die Frage auf, ob in einer unwirksamen *acceptilatio* ein wirksames *pactum de non petendo* enthalten ist, ob also „der unwirksame förmliche Erlass eine wirksame Abrede hat": „An inutilis acceptilatio utile habeat pactum, quaeritur", D. 46.4.8 pr. (Ulp. 48 Sab.). Die Antwort darauf ist Opfer einer gestörten Überlieferung. Unsere wichtigste Handschrift, der *Codex Florentinus* hat einen anderen Text als die Vulgathandschriften:

F:	„Et nisi in hoc quoque	**contra** sensum est,	**habet** pactum."
Vulg.:	„Et nisi in hoc quoque	**con**sensum/-s est,	**non habet** pactum."
F:	„Und wenn man nicht auch darin	**gegenteiliger Ansicht war,**	enthält er **eine** Abrede".
Vulg.:	„Und wenn man nicht auch darin	**übereinkam**,	enthält er **keine** Abrede".

Der *consensus* könne fehlen, so heißt es im zweiten Teil der Stelle, wenn der Gläubiger die *acceptilatio* vornimmt, obwohl er (insgeheim) weiß, dass sie unwirksam ist. Die massiven Probleme, die diese Stelle bereitet, kann ich aus Platzgründen nicht *en detail* darstellen.[9] Die herrschende Meinung erklärt den kompletten zweiten Teil der Stelle zur Glosse und entscheidet sich für die Lesart des *Codex Florentinus.*[10]

Ich darf sofort zu meiner Lösung schreiten. Sie hat mit dem handschriftlichen Befund im *Codex Florentinus* zu tun. Er eröffnet neben den beiden genannten Les-

9 Die Probleme ergeben sich aus der gespaltenen Überlieferung des ersten Teils und der Aussage des zweiten Teils der Stelle. In Form eines Selbsteinwurfs schließt sich dort nämlich eine dialektische Überprüfung der Lösung an. Sie hat Generationen von Juristen zur Verzweiflung gebracht.

> „dicet aliquis: potest ergo non esse consensus? cur non possit? fingamus eum, qui accepto ferebat, scientem prudentemque nullius esse momenti acceptilationem. sic accepto tulisse quis dubitat non esse pactum, cum consensum paciscendi non habuerit?".

> „Es mag einer sagen: Kann die Übereinstimmung also nicht vorhanden sein? Warum sollte sie nicht können? Nehmen wir den, der den förmlichen Erlass erklärt, wohlwissend, dass der Erlass keinerlei Wirkung hat. Wer könnte daran zweifeln, dass es keine Abrede darstellt, derart den förmlichen Erlass vorgenommen zu haben, weil er kein Einverständnis zu einer Abrede hatte?".

Wie kann es sein, dass das *pactum de non petendo* am fehlenden *consensus* der Parteien scheitert, nur weil der Gläubiger insgeheim weiß, dass der Erlass unwirksam ist? Soll der Schuldner schutzlos bleiben, obwohl der Gläubiger den Erlass *erklärt* hat? Die Stelle wird zur „*crux* der Lehre von der Mentalreservation", cf. Krampe 1985: 14.

10 Zuletzt Krampe 1985: 10–6 mit weiterer Literatur.

arten eine weitere: Vor *nisi* findet sich dort ein durchgestrichenes *s*, das von einem *si* des ursprünglichen Textes stammen könnte.

F, vol. 2, f. 367ra/6: *quaerituret*[[*s*]]*nisiinhoc*

Bei Ulpian hätte die Stelle dann gelautet:

„Et **si** in hoc quoque	**con**sensus est,	**habet** pactum“.
„Und **wenn** es auch insofern	**übereinstimmenden** Willen gab	enthält [der Erlass] **eine** Abrede“.

Das würde heißen: Für das *pactum de non petendo* ist ein besonderer *consensus* nötig: *in hoc quoque*. Fehlt das *pactum* ausnahmsweise mangels *consensus*, heißt dies noch nicht, dass der Schuldner nicht dennoch Schutz vor einer Klage des Gläubigers erhalten kann. Denn dem Prätor steht nicht nur die *exceptio pacti* zur Verfügung, sondern auch die *exceptio doli*, die „Einrede der Arglist“. Der Gläubiger, der die *acceptilatio* vorgenommen hat, obwohl er (insgeheim) ihre Unwirksamkeit kannte, hat damit zwar kein *pactum de non petendo* geschlossen. Doch er hat den Schuldner getäuscht, sein Verhalten ist dolos. Dass bei einer unwirksamen *acceptilatio* sowohl die *exceptio pacti* als auch die *exceptio doli* in Frage kommen, wissen wir aus einer Stelle der *Ulpiani regulae* (D. 46.4.19 pr. Ulp. 2 reg.), die wir angesichts des zu D. 46.4.8 pr. Gesagten ernst nehmen dürfen.

Eines sei nochmals besonders betont: Ein *pactum de non petendo* wird von Ulpian *bejaht* bei unwirksamer *acceptilatio* und einem weitergehenden *consensus* (*in hoc quoque*). *Acceptilatio* und *pactum* können kombiniert werden.

Ein *constitutum* aber wird von Ulpian *verneint* bei unwirksamer *stipulatio* und einem Willen der Parteien, der sich auf die Vornahme der Stipulation, nicht aber auf ein *constitutum* bezieht.

Dass und ob ihr Konsens über die Begründung einer Stipulationsverpflichtung hinaus grundsätzlich *auch* ein *constitutum* erfassen könnte („in hoc quoque“ wie beim *pactum de non petendo*), wird nicht gesagt. Die Ausdrucksweise *stipulari, non constitui* spricht dagegen[11] und für ein Ausschließlichkeitsverhältnis von *stipulatio* und *constitutum*.

Die Gründe für dieses Ausschließlichkeitsverhältnis hat man in Funktionsverschiedenheiten von *stipulatio* und *constitutum* vermutet,[12] die den Schluss erlaubten: „Wer das eine will, will sicher nicht (auch) das andere“. Tatsächlich lassen sich Unterschiede feststellen:

11 Ebenso die Gegenüberstellung von *animus promittentis* und *constituentis* am Ende der Stelle; zu deren Echtheit aber o. Anm. 7.

12 Giuffrè 1965: 326–9; Talamanca 1978: 208f.

- Die *Beweislast* für das Bestehen der Hauptschuld (*pecunia debita*) trägt beim *constitutum* stets der Gläubiger; bei der *stipulatio* kann sie beim Schuldner liegen. Doch erstens ist dies nicht immer der Fall. Und zweitens ist das *constitutum* dadurch allenfalls von Vorteil für den Schuldner.
- Das *constitutum* ist nicht zur Novation fähig, die *stipulatio* hingegen schon. Aber: Eine Novation ist nicht bei jeder *stipulatio* beabsichtigt und möglich.
- Die *stipulatio* über eine bestimmte Geldsumme (*certa pecunia*) führt zu einer Klage auf das Kapital (*actio certae creditae pecuniae*), das *constitutum* führt zu einer Klage auf das Interesse, das über das Kapital hinausgehen kann. Aber: Das Gläubigerinteresse kann auch bei der *stipulatio* durch Versprechen einer Strafe oder von Schadensersatz gesichert werden.

Warum also kann eine unwirksame Stipulation, die die Beweislast beim Gläubiger belassen hätte, keine Novation bewirken sollte und dem Gläubiger außerdem Schadensersatz im Fall der Nichterfüllung versprochen hatte, nicht als *constituere* aufrecht erhalten werden? Warum schützt der Prätor hier nicht den Gläubiger, wie er bei der unwirksamen *acceptilatio* den Schuldner schützt? Warum gibt es keine Symmetrie von *stipulatio/constitutum* und *acceptilatio/pactum*?

5. Fehlende Symmetrie von Gläubiger- und Schuldnerschutz

Die mittelalterlichen Glossatoren standen hier vor einem Phänomen, das sich nur noch mithilfe einer axiomatischen Rechtsregel bewältigen ließ:

> Gl. *non animo* zu D. 13.5.1.4
> „Sed cum acceptilatio quandoque iure pacti valeat, ut diximus supra de pact. l. si unus.§.penultimo. [=D. 2.14.27.9] quare non stipulatio valet iure constituti? Respondeo: **Facilius** exceptio quam actio paratur".
>
> „Wenn aber der förmliche Erlass stets nach dem Recht der Abrede Geltung behält, wie wir oben zu D. 2.14.27.9 bemerkt haben, warum hat dann nicht die Stipulation Geltung nach dem Recht des *constitutum*? Ich antworte: Eine Einrede wird leichter erworben als eine Klage".

Die Frage, warum die Symmetrie fehlt, wird nicht beantwortet: Es gibt sie nun einmal nicht: Der Schutz des beklagten Schuldners durch Einrede stellt weniger strenge Anforderungen als der des Gläubigers durch Gewährung einer Klage. Diese Regel, die aus der Hilflosigkeit der Interpreten gebildet zu sein scheint, hat bemerkenswerte Ähnlichkeit mit regelhaften Äußerungen der römischen Juristen. In den Gajus-Institutionen (die die Glossatoren noch gar nicht kannten!) findet sich – wenn auch in anderem Zusammenhang, so doch wiederum zur Begründung eines Ergebnisses und recht axiomatisch – der Satz:

> Gai. 4.57
> „facilius (!) enim reis praetor succurrit quam actoribus". – „Denn der Prätor hilft eher den Beklagten als den Klägern".

Paulus zitiert einen älteren Juristen mit einer Regel zur Auslegung:

> D. 44.7.47 (Paul. 14 Plaut.)
> „Arrianus ait multum interesse, quaeras, utrum aliquis obligetur an aliquis liberetur: ubi de obligando quaeritur, propensiores esse debere nos, si habeamus occasionem, ad negandum: ubi de liberando ex diverso, ut facilior (!) sis (Mommsen: ex diverso faciliores) ad liberationem".
>
> „Arrianus sagt, es bestehe ein großer Unterschied, ob man untersucht, ob einer verpflichtet wird, oder ob einer befreit wird: Wo es um die Verpflichtung geht, müssten wir eher dazu neigen, sie zu verneinen, wenn wir Gelegenheit dazu haben. Wo es um das Freiwerden gehe, gelte das Gegenteil, damit man leichter zur Befreiung gelange (Mommsen: … müssten wir umgekehrt der Befreiung zugänglicher sein?)".

Man übt Zurückhaltung, wenn es darum geht, dem Gläubiger eine Klagemöglichkeit zu verschaffen. Man ersetzt nicht die zivilrechtliche Klage aus Stipulation, die der Gläubiger vergeblich angestrebt hatte, mit der prätorischen *actio de pecunia constituta*. Der Gläubiger betätigt eine Art von Rechtswahl: Mit der *stipulatio* will er den Schutz des *ius civile* erhalten.[13] Würde ihm der Prätor trotz dieser Wahl nachträglich die Klage aus *constitutum* gewähren, geriete das Nebeneinander der beiden Rechtsordnungen in Gefahr. Angesichts unserer – insofern verlässlichen – Ulpianstelle handelt es sich um klassisches Gedankengut; es spiegelt sich noch in den Institutionen Justinians wieder:

> I. 4.6.9 (entspr. Theoph. 4.6.8–9)
> „In personam quoque actiones ex sua iurisdictione propositas habet praetor. veluti de pecunia constituta …. De pecunia autem constituta cum omnibus agitur, quicumque vel pro se vel pro alio soluturos se constituerint, nulla scilicet stipulatione interposita. nam alioquin si stipulanti promiserint, iure civili tenentur".
>
> „Auch Klagen gegen die Person hat der Prätor aus seiner Rechtsprechung heraus verlautbart, zum Beispiel die Klage ‚wegen festgesetzten Geldes' … Über festgesetztes Geld wird gegen alle geklagt, sei es dass sie für sich oder für einen anderen zu zahlen festgesetzt haben, aber wohlgemerkt nur, wenn keine Stipulation geschlossen wurde. Andernfalls nämlich, wenn sie einem Stipulationsgläubiger ein Versprechen gegeben haben, haften sie nach dem Zivilrecht".

Der Schutz des Gläubigers bei formlosen Erklärungen des Schuldners, etwa in einem Brief, grenzt mit allen Konsequenzen an die Förmlichkeiten des *ius civile*. Der griechischen Vorstellung, mittels *chirographum* beziehungsweise Brief die Haf-

13 Ähnlich Babusiaux 2006: 123f.

tungslage eines Kreditschuldners zu gestalten, gibt der Prätor mit der Klage *de pecunia constituta* nach. Sie kann den Raum füllen, in dem das *ius civile* den Bedürfnissen des entwickelten Geschäftsverkehrs, insbesondere der Distanzgeschäfte, nicht mit der Gewährung von Rechtsschutz entspricht. Doch die Stipulation bleibt unangetastet. Überschritte man diese Grenze, würde das *ius civile* nicht mehr korrigiert – was der Prätor durchaus als seine Aufgabe versteht –, es würde ausgehöhlt, seine Formalismen wären überflüssig. Die Konkurrenz von ziviler und prätorischer Rechtsordnung eröffnet uns hier einen unmittelbaren Blick auf den Umgang der Römer mit dem Fremden und dem Neuen, auf ihre Rezeptionsfreudigkeit und ihren Konservativismus.

Bibliography

Andrae, W. 1907, "Aus den Berichten W. Andraes aus Assur von September 1906 bis April 1907", *MDOG* 33, 11–23.

Andrae, W. 1913, *Die Festungswerke von Assur* (WVDOG 23), Leipzig.

Andreau, J. 1999, *Banking and Business in the Roman World*, Cambridge.

Ankum, H. 1978, "Tabula Pompeiana 13: Ein Seefrachtvertrag oder ein Darlehen?", *IVRA* 29, 156–173.

Arangio-Ruiz, V. 1948, "Les tablettes d'Herculaneum", *RIDA* 1, 13–15.

Arena, E. 2003, "La lettera di Oleveni: fra Filippo II e Filippo V di Macedonia", *REA* 105, 49–82.

Arlt, C. 2009, "Die thebanischen Notare", in Gh. Widmer & D. Devauchelle (eds.), *Actes du IXe congrès international des études démotiques* (BIFAO 147), Cairo, 29–49

Arnold, W. R. 1912, "The Passover Papyrus from Elephantine", *JBL* 31, 1–33.

Astuti, G. 1938, "Studi preliminari intorno alla promessa di pagamento. Il costituto di debito", *Ann. Camerino* 11.2, 83–250.

Astuti, G. 1941, *Studi intorno alla promessa di pagamento. Il costituto di debito II*, Milan.

Aubert, J.-J. 1994, *Business Managers in Ancient Rome: A Social and Economic Study of Institores, 200 B.C — A.D. 250*, Leiden.

Babusiaux, U. 2006, *Id quod actum est. Zur Ermittlung des Parteiwillens im klassischen römischen Zivilprozeß* (MBPR 95), Munich.

Backhaus, R. 2004, "Die Gefahrtragung bei gemeinsamen Unternehmungen und ihre Modifikation durch Parteiabsprachen im klassischen römischen Recht", *ZSSRA* 121, 233–261.

Behrends, O., Knütel, R., Kupisch, B. & Seiler, H.H. 1995–2002, *Corpus Iuris Civilis, Text und Übersetzung auf der Grundlage der von Theodor Mommsen und Paul Krüger besorgten Textausgaben, Vol. II–IV*, Heidelberg.

Bergamasco, M. 1995, "Le Διδασκαλικαί nella ricerca attuale", *Aegyptus* 75, 95–167.

Bertrand, J.M. 1985, "Formes de discours politique : décrets des cités grecques et correspondance des rois hellénistiques", *RHD* 63, 469–482, republished in Cl. Nicolet (ed.), *Du pouvoir dans l'antiquité : mots et réalités* (CCG 1), Geneva 1990, 101–115.

Biscardi, A. 1999, *Scritti di diritto greco* (Pubblicazioni dell'Istituto di Diritto Romano, Facoltà di Giurisprudenza, Università degli Studi di Milano 34), Milan.

Blass, F. 1887–1898, *Die attische Beredsamkeit*, vols. I-III, Leipzig.

Bonner, R.J. 1905, *Evidence in Athenian Courts*, Chicago.

Borger, R. 1975, *Handbuch der Keilschriftliteratur III*, Berlin & New York.

Borger, R. 2004, *Mesopotamisches Zeichenlexikon* (AOAT 305), Münster.

Boring, T.A. 1979, *Literacy in Ancient Sparta* (Mnemosyne, Supplementum 54), Leiden.

Boyer, G. 1965, "La preuve dans les anciens droits du Proche-Orient", *Recueils de la Société Jean Bodin* XVI : *La preuve*, Brussels, 61–87, republished in *Mélanges d'histoire du droit oriental* II, *Recueil de l'Académie de législation série* 6, part 3, Paris 1965, 181–200.

Bravo, B. 1974, "Une lettre sur plomb de Berezan: Colonisation et modes de contact dans le Pont", *DHA* 1, 110–187.

Bravo, B. 1977, "Remarques sur les assises sociales, les formes d'organisation et la terminologie du commerce maritime grec à l'époque archaïque", *DHA* 1, 1–59.

Bravo, B. 1980, "Sulân, Représailles et justice privée contre des étrangers dans les cités grecques", *ASNP* 10, 675–987.

Brisch, N. 2007, *Tradition and the Poetics of Innovation: Sumerian Court Literature of the Larsa Dynasty (c. 2003 – 1763 BCE)* (AOAT 339), Münster.

Brisch, N. (ed.) 2008, *Religion and Power: Divine Kingship in the Ancient World and Beyond* (Oriental Institute Seminars 4, The University of Chicago), Chicago.

Bruns, C.G. 1861, "Das constitutum debiti", *ZRG* 1, 28–130 (= Id., *Kleinere Schriften I*, Weimar 1882, 221–312).

Buchanan, B. & Hallo, W.W. 1981, *Early Near Eastern Seals in the Yale Babylonian Collection*, New Haven, CT.

Buzón, R. 1984, *Die Briefe der Ptolemäerzeit. Ihre Struktur und ihre Formeln*, Heidelberg.

Cameron, G.G. 1948, *Persepolis Treasury Tablets* (OIP 65), Chicago.

Camodeca, G. 1999, *Tabulae Pompeianae Sulpiciorum. Edizione critica dell'archivio puteolano dei Sulpicii I-II = TPSulp* (Vetera 12), Rome.

Cancik-Kirschbaum, E. 1996, *Die mittelassyrischen Briefe aus Dūr-Katlimmu / Tell Šēḫ Ḥamad* (BATSH 4, Texte 1), Berlin.

Cancik-Kirschbaum, E. 2012, *Überlegungen zur Systematik administrativen Schriftguts der mittelassyrischen Zeit* I, in H. Kühne (ed.), *BATSH* 12, Wiesbaden, 39–51.

Cancik-Kirschbaum, E. forthcoming, Zum Problem der Verschuldung in mittelassyrischer Zeit.

Carawan, E. (ed.) 2007, *Oxford Readings in the Attic Orators*, Oxford.

Cardascia, G. 1969, *Les lois assyriennes* (LAPO 2), Paris.

Cardascia, G. 1995, "Réflexions sur le témoignage dans les droits du Proche-Orient ancien", *RHD* 73, 549–557.

Carey, C. 1994, " 'Artless Proofs' in Aristotle and the Orators", *BICS* 39, 95–106, reprinted in Carawan (2007), 229–246.

Carey, C. 2000, *Aeschines* (The Oratory of Classical Greece 3), Austin, TX.

Cartledge, P. 1978, "Literacy in the Spartan Oligarchy", *JHS* 98, 25–37.

Cartledge, P., Cohen, E. & Foxhall, L. (eds.) 2002, *Money, Labour and Land: Approaches to the Economies of Ancient Greece*. London.

Casson, L. 1971, *Ships and Seamanship in the Ancient World*, Princeton, NJ.

Cavigneaux, A. 2007, Review of P. Michalowski & N. Veldhuis (eds.), *Approaches to Sumerian Literature: Studies in Honour of Stip (H.L.J. Vanstiphout)* (CM 35), Leiden 2006, *RBL* 07, also available on http://www.bookreviews.org/pdf/5667_5983.pdf.

Cawkwell, G.L. 1969, "The Crowning of Demosthenes", *CQ* NS 19, 163–180.

Ceccarelli, P. 2002, "Message épistolaire et message oral au Proche-Orient et en Grèce archaïque et classique", in L. Nadjo, E. Gavoille (eds.), *Epistulae Antiquae II. Actes du IIe Colloque International "Le genre épistolaire antique et ses prolongements européens"*, Leuven & Paris, 11–21.

Ceccarelli, P. 2004, "Ecriture féminine, écriture épistolaire, parole des rhéteurs : à propos du fragment 194 K. A. de la Sappho d'Antiphane", in L. Nadjo & E. Gavoille (eds.), *Epistulae Antiquae III, actes du IIIe Colloque international "L'épistolaire antique et ses prolongements européens" (Université François-Rabelais, Tours, 25–27 septembre 2002)*, Leuven & Paris, 11–32.

Ceccarelli, P. 2005a, "Forme di comunicazione e ideologia della polis: discorso in assemblea, decreto ed epistola ufficiale", in U. Bultrighini (ed.), *Democrazia e antidemocrazia nel mondo greco. Atti del Convegno Internazionale di Studi (Chieti 9–11 aprile 2003)* (Collana del Dipartimento di Scienze dell'Antichità. Sezione storica / Università degli Studi G. D'Annunzio, Chieti-Pescara 8), Alessandria, 345–369.

Ceccarelli, P. 2005b, "Messaggio scritto e messaggio orale: strategie narrative erodotee", in M. Giangiulio (ed.), *Erodoto e il 'modello erodoteo'. Formazione e trasmissione delle tradizioni storiche in Grecia*, Trento, 13–60.

Chadwick, J. 1990, "The Pech-Maho Lead", *ZPE* 82, 161–166.

Charpin, D. 1986, "Transmission des titres de propriété et constitution des archives privées en Babylonie ancienne", in K.R. Veenhof (ed.), *Cuneiform Archives and Libraries. Papers read at the 30e Rencontre Assyriologique Internationale Leiden, 4–8 July 1983* (PIHANS 57), Leiden, 121–140.

Charpin, D. 1990a, "L'*andurârum* à Mari", *MARI* 6, 253–270.

Charpin, D. 1990b, "Les édits de "restauration" des rois babyloniens et leur application", in Cl. Nicolet (ed.), *Du pouvoir dans l'antiquité : mots et réalité*, Paris-Geneva, 13–24 (available on www.digitorient.com).

Charpin, D. 1991, "Les mots du pouvoir dans les archives royales de Mari", *CCG* 2, 3–17 (available on www.digitorient.com).

Charpin, D. 1992, "Les malheurs d'un scribe, ou de l'inutilité du sumérien loin de Nippur", in M. de Jong Ellis (ed.), *Nippur at the Centennial. Papers read at the 35e Rencontre Assyriologique Internationale, Philadelphia 1988* (Occasional Publications of the Samuel Noah Kramer Fund 14), Philadelphia, 7–27.

Charpin, D. 1996, "Maisons et maisonnées en Babylonie ancienne de Sippar à Ur. Remarques sur les grandes demeures des notables paléo-babyloniens", in K.R. Veenhof. (ed.), *Houses and Households in Ancient Mesopotamia: Papers Read at the*

40e Rencontre Assyriologique Internationale, Leiden, July 5–8, 1993 (PIHANS 78), Leiden & Istanbul, 221–235.

Charpin, D. 1998, "Noms de personnes et légendes des sceaux en Babylonie ancienne", in A.-M. Christin (ed.), *L'écriture du nom propre*, Paris, 43–55.

Charpin, D. 2000a, "Les prêteurs et le palais : les édits de *mîšarum* des rois de Babylone et leurs traces dans les archives privées", in A.C.V.M. Bongenaar (ed.), *Interdependency of Institutions and Private Entrepreneurs: Proceedings of the Second Mos Symposium (Leiden 1998)* (PIHANS 87), Leiden, 185–211.

Charpin, D. 2000b, "Lettres et procès paléo-babyloniens", in F. Joannès (ed.), *Rendre la justice en Mésopotamie, archives judiciaires du Proche-Orient ancien, IIIe-Ier millénaires avant J.-C*, Saint-Denis, 69–111 (also available on www.digitorient.com).

Charpin, D. 2003, *Hammu-rabi de Babylone*, Paris.

Charpin, D. 2004, "Histoire politique du Proche-Orient amorrite (2002–1595)", in Charpin, Edzard & Stol (eds.), 25–480.

Charpin, D. 2005, "Le statut des 'codes de lois' des souverains babyloniens", in P. Sineux, (ed.), *Le législateur et la loi dans l'Antiquité. Hommage à Françoise Ruzé : actes du colloque de Caen, 15–17 mai 2003*, Caen, 93–108 (also available on www.digitorient.com).

Charpin, D. 2007a, "Économie, société et institutions paléo-babyloniennes : nouvelles sources, nouvelles approches", *RA* 101, 147–182.

Charpin, D. 2007b, "The Writing, Sending and Reading of Letters in the Amorite World", in G. Leick, (ed.), *The Babylonian World*, New York & London, 400–417.

Charpin, D. 2008, *Lire et écrire à Babylone*, Paris.

Charpin, D. 2010a, "Un édit du roi Ammi-ditana de Babylone", in D. Shehata, F. Weiershäuser & K.V. Zand (eds.), *Von Göttern und Menschen. Beiträge zu Literatur und Geschichte des Alten Orients. Festschrift für Brigitte Groneberg*, Leiden & Boston, 17–46.

Charpin, D. 2010b, *Writing, Law, and Kingship in Old Babylonian Mesopotamia*, Chicago.

Charpin, D. 2012, "L'exercice du pouvoir par les rois de la Ière dynastie de Babylone: problèmes de méthode", in G. Wilhelm (ed.), *Organization, Representation and Symbols of Power in the Ancient Near East*, Winona Lake, IN, 21–32.

Charpin, D. forthcoming, " 'I am the Sun of Babylon'. Solar Symbolism of the Royal Power in Old Babylonian Mesopotamia", in Ph. Jones et al. (eds.), *Experiencing Power Generating Authority: Cosmos and Politics in the Ideology of Kingship in Ancient Egypt and Mesopotamia*, Philadelphia, PA.

Charpin, D. & Durand, J.-M. (eds.) 2001, *Mari, Ébla et les Hourrites. Dix ans de travaux. Actes du colloque international, Paris, mai 1993, vol. II* (Amurru 2), Paris.

Charpin, D., Edzard, D.O. & Stol, M. 2004, *Mesopotamien: Die altbabylonische Zeit* (OBO 160.4), Göttingen.

Charpin, D. & Joannès, F. (eds.) 1992, *La circulation des biens, des personnes et des idées dans le Proche-Orient ancien : actes de la XXXVIIIe Rencontre assyriologique internationale (Paris, 8–10 juillet 1991)*, Paris.

Charpin, D. & Ziegler, N. 2003, *Mari et le Proche-Orient à l'époque amorrite. Essai d'histoire politique* (FM 5), Paris.

Choe, B.J. 1993, "Die Schulkontroverse bei Überschreitung des Auftrags zum Grundstückskauf", in D. Nörr & S. Nishimura (eds.), *Mandatum und Verwandtes: Beiträge zum römischen und modernen Recht,* Berlin, 119–139.

Cohen, E.E. 1992, *Athenian Economy and Society: A Banking Perspective*, Princeton, NJ.

Coing, H. 1951, "Die clausula doli im klassischen Recht", in H. Niedermeyer & W. Flume (eds.), *Festschrift Fritz Schulz*, Weimar, 99–122.

Cowley, A.E. 1923, *Aramaic Papyri of the Fifth Century B.C.*, Oxford.

Crampa, J. 1969, *Labraunda. Swedish Excavations and Researches, vol III. The Greek Inscriptions. Part I: 1–12 (The Period of Olympichos)* (Skrifter utgivna av Svenska Institutet i Athen 4), Lund.

Crook, J.A. 1967, *Law and Life of Rome,* London.

Çığ, M., Kizilyay, H. & Salonen, A. 1954, *Die Puzriš-Dagan-Texte der Istanbuler Archäologischen Museen Teil I : Nrr. 1–725*, Helsinki.

Dahl, J.L. 2007, *The Ruling Family of Ur III Umma. A Prosopographical Analysis of an Elite Family in Southern Iraq 4000 Years Ago* (PIHANS 108), Leiden.

Dalley, S., Walker, C.B.F. & Hawkins, D.J. 1976, *The Old Babylonian Tablets from Tell al Rimah*, London.

Dana, M. 2004, "Lettre sur plomb d'Apatorios à Léanax. Un document archaïque d'Olbia du Pont", *ZPE* 148, 1–14.

Dana, M. 2007, "Lettres grecques dialectales nord-pontiques (sauf *IGDOP* 23–26)", *REA* 109 (1), 67–97.

Davies, J.K. 1971, *Athenian Propertied Families 600–300 B.C.*, Oxford.

De Cenival, F. 1987, "Répertoire journalier d'un bureau de notaire de l'époque ptolémaïque en démotique (P. Dém. Lille 120)", *Enchoria* 15, 1–9.

Deller, K.H. 1969, "Die Briefe des Adad-šumu-uṣur ", in M. Dietrich & W. Röllig (eds.), *Lišān Mithurti, Festschrift Wolfram Freiherr von Soden zum 19.4.1968 gewidmet von Schulern und Mitarbetiern* (AOAT 1), Neukirchen-Vluyn, 45–64.

Deller, K.H. 1984a, "Assyrisch *um/nzarḫu* und Hebräisch *'äzraḥ*", *ZA* 74, 235–239.

Deller, K.H. 1984b, "Drei wiederentdeckte neuassyrische Rechtsurkunden aus Aššur", *BaM* 15, 225–251.

Démare-Lafont, S. 1997, "Les actes législatifs des rois mésopotamiens", in S. Dauchy, J. Monballyu & A. Wijffels (eds.), *Auctoritates. Xenia R. C. Van Caenegem oblata* (Iuris Scripta Historica 13), Brussels, 3–27.

Démare-Lafont, S. 2003, Review of E. Dombradi, *Die Darstellung des Rechtsaustrags in den altbabylonischen Prozessurkunden,* Stuttgart 1996, *BiOr* 60, 652–661.

Démare-Lafont, S. 2008, "Aspects du commerce international des Assyriens en Anatolie", in J.G. Derckens (ed.), *Anatolia and the Jazira during the Old Assyrian Period* (PIHANS 111), Leiden, 195–207.

Depauw, M. 1997, *A Companion to Demotic Studies* (Papyrologica Bruxellensia 28), Brussels.

Depauw, M. 2000, *The Archive of Teos and Thabis from Early Ptolemaic Thebes* (P. Brux. dem. inv. E. 8252–8256) (Monographies Reine Élisabeth 8), Turnhout & Brussels.

Depauw, M. 2003, "Autograph Confirmation in Demotic Private Contracts", *CE* 78, 66–111.

Depauw, M. 2006, *The Demotic Letter. A Study of Epistolographic Scribal Traditions against their Intra- and Intercultural Background* (Demotische Studien 14), Sommerhausen.

Depauw, M. 2009, "A Sale of a House in Thebes on a Complete Papyrus Roll (P. BM EA 10678 & Brux. E 8053 & Brux. E 8051 B-A & Brux. E 8054)", in W. Claes, H. De Meulenaere & S. Hendrickx (eds.), *Elkab and Beyond. Studies in Honour of Luc Limme* (OLA 191), Leuven et al., 261–282.

Dietrich, M. 2003, *The Babylonian Correspondence of Sargon and Sennacherib* (SAA 17), Helsinki.

Dignas, B. 2002, *Economy of the Sacred in Hellenistic and Roman Asia Minor*, Oxford.

Dion, P.E. 1982, "Aramaic Words for 'Letter'", in J.L. White (ed.), *Studies in Ancient Letter Writing* (Semeia 22), Chico, CA, 77–88.

Dombradi, E. 1996, *Die Darstellung des Rechtsaustrags in den altbabylonischen Prozessurkunden* (FAOS 20), Stuttgart.

Donbaz, V. 2004, "Selected Middle Assyrian Private Letters Housed in Istanbul", in G. Frame (ed.), *From the Upper Sea to the Lower Sea. Studies on the History of Assyria and Babylonia in Honour of A.K. Grayson*, Leiden, 67– 80.

Donner, H. & Röllig, W (2002^5), *Kanaanäische und aramäische Inschriften*, I, Wiesbaden.

Driver, G.R. 1954, *Aramaic Documents of the Fifth Century B.C.*, Oxford.

Driver, G.R. 1957, *Aramaic Documents of the Fifth Century B.C.: Abridged and Revised Edition*, Oxford.

Duponchel, D. 1997, "Les comptes d'huile du palais de Mari datés de l'année de Kahat", in D. Charpin & J.-M. Durand (eds.), *Recueil d'études à la mémoire de Marie-Thérèse Barrelet* (FM 3) (Mémoires de NABU 4), Paris, 201–262.

Durand, J.-M. 1997, *Documents épistolaires du palais de Mari, tome I* (LAPO 16), Paris.

Durand, J.-M. 1998, *Documents épistolaires du palais de Mari, tome II* (LAPO 17), Paris.

Durand, J.-M. 2000, *Documents épistolaires du palais de Mari, tome III* (LAPO 18), Paris.

Durand, J.-M. 2002, *Le Culte d'Addu d'Alep et l'affaire d'Alahtum* (FM 7) (Mémoires de NABU 8), Paris.

Ebeling, E. 1933, "Aus den Archiven von Uruk und Assur. II. Drei gerichtliche Ladungen aus mittelassyrischer Zeit", in E. Weidner (ed.), *Aus fünf Jahrtausenden morgenländischer Kultur. Festschrift Max Freiherrn von Oppenheim zum 70. Geburtstage gewidmet von Freunden und Mitarbeitern*, (AfO, Beiheft 1) Berlin, 34–36.

Eidinow, E. & Taylor, C. (2010), "Lead-Letter Days: Writing, Communication and Crisis in the Ancient World", *CQ* 60, 30–62.

Edzard, D.O. 1974, *Textes littéraires de Suse* (MDAI 57), Paris.

Edzard, D.O. 1995, Review of AbB XII and AbB XIII, *ZA* 85, 141–144.

Ehrenberg, V. 1930, "Zur Verfassungsurkunde von Kyrene", *Hermes* 65, 332–355.

Fales, F.M. 1974, "L''ideologo' Adad-šuma-uṣur", *Rendiconti dell'Accademia dei Lincei. Classe di Scienze morali, storiche e filologiche Serie* 8, 29, 453–496.

Faraguna, M. 2000, "A proposito degli archivi nel mondo greco: terra e registrazioni fondiarie", *Chiron* 30, 65–115.

Faraguna, M. 2002, "Commercio, scrittura, pratiche giuridiche: recenti studi sull' « emporía » greca", *Dike* 5, 237–254.

Faraguna, M. 2007, "Tra oralità e scrittura: diritto e forme della comunicazione dai poemi omerici a Teofrasto", *Etica & Politica* 9, 75–111.

Felber, H. 1997, *Demotische Ackerpachtverträge der Ptolemäerzeit: Untersuchungen zu Aufbau, Entwicklung und inhaltlichen Askpekten einer Gruppe von demotischen Urkunden* (Ägyptologische Abhandlungen 58), Wiesbaden.

Finkelstein, J.J. 1972, *Late Old Babylonian Documents and Letters* (YOS 13), New Haven, CT & London.

Finley, M.I. 1952, *Studies in Land and Credit in Ancient Athens 500–200 B.C.: the Horos Inscriptions*, New Brunswick, NJ.

Fitzmyer, J.A. 1979, "Aramaic Epistolography", in J.A. Fitzmyer (ed.), *A Wandering Aramean: Collected Aramaic Essays* (SBL MS 25), Missoula, MT, 183–204.

Flensted-Jensen, P., Nielsen, T.H. & Rubinstein, L. (eds.) 2000, *Polis and Politics: Studies in Ancient Greek History Presented to Mogens Herman Hansen on His Sixtieth Birthday, August 20, 2000,* Copenhagen.

Foster, B.R. 2005, *Before the Muses. An Anthology of Akkadian Literature*[3], Bethesda, MD.

Fournet, J.-L. 2007, "Disposition et réalisation graphique des lettres et des pétitions protobyzantines : pour une paléographie « signifiante » des papyrus documentaires", in J. Frösén, T. Purola & E. Salmenkivi (eds.), *Proceedings of the 24th International Congress of Papyrology, Helsinki 2004*, Helsinki, 353–367.

Fournet, J.-L. 2008, "Préface" in J.-L. Fournet (ed.), *Les Archives de Dioscore d'Aphrodité cent ans après leur découverte : Histoire et culture dans l'Égypte byzantine,* Paris, 7–14.

Fournet, J.-L. 2009, "Esquisse d'une anatomie de la lettre antique tardive d'après les papyrus", in R. Delmaire, J. Desmulliez & P.-L. Gatier (eds.), *Correspondances. Documents pour l'histoire de l'Antiquité tardive : actes du colloque international, Université Charles-de-Gaulle-Lille 3, 20–22 novembre 2003* (Collection de la Maison de l'Orient et de la Méditerranée 40), Paris, 23–66.

Frankena, R. 1956, Review of H. A. Fine, *Studies in Middle-Assyrian Chronology and Religion* (Cincinnati 1955), *BiOr* 13, 140 142.

Frayne, D. 1997, *Ur III Period (2112 – 2004 BC)* (RIME 3.2), Toronto.

Freydank, H. 1976, *Mittelassyrische Rechtsurkunden und Verwaltungstexte*, Berlin.

Freydank, H. 1991, *Beiträge zur mittelassyrischen Chronologie und Geschichte* (Schriften zur Geschichte und Kultur des alten Orients 21), Berlin.

Freydank, H. 1997, " '*bitqī batāqu*' Abschneidungen abschneiden?", *AoF* 24, 105–114.

Freydank, H. 2000, "Addenda und Corrigenda zu mittelassyrischen Eponymen", in J. Marzahn & H. Neumann (eds.), *Assyriologica et Semitica. Festschrift für Joachim Oelsner anlässlich seines 65. Geburtstages am 18. Februar 1997* (AOAT 252), Münster, 67–72.

Freydank, H. 2001, *Mittelassyrische Rechtsurkunden und Verwaltungstexte IV. Tafeln aus Kār-Tukultī-Ninurta. Mit einem Beitrag zu den Siegelabrollungen von C. Fischer* (WVDOG 99), Saarbrücken.

Freydank, H. 2004, *Mittelassyrische Rechtsurkunden und Verwaltungstexte V* (WVDOG 106), Saarbrücken.

Freydank, H. 2005, "Zu den Eponymenfolgen des 13. Jahrhunderts v.Chr. in *Dūr-Katlimmu*", *AoF* 32, 45–56.

Freydank, H. 2009, "*Kār-Tukultī Ninurta* als Agrarprovinz", *AoF* 36.1, 16–84.

Friedman, L.M. 1977, *Law and Society. An Introduction*, Englewood Cliffs, NJ.

Friedman, L.M. 1990, "Some Thoughts on Comparative Legal Culture", in D.S. Clark (ed.), *Comparative Law and Private International Law, Essays in Honor of John Henry Merryman on His Seventieth Birthday,* Berlin, 49–57.

Fuchs, A. & Parpola, S. 2001, *The Correspondence of Sargon II, Part III: Letters from Babylonia and the Eastern Provinces* (SAA 15), Helsinki.

Gagos, T. 2008, "Compromissum", *BASP* 45, 59–67.

Gagos, T. & van Minnen, P. 1994, *Settling a Dispute. Toward a Legal Anthropology of Late Antique Egypt* (New Texts from Ancient Cultures 1), Ann Arbor, MI.

Gauger, J.-D. 2000, *Authentizität und Methode. Untersuchungen zum historischen Wert des persisch-griechischen Herrscherbriefs in literarischer Tradition* (Studien zur Geschichtsforschung des Altertums 6), Hamburg.

Gauthier, P. 1982, "Les saisies licites aux dépens des étrangers dans les cités grecques", *RHD* 60, 553–576.

Giménez-Candela, T. 1993, "Mandatum und Bürgenregreß", in D. Nörr & S. Nishimura (eds.), *Mandatum und Verwandtes: Beiträge zum römischen und modernen Recht,* Berlin, 169–177.

Giuffrè, V. 1965, *L'utilizzazione degli atti giuridici mediante 'conversione' in diritto romano* (Pubblicazioni della Facoltà Giuridica dell'Università di Napoli 77), Naples.

Goetze, A. 1963, "Šakkanakkus of the Ur III Empire", *JCS* 17, 1–31.

Goldstein, J.A. 1968, *The Letters of Demosthenes*, New York.

Gomme, A.W., Andrewes, A., & Dover, K.J. 1970, *A Historical Commentary on Thucydides. Volume 4. Books V (25)-VII*, Oxford.

Grayson, A.K. (et al.) 1987, *Assyrian Rulers of the Third and Second Millennia BC (to 1115 BC)* (RIMA 1), Toronto, Buffalo, NY & London.

Greenfield, J. 1982, "Some Notes on the Arsham Letters", in S. Shaked (ed.), *Irano-Judaica: Studies Relating to Jewish Contacts with Persian Culture throughout the Ages*, Jerusalem, 4–11.

Grelot, P. 1972, *Documents araméens d'Égypte* (LAPO 5), Paris.

Gröschler, P. 1997, *Die tabellae-Urkunden aus den pompejanischen und herkulanensischen Urkundenfunden* (Freiburger rechtsgeschichtliche Abhandlungen, NF 26), Berlin.

Gröschler, P. 2006, "Die Konzeption des mutuum cum stipulatione", *TR* 74, 261–287.

Guichard, M. 1997, "Copie de la supplique bilingue suméro-akkadienne 'Les malheurs d'un scribe' (texte n° 6)", in D. Charpin & J.-M. Durand (eds.), *Recueil d'études à la mémoire de Marie-Thérèse Barrelet* (FM 3) (Mémoires de NABU 4), Paris, 79–82.

Habermann, W. 1998, "Zur chronologischen Verteilung der papyrologischen Zeugnisse", *ZPE* 122, 144–160.

Hagedorn, D. 1998, "Noch einmal: Who got the Contract?", *ZPE* 123, 177–180.

Hall, M. 1983, "A Middle Assyrian Legal Summons", *ZA* 73, 75–81.

Hallo, W.W. 1995, "Slave Release in the Biblical World in Light of a New Text", in Z. Zevit, S. Gitin & M. Sokoloff (eds.), *Solving Riddles and Untying Knots. Biblical, Epigraphic, and Semitic Studies in Honor of Jonas C. Greenfield*, Winona Lake, IN, 79–93.

Hallo, W.W. 2006, "A Sumerian Apocryphon? The Royal Correspondence of Ur Reconsidered", in P. Michalowski, & N. Veldhuis (eds.), *Approaches to Sumerian Literature: Studies in Honour of Stip (H.L.J. Vanstiphout)* (CM 35), Leiden, 85–104.

Hallock, R.T. 1969, *Persepolis Fortification Tablets* (OIP 92), Chicago.

Harris, E.M. 1995, *Aeschines and Athenian Politics*, New York & Oxford.

Harris, E.M. 2000, "The Authenticity of Andocides' *De Pace*: A Subversive Essay", in Flensted-Jensen, Nielsen & Rubinstein (eds.), 479–505.

Harris, E.M. 2002, "Workshop, Marketplace and Household. The Nature of Technical Specialization in Classical Athens and its Influence on Economy and Society", in Cartledge, Cohen & Foxhall (eds.), 67–99.

Harris, E.M. 2004, "Notes on a Lead Letter from the Athenian Agora", *HSPh* 102, 157–170.

Harris, E.M. 2006, *Democracy and the Rule of Law in Classical Athens: Essays on Law, Society, and Politics*, New York & Cambridge.

Harris, E.M. 2008, "Two Notes on Legal Inscriptions", *ZPE* 167, 81–84.

Harris, E.M. & Thür, G. (eds.) 2008, *Symposion 2007, Vorträge zur griechischen und hellenistischen Rechtsgeschichte (Durham, 2.-6. September 2007)*, Vienna.

Harris, W.V. 1989, *Ancient Literacy*, Cambridge, MA.

Harrison, A.R.W. 1968, *The Law of Athens. I: The Family and Property*, Oxford.

Harrison, A.R.W. 1971, *The Law of Athens. II: Procedure*, Oxford.

Hatzopoulos, M.B. 1995, "La lettre royale d'Olévéni", *Chiron* 25, 163–185.

Hatzopoulos, M.B. 1996, *Macedonian Institutions under the Kings* (Meletemata 22), Athens & Paris.

Hatzopoulos, M.B. 1997, "Alexandre en Perse : La Revanche et L'Empire", *ZPE* 116, 41–52.

Hecker, K. 1999, " In nova... ", *ArOr* 67, 557–561.

Hedrick, C.W. Jr. 1999, "Democracy and the Athenian Epigraphical Habit", *Hesperia* 68, 387–439.

Heimbach, C.G.E. (ed.) (1833–1850), *Basilicorum libri LX*, Leipzig.

Heisserer, A.J. 1980, *Alexander the Great and the Greeks: the Epigraphic Evidence*, Norman, OK.

Heltzer, M. 1992, "A Recently Published Babylonian Tablet and the Province of Judah after 516 B.C.E.", *Transeuphratène* 5, 57–61.

Hengstl, J. 1972, *Private Arbeitsverhältnisse freier Personen in den hellenistischen Papyri bis Diokletian*, Freiburg.

Henry, A. 1991, "A Lead Letter from Torone", *AE* 1991, 65–70.

Herrmann, J. 1957–1958, "Vertragsinhalt und Rechtsnatur der διδασκαλικαί", *JJP* 11–12, 119–139, also published in *Kleine Schriften zur Rechtsgeschichte* (MB 83) (Munich 1990), 185–193.

Herrmann, J. 1958, *Studien zur Bodenpacht im Recht der graeco-aegyptischen Papyri* (MBPR 41), Munich.

Heskel, J. 1997, *The North Aegean Wars, 371–360 BC* (Historia, Einzelschriften 102), Stuttgart.

Hinz, W. 1971, "Achämenidische Hofverwaltung", *ZA* 61, 260–311.

Hinz, W. & Koch, H. 1987, *Elamisches Wörterbuch I-II* (AMI, Supplementum 17), Berlin.

Hoftijzer, J. & Jongeling, K. 1995, *Dictionary of the North-West Semitic Inscriptions* (HdO 21), Leiden & New York.

Hornblower, S. 1987, *Thucydides*, London.

Huber, F. 2001, "La correspondance royale d'Ur, un corpus apocryphe", *ZA* 91, 169–206.

Hughes, G.R. 1984, "The So-called Pherendates Correspondence", in H.-J. Thissen & K.-T. Zauzich (eds.), *Grammata Demotika: Festschrift für Erich Lüddekens zum 15. Juni 1983*, Würzburg, 75–86.

Hunger, H. 1992, *Astrological Reports to Assyrian Kings* (SAA 8), Helsinki.

Ismard, P. 2007, "La construction du fait associatif en droit athénien et les limites de la notion de personnalité juridique", *Dike* 10, 57–83.

Jacob, S. 2003, *Mittelassyrische Verwaltung und Sozialstruktur: Untersuchungen* (CM 29), Leiden & Boston.

Jacobsen, T. 1987, *The Harp That Once ... Sumerian Poetry in Translation*, New Haven, CT.

Jakab, É. 2000, "Vectura pro mutua: Überlegungen zu TP 13 und Ulp. 19.2.15.6", *ZSSRA* 117, 244–273.

Jakab, É. 2006, "Vertragsformulare im Imperium Romanum", *ZSSRA* 123, 71–101.

Jakab, É. 2008, "Vertragspraxis und Bankgeschäfte im antiken Puteoli: TPSulp. 48 neu interpretiert", in K. Verboven, K. Vandorpe & V. Chankowski-Sablé (eds.), *Pistoi dia tèn technèn. Bankers, Loans and Archives in the Ancient World, Studies in Honour of R. Bogaert* (Studia Hellenistica 44), Leuven, 321–344.

Jakab, É. 2009, *Risikomanagement beim Weinkauf. Periculum und Praxis im Imperium Romanum* (MBPR 99), Munich.

Janowski, B & Wilhelm, G. (eds.) 2006, *TUAT, NF 3: Briefe*, Gütersloh.

Janssen, C. 1991, "Samsu-iluna and the Hungry *Nadītum*s", *NAPR* 5, 3–39.

Janssen, C. 1992, "Inanna-mansum et ses fils : relation d'une succession turbulente dans les archives d'Ur-Utu", *RA* 86, 19–52.

Jas, R. 1996, *Neo-Assyrian Judicial Procedures* (SAAS 5), Helsinki.

Joannès, F. et. al. 2006, *Haradum II. Les textes de la période paléo-babylonienne (Samsu-iluna–Ammi-saduqa),* Paris.

Jordan, D.R. 2000, "A Personal Letter Found in the Athenian Agora", *Hesperia* 69, 91–103.

Jördens, A. 1990, *Vertragliche Regelungen von Arbeiten im späten griechischsprachigen Ägypten (P. Heid. V)*, Heidelberg.

Jörs, P., Kunkel, W. & Wenger, L. 1949[3], *Römisches Recht*, Berlin.

Kang, S.T. 1972, *Sumerian Economic Texts from the Drehem Archive* (Sumerian and Akkadian Cuneiform Texts in the Collection of the World Heritage Museum of the University of Illinois 1), Chicago.

Kaser, M. 1971[2], *Das römische Privatrecht. Erster Abschnitt: Das altrömische, das vorklassische und klassische Recht* (HAW 10.3.3), Munich.

Kaser, M. & Knütel, R. 2005[18], *Römisches Privatrecht: ein Studienbuch*, Munich.

Kataja, L. 1987, "A Neo-Assyrian Document on Two Cases of River Ordeal", *SAAB* I.2, 65–68.

Kaufman, S.A. 1974, *The Akkadian Influences on Aramaic* (AS 19), Chicago.

Kelly, T. 1985, "The Spartan σκυτάλη", in J.W. Eadie & J. Ober (eds.), *The Craft of the Ancient Historian: Essays in Honor of Chester G. Starr*, Lanham, MD, 141–169.

Kienast, B. 1996, "Mündlichkeit und Schriftlichkeit im keilschriftlichen Rechtswesen", *ZABR* 2, 114–130.

Kirk, G.S. 1990, *The Iliad: A Commentary. Vol. I: Books 1–4*, Cambridge.

Kirschenbaum, A. 1987, *Sons, Slaves and Freedmen in Roman Commerce*, Jerusalem & Washington, DC.

Klauck, H.-J. 2006, *Ancient letters and the New Testament: a Guide to Context and Exegesis*, Waco, TX (revisited translation of *Die antike Briefliteratur und das Neue Testament. Ein Lehr- und Arbeitsbuch*, Stuttgart 1998).

Knopf, E. 2005, *Contracts in the Athenian Orators*, New York.

Kottsieper, I. 2004, "Papyrus", *RlA* 10, 5/6, 330–332.

Kottsieper, I. 2006, "Hebräische, transjordanische und aramäische Briefe", in Janowski & Wilhelm (eds.), 357–383.

Kramer, S.N. 1952, *Enmerkar and the Lord of Aratta: A Sumerian Epic Tale of Iraq and Iran*, Philadelphia.

Krampe, C. 1985, "An inutilis acceptilatio utile habeat pactum quaeritur – D. 46,4,8 pr. (Ulp. 48 Sab.)", *TR* 53, 3–25.

Krampe, C. 2003, "Das Mandat des Aurelius Quietus. Celsus bei Ulpian D. 17,1,16 und die Kreditmandatsdiskussion", in U. Manthe & C. Krampe (eds)., *Quaestiones Iuris: Festschrift für Joseph Georg Wolf zum 70. Geburtstag*, Berlin, 125–149.

Kraus, F.R. 1965, "Ein Edikt des Königs Samsu-iluna von Babylon", in H.G. Güterbock & T. Jacobsen (eds.), *Studies in Honor of Benno Landsberger on His Seventy-Fifth Birthday, April 21, 1965* (AS 16), Chicago, 225–231.

Kraus, F.R. 1977, *Briefe aus dem British Museum (CT 52)* (AbB 7), Leiden.

Kraus, F.R. 1983, "Eine neue Probe akkadischer Literatur: Brief eines Bittstellers an eine Gottheit", *JAOS* 103 = *Studies in Literature from the Ancient Near East, by Members of the American Oriental Society, Dedicated to Samuel Noah Kramer*, 205–209.

Kraus, F.R. 1984, *Königliche Verfügungen in altbabylonischer Zeit* (Studia et Documenta ad iura Orientis antiqui pertinentia 11), Leiden.

Kraus, F.R. 1985, "Altbabylonische Briefe mit Siegelabrollungen", in J.-M. Durand & J.-R. Kupper (eds.), *Miscellanea Babylonica. Mélanges offerts à Maurice Birot*, Paris, 137–145.

Kraus, R. 1936, "Ein Sittenkanon in Omenform", *ZA* 43, 77–113.

Kunkel, W. 2001², *Die römischen Juristen. Herkunft und soziale Stellung*, 2001.

La Rosa, F. 1997, "Il formalismo del pretore: « constituta » e « recepta »", *Labeo* 43, 202–224.

La Rosa, F. 2008, "L'« adiectus solutionis causa » e il « constitutum debiti »", *Index* 36, 277–284.

Lafont, B. 1990, "Nouvelles lettres du temps des rois d'Ur", *RA* 84, 165–169.

Lafont, B. 1992, "Messagers et ambassadeurs dans les archives de Mari", in Charpin & Joannès (eds.), 167–183.

Lafont, B. 2001, "Relations internationales, alliances et diplomatie au temps des royaumes amorrites – Essai de synthèse", in Charpin & Durand (eds.), 213–328.

Lambert, S.D. 1997, *Rationes Centesimarum. Sales of Public Land in Lykourgan Athens* (Archaia Hellas. Monographs on Ancient Greek History and Archaeology 3), Amsterdam.

Lanfranchi, G.B. & Parpola, S. 1990, *The Correspondence of Sargon II, Part II: Letters from the Northern and Northeastern Provinces* (SAA 5), Helsinki.

Lang, M. 1976, *Graffiti and Dipinti* (Athenian Agora: Results of Excavations conducted by the American School of Classical Studies at Athens 21), Princeton.

Lenel, O. 1927³, *Das Edictum perpetuum. Ein Versuch zu seiner Wiederherstellung*, Leipzig.

Lewis, S. 1996, *News and Society in the Greek Polis* (Studies in the History of Greece and Rome), Chapel Hill, NC.

Liddell, P.P. 2007, *Civic Obligation and Individual Liberty in Ancient Athens* (Oxford Classical Monographs), Oxford.

Linders, T. 1992, "Inscriptions and Orality", *SO* 67, 27–40.

Lintott, A.W. 2004, "Σῦλα: Reprisal by Seizure in Greek Inter-Community Relations", *CQ* 54.2, 340–353.

Lippert, S. 2003, "Die sogenannte Zivilprozessordnung. Weitere Fragmente der ägyptischen Gesetzessammlung", *JJP* 33, 91–135.

Liverani, M. 1999, *Le lettere di el-Amarna. 2 : Le lettere dei 'Grandi Re'* (Testi del Vicino Oriente antico 3.2), Brescia.

Liverani, M. 2000, "The Great Power's Club", in R. Cohen et R. Westbrook (eds.), *Amarna Diplomacy. The Beginnings of International Relations*, Baltimore, 15–27.

Livingstone, N. 2001, *A Commentary on Isocrates' Busiris* (Mnemosyne, Supplementum 223), Leiden.

Llop-Raduá, J. 2005, "Die königlichen „großen Speicher" (*karmū rabi'ūtu*) der Stadt Assur in der Regierungszeit Salmanassars I. und Tukultī-Ninurtas I", MDOG 137, 41–55.

Llop-Raduà, J. 2009, *Mittelassyrische Verwaltungsurkunden aus Assur. Texte aus den „großen Speichern" und dem Ubru-Archiv. Mit einem Beitrag zu den Siegelabrollungen von B. Feller* (WVDOG 124), Wiesbaden.

Longo, O. 1978, "Scrivere in Tucidide: communicazione e ideologia", in E. Livrea & G.A. Privitera (eds.), *Studi in onore di Anthos Ardizzoni* (Filologia e Critica 25), Rome, 519–554.

Lozachmeur, H. 2006, *La collection Clermont-Ganneau : Ostraca, épigraphes sur jarre, éttiquettes de bois I-II* (MAIBL 35), Paris.

Luukko, M. & van Buylaere, G. 2002, *The Political Correspondence of Esarhaddon* (SAA 16), Helsinki.

Ma, J. 1999, *Antiochos III and the Cities of Western Asia Minor*, Oxford.

MacDowell, D.M. 1978, *The Law in Classical Athens*, London.

MacDowell, D.M. 2004, *Demosthenes, Speeches 27–38*, Austin, TX.

Mader, G.J. 2006, "Fighting Philip with Decrees: Demosthenes and the Syndrome of Symbolic Action", *AJPh* 127, 367–386.

Magdelain, A. 1958, *Le consensualisme dans l'édit du préteur*, Paris.

Manthe, U. 2004, *Die Institutionen des Gaius* (Texte zur Forschung 81), Darmstadt.

Martin, V & Budé, G. 1928, *Eschine II. Contre Ctésiphon, Lettres*, Paris.

Matthews, V.J. 1974, "The *Hemerodromoi*: Ultra-Long Distance Running in Antiquity", *CW* 68, 161–169.

Melville, S.C. 1999, *The Role of Naqia/Zakutu in Sargonid Politics* (SAA 9), Helsinki.

Merklein, A. 1967, *Das Ehescheidungsrecht nach den Papyri der byzantinischen Zeit*, Erlangen.

Messeri Savorelli, G. 1980, "Lista degli agoranomi di età tolemaica", in R. Pintaudi (ed.), *Miscellanea Papyrologica in memoria di Herbert C. Youtie* (Pap.Flor. 7), Florence, 185–271.

Michalowski, P. 1976, *The Royal Correspondence of Ur*, Ann Arbor, MI.

Michalowski, P. 1980–1983, "Königsbriefe", *RlA* 6, 51–59.

Michalowski, P. 1993, *Letters from Early Mesopotamia* (Writings from the Ancient World 3), Atlanta, GA.

Michalowski, P. 2011, *The Correspondence of the Kings of Ur. An Epistolary History of an Ancient Mesopotamian Kingdom* (MC 15), Winona Lake, ID.

Michel, C. 2008, "La correspondance des marchands assyriens du XIXe s. av. J.-C. De l'archivage des lettres commerciales et privées", in L. Pantalacci, (ed.), *La lettre d'archive : communication administrative et personnelle dans l'antiquité proche orientale et égyptienne : actes du colloque de l'Université de Lyon 2, 9–10 juillet 2004* (Topoi, Supplementum 9), Cairo, 117–140.

Millender, E.G. 2001, "Spartan Literacy Revisited", *ClAnt* 20, 121–164.

Mirhady, D.C. 1996, "Torture and Rhetoric in Athens", *JHS* 116, 119–131, reprinted in Carawan (ed.) (2007), 247–268.

Mirhady, D.C. 2000, "Demosthenes as Advocate. The Private Speeches", in I. Worthington (ed.), *Demosthenes: Statesman and Orator*, London, 181–204.

Missitzis, L. 1985, "A Royal Decree of Alexander the Great on the Lands of Philippi", *AncW* 12, 3–14.

Mitteis, L. 1912, *Grundzüge und Chrestomathie der Papyruskunde, II: Juristischer Teil, 1. Grundzüge*, Leipzig & Berlin.

Moran, W.L. 1987, *Les lettres d'El-Amarna : correspondance diplomatique du pharaon* (LAPO 13), Paris.

Muhs, B.P. 2005, "The Grapheion and the Disappearance of Demotic Contracts in Early Roman Tebtynis and Soknopaiou Nesos", in S. Lippert & M. Schentuleit (eds.), *Tebtynis und Soknopaiu Nesos. Leben im römerzeitlichen Fajum, Akten des internationalen Symposions vom 11. bis 13. Dezember 2003 in Sommerhausen bei Würzburg*, Wiesbaden, 93–104.

Muhs, B.P. 2009, "The Berkeley Tebtunis Grapheion Archive", in G. Widmer & D. Devauchelle (eds.), *Actes du IXe Congrès International des Études Démotiques, Paris, 31 août – 3 septembre 2005* (Bibliothèque d'étude de l'Institut français d'archéologie orientale 147), Cairo, 243–251.

Muir, J.V. 2009, *Life and Letters in the Ancient Greek World*, London.

Murray, A.T. 1939, *Demosthenes V*. Cambridge, MA.

Nelson, H.L.W. & Manthe, U. 1999, *Gai Institutiones III 88–181. Die Kontraktobligationen: Text und Kommentar* (Studia Gaiana 8, Freiburger rechtsgeschichtliche Abhandlungen, NF 35), Berlin.

Neumann, H. 1992, "Nochmals zum Kaufmann in neusumerischer Zeit: die Geschäfte des Ur-DUN und anderer Kaufleute aus Nippur", in Charpin & Joannès (eds.), 83–94.

Neumann, H. 2006, "Sumerische und akkadische Briefe des 3. Jt. v. Chr", in Janowski & Wilhelm (eds.), 1–20.

Nicholas, B. 1962, *An Introduction to Roman Law*, Oxford.

Nicolai, R. 2004, *Studi su Isocrate. La comunicazione letteraria nel IV sec. a.C. e i nuovi generi della prosa* (Quaderni dei Seminari romani di cultura greca 7), Rome.

Nora, P. (ed.) 1987, *Essais d'égo-histoire*, Paris.

Nörr, D. 1993, "Mandatum, fides, amicitia", in D. Nörr & S. Nishimura (eds.), *Mandatum und Verwandtes: Beiträge zum römischen und modernen Recht,* Berlin, 13–37.

Nouhaud, M. & Dors-Méary, L. 1990, *Dinarque, Discours*, Paris.

Owen, D.I. 1975, *The John Frederick Lewis Collection* (MVN 3.13), Rome.

Palme, B. 2007, "Antwort auf J. Urbanik", in E. Cantarella (ed.), *Symposion 2005, Vorträge zur griechischen und hellenistischen Rechtsgeschichte (Salerno, 14.-18. September 2005)*, Vienna, 401–410.

Papazoglou, F. 1998–1999, "L'inscription d'Olévéni", *Tekmeria* 4, 89–100.

Parpola, S. 1983, *Letters from Assyrian Scholars to the Kings Esarhaddon and Assurbanipal. Part II* (AOAT 5.2), Neukirchen-Vluyn.

Parpola, S. 1987, *The Correspondence of Sargon II, Part I: Letters from Assyria and the West* (SAA 1), Helsinki.

Parpola, S. 1993, *Letters from Assyrian and Babylonian Scholars* (SAA 10), Helsinki.

Parpola, S. 1997, *Assyrian Prophecies* (SAA 9), Helsinki.

Parpola, S. & Watanabe, K. 1988, *Neo-Assyrian Treaties and Loyalty Oaths* (SAA 2), Helsinki.

Partsch, J. 1909, *Griechisches Bürgschaftsrecht. 1. Das Recht des altgriechischen Gemeindestaats*, Leipzig & Berlin.

Pébarthe, C. 2006, *Cité, démocratie et écriture. Histoire de l'alphabétisation d'Athènes à l'époque classique* (Culture et cité 3), Paris.

Pecha, L. 1999, "Das Amt des *šassukkum* in der altbabylonischen Zeit", *ArOr* 67, 51–71.

Pedersén, O. 1985, *Archives and Libraries in the City of Assur. A Survey of the Material from the German Excavations. Part I* (Acta Universitatis Upsaliensis, Studia Semitica Upsaliensia 6), Uppsala.

Pedersén, O. 1998, *Archives and Libraries in the Ancient Near East 1500–300 B.C.*, Bethesda, MD.

Pestman, P.W. 1985a, "Registration of Demotic Contracts in Egypt. P. Par. 65; 2nd Cent. B.C.", in J.A. Ankum et al. (eds.), *Satura Roberto Feenstra, sexagesimum quintum annum aetatis complenti ab alumnis collegis amicis oblata*, Freiburg, 17–25.

Pestman, P.W. 1985b, "Agoranomoi et actes agoranomiques : Krokodilopolis et Pathyris, 145–88 av. J-C.", in P.W. Pestman (ed.), *Textes et études de papyrologie grecque, démotique et copte* (Pap.Lugd.Bat. 23), Leiden, 9–44.

Pestman, P.W. & Vleeming, S.P. 1994, *Les papyrus démotiques de Tsenhor (P. Tsenhor). Les archives privées d'une femme égyptienne du temps de Darius Ier* (Studia Demotica 4), Leuven.

Piepkorn, A.C. 1933, *Historical Prism Inscriptions of Ashurbanipal I* (AS 5), Chicago.

Porten, B. 1968, *Archives from Elephantine: The Life of an Ancient Jewish Military Colony*, Berkeley & Los Angeles.

Porten, B. 1980, "Aramaic Letters: A Study in Papyrological Reconstruction", *JARCE* 17, 39–75.

Porten, B. 1996, "Aramaic Texts", in B. Porten (ed.), *The Elephantine Papyri in English: Three Millennia of Cross-Cultural Continuity and Change* (DMOA 22), Leiden & New York, 74–276.

Porten, B. & Yardeni, A. 1986–1999, *Textbook of Aramaic Documents from Ancient Egypt A-D*, Jerusalem.

Postgate, J.N. 1988, *The Archive of Urad-šeru'a and His Family: a Middle Assyrian Household in Government Service*, Rome.

Praag, A. van 1945, *Droit matrimonial assyro-babylonien* (Allard Pierson Stichting, Universiteit van Amsterdam. Archaeologisch-historische bijdragen 12), Amsterdam.

Pringsheim, F. 1950, *The Greek Law of Sale,* Weimar.

Pritchett, W.K. 1974, *The Greek State at War*, Vol. 2, Berkeley.

Raaflaub, K.A. 2009, "Learning from the Enemy: Athenian and Persian 'Instruments of Empire' ", in J. Ma, N. Papazarkadas & R. Parker (eds.), *Interpreting the Athenian Empire*, London, 89–124.

Reed, J.T. 1997, "The Epistle", in S.E. Porter (ed.), *Handbook of Classical Rhetoric in the Hellenistic Period, 330 B.C.-A.D. 400*, Leiden, 171–193.

Reynolds, F. 2003, *The Babylonian Correspondence of Esarhaddon, and Letters to Assurbanipal and Sin-Šarru-Iškun from Northern and Central Babylonia* (SAA 18), Helsinki.

Rhodes, P.J. 1972, *The Athenian Boule*, Oxford.

Rhodes, P.J. 2001, "Public Documents in the Greek States: Archives and Inscriptions, Part II", *G&R* 48, 136–153.

Rhodes, P.J. & Osborne, R. 2003, *Greek Historical Inscriptions 404 – 323 BC*, Oxford.

Ricart Martí, E. 1994, "Constitutum debiti", in J.M. Serrano Delgado (ed.), *Derecho Romano de Obligaciones. Homenaje al profesor José Luis Murga Gener*, Madrid, 695–708.

Rigsby, K.J. 1996, *Asylia. Territorial Inviolability in the Hellenistic World* (Hellenistic Culture and Society 22), Berkeley.

Röllig, W. 2004, "Eponymen in den mittelassyrischen Dokumenten aus Tall Šēh Ḥamad / Dūr -Katlimmu", *ZA* 94, 18–51.

Rosenmeyer, P.A. 2001, *Ancient Epistolary Fictions: The Letter in Greek Literature*, Cambridge.

Roussier, J. 1958, "Le constitut", in *Varia. Études de droit romain, t. 3* (Institut de droit romain de l'Université de Paris 16), Paris, 1–154.

Rowe, G.O. 1968, "Demosthenes' First Philippic: The Satiric Mode", *TAPhA* 99, 361–374.

Rubinstein, L. 2000, *Litigation and Cooperation: Supporting Speakers in the Courts of Classical Athens* (Historia, Einzelschriften 147), Stuttgart.

Rupprecht, H.-A. 1967, *Untersuchungen zum Darlehen im Recht der graeco-aegyptischen Papyri der Ptolemäerzeit* (MBPR 51), Munich.

Rupprecht, H.-A. 1971, *Studien zur Quittung im Recht der graeco-ägyptischen Papyri* (MBPR 57), Munich.

Ryholt, K. (ed.) 2002, *Acts of the Seventh lnternational Conference of Demotic Studies. Copenhagen, 23–27 August 1999 = C.Dem.Conf. VII* (CNI Publ 27), Copenhagen.

Sachau, E. 1911, *Aramäische Papyri und Ostraka aus einer jüdischen Militär-Kolonie zu Elephantine: Altorientalische Sprachdenkmäler des 5. Jahrhunderts vor Chr.*, Leipzig.

Saggs, H.W.F. 1960, "An Unaddressed Old Babylonian Letter", *JCS* 14, 56–58.

Sallaberger, W. 1999, '*Wenn Du mein Bruder bist, ...' : Interaktion und Textgestaltung in altbabylonischen Alltagsbriefen* (CM 16), Groningen.

Salonen, A. 1971, "Gruß", *RlA* 3, 668–670.

Sanmartí-Grego, E. & Santiago-Álvarez, R.A. 1987, "Une lettre grecque sur plomb trouvée à Emporion (Fouilles 1985)", *ZPE* 68, 119–127.

Sanmartí-Grego, E. & Santiago-Álvarez, R.A. 1988a, "La lettre grecque d'Emporion et son contexte archéologique", *RAN* 21, 3–17.

Sanmartí-Grego, E. & Santiago-Álvarez, R.A. 1988b, "Notes additionnelles sur la lettre sur plomb d'Emporion", *ZPE* 72, 100–102.

Santiago-Álvarez, R.A. 1990a, "Encore une fois sur la letter sur plomb d'Emporion (1985)", *ZPE* 80, 79–80.

Santiago-Álvarez, R.A. 1990b, "Notes additionnelles au plomb d'Emporion 1987", *ZPE* 82, 176.

Santiago-Álvarez, R.A. 1993, "Epigrafía dialectal emporitana", in E. Crespo (ed.), *Dialectologica Graeca, Actas del II Coloquio Internacional de Dialectología Griega, Miraflores de la Sierra [Madrid], 19 – 21 de junio de 1991*, Madrid, 281–294.

Saporetti, C. 1978–1979, "Il prestito nei documenti privati dell'Assiria del XIV e XIII secolo. Parte I. Analisi dei testi", *Mesopotamia* 13–14, 5–90.

Sasson, J. 2001, "On Reading the Diplomatic Letters in the Mari Archives", in Charpin & Durand (eds.), 329–338.

Schwiderski, D. 2000, *Handbuch des nordwestsemitischen Briefformulars: Ein Beitrag zur Echtheitsfrage der aramäischen Briefe des Esrabuches* (BZAW 295), Berlin & New York.

Schwiderski, D. 2004, *Die alt- und reichsaramäischen Inschriften. Bd. 2: Texte und Bibliographie* (FoSub 2), Berlin & New York.

Seidl, E. 1962, *Ptolemäische Rechtsgeschichte*[2] (Ägyptologische Forschungen 22), Glückstadt et al.

Sherwin-White, S.M. 1985, "Ancient Archives: The Edict of Alexander to Priene, a Reappraisal", *JHS* 105, 69–89.

Sickinger, J.P 1999, *Public Records and Archives in Classical Athens*, Chapel Hill, NC.

Sickinger, J.P. 2007, "The Bureaucracy of Democracy and Empire", in L.J. Samons II (ed.), *The Cambridge Companion to the Age of Pericles*, Cambridge, 196–214.

Sickinger, J.P. 2009, "Nothing to Do with Democracy: 'Formulae of Disclosure' and the Athenian Epigraphic Habit", in L. Mitchell & L. Rubinstein (eds.), *Greek History and Epigraphy, Essays in Honour of P.J. Rhodes*, Swansea, 87–102.

Sigrist, M. 1990, *Old Babylonian Account Texts in the Horn Archaeology Museum* (AUCT 4), Berrien Springs.

Simon, D. 1964, *Studien zur Praxis der Stipulationsklausel* (MBPR 48), Munich.

Slings, S.R. 1994, "Notes on the Lead Letters from Emporion", *ZPE* 104, 111–117.

Soldt, W.H. van 1994, *Letters in the British Museum, vol. 2* (AbB 13), Leiden & New York.

Sollberger, E. 1966, *The Business and Administrative Correspondence under the Kings of Ur* (TCS 1), Locust Valley, NY.

Spiegelberg, W. 1928, "Drei demotische Schreiben aus der Korrespondenz des Pherendates, des Satrapen Darius I., mit den Chnum-Priestern von Elephantine", *SPAW* 30, 604–622.

Starr, I. 1990, *Queries to the Sungod. Divination and Politics in Sargonid Assyria* (SAA 4), Helsinki.

Ste.-Croix, G.E.M. de 1963, "The Alleged Secret Pact between Athens and Philip II concerning Amphipolis and Pydna", *CQ* 13, 110–19.

Steinacker, H. 1927, *Die antiken Grundlagen der frühmittelalterlichen Privatrechts-urkunde* (Grundriß der Geschichtswissenschaft, Ergänzungsband 1), Leipzig.

Steiner, D.T. 1994, *The Tyrant's Writ. Myths and Images of Writing in Ancient Greece*, Princeton.

Steinwenter, A. 1935, "Das byzantinische Dialysis-Formular", in *Studi in memoria di Aldo Albertoni* (Studi di diritto privato italiano e straniero 17), Padova, vol. I, 73–94.

Steinwenter, A. 1936, "Aus dem Gesellschaftsrechte der Papyri", in *Studi in onore di Salvatore Riccobono nel XL anno del suo insegnamento*, Palermo, vol. I, 487–504.

Steinwenter, A. 1955, *Das Recht der koptischen Urkunden* (HAW 10.4.2), Munich.

Stirewalt, M.L. Jr. 1993, *Studies in Ancient Greek Epistolography* (Resources for Biblical Study 27), Atlanta, GA.

Stolper, M.W. 1989, "The Governor of Babylon and Across-the-River in 486 B.C.", *JNES* 48, 283–305.

Sykutris, J. 1931, "Epistolographie", in *RE,* Supplementum V, cols. 185–220.

Talamanca, M. 1978, " 'Conventio' e 'stipulatio' nel sistema dei contratti romani", in H. Kupiszewski & W. Wołodkiewicz, *Le droit romain et sa réception en Europe : les actes du colloque organisé par la Faculté de Droit et d'Administration de l'Université de Varsovie en collaboration avec l'Accademia Nazionale dei Lincei, le 6–10 octobre 1973*, Warsaw, 195–266.

Thomas, R. 1989, *Oral Tradition and Written Record in Classical Athens* (Cambridge Studies in Oral and Literate Culture 18), Cambridge.

Thomas, R. 1992, *Literacy and Orality in Ancient Greece*, Cambridge.

Thür, G. 2005, "The Role of the Witness in Athenian Law", in M. Gagarin & D. Cohen (eds.), *The Cambridge Companion to Ancient Greek Law*, Cambridge, 146–169.

Todd, S. 1990, "The Purpose of Evidence in Athenian Courts", in P. Cartledge, P. Millett & S. Todd, (eds.), *Nomos. Essays in Athenian Law, Politics and Society*, Cambridge, 19–38.

Too, Y.L. 1995, *The Rhetoric of Identity in Isocrates: Text, Power, Pedagogy*, Cambridge.

Trapp, M. 2003, *Greek and Latin Letters, an Anthology with Translation*, Cambridge.

Trevett, J. 1992, *Apollodoros, the Son of Pasion*, Oxford.

Tsetskhladze, G.R. (ed.) 1998, *The Greek Colonisation of the Black Sea Area, Historical Interpretation of Archaeology* (Historia, Einzelschriften 121), Stuttgart.

Urbanik, J. 2007, "Compromesso o processo? Alternativa risoluzione dei conflitti e tutela dei diritti nella prassi della tarda antichità", in E. Cantarella (ed.), *Symposion 2005. Vorträge zur griechischen und hellenistischen Rechtsgeschichte (Salerno, 14.-18. September 2005)*, Vienna, 377–400.

Van De Mieroop, M. 1987, *Crafts in the Early Isin Period. A Study of the Isin Craft Archive from the Reigns of Išbi-Erra and Šū-Ilišu* (OLA 24), Leuven.

Vandorpe, K. 1997, "Seals in and on the Papyri of Greco-Roman and Byzantine Egypt", in M.-F. Boussac & A. Invernizzi (eds.), *Archives et sceaux du monde hellénistique. Torino, Villa Gualino, 13–16 Gennaio 1993* (BCH, Supplementum 29), Paris, 231–291.

Vandorpe, K. 2000, "Two Agoranomic Loans with Demotic Summary", in H. Melaerts et al. (eds.), *Papyri in honorem J. Bingen octogenarii* (Studia Varia Bruxellensia ad Orbem Graeco-Latinum Pertinentia 5), Leuven, 195–204.

Vandorpe, K. 2002, "Un ancêtre de l'estampillage : les cachets encrés sur papyrus (IIe siècle av. J.-C. – IIe siècle apr. J.-C.)", in A. Mercier (ed.), *Les trois révolutions du livre, catalogue de l'exposition du Musée des arts et métiers, 8 octobre 2002–5 janvier 2003,* Paris, 37–41.

Vandorpe, K. 2005, "A Greek Register from Pathyris' Notarial Office. Loans and Sales from the Pathyrite and Latopolite Nomes", *ZPE* 150, 161–186.

Varvaro, M. 2007–2008, "Sulla storia dell'editto *De pecunia constituta*", *AUPA* 52, 327–366.

Vatin, C. 1985, "Lettre adressée à la cité de Philippes par les ambassadeurs auprès d'Alexandre", *Πρακτικὰ τοῦ Η΄Διεθνούς Συνεδρίου Ἑλληνικῆς καὶ Λατινικῆς Ἐπιγραφικῆς, Ἀθήνα 3-9 Ὀκτωβρίου 1982,* Athens, I, 259–270.

Veenhof, K.R. 1987, " 'Dying Tablets' and 'Hungry Silver': Elements of Figurative Language in Akkadian Commercial Terminology", in M. Mindlin, M. J. Geller & J. E. Wansbrough (eds.), *Figurative Language in the Ancient Near East*, London, 41–75.

Veenhof, K.R. 1995, " 'In Accordance with the Words of the Stele'. Evidence for Old Assyrian Legislation", *Chicago-Kent Law Review* 70, 1717–1744.

Veenhof, K.R. 1997–2000, "The Relation between Royal Decrees and Laws in the Old Babylonian Period", *JEOL* 35–36, 49–84.

Veenhof, K.R. 1999, "Silver and Credit in Old Assyrian Trade", in J.G. Dercksen (ed.), *Trade and Finance in Ancient Mesopotamia: Proceedings of the First Mos Symposium* (PIHANS 84), Leiden, 55–84.

Veenhof, K.R. 2005, *Letters in the Louvre* (AbB 14), Leiden & Boston.

Veenhof, K. 2008, "Communication in the Old Assyrian Trading Society by Caravans, Travelers and Messengers", in C. Michel (ed.), *Old Assyrian Studies in Memory of Paul Garelli* (OAAS 4, PIHANS 112), Leiden, 199–246.

Velaza, J. 1992, "Basped- sur plomb grec d'Emporion : un anthroponyme iberique?" *BN* 27, 264–267.

Verboven, K. 2000, "L'organisation des affaires financières des C. Sulpicii de Pouzzoles (Tabulae Pompeianae Sulpiciorum)", *CCG* 11, 161–171.

Verboven, K. 2003, "The Sulpicii from Puteoli and Usury in the Early Roman Empire", *TR* 71, 7–28.

Villard, P. 1994, "La disgrâce d'Urad-Gula et la datation de LAS 122 et 125", *NABU* 1994.3, 66–67.

Villard, P. 1997, "L'éducation d'Assurbanipal", *Ktema* 22, 135–149.

Villard, P. 2001, "Les administrateurs de l'époque de Yasmah-Addu", in Charpin & Durand (eds.), 9–140.

Villard, P. 2007, "L'(an)durāru à l'époque néo-assyrienne", *RA* 101, 107–124.

Vinogradov, Y. 1998, "The Greek Colonisation of the Black Sea Region in the Light of Private Lead Letters", in G.R. Tsetskhladze (ed.), 153–178.

Vleeming, S.P. 1980, "The Sale of a Slave in the Time of Pharaoh Py", *OMRO* 61, 1–17.

Vleeming, S.P. 1981, "Een lang uitgestelde benoeming", *Phoenix* 27, 82–91.

Vleeming, S.P. 1992, "The Tithe of the Scribes (and) Representatives", in J. H. Johnson (ed.), *Life in a Multi-Cultural Society: Egypt from Cambyses to Constantine and Beyond* (SAOC 51), Chicago, 343–350.

Von Reden, S. 2007, *Money in Ptolemaic Egypt: from the Macedonian Conquest to the End of the Third Century BC*, Cambridge.

Waelkens, L. 2008, "Pecunia constituta, un mode de paiement du droit romain", in A. Girollet (ed.), *Actes des Journées internationales de la Société d'Histoire du Droit, Dijon 2007 : le droit, les affaires et l'argent, célébration du bicentenaire du Code de commerce* (Mémoires de la Société pour l'Histoire du Droit et des institutions des anciens pays bourguignons, comtois et romands 65), Dijon, 67–79.

Walker, C.B.F. 1983, "Another Babati Inscription", *JCS* 35, 91–96.

Weidner, E. 1939–1941, "Studien zur Zeitgeschichte Tukultī-Ninurtas I", *AfO* 13, 109–124.

Welles, C.B. 1934, *Royal Correspondence in the Hellenistic Period. A Study in Greek Epigraphy*, New Haven, CT.

Welles, C.B. 1938, "New Texts from the Chancery of Philip V of Macedonia and the Problem of the 'Diagramma' ", *AJA* 42, 245–260.

Wenger, L. 1953, *Die Quellen des römischen Rechts* (Österreichische Akademie der Wissenschaften. Denkschriften der Gesamtakademie 2), Vienna.

Westbrook, R. 1997, "A Matter of Life and Death", *JNES* 25, 61–70.

Westbrook, R., (ed.) 2003, *A History of Ancient Near Eastern Law* (HdO 72), Leiden & Boston.

Whiting, R.M. 1976, "Tiš-Atal of Nineveh and Babati, Uncle of Šu-Sin", *JCS* 28, 173–182.

Wilcke, C. 2007^2, *Early Ancient Near Eastern Law. A History of its Beginnings. The Early Dynastic and Sargonic Periods*, Winona Lake, IN.

Wilcken, U. 1913, "Papyrus-Urkunden", *APF* 5, 198–300.

Wilson, J.-P. 1997–1998, "The Illiterate Trader?", *BICS* 42, 29–56.

Winter, I. 1987, "Legitimation of Authority through Image and Legend: Seals belonging to Officials in the Administrative Bureaucracy of the Ur III State", in M. Gibson. & R.D. Biggs (eds.), *The Organisation of Power. Aspects of Bureaucracy in the Ancient Near East* (SAOC 46), Chicago, 69–106.

Wolf, J.G. 2003, "Aus dem neuen pompejanischen Urkundenfund: Die 'Naulotike' des Menelaos – Seedarlehen oder Frachtvertrag?", in *Iuris Vincula, Studi in onore di Mario Talamanca*, Naples, 421–463.

Wolff, H.J. 1957, "Die Grundlagen des griechischen Vertragsrechts", *ZSSRA* 74, 26–72.

Wolff, H.J. 1961, "Der byzantinische Urkundenstil Ägyptens im Lichte der Funde von Nessana und Dura", *RIDA* 3e série, 8, 115–154.

Wolff, H.J. 1978, *Das Recht der griechischen Papyri Ägyptens in der Zeit der Ptolemaeer und des Prinzipats, II: Organisation und Kontrolle des privaten Rechtsverkehrs* (HAW 10.5.2), Munich.

Wolff, H.J. 2002 (†), H.-A. Rupprecht (ed.), *Das Recht der griechischen Papyri Ägyptens in der Zeit der Ptolemaeer und des Prinzipats, I: Bedingungen und Triebkräfte der Rechtsentwicklung* (HAW 10.5.1), Munich.

Worthington, I. 1999, *Greek Orators II. Dinarchus and Hyperides, an Introduction, Text, Translation and Commentary*, Warminster.

Yiftach-Firanko, U. 2003, *Marriage and Marital Agreements. A History of the Greek Marriage Document in Egypt. 4th century BCE – 4th century CE* (MBPR 93), Munich.

Yiftach-Firanko, U. 2007, "The Rise of the Hypomnêma as a Lease Contract", in J. Frösén, T. Purola & E. Salmenkivi (eds.), *Proceedings of the 24th International Congress of Papyrology, Helsinki 2004*, Helsinki, 1051–1061.

Yiftach-Firanko, U. 2008, "Who Killed the Double Document in Ptolemaic Egypt?", *APF* 54, 203–218.

Yiftach-Firanko, U. 2009, "The *Cheirographon* and the Privatization of Scribal Activity in Early Roman Oxyrhynchos", in Harris & Thür (eds.), 325–340.

Youtie, L.C., Hagedorn, D. & Youtie, H.C. 1971, "Urkunden aus Panopolis, I", *ZPE* 7, 1–40.

Zauzich K.-Th. 1968, *Die ägyptische Schreibertradition in Aufbau: Sprache und Schrift der demotischen Kaufverträge aus Ptolemäischer Zeit* (Ägyptologische Abhandlungen 19), Wiesbaden.

Zelnick-Abramowitz, R. 2005, *Not Wholly Free: The Concept of Manumission and the Status of Manumitted Slaves in the Ancient Greek World* (Mnemosyne, Supplementum 266), Leiden & Boston.

Ziegler, K.-H. 1971, *Das private Schiedsgericht im antiken römischen Recht* (MBPR 58), Munich.

Zimmermann, R. 1990, *The Law of Obligations. Roman Foundations of the Civilian Tradition*, Cape Town.

Zweigert, K. & Kötz, H. 1996, *Einführung in die Rechtsvergleichung auf dem Gebiete des Privatrechts*, Tübingen.

Index Locorum

Cuneiform Texts

Akkadian Texts

Elamite Texts

Sumerian Texts

Greek Literary Sources

Roman Literary Sources

Roman Legal Sources

Greek and Latin Inscriptions

Aramaic Documents

Biblical Sources

Papyri, Ostraca and Tablets

fig. 1a

fig. 1b

fig. 2a

fig. 2b

fig. 3a

fig. 3b

fig. 4a

fig. 4b

fig. 5a

fig. 5b

fig. 6a

fig. 6b

fig. 7a

fig. 7b

fig. 8a

fig. 8b